Forward Press

POETS 2008

Wales, Northern Ireland & Scotland

Edited by Forward Press Editors

Forward Press 20th Anniversary
20 Years
Poetry for the people, by the people

forwardpress

First published in Great Britain in 2008 by:
Forward Press Ltd.
Remus House
Coltsfoot Drive
Woodston
Peterborough
PE2 9JX

Telephone: 01733 890099
Website: www.forwardpress.co.uk

Book Design by Ali Smith & Tim Christian
Edited by Forward Press Editors

HB ISBN 978-1 84418 477 4

Foreword

So often poetry can leave the common reader alienated. Since our establishment in 1989, our goal at Forward Press has always been to remove the barriers of elitism and provide a platform for poets from all walks of life. We believe poetry should not be obscure, introverted and as cryptic as a crossword puzzle: it is the poet's duty to reach out and embrace the world. This is exactly what our talented writers achieve with this collection of verse that is both entertaining and inspiring.

The main criterion for selecting the poems within this anthology is very simple: they communicate. They express feelings, emotions and ideas to the reader and most importantly they ensure the experience of reading poetry is one that can be enjoyed by all.

Contents

The Poems

The Colours Of My Life

Come sit down by my side while I paint for you
Pictures on this canvas from my life
Scenery ever-changing, constant rearranging
Taking me through childhood, then captures me forever as daughter, mother, wife

I've had to wear so many different mantles
The requirements that were needed on my journey through the years
My sojourn here on Earth reflecting nature's seasons
Emotions cold as winter, or uplifting as the summer's healing warmth
And the lonely isolation by the river of my tears

I feel an aching sadness for the girl that once was me
Who held onto the dreams she had that never came to be
Always painting rainbows around those future distant plans
Never doubting all these precious dreams slumbered safely in her hands

No pretty clothes, just hand-me-downs, someone else's shoes
Trudging every day to school with each season's changing hues
No happy memories filter through of friendships made to last
For sickness altered all the plans and so the die was cast

Poverty took precedence preventing carefree teenage years
And shouldering family burdens created a multitude of fears
We are Mother Nature's players upon this stage called life
The parts we're given preordained, and to live demands a tithe

So I took the dice and threw them, accepted where they lay
And knew the path I'd chosen meant a price for which I'd pay
Then I put aside my longings and the dreams I'd held inside
And turned them into colours for the hopes I'd been denied

But now along came motherhood young blossoms to unfold
And with these precious children weaving memories yet untold
I knew they'd be the rainbows I would find around each bend
And the paths they chose I would follow until the very end

Now I saw my life as paintings upon the canvas in my mind
Each brushstroke painted differently, an imprint left behind
Every theme a brilliant facet attempting to define
The many roads I'd walked upon on my journey throughout time

The mistakes I'd made are shaded grey and some are outlined black
For love cannot compensate for the wisdom one may lack
But if you suffer losses, there are also many gains
Life often hands out happiness to balance out the pains

I've pursued so many rainbows that never yielded up its gold
And my dreams like fragile fireflies never close enough to hold
But maybe a memory of who I was will chance to linger on
And filter all my colours to my children and grandson

So I come visiting my gallery, each time my senses call
To view my greatest masterpieces there upon the wall
Because my children and my grandchild are the colours of my world
And I hope they will see the beauty as my canvas is unfurled.

M W Grainger (Cardiff)

The Volcano

A distant rumble
A tremor
The earth moves
An olive tree, black with larks
Is suddenly empty.

A solitary seagull
On the lookout for fish
Violently swerves
Flies inland
In panic
No fish there
Something has thrown it
Off course.

Goats, grazing happily in the foothills
Now run, helter-skelter
To the safety of trees.
Deepening rumble
More prolonged
Underground explosions
Several
Crockery on dressers
Shake
Crash to stone floors
Splintering.

A spiral of smoke
Not seen for years
Unleashes itself
Like a giant Cherokee warning
High into the clear blue sky.

Peasants gaze upwards
Nervously
Unbelievingly
To the peak
Mouths hang open
Surely not again

And on such a bello giorno?
A terrifying roar
Like ten thousand wounded lions
Then flaming rockets shoot skywards
To mingle with the smoke
Already there.

Then it comes!

Like pus oozing out of an enormous boil
Slowly at first
Molten matter drips out of open wound
In Mother Earth
To gather momentum
And pour over the lip
Of the crater.

A red lava road!

Run Bruno
Quickly
Tell Benito and Pia
Gather il bambino
Make for the sea
You'll be safe there!

An overpowering smell of phosphorus
Fills the air
So pungent
It precludes breathing
The lava road speeds down dark mountainside
Faster, ever faster
Sweeping all before it
Shaping itself into a merciless triangle of red death.

Luigi's cottage is covered already to the roof!
Striped rivers of phosphorescent light
Break away from the main flow
To roar down sunlit gorges
Fiery, smoky red

In places
Bubbling white hot
Like a huge blanket of Russian snow
Only redder and more dangerous than
Anything on Earth.

Craftily gaining confidence as it speeds towards
The unsuspecting town below
A mammoth anaconda
Twisting, turning, squeezing, suffocating
The life out of
Everything in its path.

Cracks like machine gun fire
As huge trees
Come crashing down
Under the weight of
The anaconda
Distracted birds wheel and dive high in the sky
Not knowing where to land
All their nests have been raided
By this awesome fire blanket
A blanket with an insatiable appetite for
Destruction!

Paul Harvey Jackson (Bangor)

Wartime Romance

I met her one day, in forty-one
And it's the best day's work I've ever done
We married while on army leave
Knowing that we soon would grieve
At parting from this love of ours
Counting the days, counting the hours
Till once again we soon would meet
And both our hearts would miss a beat
In forty-three our son was born
To leave them both, I felt forlorn
They braved the Blitz in London Town
And never let Hitler get them down
In forty-six came my demob
Then back in print, to my old job
The money was small and times were hard
And food only obtained on ration card
We lived in two rooms as cold as ice
We had some companions, a family of mice
Hard times lay ahead, but we stuck it together
As we have done since, whatever the weather

Now old age is upon us, but we've had wonderful years
With plenty of sunshine and a great many tears
We've always had a good table and a lovely warm bed
And material things have never gone to our head
We don't own a car, but what does it matter?
We would rather sit by the fire and have a good natter
She has stuck by my side, it matters so much
And to me she will always be my Old Dutch
We've been together now for sixty-two years
And there ain't a lady living in the land
That I would swap for my dear Old Dutch

Time is passing quickly, my life is ebbing away
Sometimes it's quite frightening and I don't know what to say
Cancer was a bit of a problem and diabetes too
But when the blinking strokes came on, I had a bit of ado
My left side went all wobbly, my brain went on the blink

But I really must stop moaning and pause to try and think
Of people who are worse than me and have a harder life
I could have been the same as them, if it wasn't for my wife
She has been the backbone of our marriage for sixty-two years
The best complement I can pay her, is to break down in bloody tears

And now she is in hospital, it's such an awful shame
She really doesn't deserve it, but cancer is to blame
It breaks my heart to watch her, as she struggles to survive
My thanks to the doctors and nurses, who are keeping her alive
But we really can't live forever, it wouldn't be much fun anyway
We must be like old soldiers and simply fade away.

Frank Tampin (Carmarthen)

Father Christmas

'Are you old Father Christmas?'
The little girl said.
'Cos your hair and your beard are white
Your robe is all red and it covers your head
Mummy said you'd be coming tonight.'

When you come Father Christmas
In the still of the night
Perhaps you'll find I'm not fast asleep
I'll be ever so quiet and not say a word
Will you mind if I just have a peep?

I wrote you a letter
About four weeks ago
Saying the things I would like you to bring
Maybe a doll, or a pram or some books
Or perhaps you could manage a swing

My little brother Billie
He wrote to you too
But he cannot write very well
He'd like a fire engine, all red and white
But make sure it's got a loud bell!

Now Mummy and Daddy
I'm not very sure
They're too busy to worry, I suppose
Daddy'd like a new jacket, and Mummy some beads
Or, I know, she would like some new clothes.

With all the excitement
Tomorrow will bring
I think of the lonely at home
No one to talk to and no one to love
I wish I knew someone to phone

You know Father Christmas
I still have some doubts
And I say to my daddy, 'That's odd'
But he says, 'Not now darling, it's time for your bed
I can see you're beginning to nod.'

When my hands are together
And I'm down on my knees
I'll remember the things that you do
I'll ask Jesus to help you, I know that He will
Your work will be easier with two

You'll be tired Father Christmas
When you've finished the day
But will you do something special for me
Mummy'll make some mince pies, they'll be ever so hot
Will you join us at our Christmas tree?

Norman Howells (Bridgend)

Words From My Heart!

Bumming around, my heart out of sync
My head filled with thoughts - too much time to think
The realisation that the end is nigh
Disturbed, I don't know whether to laugh or cry
A week in our time, thousands dead
In a world where they say God is good
Gas explosion, earthquake, flood
Nations surviving on minimal food . . .
But government, leaders, the infrastructure
Are working together for a 'better' future
Weapons, warheads, germ manufacture
A crack in the system - no - it's a multiple fracture
The truths they tell us are a load of crap
We believe, we choose them, we've set our own trap
Advertisers tell us what we need
They instil in us a sense of greed
Who cares if millions live on the street
And global warming an obvious threat?
Dying nations, AIDS, no food
Again, they say God is good . . .
Incest, rape, murder, porn
This is the world into which we are born
A chance to live and then we die
What falls between is a twisted lie
Is this Earth or a living Hell
Where nature casts a deceptive spell?
Beauty all around us lies
In the oceans, on land, or in the skies
But deception is the missing link
It cannot be seen, it's the ideas that we think
Ideas that developed one step further
Have created a world of chaos and disorder . . .
Paintings and relics, more precious than life
£6 million for Van Gogh . . . £10 for the dying
But at least we contributed, we feel better inside
Then we get dressed for a party with a feeling of pride
£100 for champagne, £5 for water
Then a talk about fashion, Chanel, 'Yes, you ought to'

'That dress is a steal at £10,000, you know'
The mood is enhanced by a few lines of snow
Discussion of couture, car, gems by the ream
These people, realisation of the advertisers' dream
TV an escapism, enemy or friend
Who's to know the power of the messages it sends
Of violence, religion, of sex and the 'real thing'
Of music, of people, whether living or dying
Religion a tough one . . . of Heaven and Hell
Are we living the latter? Not easy to tell
Is it the good that are dying the violent ends
Of natural disasters, murders and drugs
Accidents, diseases, famine and thugs.

When we think of the future, we add with a sigh
What future? We ask, when we sense end is nigh
Devine retribution, remaining in Hell
So different from life, sometimes hard to tell
To live the destruction of Earth in our time
To be honest, punishment fit for the crime
Of hatred, power, lust and of greed
The ones that are dying, are those that are freed
In the words of a leader of youth in our time
'Death makes angels of us all
And gives us wings where we had shoulders
As smooth as ravens' claws'
His name, Mojo Risin, his lyrics digress
The subjects of life, love, sex and of death
The latter, his escape from life's screwed-up mess
His friend 'The end', he decided was best
But so many have followed his coward's way out
From the famous, to children, with heads full of doubt
About life's many questions, death's ravenous jaws
How long have people been aware of the flaws?
We've had several warnings, the signs are all there
Are there enough people remaining - people who care
Enough to repair the damage and disgrace?
I really don't think so, ah well, what a waste . . .

Janet Boyce (Port Stewart)

Sing A Song Of West Street

Let's cast our minds back a few years
When a megabyte was a big bowl of stew,
There was a bar at the bottom of West Street
Called Hook'sies, you remember? You do.

In the village of sweet Ballycarry
For a long time it stood, one of two,
Its décor was sparse, some would say, 'Badger's arse'
And for refinements, it had very few.

But for the boys that sang in the bar room
And for the 'craic'ach, spare a minute or two,
For I'd like to relate some names for debate
And who knows, there might even be you.

Of talent, this pub had aplenty
Bomber Brown, John Glover, Jerry D,
One singer, one song, less invited to sing along
Was the way that things had 'te' be.

But when Eric Mullholland sang, the whole pub rang
To the tune of 'The Red River Valley'
And we'd be singin' along to the words of the song
And in the meantime, havin' a 'swally'.

Next was Jeff King, to give his 'rending'
Of the Turfman from Ardee,
Then along with the Rancher, Billy Macdonald and co.
We'd burn bridges with Affee Mac C.

Stevie King would sing 'Peggy Gorden'
His Galway Shawl would always get a 'big han',
And Wull Hall would court lovely Molly
The flower of sweet Strabane.

And do you know when I think about it
We didn't do no one harm,
Just a drink and the joy of the music
With friends, by the fireside so warm.

Sure, the way Hooksie called, 'Time!' 'twas effective
Although it was basically 'cruid',
When the mop hit the 'flur' you moved to the 'dur'
Or be swamped by the o'ul 'Jasus' fluid.

Well, in truth, now times are a-changin'
And in a way, it is sort'a sad,
In a village serene, midst town lands so green
The developers have gone 'bloody' mad.

But for me, my pleasures are simple
And do you know what would make me feel glad?
Just to stand at the bar down in Hook'sies
And to sing a 'wee' song with the lads.

Michael Johnston (Carrickfergus)

Tae A Burns Night

Wis invited tae a Burns'
I wisnae awfy keen
Bit 'twas wan o' the best nichts
At Sandy an' Jean's

The table wis aw set oot
It looked really grand
Aw that wis missin'
Wis the village Pipe Band

A wis dressed as Pussy Nancy
Held the haggis on a plate
Shower cap upon ma heed
A really wis a state

Followed in the big man Craig
An he addressed the baw
Handed him the knife then
An' he slaughtered it an aw

The man who led the ceremony
Wis Mr McIntyre
Whit a man oor Tammy is
He's like the village squire

He disnae like nae nonsense
Ye've aw tae dae yer bit
Mak a fill o Rabbie Burns
An he wid have a fit

First he gets oor Janice
As she sings her prose
Something aboot Don
Bein her red, red nose

Then John wis sittin' ready
Noo whit verse did he choose
Cannae mind but awfy smart
Cos he wore his tartan trews

Then they pit the lichts oot
Are they jist bein silly
Naw it's time fir Sandy
Dae'n his special 'Holy Wullie'

Wis wan aboot two dugs
Wan rich the ither poor
Tammy minded every line
Professional fir sure

Alas it hid tae finish
Bit whit a smashin time
Then roond the road wi 'tipsy Chic'
As he blethered drunken rhyme.

Janis Robertson (Cardenden)

To Someone Very Special

No matter whatever happens between us,
You are and always will be, a friend to me
Because you are the type of person
Who is thoughtful and loving, caring and so kind
I hope that what I have said to you so far
And don't you ever doubt it, you will agree
You always have everyone else's welfare and feelings
Apart from your own, in mind

When you stand so close to me in work
I get really nervous and get ever so excited
All I want to do is to take you in my arms
And passionately kiss you so, so much
I want to tell you these things when I see you
And for you to be and feel so delighted
I do look forward to the day that we will both
Be able to feel and to kiss and to touch

When we're together, just a short time
I really feel so happy; hope you feel the same
When I look at you across the shop floor
And you are smiling, I like to smile with you
When I am by myself at night just thinking of you
I like to say out loud your name
I hope that when you read this poem
You'll think of me, you will feel the same as I do

When I am not with you, I will often wonder
What you're doing at that moment in time
Will you be feeling the way I am?
Will you be thinking of me?
What are you doing now?
I know that our situation will be a struggle
For us it will be a big, steep hill to climb
But I know that we will make it through all this
The good times and the bad, somehow

You're my true soulmate;
Through the thick and thin of life, you are my one and only
For no matter whatever happens between us both
You know that I'll be there for you
And I know that you will always be there for me;
We can talk when we're both lonely
My heart will always be for you to keep forever
In everything that we both shall do

I think that you are so beautiful, gorgeous, sexy
And so much fun to be around always
I want to hold you close to me and to feel your body
Next to mine all day and all night
You fill me with joy and excitement
You fill my thoughts and my heart in all my days
When I travel through the night to be with you
You will always be my guiding light

As my feelings for you grow stronger and stronger
At the passing of every single day
Please believe me when I tell you all these words
For, to you, I would never ever lie
It is because that I would want you to feel
So glad and happy and so nice in every way
And it is because of my feelings for you
That I would not want you to tell me goodbye

One day in the future, I hope that I can take you out
For a nice, romantic candlelit meal
Then go for a long walk, hand in hand
Under a clear, summer's night sky, in the park
I do really hope that you do not mind me telling you
All these things about how I feel
You've given me something back into my life
I know between us there is some spark

I do hope that when you do read this
It will make you feel happy and make you smile
Because I do really like to be around you all the time
Because you are so full of fun
You know I would do anything at all for you
I will always go, for you, that extra mile
Because for me, you will always be, for all of time
Truly be that very special someone.

Brian Walker (Glasgow)

The Tender Hours

Every night from 'ten 'til one',
The telly goes off and the radio on.
It's Chris Needs' 'Friendly Garden',
On friendly Radio Wales,
He plays us lovely music
And listens to our tales!

Eirlys Evans (Rhos-on-Sea)

The Ghost

Destined to walk in the shadows,
Away from the sun,
Its rays shine on others,
Yet me, seems to shun.

This quiet and solitude
Suits me just fine,
Till I try and break out
And find I'm confined.

I peer out from dank undergrowth
And look at that light,
But then find I'm drifting
Back into the night.

The wheel of my destiny
Just drags me along
In a cyclical nightmare
Which I know is all wrong.

Dead when alive
And alive when I'm dead,
I can't break this chain
Of my fate in my head.

It just seems to drown
Any hope that appears,
Submerging my dreams
Welling up all my fears.

This wound in my heart,
This pain that I feel,
How long will it take
For it ever to heal?

You tell me it can,
I just need to let go
And fly into that sun
And the stars' night-time glow.

The vast cosmic skies
That you're talking about
You say are locked
Into my very own heart.

Yet without the right key
Your words are just hollow,
I'm fed up existing
With all of this sorrow!

But you say that this life
Is both key and both heart,
And it's always been there,
In me, from the start.

Liz Moulson (Cardigan)

Ynys Llanddwyn

Island of Solitude - of calm and gentle mood -
The winds that blow o'er rock and fell
Restore our souls and make us well
That we might continue on our way
Through one more repetitive colourless day.

The fury of the sea and storm
Beat on the shores of Llanddwyn.
Yet this shall never change the form
Of the pearl in the sea that is Llanddwyn.

The ghosts that roam the ageless paths
Speak to us of a distant past
When the pace of the world was slow yet hard
And the spirit that lived in the hearts of men
And the strength of the folk that lived here then
Reaches out to us from infinity
Enriching our hearts with its purity.

As we sit in the rocks with the spray and foam
We smile in the wind and know we are home.
Our bodies are weak - our feet are of clay
But our hearts and souls are flying away
From the prison of life in this present day
As we sit in the rocks of Llanddwyn.

We roam through the coves of shell and stones
We gather collections of fossils and bones -
We run like children as free as air
The wind in our faces and streaming hair.
We jump and we leap, we laugh and we weep
We shout and we sing - we can do anything -
Away from the eyes of the critical world
Our wings spread wide, our mainsail unfurled
On the beaches of Llanddwyn.

We lie in a ring on the shingled shore
And gaze at the colours there
Trying to count the countless shades
On the shingle beneath us there.
The smell of each stone is one of its own
And the feel of the beach is more like home
Than the warmth and comfort of the house far away
That we must return to after today.
What paintbrush or palette could ever express
The wonderful feeling of happiness
That exudes from each rock - from each blade of grass
No one shall capture the mood that is here
Of glory, enchantment, challenge and fear
In the secret places of Llanddwyn.

Marjorie Richards (Gwynedd)

For Pippa

When tomorrow starts without me
And I'm not there to see;
The sun will rise and find your eyes
All filled with tears for me.
I wish so much you wouldn't cry
The way you did today,
Remembering how I'd lay my head
In your lap that special way.
I know how much you loved me,
As much as I love you
And each time that you think of me,
I know you'll miss me too.

But when tomorrow starts without me,
Please try to understand,
That an angel came and called my name
And petted me with her hand.
She said my place was ready,
In Heaven far above
And that I'd have to leave behind
All those I dearly love.

But, as I turned to heel away,
A tear fell from my eye.
For all my life I never thought
That I would have to die.
I had so much to live for,
So many dances and laughs to do,
It seemed almost impossible,
That I was leaving you.

I thought about our lives together,
I know you must be sad.
I thought of all the love we shared
And all the fun we had.

Remember how I'd nip your hand
And poke you with my nose?
The ball I would gladly chase,
Our grandparents I'd bite and hold.

If I could relive yesterday
Just even for a while,
I'd jump around and lick you,
Just so I could see your smile.

But, then I fully realised
That this could never be;
For emptiness and memories
Will take the place of me.
And when I thought of treats and toys
I might miss come tomorrow.
I thought of you and when I did,
My ferret-heart filled with sorrow.

But then I walked through Heaven's gate
And felt so much at home;
As God looked down and smiled at me
From His beautiful golden throne.
He said, 'This is eternity
And now we welcome you.
Today your life on Earth is passed,
But here it starts anew.

I promise no tomorrow,
But today will always last;
For you see, each day's the same day,
There's no longing for the past.
Now you have been so faithful,
So trusting, loyal and true;
Though there were times you did things
You knew you shouldn't do.

But good ferrets are forgiven
And now at last you're free;
So won't you lay here by my side
And wait right here with me?'
So when tomorrow starts without me,
Don't think we're far apart,
For every time you think of me,
I'm right there, in your heart.

Eve Leah Roberts (14) (Treharris)

The Great Salt Lake Desert

The winds are high and the desert is dry
The sun shines down and burns the ground
The birds fly low and the snakes move slow
As the sun goes down and the moon goes up
And the wind blows slow the desert goes cold
As the clouds cover the moon and the birds fly north.

Alex French (Cardiff)

Peace, Be Still

I'm home alone
As winter winds are blowing
Strong and wild
I lock the door, close the blinds
And sit frightened as a child
The windows shake, the lamp posts sway
The trees are pushed and tossed
The wind, it howls and whistles
As if saying, 'I'm the boss!'

Then a story comes to mind
Of long ago, in Galilee
How the disciples too were troubled
As they sailed the stormy sea
They thought the winds
Would surely break
Their fishing boat in two
The wind just seemed to howl at them,
'There's nothing you can do!'

They cried for help
And immediately
Across the stormy sea
The Saviour's gentle voice was heard,
'Don't be afraid, I'm here!
Peace - be still!'
The Saviour said
The winds and the waves obeyed,
'Peace to you - be still my friends
And listen to what I say.
When wind and rain and rolling seas
Bring to you such fear,
Just close your eyes
And think of me
Remember - I am near.'

So, when the stormy winter winds
Are howling at the door
Just raise your voice

And shout right back,
'You'll frighten me no more!'
Now winds may howl
And winds may blow
The only thing I hear
Is the Saviour
As he says to me,
'Peace, be still -
I'm here!'

Julie Lambe (Newtonabbey)

Speaking In Tongues

Are you sure, Fiona asks, you're not a priest? Ten minutes left
before her next, and she lies on her back, knees bent up, her red hair
fanned across the lilac sheet, dabbing her chest with a wet wipe.
I pour her a warm Coke. Outside it's eighty-eight degrees; inside,
the fan grinds back and forth. From one wall come the usual sounds,

from the other, Caprice, ten hours into a twelve hour shift, saying,
trust me, it happens all the time. Have it your way, Fiona says
I've been around too long. They come in here around Lent,
the young ones, before they take their vows. And then I see them after.

Two pigeons flurry at the skylight, fall exhausted and Caprice
is trying again when Fiona says, You know this place was haunted?
Lights coming on and off, ashtrays flying round. All that stuff. Bloody
punter, of course. Dead and nowhere better to hang around than here the bxxxxxd. Didn't
bother me. I says, *if you can move*
plates about, why don't you do the washing up? But the wee girlies
were getting frightened. Voices. Touching their hair. And then it's bad

for business. So there's this one guy - one of my regulars.
I had a feeling about him. I didn't ask, cause then it makes it
awkward. I just says to him, *I've got a problem.*
Now could you maybe do something, just as a favour?
Looks that damn surprised, I tell you.
Then all serious, he says, *I'll need to be alone, Fiona.*
She passes me some tissue, sips her Coke, and I see

him standing in this room, naked, his right hand lifted, quartering
the air. His breath slowing, the pulse of the fan, the cars outside,
all slowing, beginning the Liturgy of Deliverance and as he speaks
something growing present, clawing at his nerves, a burden in the air
an outline at the edge of vision, the muscles in his neck tensing,
sweat glistening on his temples, running in the hollow of his spine
and then, unasked, his throat convulsing saliva

flooding in his mouth and breaking in the room the tongue of angels,
harsh with the arid rhythms of the desert
the air opening to his words the way that eggshell opens for a bird
or snake. His palms scorching and all this, the bed,
the table with its folded towels, the plate of Durex, Asda talc, blazing
holy, their colours scalding, the light of everything awoken, and then the peace
of nothing, the carpet, walls, fading to dullness, and him standing
here, the air chilling on his skin, the damp prints of his feet, his hair
matted, limp and outside the shrill summons
of pelican lights on Dundas street.

Right enough, Fiona says, he did the job. Not that I'm religious -
Christmas and wedding, me. But I could tell, he'd cleared it out.
I owe you, I says to him and then he says to me, *Fiona, you realise,*
he says, *I'm really sorry hen. I can't come back here now.*

Edmund Cusick (Llandrillo)

Our Sister, Kate

To get our Kate out for a night caused many a fight,
It's the last time I'm going, she'd warn
And when we got there, she said with a stare,
We're at the bloomin' Glencarn.
It was late when we arrived, we felt deprived
And the cars had started to freeze,
The car park was full, there was certainly no lull,
Of tractors or JCBs.
I said, sure we're single, we might as well mingle,
She said I'd rather be darning my socks,
Take a look at that crowd, there is some in the shroud
And the rest would give you chickenpox.
Then along came Slim Jim, with a wide, open grin,
Saying excuse me, would you like to dance,
I'm sweating with the heat, I've got two left feet,
But do you think you might take a chance?
From that day to this, she's been on the missing list
And she hardly ever comes home
And what would Jim do, if he couldn't get through,
Sure she had to get the mobile phone.
She said, I think that he's keen, or so it would seem,
He's asked me to spend the night
And what do you know, I think I might go,
It could put an end to my plight.
She came back with a grin, her face full of sin,
Isn't she the sly fox,
My heart is sore, my life is a bore,
For now I'm the one darning the socks.
Though I don't complain, only now and again,
About her taking care of his stuff
And they come visit me, about once a month, for tea
And he brings me the odd bag of turf.
Kate would like him to stay, until the next day,
That's what started all the rows,
But Jim had to leave, wipe his tear on his sleeve,
Who else would milk the cows?
So Jim, you stay at home, look after the farm,
Just think of the financial gains,
Kate and I will go abroad, get an all-over tan,

To help camouflage the varicose veins.
He thinks he's well got, with me and my lot
Says she to me with a wink,
I'm no slave, he'll not work me into the grave,
I'll put him in front of the sink.
Now you're going taa, greaghcashel or Donagh,
But remember, you're from Armagh,
We've got something to say on your wedding day,
Yes, it's us, your Ma and Da.
You're on your own long enough, you were so good to us,
We love you, you're special, my dear.
Now eat and be merry, let the laughter be plenty,
But no drinking and driving, look-see-here.
Some might say you were hard to please, other men you did leave,
But this match was not made on a whim.
Would you like to know, before your Ma and me go,
What we think of your Mr Jim?
Well, you know he's not bad for a middle-aged lad
And he does have a wee farm of land,
Be sweet and be nice, don't think twice,
You'll have him eating out of your hand.
You've exchanged your vows, amid these crowds,
You've said, 'I do' and 'I will,'
Now you can whisper to me, on the QT,
Is Patrick footing the bill?
Slainte to Borde Failte, Marie and what-ya-call-ya,
I'm combing my pursuits,
I'm milking the cows, cleaning the turkey house,
Knee-deep in my welly boots.
So, now you all know, how their love did grow
And it all started off with one date,
So, these words just had to be said, especially now that they're wed,
About Jim and our sister, Kate.

Esther Bernadette McKevitt (Newry)

Where

I'm sitting here, I'm sitting here, I'm sitting here
But I'm not here, I'm not here, I'm not here
I cannot think, I cannot feel
It must be true, but it's not real.

His loving hand in mine, so warm - he smiled
No words, just closeness -- then he died . . .

Linda Laugharne (Newport)

The Crab

I looked out of the waiting room window,
Cancer is a frightening word.
I'd seen my father go from robust health
To die just skin and bone,
Some people have cancer;
They have cancer;
He had cancer;
Such different words - when the surgeon said to me,
'You have cancer.'

The chair had the hardness only patient seats provide.
I looked out at the sky.
As I gazed the clouds took human form,
I saw my father shrink again,
I saw myself boy *bach* again;
The clouds changed form again.
The boy, a youth, was without hair -
Chemotherapeutically bald.
'You have cancer.'

Cancer's a nasty name,
I tell myself I'll beat it.
Think, think, think positively,
Out of the waiting room window
I can see the scanner room;
Its maw agate, it waits for me.
I'll greet it with a grin.
I'm not afraid of claustrophobia,
I'm not afraid of anything.

I know my Mabinogion.
With the help that my cloud friends will give,
I'll return from the Land of the Dead.
I start with a trip to the scanner,
'Do your worst, I'm no longer afraid.'
Piss on the words like therapy
Whether chemo, radio or video,
Some other one I don't yet know.
Arthur's cloud knights will keep me safe.

The power of words will sustain me.
The mother in che*mother*apy
Will guard me from serious harm.
She'll make a fish paste of
The crab that's invaded my body
And help me recover my health.
She'll watch over me during my sleep.

Gordon Lowden (Colwyn Bay)

Dreadful Diet

Today I start my diet
I'm feeling very keen
Instead of stuffing my fat face
I'll treat myself real mean
For breakfast I'll have porridge
Instead of cake and tea
The weight will just drop off me
And skinny I will be
The porridge was real filling
But then I feel my eye
Drawn to the biscuit tin
I hid away up high
Oh no you don't, you fatty
No biscuit you will take
Just look at your enormous butt
And try, for goodness sake
For lunch I'll have a salad
Instead of steak and chips
I'm sure that's bound to do the trick
And burn weight off my hips
But still I feel quite peckish
Not feeling really full
My eye is on the biscuit tin
So I pull across the stool
I manage to withdraw myself
I'm doing really well
Even though this dreadful diet
Is putting me through Hell
For dinner I'll have salad
Instead of chips and pie
Just after I have finished
Comes the roaming of the eye
Just then I heard a crash and bang
And what came tumbling down?
The biscuit tin with such a force
It knocked me to the ground
The biscuits, they were scattered
Around me as I lay

I picked them up and one by one
I put them on a tray
Feeling hurt and very hungry
I rubbed my swollen head
I grabbed the tray of biscuits
And ate them all in bed!

Tina Kelly (Maghera)

The Other Side Of The Wire

I notice that you smile
And raise an eyebrow at the mention
Of how an everlasting sun shone down
Upon our childhood summers
To the never-breaking rhythms of a cheerful seaside tide
Or how the snow and ice that blanketed
Each and ev'ry winter's day
Could always be relied on
To reinforce accepted wisdom
Like the benevolent domination
Of colony and empire
Spreading knowledge and enlightenment
To the furthest reaches of a boundless Earth
Where faithful guardians of stability
Were holding off the baying house of chaos
In the 'Here-Be-Dragons' realm beyond the wire

Maybe you find it all
A bit too difficult to credit
That we should chase so readily across
Those well-thumbed schoolroom pages?
Without raising hands to question where the real distinctions lay
Between adventurers and brigands?
What turned explorers into thieves?
Our teachers hailed achievements
And offered praise in equal measure
To men of principle and conquerors
To still, small voice and fire
For, of course, the Sunday stories
Still urged the true believer to take up the sword
And, with a righteous hand, as the Scriptures say,
To sweep away the pagan man's damnation
And dispense a new salvation through the wire

Perhaps you will agree
That those in power make pretty statements
Until self-int'rest spies an op'ning
Where the spoils are too inviting
Do they ever pause to wonder whether frontier lines divide
Their moral high ground from the dogma
That says, our wars are always just -
The other side is evil?
And thus a further generation
Must live or die for noble causes
And the peace that all desire
Young men marching under orders,
Dispatched to levy vengeance on this latest foe
And grind the dust of his broken cities
Blotting out the pain that's etched upon the faces
Of the children staring vanquished through the wire

What course would you select
if you were standing at that crossroads?
When the last hand had waved surrender
And the battlefields were silent?
Would you settle for forgiveness, or demand some reckoning?
Would it be your preferred solution
To go in search of missing sheep
And fetch them back to safety?
Or to devote your time to judgement
Calling for hunting down of guilty goats
To cast upon the pyre?
Which of us can say the road we'd take -
Towards hate or mercy - till that moment comes?
Most often justice is what the mighty say
And history the fiction of the victors
Leaving truth to squeeze through underneath the wire

It seems to me these days
The world's become so hard to fathom
With talk of profit and consumption
Without hint of moderation
Now that lines are drawn by markets and restraint's become a crime
They call for guards and higher fences
To stop the hungry and oppressed
Encroaching on our fortune
Whilst elsewhere preachers of a diff'rent truth
Underline our moral shortcomings
And men of faith conspire
As the gathering corporations circle
The spoils in their pragmatic shades of grey
Where past atrocities are repaid a thousand-fold
And lands are shaped by peacemakers
Who thrust their snarling faces hard against the wire.

David Gasking (Carrbridge)

Untitled

Green hills concealing still lakes
Vast sea views observed from snaking mountain roads
Wet nights on eight-lane motorways
Warm summer days sinking a beer with friends
Sky, which matches the black/grey colour of the tarmac
For better or worse
Home.

Paul Gray (Bangor)

Plant A Tree?

They march in rows across the frozen waste
Dragging branches in their frightened haste
The ice-bound soil beneath their roots displaced
As global warmth accelerates its pace

Arid sands replace the jungle green
And chattering, leaping apes no more are seen
The lifeless trunks raise high their limbs to keen
Their silent cries bewailing life's lost dream

The coral seas once filled with vivid life
Lie stark and still as skeletons bleached white
Gone are the dancing, flashing fish once rife
As though excised beneath a surgeon's knife

The pretty cottage garden is no more
As swarming locusts thrive outside our door
Driven further from their place of yore
To distant countries never seen before

Savage winds bring fear throughout the land
Ripping life from soil with violent hand
As crop-filled fields rot in endless rain and
Clean fresh water cannot meet demand

Countless species filled this planet Earth
A paradise alive with vibrant mirth
But human kind rose up from out the surf
And selfishly took everything of worth

We spread unchecked across our planet's face
Our actions caused disfiguring disgrace
And selfishness took every inch of space
So many creatures vanished without trace

'What have we done?' I hear your plaintiff cry
As millions starve and waters run stone dry
Our greed destroyed our home, our end is nigh
As climate changes fast and then we die

Is there some way to change our pending fate?
To bring back hope instead of fear and hate
To save our world our efforts must not wait
Let's work together lest it get too late

Treat nature as a friend and not foe
Respect all life and learn how best to grow
The trees hills need so soil will not erode
To save a world that thrived not long ago

Karen Carmichael-Timson (Carmarthen)

A Cry From The Grave

You have all been babies
Babies just like me
Little cuddly bundles of joy
A marvel for all to see

But your life has been so different
Of that I am so glad
Because my life was brutal
And it made me oh so sad

Even when I went to school
And some of those kids were losers
None of them could ever compete
With my number of hideous bruises

Some of my teachers noticed
Of that I'm pretty sure
But it wasn't even in their power
To find an effective cure

They did report it to officialdom tho
No more could they do
And those who were responsible
Said they would see it through

O yes, they did come and visit
They came again and again
Could they not see the state I was in
See all those bruises and pain?

As I lie here sleeping now
Their attitude drives me wild
Surely only the Devil could have blinded their eyes
Not to see the state of this child

But now peacefully I sleep
I can no longer hear them murmur
But tell me, could anyone possibly be
An accomplice to my murder?

I suppose when that person sleeps at night
They will have no need to worry
For tomorrow night on the television
Someone will say, 'We are sorry'

As I said before, I lie here peaceful now
I have breathed my very last breath
And in a few weeks time, not even remembered
This child that was beaten to death.

Artie Salopian (Orkney)

A Day At The Tattie Picking In The 1950s

We're really needing half a crown,
To have a daunder round the town,
We didn't do so well at school
And always played the bloody fool,
So me and my pal, Plookie Jean,
On tattie picking we were keen,
Jean says it near ten bob they pay,
We'll try it out - just for a day.

A flask of tea with bread and spam,
We hurried out to meet the gang,
We're sweet sixteen with not a worry,
We wanted on the tattie lorry,
With trousers and our big black wellies
We wanted to impress the fellies.

We're jammed together in a pack
My legs are dangling o'er the back
I'm terrified I'm going to fall
While Pookie Jean, she has a ball
She has to sit on Paddy's knees
I bet he's giving her a squeeze.

We're full of life, we're full of wit
The songs we learn you'd have a fit
We're full of vigour and with vim
For ten bob we'll do anything

We're on the field, we're at our bit
The gaffer's howling like a git
'Now pick these tatties, nice and clean
Or you'll feel my boot upon your beam.'

We pick our bits, it's all great fun
The digger's got us on the run
By piece time our backs are aching
And all our fingernails are breaking.

There's something else we didn't savvy
Till Jeanie shouted, 'Where's the lavvy?'
Paddy stands there with a grin
And rubs the stubble on his chin,
'Now listen here, wee Jeanie, lass
This tattie field is not first class
Just go o'er there, among the trees
And air your backsides in the breeze.'

By dinnertime we're on our knees
Our aching backs they will not ease
The bits they seem to get much bigger
Wish somebody would shoot that digger.

We have a laugh, we have a joke
We lassies fancy all the blokes
The tractor boy, a no bad looker
Offers me a granny sooker
My stomach feels like it's been kicked
I can't believe I've really clicked.

Loads of dirt and old cow patties
Is what you get when picking tatties
Me and Jeanie think it's great
Ten whole shillings and a date.

It's not the bits that seem much bigger
Or chuckie stains and double diggers
Our aches and pains that make us frown
It's just not worth it - four half crowns.

It's lousing time - it's nearly five
We can't believe we're still alive
Plookie Jean now she's pot black
And screaming, 'I'm not coming back.'

Now I tell you all so you'll be quicker
And not end up a tattie picker
Please never ever act the fool
Learn all you can when you're at school
You'll always have your half a crown
To have a daunder round the town.

Viga Walker (Perth)

Empty Eyes

E verything, all is mirrored in our eyes
M emories good, by smiles. Or bad, by sighs
P atiently hoping, a good day, will it be?
T omorrow our actions will set one free
Y earning for yesterday, when life was full.

E very day happy, one was so cool
Y esterday, so long ago, played by the rules
E cstasy was, something, someone else, life is now cruel
S o be it, please, I wish back, but I am the fool.

Sheila Macdonald (Fraserburgh)

Down By The Brook

Down by the brook
in the bluebell wood,
little foxes roam
where the old oak stood.

Down by the brook
in the dappled shade,
seek hiding places
where dreams are made.

Down by the brook
hear the wind in the trees,
where the blackbird sings
through the trembling leaves.

Down by the brook
where the willows dip,
from the soft mossy bank
where we watch and sit.

Down by the brook
where the swallows fly,
little frogs leap
as the fish swim by.

Down by the brook
on a summer's day,
if you keep very quiet
little fairies will play.

Down by the brook
all covered with snow,
rabbits' footprints cross
where the snowdrops grow.

Down by the brook
as the night begins,
the moon glows yellow
whilst the nightingale sings.

Down by the brook
where we fall asleep,
looking up to the stars
counting lots of sheep.

Down by the brook
as the stars shine bright,
creatures of the woods
bid us all - goodnight!

Louisa Middleton-Blake (Llandysul)

Orlock Bay Of Ulster's Way

I walked through rugged paths today
Where stones of Earth's upheaval lay
From far off times they lean inclined
Layered rock and shale combined

And as I walked and studied more
Each crack within a world is stored
With flowered beauty our display
To them the clouds that line their day

A microscope world of gems
That lends my heart to lift this pen
A poet's view, a special way
To see, then tell, for all that may

Reflect with me within these lines
As I involve each reader's mind
A dwell of sands of homes so small
Are we, to them, their faith and God?

Yes, life can thrive in scars of old
A struggle born of timelined shores
For deep within each delve life hides
As in our world we too survive

What is a world, what is its dwell?
Are we the world where they are held?
Just maybe then, the chance that we
A hidden crack set by a sea

The universe, its sandy beach
With pebbles, shells, its worlds are each
All galaxies are ponds that hold
A million stars of grain-like souls

For me, it's just a part of space
This world I know it's just one place
A tiny speck like they to me
As most that walk this path don't see

Of countless worlds and endless lines
The marks of prehistoric times
We all evolve, we all can end
It matters not what time or when

So, as you fathom all you've read
Before you say your prayers in bed
Look out your window to the sky
To see our stranger walking by.

Colin Thomas Coffey Mercer (Bangor)

From Nature: The Creative Into Enlightenment

'Twas balmy and still, ripples upon reflections
birds in tune with the sunset, distant recollections
of harmony, stillness, amid peace, the unity of nature
telling me the synchrony of this scene has to be in my future.

I sat upon the stump . . . pondering about this synchrony
life in nature had an elegant perfection within its alchemy.
Signets swam collectively, somehow guided along the way
how could I take these reflections as a learning for each day?

Musing that creativity was somehow in the design of this scene
one often taken for granted . . . but now from it, what did I glean
that could help my journey become aligned with divine purpose
imbued with the richness of balance in needs and rightful choice?

The air was drifting towards cool yet it remained quite gentle
as the wafting of leaves and plaintive birdsong calmed the mental.
I wondered if the creative mind could come from alert restfulness
through our association with the novel, being in a state of playfulness?

I thought I would try to germinate some new patterns in design
where my mind ignored the needs and concerns of the usual line
allowing the distillation of sensual osmosis through this synchrony
to be open to receive through a peaceful yet energising harmony.

Giving acceptance for new schemas to play out their part
gestalts of idiosyncratic connections emanating from the heart
novel associations being caressed with respectful tenderness
from the bed of humanity awkward questions posed in calmness.

Where any answer was safe, free to be fully expressed
in social intercourse without the fear of being oppressed
the beauty in being oneself, connecting with synergy and acceptance
the germination of new health, a new world of faith and expectance.

Creativity and camaraderie thus conjoin in a spirit of quest
first there is dialogue, then incubation through play and rest
connections of interdependence become the basis of structure
integrous design and unity of purpose translate into manufacture.

I wonder if creativity could also be about creating a space
where freedom percolates in our mind, thence we can espouse
our wonderings and disconnected thoughts, our many doubts
and regrets, not forgetting those meanderings we call wants.

And within that space, the fullest acquiesce is given
that anything may be expressed, that anything could happen
for this space is like the ballroom of design and practice
the mind is free to play with ideas . . . we reflect and notice.

These scenarios are then replayed and considered
could they fit with the world out there and be heard
are there other minds attuning to this creative frequency
construing their future from like vibrations and potency?

We cannot idealise specific attracting entities in human form
but we will connect and kindred spirits who have flown
into our transmission receiving area, our zone of proximity
energies communing, thus creating an ambience of synchronicity.

Respecting one another through care and tolerance
recognizing that freedom must reside in an ambience
that accepts without condition opposing points of view
where dialogue replaces monologue as prerequisite for the new.

Something in my reflections began to connect states of mind
to observe that creativity, peace, and lovingness are like in kind
. . . as they coalesce, the energy of spiritual transformation
manifests as change in core consciousness and maturation.

Slowly the balm of nature permeates its presence in mental pores
distilling the emotions with a consciousness found in spiritual laws
enlightenment thus began as energy flowed in human transmission
radiating the radiance of effortless change within society's mission.

The soul of nature had touched the mind of Man at its essence
clearing neutral pathways for novel associations of luminescence
giving birth and expression to the creative process in human living
as slowly the souls of this enlightened energy became one in sharing.

Bob Gleeson (Glasgow)

Forever In Our Hearts

It seems like only yesterday that
With a sad heart we said our goodbyes,
To a mother and friend who was very special.
She suffered in silence without complaint,
But she lost the battle and the will to live.
Without her our lives will not be the same,
She is sadly missed by one and all.

Time passes and the pain of grief subsides,
She will be remembered in those happier times,
By her children and grandchildren and great grandchildren,
She will be remembered for the joy and happiness,
The unconditional love she shared with us,
And as long as we live in our hearts she will forever stay.

Sue Peach (Rhos-on-Sea)

Surely Thou Did Know

High in the celestial sphere
I spied a saddened angel
Shattered wings, halo dulled, fading smile
Trying to reach a falling star
And was that thee

Then I saw a twilight moth
The moonlight caught its sheen
And as its wings were gently stilled
The moon, it lost its beam
And was that thee

The mighty oak did tremble
Stretching its weary limbs
Heavenly bent, crumbling within
On its last summer day
And was that thee

Cruel was my day of awakening
The sun, it tumbled down
Melting with my destiny
Surely though did know

If I could turn the searing heat
Into a drizzling rain
And fix the broken angel
Much solace would I gain
For then the mist would wash my tears
And make my eyes aglow
Perhaps thou did know

The rain would wet the thirsty tree
The moth would flutter and be free
The angel would be over thee
Surely thou did know

Now treading a sacred path with healing heart
In stillness and serenity do I dwell
My soul withdrawn from the vast wilderness
Of loud confusion
The light did shed my darkness
My spirit soothed in silent adulation
And did thou know
    Horizons, nay many, mingled with sky
    Now blazing scarlet, filling my ocean of emptiness
    And fear will not dare to creep upon me now
    Surely it was thou

F Crosby (Abergele)

Lough Neagh's Discovery Centre

Lough Neagh must be in your plan,
If you wish to visit Northern Ireland,
The marina is located on the southern shore,
When you visit it, you will love it even more,
The largest marina on the Lough is Kinnego,
Harbour Master Paddy Prunty is in control,
With over 100 berths and 30 hard standing spaces
And on many occasions you will witness boat races,
In the provision of royal yachting,
This marina is in the recognised leading,
There are powerboats, personal watercraft, sailing
And shore based courses for your learning,
It is one of Northern Ireland's oldest sailing club's home,
Eighteen seventy-seven was the year it did come.

Within the surroundings of Lough Neagh shore,
There is Sands Boatyard and a Chandlery store.
The Life Boat station, caravan park and ducks to feed,
Plus a nature reserve and a café to meet your need.
The Loughside Café offers a wide choice of cuisine,
From its ground and mezzanine floors, the views are extreme,
The well-stocked gift shop at the Discovery Centre,
Will give you a warm, friendly welcome, when you enter,
There is a Tourist Information Office at the reception,
Helping visitors to enjoy their expedition.
Contact the Discovery Centre throughout the year,
Free of charge, innovative exhibitions will appear,
Corporate visitors will enjoy the state-of-the-art meeting facilities,
In a unique and tranquil setting that will share happiness.

With the successful lowering of Lough Neagh
And a lot of water being drained away,
Oxford Island National Nature Reserve was created
This peninsula is a haven for wildfowl being wintered.
Song birds abound throughout the woods,
Making your walk boost all your good moods,
On the flower-rich pastures and meadows
Graze the Irish breeds of Moiled and Dexter cows,
The Conservation Service is based at Oxford Island,

Giving information and guidance if you wish to plan.
The Discovery Centre will supply maps of the site
And interpretive panels that illustrate the wildlife.
Hope you will enjoy all this when you come
And won't be so tired when it's all done.

Maureen Dawson (Craigavon)

Glamorgan Sheep

As dawn broke over the valley
They would amble down the street,
One by one with a *ba, ba, ba*
Came the Glamorgan sheep.
They were experts at tipping the buckets,
Leaving ashes all over the place,
They would nose out the cabbage and peelings
And emerge with a dust-covered face.
If you went out and shooed them, they'd stand there
With a nonchalant look they would munch,
If you rose up your hand, they would just turn away
Then leave you their yesterday's lunch.

I remember my friend Mary's mother,
Edith Maud, who had bought a new hat,
She had bought it for our Gymanfa
Or, some big occasion like that.
But Edith Maud was never to wear it,
And the reason is you see,
She left her front door open
And went next door for a nice cup of tea.
The sheep ambled in through the doorway
To the parlour and saw Edith's hat,
They chewed it all up, then, gulped it all down
And that was the end of that.

One morning our mam was unlucky
She was faced by a curly horned ram,
He dropped his head all ready to butt her,
But our mam slammed the door with a bang.
The ram, he was very persistent
He butted the door constantly
Until Dad took the cane-brush and poked him
Said, 'Get away or we'll have you for tea.'
Sheep were also quite partial to gardens,
Like ghosts they'd arrive in the night,
They'd vault over the wall like Olympic stars
Then destroy everything within sight.

I've seen many a gardener in tears,
Swearing vengeance to farmer and ewe,
But in those days, three was no compensation
There was nothing the gardeners could do.
If they went and complained to the farmers,
They would just shrug their shoulders and say,
'The Glamorgan sheep, they have minds of their own,
It's not our fault if they want to stray.'
'But the sheep should be fenced up on the mountain,'
They'd cry, 'Or kept 'tidy like' locked in a pen,
Not stuffing their guts on our Delia's
And our lettuce and carrots as well.'

One day I awakened quite early
To a commotion outside on the road,
When I opened the curtains and peered out,
It was Glam-or-gan sheep swr y fod
The sheep was wearing ma Moses' front gate,
That had finally come off its hinge,
The ewe staggered and fell in the gutter,
With the gate round its neck like a fringe.
Dai and Harry, they carried the sheep off
To Twm's carpenter shop up the lane,
Twm cut off the gate with a hacksaw,
But we never saw that sheep again.

My Bopa, she had her suspicions,
When Twm's wife bragged about her new mat,
'It's woolly and white for the bedroom,' she said
And my Bopa said, 'Well fancy that,
No doubt the mince sauce has been flowing too,'
My Boba said, nodding her head,
'Goes nice with a slice of fresh, Welsh lamb,'
Twm's wife's face turned a bright shade of red.
Now, those days of ash buckets and sheep mess,
And irate gardeners, who tore out their hair,
Like the innocent pleasures of childhood
They sadly, no longer are there.

Anna Brown (Treorchy)

Sleeping Man

Sleeping man
on a library chair
your snores are heard
pervading the air.
Have you no home
why are you there
beside the table
on a library chair?
Friends meet to read
but stop to stare
at the snores
from the man
who is unaware
and is fast asleep
on a library chair.

R Hanna (Glasgow)

Greetings

Cards of every shape and colour
Elegantly printed, huge,
Homemade, tiny,
Cobbled up
From last year's
Collection.

Robins, robins, endless robins
Wait a minute - here's a fox!
Oh, a squirrel!
Hey, a badger!
Oh dear, one more
Robin.

Sheep and shepherds, donkeys, camels,
Magi, Holy Family,
Mixed up with
St Nicholas
Sledges, reindeer
Christmas trees.

Curious conglomeration
Of the sacred and profane
Witty, poignant
Sentimental
Sugary
Unreal.

Millions, millions, still more millions
Year on year, cascade anew
Friendly greetings
Crossing oceans
Or from neighbours
Down the road.

These, because a village girl
Screamed in labour in a cave,
Brought a baby,
Boy to birth
On a mucky
Stable floor.

Or maybe
You can provide
A different
Explanation.

Frank Hooley (Powys)

Glastonbury Song

Hello, it's good to be here!
(Wherever here is)
The chopper just landed backstage -
How are you all?
Waiting since dawn yesterday,
In the wind and the rain?

Well, now you can vent all your rage;
Throw caution to the wind
And your cash at the stage.

Is this a place of unity
Or the scene of a crime?
Fifty-odd thousand young souls
In a field used for sheep.
And I'm just like you, don't you know?
We're in this together.

I'm here, with my personal beasts,
You're here, and you're certainly fleeced.

Behind this scaffold and steel
Is a simple heart beating.
Our music gets straight into charts,
And girls into bed.
And this next song is just for you,
(If you're good-looking).

All that, and art for art's sake,
Be sure and buy a shirt at the break.

Here comes a song that you know.
Including the half hour
. . . obligatory
. . . Freudian
. . . erectile
. . . guitar solo.

Well, goodnight, you've all touched our hearts.
(We almost mean that)
And, just like thieves in the night,
We'll say bye-bye.
Tomorrow the garbage will blow,
The rags of the real world.

But we'll meet again, mon ami,
(Not personally, obviously.)

Scott Perrie (Lanark)

In The Boat

I'm not a real fisherman,
But my uncle is
And sometimes, if there's room
In the boat, he takes me out with him.
He even allows me
To help haul in the nets
So I suppose that makes me
A sort of apprentice fisherman.
I love the sea, even when it's rough,
And the Sea of Galilee, as You know,
Can be very rough at times.
Once, when I was in the boat,
A really bad storm blew up
And I thought we would never get back
To the shelter of the small inlet
Where the boats are moored.
It was a bit too rough for my liking.
I found myself wishing that
You were in the boat with us
Because my uncle had told me,
Many times, the story of how a
Big storm blew up one day
When You were out with them.
By all accounts, it was an even worse
Storm than the one I had experienced.
So violently was the boat being tossed
By the wind and the waves
That my uncle and the other fishermen
Feared that it might capsize.
You were asleep and unaware
Of the danger. They awakened You
And You reassured them,
Telling them not to be afraid.
They were amazed when
You went to the prow
Of the boat and rebuked
The wind and the waves,
Commanding them to be calm;
Instantly the storm abated

And my uncle said that for a long time
Afterwards the silence was
Deep and beautiful and unbroken.
Later, my uncle told me
That the story of how You calmed
The wind and the waves
Could be used as a prayer,
A prayer to calm the storms
Of life which everyone,
Not just fishermen,
Have to face at some time or another.
He also told me that on one occasion
You spoke of making them
'Fishers of Men' if they were willing
To give up the sea and follow You.
I've been thinking a lot about
Those words of yours,
Especially now I'm a little older.
Maybe that's why, whenever I can,
I like to walk, by myself,
Along the shoreline,
By the Sea of Galilee, hoping
To catch the sound of Your voice
In the deep and beautiful silence.

Maurice McAleese (Portstewart)

The Intimation

I felt strange warmth within my heart
From one no way remote:
He showed me that eternity
Of which I was a part
Was loving, good and beautiful
While fret and strain would be redeemed
By his most subtle art.
Security could reign, it seemed,
Give joy a flying start.

I can't forget this startling gift
That came one autumn day
And cherish still the memory
And also always pray
With confidence all will be well
Whatever people say.

Peter Spurgin (Edinburgh)

The Fiddle

The
fiddle
warps upon
the wall
since he has
gone it
does not
bring
its joy
to any
one at
all For
no one
else can
make it
sing The
lilting
love songs
that he played The merry jig
and wild schottische The Shetland
reel and paced strathspey For now
he plays entombed beneath The
fertile ground and out of sight Playing
for the fairy king And swaying
through eternal night Made
glorious by the singing strings
While our feet tread
heavy on the earth
We scrape existence
from the soil This clay
our origin of birth And life
is naught but pain and toil But old age
with not etch his face Nor winter ache
deep in his bones The fiddle warps there
in its place While he bides preserved within the
loam And we may never know of his delight And
we may never see such things But listen when
you walk at night And you may hear his fiddle

ring Petrichor is in the song The cyclical
cadence of the land Defining the place
where we belong Just bring a
fiddle; take his hand.

Emma Grieve (Orkney)

How Men Who Built A Mountain Could Make A Village Cry

At a place called Aberfan, little children played
They were unaware a debt had to be paid
For men had built a mountain, so big, so black, so high,
In their search for coal, Man made that village cry.
God gave Man skill and knowledge, he bid us use them well,
Men dug and dug so blindly, the result we live to tell,
They took the prize from under, the waste they piled on high,
By chasing bigger profits, Man made that village cry.

Now they no longer dig for coal, the killer mountain's gone,
Sad memories are fading, but for some the grief lives on.
There's a question still unanswered, folk still wonder why
Those men who built that mountain, could make that village cry.

The rain came down so heavy, on that mountain high,
It turned the waste to water, the waste that once was dry,
Came down and took the children, and made us wonder why
Men that built a mountain, could make that village cry.
Those children played and perished, there on that awful day,
The hand of fate took over and washed them all away.
Now as we sadly wonder and ask each other why?
Men that built a mountain, could make a village cry.

Though they no longer dig for coal, the killer mountain's gone,
Sad memories are fading, but for some the grief lives on.
That question's still unanswered, folk still wonder why
Those men who built that mountain could make that village cry.

They picked them up and laid them in graves dug, side by side,
For each life that had ended, grown men and women cried.
Now as we sit round fires, piled high with glowing coal,
Let's say a prayer to Heaven, God rest each tiny soul.
They still no longer dig for coal, the killer mountain's gone,
The sad memories are fading but for some the grief lives on.
There's a question still unanswered, folk still wonder *why*
How men that built *that* mountain, could make that village cry!

Yes the question's still unanswered, folk still wonder why
Men who built that mountain could make that village cry!

Robert W M Bassett (Newport)

Equality

Equality and brotherhood for Man;
The extremist's thoughtful plan.
Equal pay with equal say,
Equal cars and equal bars,
Equal houses, equal spouses,
With children going to equal schools
All with equal ten-inch rules.
No more Jones' live next door
To make their neighbours wish for more.
But those who would partake in vices
Cannot invest in small devices
To make their homes or cars look quaint,
For this would only breed complaint
From others who would stop and see,
Then say, 'Why does he have more than me?'
Promotion, of course, would never be
As all jobs would have equal pay.
Equal men in equal trades
All with equal things to make,
Working hard, but never harder
For what's the point of being a martyr?
All causes are just and all just causes,
So all must be a bed of roses!
Top men would no longer be.
They'd all be middle men, you see.
So, if the firm should rise or fall,
It's all to blame, or none at all.
No man's grass could e'er be greener
And no man dare be keener
At doing work to win him favour
Lest he should offend his neighbour.
The rich would sacrifice their land
For little boxes to expand,
To house the poor, who live in squalor,
Who then would be content to follow
Every equal middle man's dream,
But what exactly would this scheme
Do to benefit mankind
And enlighten every learned mind?

With equal homes and education,
Equal rights and dedication,
Would every character equal be,
Or would some still persist to see
Some fault in this society?
Would those inborn instincts still persist,
To make some crave what others resist,
Or would some people still want more
Than others and still get bored
With life in such a tranquil state
And therefore find some fault to make?
Would not the strong still rule the weak
And would industrious beings cease to seek
(By instinct given to him by nature),
A higher place than other creatures?
Or would a man of cunning brain
Stop cheating those of lesser frame?
So, when we look at every man
One wonders how we ever can,
Be equal, except as child or babe,
Or perhaps just when we reach the grave.
But even then, our earthly status
Is shown by where our epitaph is!

Ruth E. Adam (Dollar)

A Loss

(In memory of Reg)

I am bereft today
Of a best friend, a father of my dreams

You have suffered a loss
Of a cherished lifetime part of you

His issues will now endure
The empty space, once filled with his noble grace

World will forever mourn
The loss of paragon, of humanity, of excellence

But it gives me some comfort
When my thoughts transcend to the heavens
And see him at peace
At a place better than mine
Yours and this motley world.

A Jamil (Abergele)

If You Own A Puppy

If you own a puppy you'll know their life goes in fast
When his or her life ends you'll wish it would last
You'll know that if you've ever had a dog for a pet
If you lose man's best friend, it'll be your only regret
Remember he or she walked by your side in the park
And you'll realise how much you felt safe in the dark
Now you've just put away his or her collar and chain
But you're still remembering those long walks in the rain

If you own a puppy you have to treat him or her with affection
You'll remember how he or she always gave you protection
Your pet would even take your side in a pretend fight
Your pet got a sweet for his or her loyalty every night
Remember he or she barked if you didn't hear the phone
With man's best friend at your side you never felt alone
You don't want to look to find his or her collar or chain
Because you'll cry when you remember walking in the rain

If you own a puppy, he or she will always want a walk
You'll have told your pet your secrets because he or she can't talk
You'll remember winter when there was snow on the ground
You asked if he or she wanted out, his or her tail went round
Your favourite pet carried his or her dog biscuits or can
And you wonder why they're called the best friend of Man
Somewhere in the cupboard lies his or her collar and chain
With such a lot of fond memories like walking in the rain

If you own a puppy, then you'll know these things are right
If he or she feels ill, you'll know your friend is unwell tonight
That's because you and him or her know each other so well
He or she doesn't need a tongue to say what there is to tell
That's because you can easily see he or she is walking slow
When you realise he or she is ill the tears start to flow
Nobody can blame you for hiding his or her collar and chain
Because you're sad when you remember walking in the rain

If you own a puppy you'll know when the time comes it's sad
When he or she has passed away, you can't help feeling bad
There isn't any more I can add to this song or poem to say
How sad you feel in your saddest of hearts this day
Because there's nothing anyone can write down anyway
No amount of words can express how sad you feel today
Remembering your old pet wearing the collar and chain
When your new pup will keep you company walking in the rain.

Andrew S Gibson (Glasgow)

My Belòved Isle

There is an isle where sunset
Like a flaming, fiery cauldron glows
On a blue and restless sea
That shimmers like a ruffled cloth of gold
As gentle breakers lap
And kiss the shingle shore:
This is my beloved isle, Tiree;
Land of wind and sun and the eternal sea.

Here is where the billows roar
And ride before the howling winds
That lash the cold Atlantic shore
As Kenavara's fortress cliffs in echo ring
As seabirds glide and soar
And float on silent wings:
This is my belovèd isle, Tiree;
Land of wind and rain and the eternal sea.

This is the isle with skies so blue
Where the scented clover grows
And many flowers of various hues;
Where the machairs lie above the shore
And in the summer falls the dew,
As in the fields the cattle low:
This is my belòved isle, Tiree;
Land of wind and sun and the eternal sea.

Here the autumn moon at twilight glows
To cast its silvery light
On the ripened fields of gold
Where laden sheaves stand row by row
As a wraith-like mist enshrouds
The moor and bog below;
This is my belovèd isle, Tiree;
Land of moon and mist and the eternal sea.

Here I first saw the first light of day
And here I grew to manhood ways;
Here lies my kin in God's good Earth -
No more thy blessed sward they'll tread:
Here they toiled in honest sweat;
Here they laughed and here they wept
In my belovèd isle, Tiree;
Land of peace and rest and the eternal sea.

Niall M Brownlie (Larbert)

Eventide

(This poem is based on Luke 24 verse 13)

It was drawing to the close
Of the evening
Two disciples on the road
To 'Emmaus'
Discussed the happenings
Of Jesus
They heard from the dead
He was raised

So deep were they in
Conversation
They scarcely the stranger
Did see
Till He asked of them
One simple question
Tell me, what troubles thee?

They looked at Him, all
Astonished
Is it only a stranger thou art?
Have you not heard the thing
That has happened
Just lately, around in this part?

He asked again of them
What things?
Why Jesus of Nazareth
We mean
Surely you've heard of the
Prophet
If to Jerusalem at all
You have been

We thought He would have
Redeemed Israel
For He seemed all the
Law to fulfil
But our hopes are all
Scattered and vanished
He was crucified
Outside, on the hill

It's just now three days since
This happened
Some woman made us amazed
For early this morning
At the tomb side
An angel declared He
Was raised

The stranger silently
Listened
The spoke from a heart
Full of love
Ought not Christ to have
Suffered these things
And enter His Glory Above?

Their hearts burned like fire
As they listened
To the stranger who walked
By their side
As they came to the end
Of their journey
They asked Him, with them
To abide

As they 'dined', He took
Bread in their presence
The stranger then was
Made known
It was Jesus the Blessed
Redeemer
Revealing Himself to his own.

Mary Gilchrist (Craigavon)

Oscar Wilde

Oh, come again and charm us with your wit
Your prose, your poems and a play,
Too soon, too soon, you passed away.

Oh, how much more delight you could have given,
With such light-hearted works of art,
Too soon, you left, it breaks our hearts.

How long ago it seems, but still today,
Upon the stage, his art we see,
Too soon, however could it be.

The story of his life, his loves, his days,
So gifted, so sincere and gay,
Too soon and how much more to say.

The long years roll away, he haunts us still,
We grieve for long-lost times and words,
Too soon, to never more be heard.

E Hawkins (Denbigh)

Birds That Fly

Birds are flying in the sky
As I watch the world go by
Fish are swimming in the sea
Like you, they take no notice of me
And when I hear the sound of the rain
Oh, how I wish I could see you again
I first saw you when we were at school
And fell for you just like a fool
But I knew I didn't stand a chance
As you never once gave me a glance.

Sometimes I feel so all alone
Knowing you will never phone
Snow reminds me of a wedding dress
Oh, how I miss you, I must confess
And though the years have past by
When I think back, I wonder why
You never once glanced my way
And so never had anything to say
Sometimes I still think of you
And often wish that you knew.

If only things had gone my way
And we were together today
I imagine what it would have been like
If you had asked me to be your wife
I imagine how happy I would be
To see you smiling back at me
And still birds fly in the sky
As the world just passes me by
And those fish still swim in the sea
Oh, how I wish you were here with me.

Some dogs bark as if to say hello
I'm scared of them but they don't know
My heart beats fast and skips a beat
Sometimes as I walk along the street
But of all the people that pass me by

I never see you, I wonder why?
Yet I still hope though it may be in vain
That some day I will see you again
So we can watch the birds flying in the sky
And together watch the world go by.

Eileen Kyte (Newport)

This Wonderful World

When I go out on a winter's night
To watch the sun sink in the west,
The sky is red and banded gold,
And black fingers of the naked trees
Trace their paths throughout its glory.
And I hear God say,
'This is Mine and this is thine.'

When I get up to greet the dawn
And watch the sun rise in the east,
Against the buttermilk backdrop
Of the sky, black silhouetted trees
Point their fingers to the heavens
And I hear God say,
'This is Mine and this is thine.'

And in the noonday summer's sun,
Birds sing and children laugh at play,
And the sky is blue as a baby's eyes,
And the grass is green and flowers frolic
And turn their faces to the sun.
And I hear God say,
'This is Mine and this is thine.'

And when the winter sky is denim-grey
And from the north, winds blow
Arctic frosts to chill the bones,
The snow is white and clothes the earth,
And berries, bravely crimson, glow
On glossy holly leaves,
And I hear God say,
'This is Mine and this is thine.'

And all this tiny world's
Forests and deserts,
Plains and swamps,
Orchids and hummingbirds
Flying backwards,
Long-necked mammals
And fish with lanterns,
And all the myriad galaxies
In eternity,
'Are Mine,' says the Lord,
'And thine,' says the Lord.

Mary Dwerryhouse (Llandeilo)

The Gallant Fifty-Five

(A tribute to members of the Dunedin Self-Build Group)

A few young men of our hometown
Decide it's time to settle down
But where or when, did raise a frown
To buy or rent, would cost us pounds.

So if we wish to have a home
We must decide to build our own
Our mind's made up, we will not roam
We go forthwith and ask a loan.

Here was a vacant piece of ground
Here were the plans, all safe and sound
Fifty-five members gather round
Feeling happy, feeling proud.

A home, a home is all we ask
Somewhere to live, to love, to laugh
Here was our chance, a chance at last
Hoping with hope we could build them fast.

We took advice from Mr Kay
And marked the site out one fine day
With picks and shovels, we dug through clay
We dug and dug to our dismay.

For days, for weeks and even years
Enough to make some good men swear
We toiled away, the end not near
Some members left and left their fears.

The numbers sank to but a few
But we resolved to start anew
Blame us not for feeling blue
As we set out to rebuild our crew.

Some of our troubles are best untold
As men work out in bitter cold
Enough to break both young and old
Each man deserving a pot of gold

Materials gather on the site
Men now work with all their might
Economise for money's tight
At last we see the end in sight.

Bricks and mortar, nails and wood
Members now are feeling good
Stopping only for their food
Everyone now, is in the mood.

A flag flies high from our last house
Our members gather round the houff
A cheer arose from every mouth
Which could be heard from north and south.

Our last house done, all tenants in
Invites go out, to knock or ring
Outside our children made a din
Upon our roofs, the birds do sing.

The years roll on as time ticks by
Alas, some members fade and die
And as we stand and bid goodbye
Who can blame us, if we cry.

Some members pack their bags and go
For reasons we may never know
We shake their hands and speak so low
Hoping our feelings do not show.

We welcome those who take their place
And hope to see a smiling face
The wives all dressed in silk and lace
A husband fit to stand the pace.

Now take a walk around our scheme
And see our copper roofs turn green
As nice a house as we have seen
Realising all our members' dreams.

Peter McKernan (Edinburgh)

He Who Dared

(A tribute to Lt Colonel Robert Blair (Paddy) Mayne)

As I stand alone in Conway Square
A book held within my palm
I watch the people, stop and stare
They wonder just who I am
A noble figure some will say
Whilst others question why
Then they will talk of another day
When I was young and spry
But World War II remembers me
Like others of my kind
Who fought for life and liberty
For those we left behind
Oh, life is one great mystery
From the cradle to the grave
Yesterday is history
But lonely are the brave.

Alexander Bailie (Newtownards)

To My Granddaughter

From graceful lilies
Pure and white
God fashioned lovely skin
Forget-me-nots
He chose for eyes
Then formed your baby chin

He took a tulip
Bright and red
It was one that
Did not fade
A softer, sweeter
Little mouth before
Was ever made

Another flower next he used
A rosebud pink and fair
Touched it to your
Dimpled cheeks
And bade it blossom there

Then with his magic fingers
Picked two morning
Glories white
To curl and shape
Your little ears
Soon they were fastened tight

He gathered the pollen
From the flowers
And sprinkled it with care
That crowning bit of
Golden down
Will soon become your hair

For dainty little fingers dear
And precious tiny toes
He used the slender
Daisy frills
And a snowdrop made your nose

This world and all within it
He created here for Man
But a baby was God's masterpiece
Since time and life began

R Finnighan (Helensburgh)

Flames Reignited

Trembling hands like a leaf
On a tree.
Trembling heart will he remember me?
Afraid to stand in case I should fall -
I remember the love -
I remember it all.

Afraid to be near him
After so many years,
Confused with the feeling
Afraid of my tears.
I remember the hurt,
I remember the joy,
Maybe he'll see me
As just a play toy.

At last our eyes meet
And the fears melt away -
Consumed in the moment
It's like yesterday.
We talk and we laugh
About so many things
I remember our love,
I fly on his wings.

And now we have met
It's like a new start
Both knowing we live in
Each other's hearts.

We both have new lives
And loves of our own -
We live separate places
The place we call home.

Not afraid of the future -
Or trembling hands,
Our love and our friendship
We both understand.

We're now above love
Like the birds that fly free
Like a pair of white doves
We make our own destiny.

Vanessa A Hulme (Cemaes Bay)

The Cicada In The Cinnamon Tree

(In memory of Jean Ogilvy)

Her eighty-year eyes
Of Wedgewood-blue
High in the morning sky of Kandy.

Her skin of palest porcelain
Softens her sun
Through coral lace.

To touch her hand
Is ivory:

The firm and fragile filigreed tusk
Of tropical Taprobane.

Her past is an arrangement
Of broken orange pekoe
Finely flavoured,
And caught on the cusp
Of a Crown Derby cup.

Serendipity of shortbread crumbs
On heirloom china;

A silver teaspoon with a faded crest.

Then she was sweet as frangipani,
Bright as bougainvillaea,
Tiptoeing the dappled trout streams
Of Nuwara Eliya,

The Perahera passed her
On the veiled verandah of the Queen's Hotel,
The bare-backed drummers and the dancing flames,

The silhouetted elephant,

The gilded casket,

And the lotus moon afloat
Above the Temple of the Tooth.

Silverfish scampered the musty pages
Of her jungle books;

Muskrat and mongoose,
Giant cat claws on the forest floor,
Cobra coiled in the green camellia
Where the saried women groom.

Pungent guava pulped by rains,
That swept her paper boats in the sluices.
Roaring torrents in the wood-fired dark;
Blue-bolt lightning banging
On the ozoned air.

Fruit bats lapped the velvet dawn
Through rooted ruins.

The cicada in the cinnamon tree.

In an antiseptic ward of ancients
We made our last formalities.

Outside the North Sea haar
Sagged grey to the horizons.

The TV soap turned loud
And no one listening.

Together we conspired
To conjure our illusion
Of the East,

Seeing the serried tea slopes
Of Ceylon and Java,

Sending a whiff of spices into
The ebbing, cold, insipid air.

Angus D H Ogilvy (Edinburgh)

Pre-Futurism

I've lived a century of isms
Within a quarter of the same

I've been a Mod, a post-modern
And now I'm helping build the new frame

I've had regression and progression
Both attached cynically to my name

I've had the *'opium of the masses'*
Injected straight into my veins

I've had the disillusionment of the few
The opium's effects begin to fade

I've enjoyed the placebo of the po-mo
When on this pill I've fed

I'm building for the future
Constructing scaffolding in my head

I've lived a century of isms
Within a quarter of the same

Pre-futurism is the present ism's name.

Ray J Dowling (Belfast)

Mouse

It's hard being mousy -

You are one big flaw
You trust your coiffeur
Believe in 'Hello' ads
You are *so* 'worth it'
Bleach and be glam
But after a week
You're left with a thatch
Of parched, lax straw -

It's hard being mousy -

You rub in henna foam
And leave it for hours
No measly half-measures
But it's like carnage
An Apache with psoriasis
Men cross the road
You don a cloche hat
Dark glasses in your home.

It's hard being mousy -

So you copy Katie Price
Eyebrows relocated
Face buffered, teeth capped
Hair salon-straightened
But in less than a month
You need a strimmer for
Three-day chin growth
Your wig has head lice -

It's hard being mousy -

It's costly when you're drab
A mouse just pays out
If she wants to be counted
My dog chewed my wig
My Botox went wrong
This trout really pouts
Could I sue 'Hello'?
My 'rural look' *ain't* fab -

It's hard being mousy.

Chris Ross (Strathaven)

Gairloch

On holiday in Scotland
Quite recently
My father, my sister
And of course me,
We were out for a drive
Along the west coast
We went over to Applecross
I've driven twice, was my boast.
But my dad had been
On one of these trips,
He'd paled quiet a lot,
It scared him to bits.
'OK,' I said,
'Onto Gairloch we'll go
There's no cattle pass
So the road will be low.'
Then after a walk
On the wee fishing pier,
We went for a coffee
The café was quite near.
After the drinks
And scones were all gone,
'Come on,' I said,
'We'll go further on.'
So back to the car
And drove up the hill,
The view that met us
Made us all stand stock still.
The golden sand,
The turquoise seas,
We could be in Greece,
My dad, sis and me.
I dipped my toes
In the sea, crystal-clear,
This beautiful place
I'm so glad we came here.

So when you think
You're at your journey's end,
Just go have a look
What's around the next bend . . .

Ruth Grant (Barry)

Eulogy for Sam Munster In Three Parts

This Winter

This winter,
The snow lies heavy on the hills,
This winter,
A sadness heavy on my heart,
This winter,
The golden glow of summers past,
This winter,
Never again to return,
This winter,
My heart is heavy, weary,
Longing for my summer's son,
He's taking the long road home,
This coldest, darkest winter is gone,
This winter.

Greater Call

Deep within your chest of gold
A beating fury lay
Not one man could dowse that fire
It would always stay that way
I held you close and called you 'friend'
Proud to use that word
Your precious breath left one last time
And we were left alone

You broke my heart
When you went away
It wasn't your choice
You had no say
You heard a greater call
From a better place
Safe in your Lord's embrace

Here, left on this embattled rock
For the Lord has called His angels home
Leaving a dark and lonely place
That fallen men now roam

Yet we all will meet again one day
And at that fateful time
I will sing, rejoice and praise
And hold you close my friend.
You broke my heart
When you went away
It wasn't your choice
You had no say
You heard a greater call
From a better place
Safe in your Lord's embrace

There For You

Just because I can't bring you to my mind
Doesn't mean that I don't love you
You know you might just find
No one is above you

I will be there
Be there for you
'Til the lies of Man come true
I'll be there for you

I know I drink a little too much now
It helps to ease the constant pain
Brings me closer each day now
To be with you again

I will be there
Be there for you
'Til the lies of Man come true
I'll be there for you.

Thomas Ramsay (Glasgow)

This Is What Democracy Sounds Like!

(Aberdeen City Council's budget cuts 2008)

Rum tee tum tee tum tee tum tum
This is what democracy sounds like!
Protests the sound of marching drum
Bureaucracy better change its beat now
Shouts the people through the town
You closed our schools and swimming pools alike
The drums send out a message from the Castlegate
Think again Aberdeen before it is too late
This is what democracy sounds like
Rum tee tum tee tum tee tum tum

You say your budget cuts will bring an end
To the previous city council's crazy spend
The homeless and the helpless folk already know
Thanks to you they have no place to go
Likewise the blind and vulnerable are not to blame
While administrative incompetence must hang its head in shame
Should you try to leave this at the door of those who have gone before
Here is a promise from the voter which you simply can't ignore
Democracy remembers those who say, 'There is nothing we can do'
One day these angry drums will march again and beat retreat for you

BC May '08 (Newmachar)

User Friendly - I Don't Think So!

I've struggled each and every week,
With something called 'computer speak',
My learning skills are at a loss
And all because of MS DOS.
A 'cursor' isn't what I think,
'It' cannot curse, but only 'blink',
So, if 'it' blinks, is 'it' alive?
And what is it I have to drive?
Any letter, A to Zee,
With paths and files and directory.
I can't compute, I'm so frustrated
User friendly - *overrated!*
'It' has a ROM, 'it' has a RAM
And still 'it' doesn't give a damn.
I'll try to type, oh no! That's wrong
It's 'input', now letters take me twice as long.
(Oh, good, I've made a letter,
Maybe things are getting better!)
I'll try another one of those . . .
'Backspace' - oops! There it goes!
I've lost the single letter aitch,
It's disappeared, to unknown space,
Press again and it appears . . .
This could go on for bloody years!
What's an 'address', 'loop' or 'buffer'?
Am I such a simple duffer?
That I can't find a 'database',
An 'icon' or a friendly face?
Give 'it' a boot (what good advice),
But no, I can't, not at this price.
Not a 'kick' but 'reset' then 'logon',
Password next . . . damn! That's gone!
Oh, for the days of Miss Jones
With pearly skin and curvy bones,
With thrusting breasts and dainty feet.
She had this damn computer beat!

My CPU may think it's smart,
But it can't stir my beating heart
Frustrate, annoy and friendly . . . not!
It's banished to a place to rot!

Joseph Lucock (Bridgend)

Saline Sunset

Tomorrow I sail into a heavy forest,
and shall learn
what poets seek in life,
the mysterious trick
of shadow fire
And I will be of flame.

For the Ancients
let justice be done in unholy disgrace.
Hang my wretched body
with boiling furies,
lay it down before miserable laws.
Honour the hood and lunette!
Meat machines
all we are.

Devour this bloodied Saint
you paper judge,
God in cannibal skin!
Let his pallid life and rotten bone
be your terrible soup.
Gut me in sleep,
throw my arms to priests
so they may fold them in prayer
and give these legs to children
to skip beyond chains.
But my heart I keep from the howl,
for fires of heroes
will dry my veins.
Parched flesh holds no sin.
So to fiery crowds
tomorrow I go,
in a perfect pose
for the death-obsessed.

Send for hail and thorn,
come see the gallows buckle
under my flabby skull.
My exit,
dying alive!
A blizzard for chapel idols,
owls and gulls be funeral coal . . .

Steven Francis (Carmarthen)

Hearts Beating In An Empty Room

Jealousy is a dying shame
Beating away at a healthy heart,
Leaving the pain to carry on
Even though we are still apart.
My mind is deadened, I cannot work,
Or sleep at all by night,
I see her face wherever I look
In that hour before the light.

I watched her grow, I saw her bloom
And laugh with different guys,
I snarled and fretted and shouted
Until she was confused and telling lies.
In fear she smoked and even drank
Then stayed out every night
Wearing clothes not suitable,
I was angered at the sight.

She went in bars and dancehalls,
What else I dare not know,
But the thoughts of men are lewd, dear God,
And Lord, I miss her so.
I tried to tell her that the hearts of man
Are mainly made of stone
And shattered away her innocence
So now I am alone.

I saw her through each window,
Followed close on every street,
Watching where she went at night
To see who she would meet.
I saw her lean against a wall,
Pressed close to his side,
Arms about his body, Lord,
Lips and blue eyes wide.

I put out a hand to stop her,
Saw her back against the wall,
I did not mean to touch her,
But I saw her start to fall.
Over the shouting and the footsteps,
That echoed all about,
The beating of my heart began,
Suffocating all other sound.

There is silence in our empty house,
Except the sound my heart makes,
No chatter as we break our bread,
Just memories in my head.
I can walk the rooms in a frenzy,
With no one who cares to see,
Hearts beating in an empty house,
All that is left of me.

I have walked the streets of London,
Seen sights to freeze the blood,
Name a price and you can buy
Things I don't think you should.
Please, let me kiss her better,
Don't let us stay apart . . .
Lord, let Daddy's girl come home,
She's breaking Daddy's heart.

Joan Hilditch (Pontypridd)

The Parting Road

Not here beside us as we would wish, but a little way further
along the road we all must travel in due time:
the road that leads from the imperfections of this world into the
perfect realm of celestial bliss: where peace reigns sublime.

Parting inevitably brings deep sorrow;
and grief seems almost too hard to bear
but God is ever present; His comforter ever near.

Friends, family all surround us with their love
and momentarily calm the fear.
Alas the night returns too soon bringing back
emptiness and the straying tear.

Time will heal! God's time! Time when fond memories will take
the place of sad remembrance:
then the road will not seem so dark ahead, and in a glance
we shall see bright footprints of those who have gone before . . .

Those whom we long to meet with again, and
most certainly will in the reunion God has planned.
What joy before us! To once again be with our loved ones,
together in the hollow of God's protective hand.

All our roads whether long or short lead but one way:
to God and our eternal home.

Ann Davies (Ebbw Vale)

Diaries

Diaries - are great wee things
Possessed and prized by commoners and kings
A paper trail, on all life brings
Full of agony and pleasure
Where births, deaths and wedding rings
Punctuate adventure

A private - never-ending list
Of memories - when first we kissed
A friend, appointment, loved and missed
Thought worthy to remember
Desires and dreams, that once were wished
Remain as glowing ember

To remind us of the times gone by
That bring a teardrop to our eye
The bitter truth, the wee white lie
In which we played our part
Unwelcome fingers, in the pie
That strain a secret loving heart

We select, and catalogue a thought
With a sculptured 'T' and a well-placed dot
And take pride in the little wars we've fought
Spread like shrapnel, through the pages
Then survey and castigate our lot
As we have others, through the ages

To the future we oft' speculate
As to our preference, upon our plate
And we hope, determining our fate
With each entry in our book
That joy abounds, with every date
Good luck, may never overlook

So, we play our role in the human race
Not always, with a fond embrace
But God willing, we may keep the pace
Each January to December
With our little book of arsenic and lace
That helps us plan and to remember

Archibald Macdonald (Clydebank)

Ripples In A Pool

One hundred years from now many things will be the same
Mountains, glens and rivers will survive
We will have moved on then, no matter what our name
All of us who now are so alive

Just like flowers we bloom for a period of time
Then disappear when our span slips away
No matter how high up on the ladder we may climb
No human ever gets an extra day

I feel it is important to do the best we can
To make our lives good and full of love
There is no second chance once the pattern's begun
To make deals with whoever is above

Some think they are important and can't be done without
And indeed some people well may be
But if they went tomorrow the world would still revolve
Even though their spirit has flown free

If you dip your hand into a pool that's still and clear
A ripple you will make without a doubt
Agitate some more and you make a bigger splash
Living life is just a bit like that

But when the hand's withdrawn and moments have elapsed
The pool is very still and clear once more
Our lives are merely ripples in the ocean that is life
We cannot turn the tide out from the shore

To have success in life is a very precious thing
To be needed fulfils the very heart
But we leave no lasting mark on the paper of the world
We are missed such a short time when we depart

We do pass on our heritage in those we leave behind
Our children and those who follow on
Part of us will live in generations yet unborn
Even when our time on Earth is gone

So never think the world will stop right in its tracks
If something you miss causes you fear
No one is indispensable, ripples do not last
The water will once more be still and clear

Fran Thomson (Campbeltown)

Ice Sculpture

I'm almost level with the clouds.
Cascading mountains surround me.
I have been here for years,
inching down the valley,
so, so, slowly.
I see trees fall,
hear them grinding into pulp
down deep beneath me . . .
Translucent blue crevasses
split my surface.
Rivers disappear,
running down into me,
scouring, shaping my underbelly.
I am old.
Snowstorms renew me with pristine whiteness.
My journey is tedious,
unstoppable.

There are sounds, around, within me,
thunderclaps of splitting and breaking.

In the distance I see the rise and fall of an ocean.
There lies my destiny.
I shall find a new identity within its waters
and freedom from this snail pace grinding journey
down the mountainside.
My brothers and sisters are floating there now,
their sides sculptured by waves,
smoothed, sharpened, curved,
fantastic towering statues,
morphing continuously,
turning, rolling in ecstatic movement.

It is almost time for me.
My sides are weakening.
The river beneath me has cut away my foundations.
I fall, midst a cracking confusion of ice and water.
Fountains rise up around me

Gradually I settle and look back
up the mountain pass where I was born.
Fingers of the mother-glacier
reach out towards me
but I am free, floating out into the bay,
onwards towards the ocean.
I will diminish slowly as I travel
for this new found freedom is also
my death knell.
Until that time comes
this enigmatic sculptured form that I have become
will wander the ocean, host to seabirds and seals.
Passing ships will marvel at me
but they will keep their distance
for I carry the gene of destruction.
I have become a dangerous, beautiful iceberg.

Meg Macleod (Thurso)

Before The Snow Melts

(Dedicated to the magic of childhood)

I woke up one morn to a chill in the air
A watery snowfall lay round everywhere
I dressed in a hurry, some breakfast to eat
Looking out of my window my heart got a treat

Children built snowmen, their father looked on
Before the snow melted and it was all gone
A little boy charmed me by running around
Exciting and chirping all over the ground

I thought I would go for a draught of fresh air
To raise my heart further and free it from care
I passed little Chloe who waved as I passed
As Daniel made snowballs, the snow may not last

At the end of the street, two tiny tots stay
Two snowmen were standing around they made play
One was a cowboy, his hands by his side
I stopped and I watched them, my heart open wide

Wrapped up head to toe they glowed on the snow
Then waved o'er and smiled, all time seemed to slow
At peace with the world on the snowfall outside
My heart glowed inside with this timeless ride

Roy A Millar (Alexandria)

Under A Tree In The Park

His life began in a cardboard box
Under a tree in the park
He whimpered as he lay there
All alone in the dark

Although it was a cold night
He was cosy and warm
And managed to sleep quite soundly
Until the break of dawn

A jogger found the cardboard box
And took care of little Sam
That was the name the hospital staff gave
To the blue-eyed little man

In spite of police efforts
His mother was never found
So Sam had a new family
A Mr and Mrs Brown

Time passed and Sam grew up
And was happy with his life
He had a nice house, a well-paid job
And a lovely adoring wife

But on a cold, wet, windy day
For Sam, disaster struck
His beloved wife was killed
When his car hit a truck

Sam went to pieces
Started drinking in the pub
Because he was never sober
He lost his house and his job

Everyone tried to help him
But he didn't seem to care
He was last seen wandering round the town
And then he wasn't there

Sam couldn't take anymore
Just walked off in the dark
His body found where his life began
Under a tree in the park.

Mary Paterson (South Queensferry)

To Whicherwhateroo

(A nonsense poem)

A *timid* whicherwhateroo
sat on a rock, and huffed and blew
upon rusty trumpet he had found
amongst the debris on the ground.
He thought that this would make it bright
but - then he got a *dreadful* fright!
The noise it made filled him with fear -
it shattered right, then his left ear.

He fled - and hid behind some trees
to still the quaking of his knees.
Then, first an eye, and then his nose
followed by his tum and toes
emerged from out behind the trees -
his eyes rolled round with *great* unease.

The trumpet still on ground did lie
but - nothing more 'cept rock and sky!
With utmost caution, inch by inch
he sidled forward - did not flinch -
until he was upon his foe -
then grabbed it tight - did not let go!

It made no noise, not single peep,
but - was it safe - was his to keep?
With addled brain he pondered long -
if quiet *now* where did he go wrong?
If it happened when he *blew*
the only thing that he could do
was - not to blow! Puffed up with pride
at his great brain and satisfied

he stuck it on head, between his ears
and ventured forth without his fears.
He reasoned if he himself had fright
from the noise then it just *might*
make his enemies turn and *run* -
oh he could see such *endless* fun!
In fact he could not *wait* to see -
so sallied forth with greatest glee.

Joyce Hockley (Stirling)

A Wasted Life!

What is wrong with the youth of today?
'There's nothing to do, I'm bored,' you will hear them say,
Do they carry a knife just to act cool?
When sentenced to prison, now who's the fool?
The number of stabbings has greatly increased,
The latest victim's name has not yet been released,
The newsreader said, with sadness in his voice,
A young life wiped out and it was not through choice,
Another family left shattered to grieve,
Wasted young lives, it's hard to believe,
When you hold your new baby, your heart filled with pride,
But you have no reason now, why he has died.
It's hard to imagine life without him,
Where do I start? How can I begin?
He was only fifteen years old with his whole life ahead,
I just cannot believe now he is dead.
Went out for a walk to meet with his friends,
Up a wee alley, is where his life ends,
To identify your son's body, is no easy task,
To see lifeless, closed eyes, face as white as a mask.
You just want to hold him, bring him back to life,
Instead, all you're left with, is sorrow and strife,
The day of the funeral, hundreds came;
Trying to console me and somehow ease my pain,
There's an empty chair at the table,
No clothes on the floor,
Remember the mess of his room,
I'd shake my head, smile, just close the door.

Make sure you do your homework before you go out,
Back by nine-thirty, I would so often shout.
Now I sit in his bedroom and just stare at the floor,
Just wishing and praying he'd come through the door,
He loved his football, was a potential star, all I'm left with,
Are memories, my darling son's body in an awful black jar.
When I meet his friends still out and about,
My stomach feels sick, like my heart's been ripped out!
My angel is gone and I can't bring him back,
But oh, how I wish I could do exactly that.

Instead, I'm just left here, to grieve all alone,
But what is my future, now my angel is gone?
Young people just think of what you are doing,
Look to the future, what career you're pursuing.
A youth has been caught, will be sentenced to jail,
Only three years for a life, I feel the court system has failed.
Is that all they feel my lad's young life was worth?
It doesn't seem right now, I can't trust the courts.
To rehabilitate the youth who took a young life,
Will cost taxpayers thousands, surely this can't be right?
I am supposed to move on, been told, on my son's death not to dwell,
Every single day without him, is just pure living Hell.

Joan Cardwell (Dungannon)

Promise

By early morning, nature brings,
Night's curtain drawn, the vast sunrise.
Grey, tinged with rose, then gold, azure, swan's wings,
The evolving drama of the skies.

Yet all this scene, without intent,
Takes no direction, heeds no cue,
No loving brush nor ages spent,
In fervent search of line and hue.

Life's precious fountain have I sought,
Yearning to find a God, to prove
Nil, the accusing ploy of fate.
Yet promise lies in this one thought.
Inventive skill, love's power to move,
Might with a God of worlds relate.

I knew a man, long time ago, came by,
Whose bloodstained hands drew all the nations high.
He walked in simple raiment too,
To let His shining spirit through.
And He, once subject to Man's worst hostility,
Drew to Himself, one suffering like as He.
In that fierce moment love in essence came,
And banished fear with a sweet promise true.
Then human pain to Heaven's peace gave way;
Sure 'twas no mortal love was found that day.
If this is truth not pen nor tongue can quell,
How safely in that precious thought I'd dwell.

Florence Lyster (Holywood)

Aberfan October 1966

The mountain was shrouded in mist that dark day
When the colliery waste tips moved and gave way
Huge waste tips piled high by the working of man
They roared down the mountain to engulf Aberfan

It swept all before it that tragic Friday
Dealing death and destruction to all in its way
Onward it roared to the school of Pant-Glas
Where all the school children were sitting in class

They stood no chance to escape this black hell
As this thundering great mass dealt out its death knell
The school of Pant-Glas and all in it were gone
As the colliery tips moved relentlessly on

At last they slowed down and finally stopped
People ran to the scene and were so deeply shocked
At seeing the carnage wrought by these tips
Cries of horror and anguish poured from their lips

They dug with bare hands if having no tool
To get at buried children in Pant-Glas school
Frantically digging while gasping for breath
As they clawed at this tomb of destruction and death

A big burly miner went stumbling by
A dead child in his arms, tears in his eye
He threw back his head to shout up to the sky
Lord God almighty why did they all die?

When digging had ceased after all had been found
Aberfan was so silent devoid of all sound
No birds sang in trees, no children played around
Despair and disbelief cloaked this grief-stricken town

A generation of children were lost that sad day
When the colliery waste tips moved and gave way
The full scale of the horror was made known worldwide
As they laid out the small bodies in rows side by side

Aberfan laid to rest their little lost souls
On each headstone the tale of what happened is told
When on that terrible cruel black day
The colliery waste tips moved and gave way.

Desmond Williams (Blaenavon)

The Piano

I said I'd buy a piano
One day when I got old,
I thought, *that day's not far away,*
So shopping I went, feeling bold.

Now a piano is not as we know it,
All wood, all teeth quite smiley,
They're now all shiny and digital,
All singing, all dancing, all wily.

It arrived on a Monday morning,
All boxed and looking so smart,
The men set about erecting it,
Till it looked like the state of the art.

Oh! I forgot to say, that I can't play,
The books look like dots gone mad,
A teacher is now what's needed,
My knowledge of scales quite sad.

I found a man, a tutor guy,
Who's patient and clever as well,
He hasn't yet lost his will to live,
While teaching this Mrs Bell.

Now Thursday is my lesson day,
It's the very greatest thing,
I'm learning to scale the music notes,
Of sharps and flats and swing.

My love of music has always been great,
But the knowledge had just gone to pot,
So just to hear what I now can play,
It's wondrous, it's fab, it's hot.

A maestro, I know I'll never be
My audience will all be at home,
I'll stick to the things I know when away,
The piano my fun when alone.

So here's to all those composers,
Whose music I must get the gist,
I wonder if I'll do any better,
When playing quite Brahms and quite Liszt.

Susan Bell (Alness)

The Tale Of The Auld Married Pear

He admired her melons, she liked his nuts
It was true love, no ifs or buts
On his first date, he had to leave her alone
The sour-faced lemon was the chaperon
He tempted her with strawberries, an apple and a lime
And said, 'Stay the night, you'll have a good time'
The oranges and the grapefruit warned her about the trip
Then said, like a banana skin, she was likely to slip
She ignored their advice and went instead
And Granny Smith made sure they got wed
So, if it's the fruits of love you're after and don't take care
You're going to end up an auld married pear
The tomatoes and mushrooms, they started to talk
So the auld married pear decided to walk

They arrived at the butchers in the middle of a row
He was calling his wife a silly old cow
She was expecting a visit from nephews and nieces
And the poor woman's nerves had gone to steak pieces
Out came their sow, a pork chop called Sam
Unlike his dad, he was as quiet as a lamb
'Would you like some steak? We have braising or frying'
'No thanks,' said the pear, 'it looks like it's been lying'
'What about some stewing or sirloin instead?
Or a nice, fresh chicken that comes from Farm Fed?'
'We'll have some sausages, give us pork and leek
Then we'll head to the provisions, more goodies to seek.

We'll buy some ham or maybe some veal
We only want a sandwich, not a main meal'
The girl behind the counter, she is such a tease
'Oh that reminds us, we'll have to buy cheese
We'll get some bacon and black pudding for a fry
Or a side of pork ribs, that have taken our eye'
They bought some coleslaw, it was in a nice dish
They then moved over to look at the fish.

There were mussels and prawns, both sold in their shell
Five flavours of cooked salmon, they also did sell
The fishmonger was a big salmon, who was knocking about
With a young thing from Antrim, a little rainbow trout
Within a week it was over, it ended in disgrace
So he went back to sea and moved in with a plaice
He was a DJ at night, his favourite music was sole
While during the day, he was claiming the dole
The eel was a slippery customer, always looking for a thrill
He ran off and was chopped with a brill
By now, some of the fish started acting the cod
While the prawn-again Christian thought he was god
The pear then moved on, while they got the chance
And were tempted by the smell coming from Cuisine de France.

When they arrived, the pear started to scream
The aunts and uncles were in a trifle covered with cream
While going into an oven, ready to bake
Were their cousins, the Bramleys, inside a big cake
To save the Bramleys, they needed a plan
And were helped by the pastries lead by a flan
The breads and the rolls who were mostly French
Were to ambush the assistant, a young serving wench
They all blocked their way as she came across the store
And the apple cake headed for the fins exit door
The pear held it open and they both ran away
And neither has been seen, since that fateful day.

Pat Leonard (Belfast)

Invitation

Poplar leaves pulsate and plead with me:
'Leave your place of safety and dance with us on the wind.'
The wind whispers:
'Do not fear; let me waft you into a wonderful world
that you will barely believe.'
Lush lilies and passionate pinks murmur:
'Lose yourself in our land of bountiful beauty
and perfumed perfection.'
Darting deer and skittish squirrels
invite me to give playful chase into their universe.
Diving dolphins and soaring seabirds call to me:
'Come into our realm where the rainbow rings
as the radiant raindrop sings.'
Ocean waves surge at the shores, urging me:
'Dare to discover the distant depths
that we can reveal to you.'

The ebbing embers of the fading fire crackle:
'What are you waiting for?'

I hesitate. What is this mysterious state
that all of nature knows about?
I still myself and listen.
Together they slowly encircle me.
And with one voice they tell me:
'This is the place of pure and simple existence.
No doing, just *being.'*

'Come.'

Sheila Phillips (Dundee)

A Rivitt-ing Encounter

I sat down to talk
to a frog in a frock
by the edge of a murky river.
The moon floated high
in the black of a sky,
peppered with stars of silver.

Now while I was there
we tried to compare
our views on grand worldly affairs.
To my dismay
I heard the frog say,
'Men are no better than bears.

They claw and they fight,
they scratch and they bite
they're spoiled
wanting all their own way.
They ruin our Earth,
devalue its worth,
then pretend that all is OK.'

With a sidelong glance
the frog rose to dance
and waltzed with a delicate grace,
the dress held out
swirling about,
a smile wide-lipped on the face.

I heard the frog cry
as it danced by,
calling to me, 'That's life.
Yes, you guessed right
I'm a transvestite,
and the frock belongs to the wife.'

On the frog danced
while I sat entranced
wondering whether to say
some light badinage
to this riverbank sage,
but the frog in the frock pranced away.

Isabel Findlay (Glasgow)

Compelled

She had to go down
and some of the stairs
were crumbling in places
making her grasp the wall rail
to prevent herself from falling
into the darkness below.
Fearfully she descended
afraid of being alone in the dark
yet compelled to find out where
the sound of moaning came from.
At the bottom of the stairs
she was relieved to see
a ray of light shine through
the small window
in the cell door facing her.
Trembling she went forward
peered through the window
and saw the figure of a man
head buried in his hands.
Quickly she lifted the key
from a nail in the wall
unlocked the door and threw it open.
The prisoner's eyes met hers.
With a start she recognised him.
Here was the man
who'd betrayed her years ago.
She fingered the key
thought to lock him in again.
Instead she stepped aside
allowing him to pass.
And as she watched him
ascend the stairs to freedom
she realised that this place
was her dungeon
the moaning inmates her prisoners
guilty of past offences against her.
Now she knew why she was here.
She had to be here
to set the prisoners free.

Fay Smith (Glenrothes)

Laminations

I am an onion,
Many layered.
To others of the human race
I show a brown and shiny, smiling face,
Exchanging the trite trivia
Of the market place:
How are you? Going away!
How nice to go away in May,
We'll meet again another day:
How little words can sometimes say!

Peel it off!
Below that brown and shiny skin
Another lies, more cerebral, wherein
There's talk of dull domestic cares,
Of stocks and shares
And parliamentary affairs,
Vexed questions of the day
Tossed around in verbal fray.

Peel it off!
Beneath that layer of mental dice
A world of sensibility lies
Where poems are read and time flies
As music floods the soul
With inexpressible delight
And rich tapestries of sight and sound
The senses fill with joy profound.

Peel again!
For deeper still, there lies
A layer of inner feeling, much
Too sensitive to touch;
A world of shared affections,
Regrets, remorse and separations,
Of hopes and doubts and fears
And barely hidden tears,
Told - if told at all -
But to one's dearest.

Another layer, you ask?
Oh, yes!
Within the secrets recesses of my heart
Lie truths I dare not contemplate
And little comprehend;
The quintessential essence of my being
Is too fragile, too terrible, to uncover.

To no comforting illusion
Of perpetually I cling,
No songs of paradise I sing;
Enough to know *I am*
Myself, alone, unique;
No other solace need I seek,
For in this unfathomable reality
May lie my immortality.

I am an onion,
Many layered,
You too?

Rodney Bambrick (Bangor)

Great Britain?

What's gone wrong with Britain?
It's all got out of hand
It used to be so great here
This old but peaceful land

A stabbing here, a stabbing there
We hear it every day
What's gone wrong with Britain?
Why has it gone this way?

I read it in the paper
An unprovoked attack
He simply walked away from them
He got stabbed once in the back

What's gone wrong with Britain?
Why has it got so bad?
Another life's been taken
Somebody's special lad

A young man's life has ended
And the boy who stabbed him too
Now I've put pen to paper
That's why I'm telling you

It only takes a single strike
To kill somebody with a knife
So come on all you people
And try hard to unite
Let's make Britain Great again
By laying down your knife.

Carol Rance (Southsea)

A Spanish Memory - Olé!

Whene're I gaze at the sky so blue,
My thoughts forever turn to you
And the happy days we shared in Spain,
Lots of sunshine and little rain,
First time we went by boat and bus,
'Twas such a thrill for both of us!
We travelled o'er the foreign land,
Sometimes boring, sometimes grand.
We spent a week or nearly two,
Going to places, admiring the views,
Rides on a train, a boat and a bus,
Oh! How exciting, hooray for us!
Lloret and Blanes and Tossa-de-mar,
Beautiful places, though not very far,
The days we spent lazing,
Were days you spent gazing,
At all of the girls who were 'new',
The ones you liked best -
Were only half dressed -
And of those there were more than a few.
The boat ride we had -
When the weather was bad
And the sea and the sky was quite stormy,
The captain and crew - just grabbed hold of you
And really, they did so quite calmly,
The captain got bolder - with you on his shoulder,
By golly, it petrified me!
I kept pulling you back;
You were just like a sack -
Head first I thought, straight in the sea!
I just held my breath
As he struggled to get you ashore,
He dumped you on land - by gum! It was grand,
To feel 'terra firma' once more!
We were really amazed, at the strength of the waves
And the men who were part of the crew,
If they hadn't been steady,
As waves churned and eddied,
We'd still have been looking for you!

Rose Selby (Tonypandy)

Outburst, Cynheidre Colliery

Here, underground, it is never spring.
Black-studded, ridged branches of trees
Broken multi millennia ago, strewn abjectly:
And ferns lying folded,
All glistening as black as glass,
In the deep anthracite seam:
Ferns, in layers, patterns traced,
Flat on rock, fossilised forever in time.

Suddenly the coal seams are cold;
Touch cold - this is the signal.
It is dark and oppressive, when the earth
Trembles, before the black wall
Of brittle coal ruptures into powder,
And shoots out in all directions.
It is so claustrophobic
In the fetid, dust-choked curtain
Of methane fumes, too dense
For normal clear vision.

With haste and consternation,
Well-drilled routines, voices shouting
In the dark, for the safety of their mates.
In desperation, a true comradeship;
Gigantic power machines on standby,
To clear up any splintered shards.
The Linley fresh breathing sites
Bringing some sense of law and order
For a safe breath of life.

Counting those present,
Checking always, with shouts for help,
Testing for gas all the time, waiting for
The surges to subside.
But checking again and again.
Now, after all the devastation,
No one hurt - this time,
No one with lungs clogged black with dust,
Just cleaning up.

Now then the question, *why?*

Phyl Jones (Pontyberem)

The Road To Wales

The owl hooted eerily in the sky
The field mouse silently gnawed
His banquet consisted of barley and rye
Somewhere a wood pigeon soared

As dawn came over the silent slopes
I tramped my weary way
Something within raised my hopes
And promised a better day

My limbs ached from walking
From Bristol and the west
Ah, you've guessed, my life was tramping
And poaching with the best

I hailed a passing lorry
And used my hard luck face
The driver said
'Sure mate, sit on this packing case'

As we crossed the River Severn
He spun some lively tales
Of how he'd come from Devon
But had settled now in Wales

We passed a place called Newport
Then Cardiff came in sight
The Castle like a fortress
Silhouetted the morning light

The battlements stood in sharp relief
Against the crimson dawn
The ancient courtyard stretched below
Replaced now by a lawn

I tried to visualise the men
Who once lay down their lives
Who had fought for Henry and Elizabeth
With sabres, swords and knives

From here, we went to Margam
Past a big industrial plant
And I began to take an interest
In this land of Dewi Sant

From there we came to Swansea
Grey in the light of day
But I've learned to love this city
In an adopted sort of way

I love the great big marketplace
Entirely roofed in glass
Where congregating Saturdays
Are every creed and class

The women sitting patiently
Selling cockles in their shells
The interruption frequently
Of St Mary's midday bells

But the place which pleases me the most
Is the scenery on the Gower coast
I tell you folks, it makes my day
To see the sun go down on Three Cliffs Bay.

So, dear friends, if all else fails
Pack up your troubles and come to Wales.

Audrey Morris (Swansea)

Star Gazer

With windswept hair and foreign grace,
She stands alone, and face to face -
With the evening sky.
Dawn is her name, and
So great is her fame,
That none may ever touch her.

Eyes like fire reflect the stars,
With a longing for their freedom;
For endless years, with countless tears,
She's tried so hard to reach them.

Her dress is light and many-coloured;
It flies like silk in the breeze around her.
A foreigner, a traveller from the sky;
A princess, soldier and a lover -
But like a songbird - trapped in an iron cage,
She is helpless now, and silent.

So she is there each night
On that cliff, by the sea -
Perhaps she waits, and looks out
For me . . .

But none have ever found her,
As my mind is all there is around her;
And as I watch her from afar,
She hangs her head in sorrow;
And as she turns to walk away,
I know I'll dream of her again
Tomorrow . . .

John S M Evans (Largs)

Good Verses Bad

All the time
In every kind of place you can imagine
In all the different corners of the world
Bad things are happening to good people

And if when you hear or know of these times
One cannot help but question why they come around
Because surely if God was real and true then these situations would not be happening

To hear that your sister is in hospital
Fighting a strange virus that is attacking her
In a way that we do not know any more what is going to happen tomorrow
Thinking to myself about the last few words I said to her
Then kicking myself to realise that I should have said something better
When was the last time I told her that I loved her?

Coming home to find my world turned upside down
With screaming words being thrown across the room by my parents
Each trying to make the other see their side clearer through
the midst of unsolved arguments from the previous weeks
Then my name is brought into the argument
As the next round of ammunition
What shall I do this time?

One day hanging out with my best friend
Laughing making jokes
The next day I receive a phone call
Last night my friend did not make it home
I hear the soft mechanical calm voice of her father
But I can still hear the pain seeping through his voice down the phone receiver, into my ear
His daughter, my best friend is dead
Killed
As a consequence of her last action carried out in this world

I feel my thoughts spiral out of control
Trying with all my might to cling to some sense of normality
What did I let happen?
Why didn't I see it coming?

But after all
Bad things happen all the time
Why should these times be any different?

Rosie Phillips (Clunderwen)

I Wonder

I wonder are you happy, are you free
I wonder if you ever think of me
I wonder if the pain I feel when I think of you will ever go away
Or will it be here forever because I feel like this every day?

When the pain comes from deep inside
I just want to disappear and hide
I didn't think after all this time the feelings would still be here
But I was wrong, they still go on year after year

When I see people in love holding hands and kissing
I cry for the life I have lost, the one that I'm missing
Why didn't you tell me what I did wrong?
I could have fixed it and made it strong

Instead I didn't know I was unaware
You didn't think it was worthwhile to share
I never imagined feeling this bad
You took all the love that I ever had

I feel lonely and empty inside
What has happened to me, where is my pride?
But like you it has gone away
And in its place is misery which is here to stay

Why can't I get over you, why is it a long fight?
Why can't you stay out of my head so it will be alright?
Because I guess the day I don't think of you
Will be the day that I stop loving you

When will it happen, when will I be free?
Surely all this pain wasn't meant to be
Do I want to stop loving you, you will always have my heart
Because I have always loved you, always from the very start

When you went away, when you were there no more
I didn't realise what was left for me what was in store
All the hurt, the loneliness, the pain, it didn't matter
It was the fact you didn't want me, that's what made my heart shatter

So maybe it will be better when I am free
And not hold onto memories that were not meant to be
I wonder.

Nancy Tamagno (Livingstone)

The Bobby And The Urchin

You will find him everywhere
In towns and cities without a care
An angel or devil who can guess
He's an urchin nevertheless
Our urchin has a favourite shop
From home to school he's bound to stop
There on show for his favourite sweets
Some in a box and some in a heap
An unwashed face and combless hair
Together with eyes that stare
He's really deep in thought you know
Although he hopes it does not show
His tongue comes out to moisten lips
Then wipes sweated hands along his hips
He's swallowed the first imaginary choc
Bending down to pull up his socks
Much nearer to the sweets at last
Squashed nose and lips against the glass
A reflection appears on looking through
Someone there in familiar blue
No fear shows on our urchin's face
As a policeman nears without haste
Both of their eyes meet and hold
One not so young - one not so old
The policeman glances at the sweets
Then down to our urchin's booted feet
His hand then explores beneath his coat
Coughing as if to clear his throat
His hand withdraws and travels down
Nails so clean and skin all brown
So tall with his helmet grand
He places a coin in the urchin's hand
With a smile he strokes unruly hair
And gives a tug that breaks the stare
Two smiles exchanged no word is told
From one so young, one not so old
The policeman then moves slowly on
Leaving behind a heart in song

Coin in hand now clenched tight
Watching the policeman move out of sight
A turn of the head towards the door
Eyes down to the coin - to make sure
He turns it over once or twice
Then enters the shop for something nice

AD 1950

I was that urchin many years ago
The policeman and shop I still know
That coin and act has magnified
Showing the way with trust and pride
Another policeman pounds the beat
With memory of that simple treat
Who knows why that coin was given
Pennies I know don't come from Heaven
So I'm the richer by far this day
Trying to follow the policeman's way.

E W Smith (Barry)

Bird Talk

'But, how can you find that
which is not lost?'
asked the robin.
'Because little friend,'
said the magpie,
'until I find it, it is not yet lost.'

'Tell me all that you know,'
asked the robin.
'Please tell me all that you know.'
'What would you give me,'
asked the owl,
'if I tell you all that I know?'
'I would tell you where the little grey mouse
nests with all her babies,'
said the robin importantly.
'Indeed,' said the owl,
'and can these babies yet
run in the bright moonlight?'
'Oh no!' said the robin,
'For their eyes are still shut tight.'
'Pity,' said the owl.
'I think I'll wait for I like the fun of the chase.'
'Then you may be disappointed,'
said the robin shaking his head.
Asked the owl,
'Why is that?'
'Because,' said the robin,
'by that time they will probably
be eaten by the farmyard cat!'

Marjorie J Matthews (Penarth)

Tsunami South-East Asia, Dec 26th 2004

Families playing on an idyllic beach,
Palm trees swayin' too high to reach,
Villagers sleeping on their hammock sacks,
Unaware, a thousand miles away, the ocean bed cracks,
Warm white sandy beaches and broken shell
Paradise is going to turn to Hell,
People on the beach, don't have any notion
There's death heading under the Indian Ocean,
A wall of water, heads for the shore, ripping up beaches to the core,
Frantic mothers on the beach, babies' fingers just out of reach.

The tsunami strikes, destroying everything in its wake,
Whole villages wiped out, nothing left to pick or take,
Palm trees ripped out by the roots at least
Ending up flotsam to the relentless beast,
Bodies flung fifty feet into the air,
Mothers with empty eyes can only stare,
Impending disaster looms, thousands sent to their doom.
Broken bodies lying twisted and astrew,
Boats upturned, no hope for the crew,
No place to run or hide,
Hundreds more got sucked in by the receding tide.
How much more can be said? 150,000 people dead.

How many more lie on the ocean bed?
World leaders pledge vast amounts of money,
Humanitarian helicopters drop food, water and honey,
Mass graves dug to prevent disease in the tropical sun,
Before another 100,000 die with cholera, a race had to be won.

Appendix
Eight prison ships holding Osama Bin Laden's most trusted
lieutenants were given an hour's warning of the tsunami.
The terrorists were aboard vessels 1,000 miles south of India
anchored off British-owned Diego Garcia.
Diego Garcia is an island stretch leased to the US Military.
They used it for bombing runs on Iraq and Afghanistan.
Officials at the US Pacific Tsunami Warning Centre in Hawaii
alerted the base,
but failed to warn the affected nations!

Angus McInnes Gus (Elderslie)

Destiny's Trauma

That lump o' dodgy royal stane
Has hit the headlines once again
By controversy tae sustain
Frae where it came.
It seems it can't be left alane
In its true hame.

Scots Nats boast its hame wis Scone
Where a' oor kings were gied their croon,
Afore the Hammer nicked it doon,
As Saxon prize;
Westminster Kirk in London toon
For Sachenach's eyes.

But ane dark night a darin' deed
Wi perpetrated there wi' speed,
When Scottish students used the heid
Tae nick it back
An' left sair English herts tae bleed
O'er this hijack!

Tae sich extent is wis returned,
though patriots were shocked but spurned;
Their protests raised, but swift adjourned
Tae future fate.
Deliberations noted well, then burned,
And left tae fate.

But noo the stane is back in place,
But no' in Scone's much-honoured base
An' while they argue o'er the case
For legal right.
A Roman claimant jined the race -
Augustan might!

So is it really worth a dime
Aboot a stane no' in its prime;
Hacked wi' age an' ful' o' grime?
Break in it three.
Gie each a dod . . . forget the crime
An' family tree.

Neil Gill (East Kilbride)

I Remember

I remember the road I was born in,
Red-bricked houses with pebble-dash awning,
Bay windows above and below,
Which gave them a bit of class.

There was a lean-to porch at the side,
Where Mam put our bikes to keep them dry,
A bit of a garden at the front and the back,
Concrete steps which led to a concrete path.

I remember we played on the streets until nine,
When the days were long and the sun used to shine,
We'd all gather round choosing teams,
Played cricket and rounders while young babies dreamed.

I remember climbing my shale-tip mountain,
Then lie on the top just daydreaming,
I didn't know then I'd have to grow up,
Life was such an adventure, I wanted to know so much.

After sliding back down my shale-tip mountain,
I'd build dams in the stream that I called a river,
My shoes and socks I'd dry in the sun,
The leather turned hard, my socks turned brown.

A smack and a telling off, I was sent up to bed,
My belly grumbled as I sat on the stairs,
I imagined all the food I could buy in the shop,
While the scent of toast wafted up.

I remember the moors which seemed to go on forever,
And my dreams of finding a chest full of treasure,
The mountain ponies would gallop away nervous,
But soon came to trust me when I fed them lump sugar.

I remember one pony a little grey mare,
I jumped on her back as a dare,
We rode with the wind our spirits were high,
And a tremendous sense of awe hit me as the world rushed by.

I remember my valley, my Ebbw Vale,
The mines and the steelworks and its decay,
Now when I visit all I see are lives crumbling,
Holes in the mortar, no one is mending.

No hope in the faces, old when they're forty,
A multitude of ailments brought on by poverty,
Men who've not worked for a quarter of a century,
They live for the bacco, beer and bingo.

Children growing up without proper family values,
Hang about on the corners just doing nothing,
Fag in one hand, pushchair in the other,
Apprentices, of the gloom they're about to encounter.

I remember once seeing hope and ambition,
Pride in themselves and what they were achieving,
It's all gone now even though they breathe in fresh air,
The loss of employment has left an air of despair.

I remember my valley, the home of my roots,
And remember those people who to me meant the most,
Some of them gone now, I place flowers on their graves,
Before my return journey to the heart of Mid Wales.

Jane Margaret Isaac (Ystrad Meurig)

Depression

A life I've lived
With constant struggle
The here and now
Is such a muddle
Maybe if I'd followed a dream
The life I have now
Would be unseen
Troubles I've had
Every day of my life
I wonder how others
Deal with this strife
Five children I've had
Only two remain
I only wish
I could break the chain
I wish I could run
I wish I could hide
I wish more than anything
That I could find
A heart that's true
A love so kind
A man who could clear
And ease my mind
I want a life
That's trouble-free
A life with love
To surround me
With so much to wish for
And nothing in sight
Will somebody hear
My desperate plight?

Sarah Hadigate (Crumlin)

The Silent Cries

I hear your voice, like an echo in my heart,
As a gentle breeze, your laughter soothes my soul,
The sound of you comes down the painful years,
Remembered smiles and kisses keep me whole.

Your tiny hands, a blessing on my face,
Your heart so full of wonder, full of joy,
Your soul replete with kindness, full of grace,
Your spirit humbles me, my wondrous boy.

Still strong, still sure, in your defence,
Of all the world's rejected and despised,
Through suffering and cruelty too immense,
Your manhood yet, in goodness, realised.

When all around you cannot hear your silent cries,
Nor see the sorrow in your haunted eyes,
When no one sweeps away the lies that brought you here,
But blame you for the changes wrought in you by fear.

When all they do is ponder, scold and frown
And feel compelled to write some nonsense down,
But then no labels seem to fit your complex song,
They see you only as forlorn, call you schizoid and move on.

And if this doesn't fit for very long,
Still the travesty will stumble on and on
And someone else and someone else and someone else will proffer more,
Always blind and deaf to you, still they miss the very core.

When the years have rolled away, your life still in abeyance,
They will add some more 'success' to their evasions,
With your mind suffused with drugs in railed profusion,
'We've got it now! Psychosis! Your thoughts are in confusion!'

They cannot yet perceive your silent cries, immune to the sorrow in your eyes,
They give the complex chemistry a shake and no surprise!
Schizophrenia! As they add the last enigma to their tag of lies,
When those blinkered hearts and minds, full of ignorance and pride,
Tell themselves they're right once more, congratulations, far and wide,
They will never see they've hurt you, with their books in which they hide,
For arrogance and blindness keep them impotent, outside.

Margaret Miller (Livingston)

Heartland

I am still a stranger -
your shrouded hills,
bracken-lit mountain steeps,
(tumbling crystal, rock-strewn rain-soaked turf)
a foreign land.
Beauty smiles yet her eyes
are wary, heavy-lidded.
They see and turn the cheek
to speak in secret syllables,
sharing minds fast closed
to mine and thoughts
a world apart.

If I knew your tongue
sombre land of my adoption,
it would not make me heir,
a trueborn son.
No, though I pen my
admiration, breathe
your still cold air,
sweet and pure as it filters
golden through the pines,
though I call you mine,
yet am I not yours,
my children halfcaste still.

You bare your ancient soul,
wild and dark as the storm,
in verse and song,
and as I listen to the curlews' cry,
their lone despair
the sorrowing heartbeat
of a melancholy land,
then do my thoughts return
to the citied warmth
of an English childhood -
polluted air, a dusty sun,
family feuding
and . . . laughter.

Anna Jones (Machynlleth)

Gorton Chapel

I thought I saw God in your chapel
was lit kindness and goodness I saw?
We 'followed the fleet' on your nimble
quick feet choreography by Cliffe College elite

Who could say nay to such politeness?
such clever short finger-nailed fun
such savoir faire, if any gel fell
his mummy and daddy would come

Were there stone stairs up to paradise
or were they 'Epileptics beware'?
Did the high and the mighty start up
them and only the faithful get there?

No cathedral choir echoed roundly
along the pine-polished pews
the hymns were sincere and rose so clear
Like Beyer Peacock steam whistle blues

The others piped a lesser treble,
Crossley Motors, Armstrong Whitworths, Gorton Tank,
Brooks and Doxey, Fallow and Bate, Pernes
while Massey's played regular notes,
our bread and butter music.

There were Xmas presents for Sunday school regulars
Books of Nature embossed and inscribed, God wot
my sister loved hers particularly
if it was the only present she got

The chapel and the pawnshop shared corners
but they were both swamped by the pubs
beer and betting shop coppers flowed freely
landlords never gambled. Bookies kept out of pubs

The pawnshop would take anything saleable
the chapel preferred tender young souls
they both used pompous phrases like
'unredeemed pledge and everlasting life'
I shiver when I think of them
and cling more tightly to my wife

There was a picture of a fellow from Oxbridge
saying 'Suffer young children to me'
he wore a nightshirt and authentic 'J' sandals
my sister went forward too kindly, too blindly for me

I sat at the back with the wicked though
I'd not done owt at all bad
it was in case anyone I knew saw me
they'd be obliged to think that I had

I thought I saw Heaven thro' the fanlight
over the chip shop across the way, perhaps
it was only the reflection of life thro' my tears
as they say

The heavenly view persisted like
a light that would not go out
was it freedom I saw over the chippy?
Did a voice say it's all about nowt?

Judd Hulme (Colwyn Bay)

For You

Do not leave me to travel through this world, this life,
Because when I found you . . . when you found me.
I discovered the meaning to my life.
You brought to me, hopes and dreams that caused
My prayers to become real.
Each day is a better day with you,
I do not wish to experience that day
Without you . . .
There were too many, before you appeared.

I wish for our life to intertwine in the web of emotions
That links the threads, of our differences, together.
They meet and join with love,
With love that touches upon our very souls,
Our very beings.
That brings understanding, compassion and knowing . . .
That together, we are,
Apart, we are not.

Forgive me in my darkness,
Love me in my goodness,
Laugh with me in my craziness,
Share with me in my thirst for knowledge,
Believe in me for my wish for a better way,
Search with me to discover,
Cry with me in my sadness,
Be patient with me in my disillusions,
Be a friend to me when I need the truth,
Show me a different perspective,
Teach me what I do not know, nor understand,
Learn with me . . . grow with me,
But above all . . . accept me.

Pauline Foster (Belfast)

Ghosts

Dead now;
so many dead.

Dead and dead and dead.

Gone,
their going
unmentioned,
unmissed,
unmourned.

Except by this one,
and him old
and him wearied
but he can hold,
here,
inside his head,
within his memory,
those gone:
has held them all,
for sixty years and more,
both while they lived
and now that they are dead;
has held their glorious hopes,
has held their eager reaching for tomorrows;
has held their joy and shared their hurt of sorrows;
has held the once was brilliance
of their all too brief,
yet startling
technicolour dreams!

Aeons ago,
it seems,
when it began.
And does that sound to be a long, long time?
He wants it so,
this man;
for that,
at very least,
is what it's been.

Brian Travis (Pwllheli)

Your Grace

To the gracing
The hearing
The rhythms loving
To the moments of forgetting
The awakening to new sounds
Your heart's a jigsaw
With all its puzzling pieces
The eternal loving
Only placing together
This feeling
Yearning, twisting, burning
Testimonials of you
Neon lights and radio cities
San Fran suburbs
Those revealing frescos
Snow swept landscapes
Telescopes, Fed Ex and coliseums
Moonlight dreaming
Engraved forever your freedom in stone
Your grace.

The distant ambience
Rippling your tranquil silence
While watching your mind's lake
Relaxing to its reflections
Northern lights
Diaries of sight
Those memories of fragrances
Thinking of questions
That's never been spoken
Music I think I can articulate it
Along the beaches
Above the skylines
All these timeless atmospheres
Only to fulfil and exult your forte
Extricating and enamouring
Fresh to your future
Your grace.

Paul Kelly (Londonderry)

The Gypsy Girl

In lonely meditation
I walked down through the glen
To view the purple heather
And to see it once again
I stopped to watch the many flowers
In wild profusion there
I really was enraptured
And free from worldly care

The birds were singing loud and clear
The larks did soar above
As if to show their gratitude
To God, for His great love
In giving us this place of joy
That we could share together
Not governed by our lust and greed
But just to help each other

But as I wandered through the trees
Beside a babbling stream
There was a little clearing
Where I sat down to dream
And while I mused on nature's store
Of beauty freely given
I heard a cry of anguish near
From one whose soul was riven

I thought that I was there alone
Where serenity did reign
But here a soul in sorrow cried
As if in mortal pain
'Twas then I saw the fresh turned earth
A mound just newly made
And there I saw a gypsy
Beside where her child was laid

No tombstone there to mark the place
No coffin to surround her
Just a few wild flowers freshly plucked
And the cold clay cast around her

I turned in sorrow from that spot
And my own steps retraced
To my dying day I won't forget
Where that young child was placed

Oft I've returned to that same place
To see the little grave
And meditate on that young child
Who left this life so brave
Down in the glen within the grove
Beside the little stream
Only a little gypsy girl
With hopes that might have been.

Hugh Carton (Ballymoney)

Claret And Anger

I can weel mind the days when St John turned oot for Motherwell,
I'd just started at the Craig and taen hame my very first pay.
And I thought my heart would break the day they took St John tae Liverpool,
But noo, they've taen the Craig and wi' it taen my heart away.

I can weel mind the days when St John turned oot for Motherwell,
There were endless hours o' work, I thought it would always be that way,
And I swore I'd no' be back the day they took St John tae Liverpool
Noo, I'll no' be back tae Ravenscraig, they close the gates the day.

Nae steel, nae iron ore, nae strip-mill,
Nae King Lud, nae work.
Only empty days, the supermarket, gairden and the kirk.
I'm just waitin' for the end.
There's nae reason tae pretend nae different.
Quinn, St John and Hunter gone,
Noo Ravenscraig,
Then me.

I can weel mind the days when St John turned oot for Motherwell,
We worked wi' skill and pride, and they played wi' style and flair,
But the magic disappeared the day they took St John tae Liverpool,
They selt the jerseys then and noo they've done the same once mair.

Nae Era Bar nae Clydesdale,
Nae blast funaces - nae hope.
Only lookin' after grandwaens,
Bein' sent a message tae the shop.
I'm just waitin' for the end.
There's nae reason tae pretend nae different.
Quinn, St John and Hunter gone.
Noo Ravenscraig,
Then me.

Graeme Liveston (Milngavie)

Cheapside

It was back in 1960,
In the early morning light,
The sound of fire engines
Woke the city with a fright.
Words were echoed through the street,
As the flames grew higher and higher,
That a whiskey bonded warehouse
Was on fire.

The workers screamed in terror,
Who would answer for this sin?
For the window bars to keep thieves out,
Kept those innocents within.
They huddled in their masses,
To the door, to no avail,
The smoke was creeping onward,
As they started to inhale.

The firemen battled fiercely,
The wall was 60 feet in height,
They used every appliance to reach the other side,
Then, just on early evening, an explosion by the Clyde,
The city shook in terror,
The blast came from down Cheapside.

Nineteen firemen trapped there,
Nineteen courageous lives.
Nineteen men of honour, died by the riverside.
Nineteen families grieving, nineteen men in all,
Buried there for fighting,
A 60 foot brick wall.

Wives wept for their men folk,
Children cried out for their mums,
Firemen for their workmates,

A city for its sons.
A tragedy of errors, all over in a day,
But the memory of Cheapside
Will never go away.

Patricia Kelly (Skelmorlie)

Rhosymedre Chapel

Four square you stand -
At the top of the hill, where the roads meet;
An aged beacon to times gone by.
A marker for the local community,
Memories of weddings,
Funerals, baptisms,
Of Sunday school anniversaries -
White dresses, blue sashes -
Of 'chapel teas' and outings to local parks.
Still the same building they made,
Founded 175 years ago.
A stalwart, comfortable place,
Warmly carpeted in a way our ancestors would deride!
The copper and steel ceiling
Picked out in white and wedgewood blue.
Although the trapezium arch is now a mini arboretum
You still stand - a major monument to community,
To change and challenge.
On Saturday mornings, your walls ring,
As in older days, with children's laughter.
Sundays bring a more sombre note -
None the less joyful, just expressed more quietly!
Tuesday brings a closeness of fellowship shared -
Shown for the rest of the time by your open doors.
Here is no mausoleum to the past
But a living, breathing building,
Encapsulating lives and experiences,
Memories, joys and sorrows.
Four square you stand,
At the top of the hill, where the roads meet,
Looking through the houses to your sister parish church.
You welcome in the new and stranger, the old familiar,
Those coming often and those not been for some time,
You embrace them in the love that is your calling,
Inviting them to celebrate and share,
Together, in the community, in life.
At the top of the hill, where the roads meet.

Una McLean (Llangollen)

I Gazed Into The Glass And Thought!

Dear lady, you have lots of wrinkles
Grooves there by the mile
They may go with some twinkles
If you try on a smile

Can be caused by sorrow
Still often just with joy
Never fear about tomorrow
Let your face a smile employ

Wrinkles from a happy time
Days so long gone
The day you wed, the bells did chime
The sun it brightly shone

What of that gift so dear
A son so strong and tall
This filled you up with cheer
No wrinkles then - he had them all!

It's so much better sure
To think of happy times
With wrinkles on a tour
Your heart it really climbs

Hold on to creases
What joy do they behold
Face of smiles ne'er cease
Friends would miss each fold

Some are laughter lines
So never let them go
Are precious those designs
They will forever glow

If on your brow or face
God loves you as you are
Each one takes up space
Your looks they cannot mar

Wrinkle-free is your heart
Lines and curves all gone
The Lord irons smooth and flat
His love divine you've won

So dear lady, take a peep
Wrinkles are memories sweet
Do not sigh or weep
They fit your face a treat

So mirror, mirror on the wall
Who is the wrinkled of us all?
They'll lift up my morale
Even if I'm slow to crawl
To you they do enthrall
I feel I'm really on the ball!

I gazed into the glass and thought
Wrinkles, I have them more and more
I think I'm getting old
This only on the outside
Still I'm behind them, not in front
That's your pleasure - so I hope!
It's more than I can cope!

Erica Menzies (Aberdeen)

Flowers

Flowers are a gift from God
When seeds are planted in the sod
He saw them in his great creation
A flower for all and every nation

Flowers come in every colour
Bright yellows, pinks and greens
This makes for admiration
For they can easily be seen

Growing in a garden
Or on a window sill
Brought into a hospital
Can help the patients
Take their pills

A bunch can be a symbol
Of true love or special thought
Or given as a make up
When pardon it is sought.

Their life it goes so fast
With nothing left then for it
But to put them in a bin
Surely God in Heaven
Must think that we have sinned

Though our sins by Him all forgiven
His love for us had Him driven
He opened the gate of that garden
Asked God to give us His pardon

We shall walk with the beauty of flowers
As we watch them forever grow
Watered like us by that river
Which will for eternity flow.

Muriel Magee (Lisburn)

Untitled

The car won't go
It's slipping out of gear
This feels funny
Like it sits in fear
It can't go forward
It can't go back
It won't go zoom
It won't go pthath
The key is turned
The engine's come on
This is no choke
No automoton
Run the engine
Make a dull hum
Hum, hum, hum
This is very humdrum
Does it need oil?
What about a kick?
Try, try again
Move the gear stick
The car can't forget
Its heart can't fail
It doesn't have a soul
Its engine's not impaled
Mmmph
Turn it all off
Let's start again
Then all of a sudden
It's leapt through its pain
The engine is going
The gear is in
It's moving, it's driving
It's like it's insane
The car is working
Mechanics on form
It's no longer in fear
Now the engine is warm.

Belinda Howells (Pontypridd)

A Wedding Poem

(For every bride and groom on their special day)

Welcome to the bride and groom
On this your wedding day,
May you have blessings from above
And roses all the way.

Family and friends are gathered
To hear you say 'I do',
Love and joy in abundance
Are what we wish for you.

How lovely to see your happiness
With the rest of your lives ahead,
May you always and ever remember
The special day you were wed.

The recipe for marriage
Is plain give and take and trust,
'Old' married folk will tell you
That loyalty is a 'must'.

May the vows that you take on this day of days
And the rings that you lovingly treasure,
Fulfill all your best expectations
To the highest possible measure.

And as you set sail on the voyage
Of matrimony's sea,
If you hold very fast to each other
You'll ride out whatever will be.

'They lived happily ever after'
So ends each fairy story,
Thus may the story of your lives
Be written in love and glory.

Here's to the beautiful bride
And the handsome bridegroom too,
Follow your heart, follow your dream
May all your dreams come true!

Moira Wiggins (Neath)

Aut Inveniam Viam Aut Faciam

Down the raging torrent fell
A gushing, tumbling, foaming Hell,
Tripping and stumbling through the dell
Onward in wild ambience;
And roaring and moaning, it cast its spell
Upon the frozen audience.

Down, down the water sped
Leaping and dancing o'er stony bed,
Angry waves cursed and fled
To be replaced by yet another;
In a never-ending struggle, bred
By distant time's own mother.

Through the rocky gorge it poured,
A raving, rushing, furious horde,
Forcing its way like thrusting sword
Into the heart of its victim;
Splitting asunder the cleft it bored
With ferocious and vehement dictum.

Incensed and mad, it rode the steep,
Tossing and rolling in swirling sweep,
Bounding and vaulting, dark and deep,
It ran with terrifying force;
Unable to stop, unwilling to sleep,
Locked into its puissant course.

Excited and wrathful was its mood,
A toppling, falling, seething flood,
Enraged and infuriated, it seemed to brood
Upon its very sound;
And lurid waters turned to blood
Cascading from an open wound.

Transformed, it rose amid the storm
And donned the guise of another, torn
In true chimerical form
From the roots of imagination;
Vibrant and trembling, it seemed to adorn
The walls of admiration.

To escape this cruel and wicked detention
Appeared to be its only intention,
Yet trapped it seemed in this dimension,
Held by unyielding reason;
Descending swiftly, with augmented tension,
It made its bid for freedom.

Hopping and skipping, on it pounded,
Each murmur rising till it sounded
As though it were being pursued and hounded
By some unseen hand;
Tormented and wailing, it crashed, astounded,
Towards its destined land.

George Edward John Birbeck (Earlston)

Our Little Piece Of Heaven

(In memory of Mairi)

Take a walk up Burnhouse brae
Amidst the colourful glades in May,
Where pungent garlic heads the way
Through old Millennium wood.

Rich dense canopies of lush green trees
Branches dancing in the breeze
In dappled light, the shimmering seas
Sparkle through the wood.

Drifting 'neath the leafy bowers
Bursting banks in bathing showers
A brimming burn of deep blue flowers
Ring merry through the wood

In violet skies of speedwell blue
Golden buttercups filter through
White stitchwort clouds in pictures new
Weaving through the wood.

As the heron takes off overhead
Warm sunshine sets in campion red
Where avens sleep by the water's bed
With milkmaids in the wood.

How I love sweet summer scents in my nose
Honeysuckle cascading over beech hedgerows
Sifting the air with wild dog rose
Rambling by old Cessnock wood.

Have you heard our choir of songbirds sing?
What harmony they always bring
When they join together it is quite something
Having raised their feathered brood
In our heavenly woods.

Rosemary Gladwell (Galston)

My Front Door

(By an agoraphobic sufferer)

Today's the day I'll do it,
I'll put it off no more,
On with my coat – I've got my bag,
Now I'll just walk through the door.

But, like every other day, the doubts soon start to come,
What if something happens? *What if* I am ill?
What if my legs tremble, my stomach churns?
Maybe I'll take another pill.

Now I have to wait a while,
Until I feel more calm,
Time for more doubt yet again,
What if I come to some harm?

By now another hour has passed
And still I haven't gone.
The thoughts go round and round my head,
The fear is really strong.

Perhaps it's best if I leave it today,
I'll try when I feel well,
Off comes the coat; down goes the bag,
This is a living hell.

Other people pass the house,
They seem to be so free,
Oh why can't I be just like them?
Why has this happened to me?

Tomorrow will be another challenge,
More fears to go through,
Please live each day as best you can,
One day, this could be you.

But rest assured, I'll keep trying and trying,
Though at times it feels I can't go on anymore,
Because one day I'm going to be 'normal'
And walk through my front door!

Angela Davies (Porthcawl)

The Voices

(On the path to glory)

I've walked through pastures in my mind
And seen some wondrous places
And answered voices that called to me
But never saw their faces

Like Percival my soul was lost
Or so I thought in darkness
But found my feet did not retreat
Nor from my faith was parted

I walked the place I should not go
Where demons dwell in terror
And learned the lesson and understood
My fragile life of error

I turned to God he could not help
I'd lost my faith and reason
The voices that still haunted me
Now held me bound for treason

I prayed as habit would have me do
Not knowing if it mattered
The voices spoke to criticise
The next to leave me flattered

Borne on confusion I did go
To seek the path to glory
Then to return no hell to burn
I sought to end the story

I called to them to leave this place
To find some other dwelling
I prayed with passion in my heart
For the story I was telling

That peace can come to those who seek
The inner strength to find
To learn to face and defeat
The battle of the mind.

RTL Matthias (Aberystwyth)

Simon Cowell's Britain's Got Talent

Hello I can't believe I'm on this stage
Don't buzz me off before I turn the page
Oh! Please don't laugh
I thought of this one in the bath,
The words are coming in my head again,
Oh! My God I haven't got a pen
It always happens at the most awkward time
When in my head there is a rhyme.

Picture the scene not a pretty sight,
Covered in bubbles as I get out of the bath to write,
I stand up and put around me my towel,
Thinking all the time of Simon Cowell.

I can't dance, I can't sing,
Writing verse is my thing.
I bet Simon's thinking, *who cares*
It would be better if I sounded like Pam Ayres.

Well let me finish the story of my caper
In my towel looking for pen and paper,
I put one foot out the other on the soap,
I slipped and fell how would I cope?

So I'm on the floor still soaking wet
And I haven't written my verse down yet,
So with one hand on the bath, the other on the wall
Holding on tight not to repeat the fall,

My towel was quite big so I tucked it in like a sarong
Then the door got stuck what else can go wrong?
I pulled and pulled with all my might
How can I get out of this awful plight?

I thought I'd pull it gently instead
At last! It opened, touched my foot and banged my head,
So now I'm in the kitchen and at last I see a pen
Ouch my poor head was sore
And now there's someone at the door

'Wait a moment,' I shout, 'give me time,
I have to write down this rhyme.'
They kept knocking so I went to the door
It was someone I'd never seen before,
So with one hand on my head and a pen in the other,
At this point I was crying for my mother.
This person handed me a card
For some reason getting rid of him was hard.
At last I have pen and paper, my story now to be told

I write it down, go back to my bath, but now my water is cold
Well I give up so I go to bed
Nursing the nasty lump on my head,
The next time I'm in the tub and think of a rhyme,
I'll try and remember it and write it another time.

Linda Randell (Mountain Ash)

Luisa

(On her wedding day)

When she was born
She was little and chubby
Sausage limbs and tummy tubby
With dark curly hair
Like my sister's hubby
The Italian strain
Working against the English grain

Toddling she wore
Her cowboy gear
Waving her gun to instil fear
In her uncle and auntie
Back from France
She led us all a bit of a dance

Later a photo from school
With a few teeth missing
We had to ask
Which boys
She'd been kissing

And yet she grew
Tall and slim
Sophisticated and educated
And I must admit
Full of charm and wit

Now she has met
The man of her life
I know she will make him
A very good wife
And when they've exchanged
Their wedding bands
I also know
She'll be in good hands.

Alan Harry Francis (Llandrindod Wells)

My Little Boy

(For Dylan)

The bond that is strong between mother and son
A little angel sent from above
The wonderment of all that he does
Brings a love that only Mum can share

My little boy, with his cute cheeky smile
Looking at me through his bright coloured eyes
Watching as he toddles, just learning to walk
Sounds from his lips not quite making the words

Off he goes this tiny chap,
Waving his hand, as he looks back
Nursery is calling, he's learning to play
Making new friends, growing day by day

Painting and crayons, books to read
Balls to kick, holes to dig
Shoe laces to tie, buttons to fasten
Thomas the Tank, lunch in a minute

Excitement now as the bin man arrives
Waving and jumping he wants to go outside
Chattering away my attention to draw
To open the door and just let him go

Our first holiday, he plays in the sand
Castles to build, ice cream in his hand
The fairground is calling, which ride will he take
His laughter infectious, as he calls out again, again

The time it is precious, one day he'll be a man
High school and girls, bikes and fast cars
For now though, I keep him close by my side
Afraid of the time that is passing us by

Sleeping now I watch him, his eyes shut tight
His thumb in his mouth, teddy by his side
How I love him, tiny child of mine
God bless and keep you, my son

Jane Bessant (Pontypool)

The Raindog

I found it strange,
And strange it was.
That a simple twist of fate,
Should bring such light into a life,
So blighted, by the darkness of loneliness.
A drunken fumbling, to thoughtless obsession,
So soon.

Like a tallow candle's flame,
You cast a shadow across my heart.
Each breath I breathed,
Drawn by you,
Each thought and deed,
Inspired by only one.
So much, so soon.

I wanted to wake up where you were,
Stay forever at your side,
Lay awake to watch you breathe,
In the dark and shallow night.
But that would never be,
For I was cast aside, like driftwood.
So soon, so soon.

Driftwood floating down the river,
Beneath the burning bridges,
That once adjoined our lives.
And the twists and the turns,
And the drifts and the tides,
Took me once again.
So soon. Too soon.

And the fat, narcissist, thrice pricked,
Self-loathing, self-pity, self-doubt.
Shied away from the mirror's gleam,
To dance alone, in the garden of dreams.
Like a raindog lost,
In the torrent of life.
Too soon, too soon.

Samuel J Curry (Belfast)

Masheens

'I have a friend who has never had a washing machine.'
'How old is she, two?'
'No, she's sixty-eight.'
'I bet her clothes are in a state.'
'Probably wears black and brown.'
'Yes, quite.'
'But she has some Camilla-pink, tanzanite-blue
And cracking ice-white.'
'How does she do it?'
'Boiling water in the morning after a cold soak overnight.'

I realise that much fun is lost to her,
She cannot open a machine,
With a spiky-haired, spin-dried cat to be seen,
There are mornings, when paddling in ankle-deep foam is denied
And frantic phone calls to bring a plumber to her side
Are unnecessary.

Sets of underwear remain white,
Budding artists are denied the sight,
Of sweater-red mixed with sock navy-blue
And the baby has no backing group
To accompany his latest song.

Soap powder in chest gasping quantities
Is not on the shopping list
Clothes on the line are sun and wind-kissed
Petals float gently around
Before completing their mosaic on the ground.

A trip to the white goods store
Needs no diary to find a window
Who wants a vast wrist-dislocating iron
Based on the design of a train, fast or slow.

The shacka lasha ting of the machine
Deprives the kitchen of silence,
My friend has quiet, this can only mean
That thoughts become important and are not ignored

Here they burst through,
The subjects are roared
Loud, but not clear - for who knows the truth?
Iraq, negative equity,
Africa, bullying of our youth,
Weapons, destitution,
Sickness, stupidity,
Palestine and hubris.

I shall tell my friend
That to be green
Is not mind soothing,
'If that is all you want
Invest in a shacka lasha ting masheen.'

Barbara Phillips (Pontyclun)

A Mother's Love

(Dedicated to Paul and Michelle: from Mum, with love)

I could hardly believe the hurt I felt,
The day I heard you say,
'Mum, you know we love you,
But we must go away.'
Although it wasn't very far,
I felt a sense of loss,
All my emotions stirred up inside
And yes, you could say I was cross.

But soon the anger left me
And I thought my heart would break,
I even prayed at one stage,
The Lord my soul to take,
The home we shared felt empty now,
As empty as my heart,
But deep inside I guess I knew,
We all had a brand new start.

I accepted your decision, but why, I'll never know,
I didn't want you hating me,
So I had to let you go,
When you both were leaving,
Be good, you heard me say
Everyone was crying,
I'll never forget that day.

And as you walked away from me,
I watched with eyes that could not see
You threw me kisses, as I waved goodbye
But in my heart, I thought I'd die.

Although you're with your dad now,
I pray to the Lord above,
That you will never, ever forget,
The warmth of a mother's love.

Frances Meenan (Londonderry)

To Ex-Air Hostess Branwen, To Greet You On Your Birthday

I remember, I remember,
You came to visit me.
When I was living in Rosebush
And you were only three!

I well remember how you played,
Beside the garden wall,
Those happy days were gone too soon,
As I can well recall.

I saw you grow as time went by,
At school you did so well
And on your life it left its mark,
As we can easily tell.

All down the years I have received,
A greeting card from you,
From distant lands beyond the seas,
Where skies are often blue.

From far off lands with different tongues
And different modes of life,
From some, where peace still reigns supreme
And others torn with strife.

You've met with many famous men
And with well-known women too,
With kings and queens from distant lands
From here to Timbuktu!

So, from us all now gathered here,
To Branwen we all say,
A very happy birthday,
God bless you on your way.

Denzil Edwards (Haverfordwest)

The Ghosts Of The Min y Don

It stood for two hundred years or more, a grand old hostelry,
The Min y Don with its back to the cliff and its front to the Irish Sea,
Withstanding many a savage storm and many a spiteful squall,
Defying the wind and violent waves lashing the old sea wall.
Built to last from old grey stone, steeped in history,
The Min y Don at Red Wharf Bay on the Isle of Anglesey.
In the early days the fishermen's ways dominated the quay,
With the catch brought in they'd meet at 'The Min' and talk of their day at sea,
They'd hear the sound of plunging hooves as horses coming in
Carried weary travellers to the well-known coaching inn.
Time marches on and with fishing days gone people came to stay
To enjoy the sun and the family fun on a summer holiday.
In modern times the Min y Don was a place for revelry,
With weddings, discos, parties and Christmas festivity.
The old grey walls absorbed it all as ghosts from the past looked on,
Content with all that happened in that place called the Min y Don.
They've demolished it now to build houses, bulldozed from ceiling to floor,
Without a thought for the age-old past and the people who'd gone before.
They've put up modern buildings, very trendy and smart,
But that's only part of the story since they tore out its very heart.
The past is linked to the future so whatever is said and done
The ghosts of yesteryear will haunt that place called the Min y Don.
They will linger in shadowy corners and whisper of people who came,
Nothing has changed as far as they know so to them 'The Min' is the same.
They'll be at their posts and re-live what they did and walk where they walked before
For now they're disturbed, they're up and about, looking and wanting more.
There's the red-haired girl with the clustering curls who waits by the coach house door
For the boat coming in bringing Dafydd home but he'll come home no more.
When the boat went down he was left to drown, the one they couldn't save,
Now Dafydd, and his little pet dog sleep in a watery grave.

The old sea captain will walk the floor following his routine
When he got well-fed then went to bed and died in room fifteen.
So many spirits will linger as the cold east wind kicks in
Remembering the wintertime and evenings spent at 'The Min'.
The incoming waves will come racing reminding us as they roll
That Red Wharf Bay once had character and the Min y Don had a soul.

Betty Weaver-Lucking (Anglesey)

Be Ready

As I gaze out through my window,
I see a most amazing sight.
The awakening of the springtime
Fills my heart with sheer delight.
Hedgerows, scrubs and flowers,
All with great promise ring,
Sunshine peeping through the clouds,
Birds tuning up to sing.

Springtime turns to summer
With long relaxing days,
The awakening of the springtime,
Now reveals a wondrous maze.
Beautiful summer fragrance,
Rich, cultured land,
All in perfect harmony,
Exactly as God planned.

Autumn follows quickly,
Leaves falling everywhere,
Fade away in glorious splendour,
No artist can compare.
Evenings long and cosy,
Welcome visits from a friend,
A time of preparation,
Winter lies around the bend.

It was the bleak midwinter,
That Jesus came to Earth,
Far away in Bethlehem,
The humblest of birth,
With donkey, sheep and oxen,
In a lowly stable stall,
A babe was born, the Prince of Peace,
Jehovah, Lord of all.

Jesus grew, and walked and talked
With folk like you and me,
He healed the sick, helped the poor
And made the blind to see.
Preaching the Gospel to mankind,
Wisdom flowing free,
He died to cleanse us of our sins
On the Cross at Calvary.

He arose! Ascended into Heaven,
To reign with God above,
Tenderly watching over us,
Bestowing boundless love.
We read it in the scriptures,
He had gone there to prepare
And close behind Him, for each of us,
There stands a vacant chair.

In his word He promises,
He will return one day,
So can we all be ready
When Jesus comes this way?

E E Sheridan (Welshpool)

I Mine Fine

*(Memories of Peterhead, Aberdeenshire in the early 1940s
written by June Strachan, a Peterheid quine)*

I mine fine when I was a quine
Doon at the Giddle Braes
We'd jump ower rocks
An' weet wir socks
There were some skelpit docks
Fan we got hame!

But first we'd knock aff some limpets
Wi a steen jist made for the job
Syne pick some buckies
Find a roostie tin
Mak a fire an' bile em
An' eat em wi a pin!

Fit wye we didna get pishoned
Is onybody's guess
I dread to think
Fit the Environmental Health
wid say
If bairns did at I day!

Aye, I mine fine when I wis a quine
Fan gay meant happy
An' we got a cappie
For a treat
Nae designer labels or meals in posh hotels
An if we dar' be cheeky we'd get a clout
Ower I lug and we'd hear bells!

Aye, I mine fine when I wis a quine
Fan aids meant helpin'
An' we got a skelpin
For gaun doon tae the Giddle Braes
Those were the days
Fa else mine's fine?

June Roskell (Fraserburgh)

The Hermitage Of Braid - Edinburgh

I take the woodland path.
The gray stone bridge that spans the burn
Echoes delusions of torrential
Grandeur, fierce and rapid;
Instead of the friendly burn it is,
Gossiping away
To the stones, branches, beer cans
That find its bed; inviting dogs
And children in to play.

Beneath my feet, leaves and berries cling
Damply, in haphazard reds and golds.
Ruffled in the breeze, folds of bright water
Reflect out passing trees, out of focus.
The silence deepens, deeper in the wood,
Underlined, not broken, by the cry of gulls.
Treetop rooks, in minor key
Descant against the chorus
Of the waterfall.

Round the bend, motherhood
In tracksuit and trainers
Breaks my solitude.
A young babe, snug against her breast
Is harnessed to her heartbeat.
Wood smoke smarts my throat and eye.
A phoenix from its funeral pyre,
A livid slice of logs which lie
In half-quenched ashes, half submerged.

In the distance, sunlight
Shafting church-like
Through the trees,
Plays on the now still water,
Highlights the upper reaches of the bank
To catch in silhouette
The desolation of a park bench
Waiting for spring.

Thelma Legget (Edinburgh)

At Kings Cross Ancient Fort

(For Kate and Hugh after their visit to Arran)

Two sticks, staff-length, crossed,
ritually left alone on ancient rampart stone.
Bruised, broken bark; one end sharp;
the other bent from wielding.
Weapons for boys in play
left in truce for another day?

Or a tryst for lovers
who kissed
and used a cross for a ring
to mark their promised marrying?

Or perhaps a spirit passed that way
and left a warning sign to tell
of warriors and wives who lost their lives
and fell beneath that stone
denied their romance and their play
and, who, one day, will emerge
to claim their heritage.

Or was it here that an anxious king,
spider-inspired,
waited to cross the foam
hopeful to reclaim his home
and win his throne.

Nearby, a lad with unkempt titian hair
caused his kite to fly
pulling strings.
Was it his necromancy weaving fancy
through the wind in its wings?

Such was my meandering
standing in that cliff-top fort
feeling for history in its mystery
glad I was not alone
with that silent, fortune-holding stone.

George Baines (Isle of Arran)

The Christmas Star

I awoke on Christmas Day and what did I see?
Multicoloured lights were upon a tree
Tinsel cascaded from every windowpane
While banners hung from every country lane

Lights of colour did never end
Flags and glitter for Christmas did send
Mistletoe fell around lovers' heads
Holly draped with berries red

The Norwegian spruce so clad in snow
Did gleam with lanterns put on show
There were baubles that shone from every arm
And the Northern star kept all from harm

Streamers plastered the paveway where I walked
The rivers were champagne, the roads were of cork
Crystal trees and diamond light
Reflected the icicles shimmering bright

Horse-drawn carriages lined the road
Children's toys were delivered by the load
Festive food from stalls were sold
Next to sleighs with bells of gold

The snow seemed like psychedelic drops
That tasted just like lemonade pop
Church bells rang from the town spire
And I felt my lifting heart get higher

Those with candles did sing with joy
No one soul did another annoy
Yellow and red did fill the air
As a bonfire burnt from the centre of the square

Christmas Day heard Jesus call
Everyone laughed, no one did fall
People waved and people played
In a land that equality had made

Couples walked arm in arm
No lighted shop did ring alarm
Old people turned young before my eyes
By eating Christmas pudding and mince pies

There passed a flock of turtle doves
That praised the peace of Heaven above
This land of plenty all year round
Without even one unhappy sound

Music echoed around the Christmas star
The kids had their fill of chocolate bars
And as the carols came from open door
I warmed my hands as the fire did roar

This was a planet not up for sale
No young child did unhappily wail
And as this world did merrily feed
I walked on home for food and mead.

Richard Appleyard (Pembroke)

Go Gently And Kindly Through Life

Step gently, lest you cause hurt to those weaker than yourself.
Be not judgemental, lest you cause others to be judgemental of *you.*
Speak gently and kindly, lest you cause others to turn away.
Be tolerant always, for none are perfect.
Be steadfast in your determination to achieve your dreams.
Stand firm in your beliefs, but respect others for theirs.
Do not harbour guilt, for guilt can mask productive thought.
Dismiss hatred from your mind, for it is as a parasite
And only serves to weaken the host.

Start each day with a joyful heart,
For there are those for whom joy is a stranger.
Count your blessings and treasure them.
Life is as a flight of steps, to be climbed with anticipation and optimism.
Problems are just obstacles to be overcome as we travel through life.
Listen to the voices of others, for they have wisdom to offer you.
Be not afraid of new experiences, for they are the fabric of our lives.
Cherish all affection offered to you, it is churlish to cast it aside.

Learn to accept gifts with grace, lest you cause offence to the giver.
Be forgiving of the young who cause you irritation,
For they are but small mirrors of yourself.
Find a place in your heart, even for the reviled,
For their lives may have been hard.
Believe in your own self worth, for only then will others respect *you.*
Trust your instincts, but do not be afraid to change direction.
Open your heart to those whom you trust, for they will help you
To carry the heavy burdens in your life.

Man was not created to live a solitary life, therefore it is beneficial
To offer the hand of friendship to those who are crying out and alone.
Live each day with enthusiasm, but not forgetting the less fortunate,
A smile will suffice, or a sympathetic gesture.
Have the strength to make them feel worthy and justified
In having their place on this Earth.
Treasure this life of yours and help others treasure theirs.
Generosity of spirit will justify *your* place in this wonderful life canvas.

C M Bellamy (Caernarfon)

The Rivers Of My Life (1997)

By Findhorn's fast and sparkling stream,
I sit and ponder in a dream,
Of days gone by,
When in my youth,
I walked by rivers just as fine.

By Thames I strode,
Hand in hand,
With boyfriend bold,
To Kew and Richmond we would walk,
And even found some time to talk
And maybe steal a kiss or two.

So life passed by,
And step by step we found ourselves on Devon's shore
With rivers bounding from the moor.

We settled in an ancient town,
And found the Dart was near by hand,
To give us joy and walks galore.

But life goes on - one's love is lost,
So northward seemed to call me on.

So, beside the Yorkshire Derwent fair,
I settled with a partner there.
A smallish stream it seemed to me
But never ceasing on its way to join the Ouse eventually.

Once more alone, all loved ones gone,
I travel further than before,
To find myself on Moray's shore,
And there find home for evermore.

So here I sit by Findhorn's stream,
Keeping alive my youthful dream,
But alas! My knees are stiff,
My hips are false; I shall never do another waltz:
But looking back my life has been,
Full of honey, jam and cream.

V E Adamson (Forres)

The Infantry

Infantry is spelt with a capital I,
For these are the men who do or die,
Five years of war have given them fame,
So always put a big 'I' to their name.

The Infantry fought at Dunkirk as you know,
The Germans were then a terrible foe,
With bombers and fighters screaming down low,
It was Hell upon Earth as the Infantry know.

In African lands, on hot desert sands,
Our Infantry fought really well,
The Germans this time were driven back fine,
And the Italians were beaten as well.

On a July morn and at early dawn,
We landed in Sicily,
On Catania's plains, we wrote up the names
Of our gallant dead Infantry.

On Italian land we made our next stand,
For the cause of liberty.
The fighting was rough and the going was tough,
For the glorious Infantry.

Then from England to France,
The boys did advance,
A gigantic Army were they.
The Germans' retreat was the Axis defeat,
So the Infantry won the day.

To all other people at home and abroad,
The help you gave was swell,
And you with me will all agree,
That the Infantry's fought very well.

So Infantry is spelt with a capital 'I',
For these are the men who do or die,
Five years of war have given them fame,
So forever and ever put a big 'I' to their name.

H F Thompson (Cwmbran)

The Good Old Days

Oh how often we hear people
Talking of the times gone by.
How the good old days were better,
They remember with a sigh.

Everyone was helpful, friendly,
In so many caring ways.
You could count on all your neighbours,
In those good old bygone days.

Children played in streets quite safely,
Hopscotch, skipping, catch-me-catch.
Home from school, if parents absent:
Keys were hanging on the latch.

Doors kept open, friendly people
Just walked in for little chats.
And cats slept peaceful, mildly snoring
Near the fire, on the mats.

Yet not everything was golden,
Too many fathers on the dole.
And we often had to shiver,
There was no money for some coal.

Food was scarce, a daily battle,
Mother restless in her bed.
Worrying how on days to follow,
She could keep her loved ones fed.

Clothing was another matter,
No new shoes or pretty gowns.
Socks got darned and shoes got mended,
And we all had hand-me-downs.

Now everything has come full circle,
No more hardship, no more need.
Full employment, supermarkets,
Great prosperity indeed

Yet are people really happy
With double income and holidays?
Doing better than the Joneses,
With parties, drinks and takeaways.

Vast expanding purse and waistlines,
Yet few of us contentment know.
We strive for more of goods and beauty,
To put up a vulgar show.

There's no time for friendly chats, now,
Strangers all, who live next door.
No more caring, no more sharing,
As was done in days of yore.

That's how it is and was and will be,
Yet *our* hectic selfish ways,
For our offspring and their children,
Will *one* day be *their* Good Old Days.

Hildegard Davies (Cardiff)

Fear Of Words

I am a poem with best words in place
I am a novel that metres Man's disgrace
I am a saga that ranges ancient sense
I am an ode too odious to state
I am a prophesy too real to fake
A tale wagging a dog too full of means

I am a story told in telling ways
I am a hymn too trite for daily praise
I am a psalm the prophet used to grant
A rap across the knuckles beaten raw
I am a rhyme to reason shown to bore
I am a verse dispersed in constant rant

I am a ditty, pretty nifty told
I am a song, Solomon judged to scold
I am a romance, no one loved too well
I am a threnody that dwells too long
An epilogue that starts with teeming throng
I am a villainous villanelle

A piece of prose opposed to abstraction
Logic refusing complex reduction
A play, a thing of acts and foolish parts
I am a magazine too full of shots
A grounded flyer marred by lots of blots
A limerick rammed full of bums and farts

I am a leaflet that no tree would bare
I am a will that brooks no one to dare
I am a deed that badly deflects hope
A text where vowels r nt gvn scope
A written dogma bearing teeth to bite
A treaty weakened that gives up its write

I am a haiku
lone by this I fear to end
my nurture thus penned

Marc R Sherland (Glasgow)

Ain't I Grand!

Night approaches,
Muse encroaches
on the minds
of writers who
seek solace to
drink sorrow still
 - sip self-pity
to their fill
and dip the poisoned
tip of quill
in ink of solitude
until;
words emerge
from deepest dark
of hell (where poet souls embark)
on nightly roaming,
often time,
in rhyme of 'thee'
or 'thou'
or 'thine' -
but better this
self-loathing phase
than listen to
the endless days
of 'big up me'
and 'ain't I grand'
now metrical
is in demand
for banishment
of poet black
revives the ego
and brings back
the killer stroke
and swift attack
of the rhythmic
megalomaniac.

Lorraine Voss (Llangammarch Wells)

Rufus . . . The Red Rooster . . .

He had a fine figure, a magnificent stature,
immediately and very clearly, he was well bred,
a dominating character tho' steady and mature,
he was promptly named . . . Rufus the Red.
Rufus strutted his stuff stiffly and proudly,
to the farmyard rank and file he lay down the law,
and to ensure that all there obeyed him -
Rufus ruled his domain with an iron claw!
He had pesky hens to control; bossy Boudicca,
lumpy Jordan, capricious Carmen and Attila the Hen . . .
but by upping his intimidation tactics and some
hard pecks and their resistance was soon broken . . .
Now his morning 'song' - a nuisance to some -
enabled his male voice was well spread,
he would pull himself up to his full height
singing his song, with repeats, from atop the chicken shed.
Born to be a legend indeed, and recorded in
the sparse annals of iconic Chickendom,
the recognition, adulation and heavy respect
he wore easily with nonchalant aplomb . . .
Because of what happened one frightful occasion
and he felt he had sang his last cock-a-doodle-doo . . .
'twas deep in the night in the chicken house,
when he was sure he had met his Waterloo . . .
Came a commotion, some murmurings, then panic clucking -
through the exit shed flap some fox stuck his head,
the chicken house exploded: fearful screechings and feathers
flew - Rufus busied himself pecking the fox till it bled.
The fox howled his pain, the hens cackled with glee,
then it fled with bushy tail between its legs,
the relieved and excited hens squawked raucously and in
celebration laid a fusillade of fresh eggs . . .
Normalcy more or less returned after the Great Panic,
but the next day is Christmas Eve . . .
after Rufus the Red Rooster's courage and heroism,
surely, most surely . . . he deserves a reprieve . . . ?

J Fred Jackson (Llanelli)

Love Is In The Air

The house was full of family and friends all getting dressed for your wedding
There was laughter and excitement in every room as we took it in turns to get ready
The hairdresser was also there doing your hair with special care

The chapel was full of family and friends, all there for your wedding day
The flowers at the altar were lovely
Chosen especially to match your dresses

The organist started to play 'Here Comes the Bride'
And everyone turned to see you and your dad arm in arm
Walking down the aisle
You looked so happy

As you stood at the altar hand in hand and said your vows together
I could see the love between you both and I'm sure others did too
The placing of rings on each other's fingers, you looked into each other's eyes

The organist played and sang as you signed your names for the first time as Mr and Mrs C Way
The best man and Chris, so handsome, your best maid, your sister, so lovely
I've never seen you look so happy together as you did this special day

Your dress pale gold with pearls and veil to match the same
Your best maid dressed in yellow and flower girl shining pink
Your little son, your pageboy, dressed in black trousers with a waistcoat and tie of gold

Your flowers of pink and yellow with ribbons of pale gold
Here and there between the flowers little glittering stones

As you walked out of the chapel as man and wife
Your family and friends behind you
With greetings and good wishes
'Congratulations,' I heard them say.

The photographer took lots of pictures as the sun shone, 'what a day'
The hall was set, your guests were waiting to greet you

As you cut your cake a cheer went up and applauded you to the top table
The meal was great, although you hardly ate

The speeches were short, no one said a lot
But your son of three stood on a chair and said thank you to us for coming to Mum and Dad's wedding
He was the best speaker on the day
The DJ announced the first dance and you danced as man and wife joined by your best man and best maid

Then the parents took to the floor

Your mum had a ball as she danced all night long with most of the men in the hall
The buffet laid out, what a spread
I'm sure your guests enjoyed
The champagne toasts went down so well

The older guests got tired as it had been a long day
So they started to dwindle and say goodnight
Leaving all the young ones to have a ball

So over the years as they go by, I hope you will always remember the day that was planned for you both
To give you so much happiness and love on your wedding day

Jean Adam (Balloch)

The Hedger

As the craftsman's billhook falls,
On the gnarled and knotted stumps,
With blades that he has sharpened razor-sharp,
With precision of the eye.
That will slice a single ply
To carry forth the sap of future life.
With the brambles cleared away,
And the surplus growth that stray,
He leaves the young and upright stems to lay.
How the gold medallions quiver,
As he slices to a slither,
The best that he's selected for the fray.
Beech and hazel, maple, ash,
Mixed with dogwood make a splash.
Indigenous they thrive, they're there to stay,
He'll lay them with his skill,
Bear in mind the slope or hill,
And then he'll place them with the wind to lay.

Oh it is the craftsman's task
To make that hedgerow last,
A stock proof fence that to the eye is kind,
There are many different styles
Some are staked for miles and miles
Crooked or pleached or some have hetherings applied.
But Glamorgan, in our Vale,
It is quite a different tale,
It is called a Flying Hedge, with lots of light.
Oh, the modern youth will not
Have the skills to fill the plot,
If craftsman's gifts are left to slip away,
There is beauty, there is skill
To the craftsman brings a thrill.
An artist who achieves this task today
Father time he will not wait,
So, before it is too late,
Don't let our country crafts all slip away.

Thelma Lougher (Glamorgan)

Toybox

When all the family were asleep,
Out of the toybox they did creep,
Teddy, Golly and Ragdoll too,
Plus ten soldiers painted red and blue.
They marched across the bedroom floor,
Then straight out through the open door.
They crept downstairs one by one,
Now it's time to have some fun.
The lounge door was open wide,
So all the toys went inside.
The moon shone through the window bright,
This was their only source of light.
This made shadows on the wall,
Making the toys look twice as tall.
Ragdoll felt a little scared,
And wanted to go back to bed.
It seemed she was the only one
Who didn't think this was fun.
They started to play hide-and-seek,
When suddenly the stairs did creak!
The toys kept quiet and very still
Then into the room walked two-year-old Bill.
Rubbing his eyes and half-asleep,
Wearing no slippers and about to weep.
He rubbed his eyes once more,
Then noticed something on the floor.
It was his favourite teddy bear,
Oh Teddy I've searched for you everywhere.
Now Bill looked happy and content,
So off to bed with Teddy went.
Now downstairs the clock struck two,
What were the other toys going to do?
They didn't want to play the game,
Without Teddy it wouldn't be the same.
They all agreed to go back to bed
And play the game tomorrow instead.

L J Dhar (Swansea)

I Am Your Strongest Motive

(For M)

I am your strongest motive
and your weakest vulnerability
I can be heard
in the quietest moment
of your beating heart.
I can be found
in the look in your eye
when you say goodbye
to love.
You have often caught my shadow
in the mirror
from a worried glance,
and sensed me
in that heart-thumping moment
of dread.
You have never held me in your arms
and yet
I am the grandest passion, you will ever have.
I have been and forever will be
your truest friend
always on your side.
Sometimes I am longing
sometimes I am loathe,
whatever I decide,
it is for your benefit.
I have held your hand
and led you
down the path of your choice
- even when you ignored me.
I am your inner voice
- always on the tip of your tongue
I am instinct
I am You
- listen to me.

Caroline Rose (Glasgow)

Portrait Of A Pensioner

Here I am - at seventy-three,
The Care Home staff look after me.
Young people often come to call
And chat to make us all recall -
Times gone by - our younger days
And in wonder they all gaze
And think of us as living history
Which, to them, is quite a mystery.

Men, once upright and so straight,
Bent over, single, lost their mate.
Women try to look quite good
And weight-watch eating healthy food,
They keep old styles - like twin-sets new,
Hair well-groomed and coloured blue,
Styled in shape of days gone by,
But still quite good, despite the dye.

Favoured jewels are mainly pearls,
Just as they had when they were girls.
No cars - a tram, a bus, a bike,
At the worst, a longish hike -
If wage ran out before pay day,
'Too bad,' our parents had to say.

So different from what the young have now,
So I have made myself a vow.
To keep 'in tune' with this 'today',
By being a radio DJ,
I am allowed to leave the Home,
To do my shows - not to roam,
I play the tracks and 'scratch' the vinyl,
Probably this will be my final -
Effort at keeping up to date,
Before the time I meet my fate.

So - listen in - don't have a care
DJ Doddery is on the air!

Aileen Kelly (Aberdeen)

Precious Fields

May I be like the man of the fields,
Who, after having sown his seeds,
Does not live in painful anxiety,
But patiently awaits the time of growth,
In polite respect of the seasons.

May I have a heart like his,
With his mind that is at peace,
For he knows he has done his best
And let the rain and the sun do the rest
He knows he has sown good seed
And looks with wonder at the silent miracle of nature.

May I have a heart like his,
A mind is nothing but a field,
Who, after having toiled hard,
Leaves to you, oh Lord of all,
To make the seed give its yield,
With your divine grace,
For the ground that never held a seed
Will only grow useless weeds.

May I have a heart like his,
A mind at peace,
I knew a man who planted seeds
But in-between there were some weeds,
He never ploughed, he never hoed,
The weeds grew up and so assailed,
The good of him, until he failed.

May I have a heart like the good seed
And cultivate a fertile mind
And every seed grows tall and trim
And has a crop of wealth to find,
Only to view my soul within,
More and more convinced,
That everything depends upon me,
But nothing entirely on me alone.

James McKernan (Omagh)

The Eyes Of Eros

He stands so very high
But in a winged pose
Where his arrows fall
No one in London knows

'Cause here at Piccadilly
The God of Love does abide
Shooting little arrows
So two people will collide

Many ponder at his feet
To watch the world go past
But Eros' eyes are watching
As he takes time to contrast

Lovers pass him by
Endeared in sweet romance
Others swamped in liquid
Stagger forward in a trance

Those eyes have seen some sights
Not all enriching, I might add
When fear becomes subsumed
In a brave and drunken façade

While the nightlife comes alive
With the music pumping loud
Eros sees potential clients
In the young and sentimental crowd

Morning dawns on London streets
Early tourists grab the chance
To photograph the Love God
Posing in a semi-naked stance

When next you are in London
In amid the many crowds
Watch out for the God of Love
On one leg, standing proud.

Heather Dickey (Ballymena)

The Last Owlets?

A great forest rose from the mountainside,
The life breath of the land's heart.
Sustaining the life of Man and nature,
Holding firm the ground and purifying the air.

Three owlets nestle safely in the old oak,
Peering out from time to time, to view their world.
Parents hovering protectively overhead,
Sleek in their brown and white plumage.

Magpies, crows and jackdaws chatter noisily
While blue tits and finches feed
Tiny wrens scuttle and hide and keep safe
And field mice steal seeds from the blossoms.

This is the perfect picture, but that was *then,*
How does the picture look now?
No more forest, no life breath of the land's heart,
No sustenance for Man or nature, just destruction.

Three owlets without a world, the trees are gone,
No parents hovering above them,
No protection now, no safety now, no food now,
No tiny wrens or field mice, no magpies, crows or jackdaws.

How long before these owlets take wing? Maybe never,
Will they ever take that first faltering flight
Gliding silently and gracefully on the evening thermals?
Will they ever swoop with precision on to their unsuspecting prey?

Maybe never. Their life span is now on hold, and why?
Without the life breath of the land's heart,
Without nature's sustenance and pure clean air,
They may be lost forever.

A great forest *once* rose from the mountainside,
The life breath of the lands' heart,
And we stood on that barren sunken ground
Thinking of three small birds that once were.

C M Bellamy (Caernarfon)

MOT

I'd like to have an MOT
Upon my ageing 'bod',
I'd like to hear Doc Paton shout,
'Drag in the poor old sod.'

We'll take a sample of his blood
And look for something harmful,
But if we are not satisfied
We'll take another armful.

We'll have to do a blood count
And if it's less than nil
We'll give him the final rites
Or put him on 'the pill'.

Where's that sample of his 'wee'
Get it analysed this minute,
No - chuck it out of the window quick
There's something swimming in it.

His moans about arthritis
Are getting on my wick,
No - don't give him a plastic hip
Give him a thicker stick.

We'll belt his knees with hammers
And look at his reflexes,
Nurse - stop making eyes at him
He's too old to know what sex is.

We'll probe inside his ear 'oles
Have a dig into the wax
And we'll call in the experts
If we find some artefacts.

According to his records
His life's been full of shocks,
Well he's going to have another one
Please phone for 'Dai The Box'.

Taff Gurmin (Crickhowell)

The Lord's Day

I'd like to set the record straight
About the term 'Lord's Day'
How people call that Sunday
I really cannot say

The 'Lord's Day' in the Bible
Is not what most believed
That Sunday is the first day
So don't you be deceived

The term is in the Bible
But not what you've been told
I'll show you where to look now
If I may be so bold

Just open up your Bible
To first Thessalonians there
Chapter four will tell the story
The truth to all will bare

Then turn to verse thirteen then
And read to seventeen through
And you will see the truth there
Of what we all must do

To be in Heaven with God
There's only one way there
So if you see the truth now
I hope with others share

Then chapter five will tell you
Verse two will say it clear
The Day of the Lord is coming
It's very, very near

That is my wish to all now
To tell them while I may
Of how to be together
On this, the last Lord's Day

Doug Crick (Bridgend)

Reflection

When middle age comes around the bend,
Melancholy will be the natural trend,
In its grasp, the heart will fine,
For failed ambitious grand design.

'What might have been,' is a tortuous joke,
As catalogue of misfortunes runs memory amok,
Comes urge to unburden life's affairs,
With a sympathetic ear to share.

But where can a sufferer find an ear,
Appreciative and offering cheer,
The bustling world is loathe to waste,
Time and patience on woeful taste.

The aged grow weary, the young won't listen,
No comfort in store for heartbreak reminiscing,
Few have time to digest or appease,
Caught up in the rat race of life's trendy maze.

When is the pleasure in hot rant blame,
Or who gives a monkey about what went or came,
It's laugh together or cry alone,
No one is anxious to share in a moan.

Society in general is generous in most,
But draws a strict line against boring outburst,
'Don't bother me, man,' is the usual rhyme,
'Cry on another shoulder, there's no room on mine.'

Come to your senses, stop acting an ass,
Focus the present, not yesterday past,
A helpful hand and friendly smile,
Will beat off the blues and make living worthwhile.

Count the blessings that are yours to command,
Lighten the burden on your fellow man,
Take time off to listen and so to befriend
And you won't feel as a failure, but as a success in the end.

Alan Moore (Dungannon)

Together Forever

Can it be fifty-three whole years
Since united we said 'I do'
A privilege we were granted
Together we saw it through

Misty memories now take hold
Of the early tentative years
So full of the joy of family life
No time for trouble or tears

Somewhere along the way we found
We were no longer alone
A little miniature of us both
Decided to join our home

Amidst the overflowing hours
Our family soon became five
A full and active life we led
So happy and alive

Then teenage years and weddings came
And grandchildren a-plenty
A big extended lively group
Our days were never empty

But suddenly and swiftly too
Such darkness filled our home
A cloud called cancer shrouded us
And you, my love, have gone

Family, faith, and friends all help
To keep my spirits high
But oh what fun has left my life
Since that night we said goodbye

Time may ease this hollow space
Where my heart feels grief and pain
Until some day I will follow you
And we'll never part again.

Bertha Logie (Garve)

Granny's Gift

Let me take you back to days of yore
When Granny was eighty and I only four
An imposing creature she seemed to me
In funereal black, as she poured cups of tea.

'Don't give me tea,' I silently cried
Taking instant dislike to a drink yet untried.
Had she no orange juice or rich creamy milk
Served in a beaker which couldn't be spilt?

This room was so dark, dingy and cold.
Everything shabby. Everything old.
Granny's hands were shaky, her footsteps slow
And where was the toilet? I had to go.

Too frightened to speak, I sat in despair
Then I noticed she'd fallen asleep in her chair.
I crept out the door with scarcely a sound
Till the 'Little Girl's Room' I finally found.

When I peeped round a corner at the end of the hall
There sitting in splendour was a beautiful doll
In a red velvet dress and long golden hair
Together we played - of time unaware.

Many times we did meet and our friendship grew
But always in secret - nobody knew.
So the day Granny died, I thought - never again
Would I share my life with my beautiful friend.

Now I am eighty as Granny was then,
And my granddaughter's coming to visit at ten.
I know she enjoys the games that we play
Especially our ritual at the end of each day.

Hand in hand we walk to the end of the hall
And into the room with the beautiful doll.
All the time Granny knew how happy I'd be,
And how well I'd look after her gift to me.

Christine Kelly (Glasgow)

The Passing Of The Years

When we are ten, the days are long,
No need to think of right or wrong.
Our hopes and dreams are all so new
And many things we want to do.

When twenty comes and we still aspire
To reach the stars and fame acquire.
Romantic thoughts abound within
And rise and fall at every whim.

At thirty we have settled down.
We live in the country or in town.
Responsibility ours to share
With other lives to love and care.

Now forty is the strangest age
Our fading youth - our middle age.
The extra weight, the loss of hair
The time has come to feel despair.

Fifty is a special age,
For sporting pastimes to engage,
A little leisure here and there,
Although some aches and pains to bear.

Sixty comes, we're unaware
Of the many, many passing years.
A slower pace is what we crave
Our strength and sight we have to save.

At seventy we hold our breath,
Afraid to contemplate our death.
The Earth so sweet, our family dear,
We wish to keep them close and near.

If to eighty or ninety we survive,
By then we're glad to be alive.
Our grateful thanks for all that's past
And the Higher Hand we'll meet at last.

Dorothy Hill Bradshaw (St Andrews)

To Try

My grandmother once told me,
You can only try your best, that's all God asks
With what you have to apply yourself
To some of life's awkward tasks

I grew up a tree-climbing tomboy
At fifteen, was a child from a broken home
With two warring parents
Felt misunderstood and all alone

I remembered her words
As I tried to help, now I'm a gran
A grandson from a broken home
Who had become an angry young man

His mother with other children
Just could no longer cope
So, I was asked would I take him in
As his last hope?

After a year and a few hissy fits
Along the way
He's a lot calmer now
And growing in confidence every day

Another month, he'll have left
His school of further education
To continue his apprenticeship
In his chosen trade vocation

A tall, hardworking young man
With his head held high
Who now knows to keep persevering
And not let life's chances pass him by

I hope for him to be independent
To grow in responsibility and maturity every day
To be there for his family
And give support to others in need, along life's way.

Ann McAreavey (Craigavon)

Ever Alone

For years she's had a secret buried deep within her mind,
A dark, dirty secret they thought she'd never find.
Despair she felt, depression too, as black as any coal,
Dark moods no one understood, for the Devil had her soul.

She'd always been a quiet child; moody some would say,
Reserved, private and very pretty in a way.
Never one to rock the boat, she would just go with the flow,
So they would do all they'd want, they thought no one would know.

The pain of childhood came rushing back; it struck her like a knife,
Everything was much clearer now, why she'd lived that solitary life.
So many uncles after father left, fat, thin, young and old,
Do what they want, it won't take long, just do as you are told.

How could she do that? What was the driving force?
What made her treat her blood like that? why did she take that course?
Her father had loved her so, Mother felt so pushed aside,
So resentment rose its ugly head, the day a mother's love died.

Mother cries now she's alone, locked up for years to come,
The shame-faced men, their families lost, no longer live at home.
On sex offenders' lists their names, black and white for all to see,
For off the street she took them, making it safe for you and me.

To be in the open, the police said, for all it was best,
Face her in court, they said, along with all the rest,
But her mind couldn't deal with it; it could not stand the strain,
So she decided to end it all, the stares, the whispers, the pain.

What a waste! Oh, what a waste! It's all so very sad,
She took them on and faced them down, with all the strength she'd had,
But all the jibes, the publicity, are what she couldn't bare,
She blamed herself for the loss, of her mother's care.

A lonely figure stood by her grave, numbed to his very soul,
To get custody of his only child, had been his only goal,
Now at least he understood, that death had brought her peace,
But he would never know the like, for his pain would never cease.

Linda J Coombes (Fraserburgh)

Dream Boat

Jack Potter was a fellow who longed to go to sea,
A bold and jolly matelot was what he yearned to be
And he realised the only way he'd ever get afloat,
Was to buy a kit and bit by bit, build his own dream boat.

In a sailing magazine that Jack subscribed to weekly,
He saw the very thing for sale and going very cheaply.
The first his wife knew of this budding tar's seafaring plans
Was when the many parts came in a fleet of PO vans.

There seemed to be enough to build an ocean-going liner
And Jack, with great ambition, could think of nothing finer.
Repairing to his garage, he hammered, glued and nailed,
From dawn to dusk he laboured, Jack's ardour never failed.

'You'd think his name was Noah,' his wife was heard to cry
And glanced with apprehension towards a cloudless sky.
Despite her protestations, he ignored her every plea,
'You get on with baking and leave this job to me.'

He dreamed of far off places and days before the mast,
Until one ne'er forgotten day, the boat was built at last.
'Nelson would be proud of me,' old Jack was heard to shout,
He opened up the garage door - and couldn't get it out!

Wedged tight inside, the splendid craft was beached like some great whale
And poor old Jack soon realised, he'd never see her sail.
'You stupid man,' his wife declared, 'It's common sense you lack,'
And from her kitchen window, threw a rolling pin at Jack.

'You've wasted time and money, whilst I'm stuck here inside,
Making scones and pastries you'd no time to eat,' she cried.
Though Jack was quite demoralised, he planned to save the day
And salvage from the wreckage, a way to make it pay.

Now it's open to the public and he charges 50p,
For folk to come and view the boat, that never went to sea.
He hopes to cut his losses and his angry wife to please,
But it's she who makes the fortune - selling fresh cream teas.

Doreen Pinder (Colwyn Bay)

Precious Moments

I went for a walk along the river one day,
With my grandaughters Fern and Tarn,
A rainbow, descended, to the river bed,
As we watched the sheep sheared for their yarn.

The sun shone on the river, quite bright,
While a dog in the distance did bark,
On our Sunday walk up the riverbank,
Passing Greenfields and Grove Park.

Sometimes we watched the rugby,
The football, and the tennis too,
With the river running clear, with trout,
There are so many things to do.

As they clutch up closely by my side,
We listen to a blackbird sing,
And I listen to their chatter full of pride
And the happiness that it brings.

Our journey took us to Sebastapool
And we seemed to have lost our way,
When we heard a splash, from a distant pool
And a heron, flew out of the spray.

Then we headed for Abertysswg,
Where we watched three ducks flying low,
We then caught a prickly hedgehog,
We fed it and then let it go.

There are no tall mountains up here Grancher,
Just whimberry slopes and streams,
But it wasn't always like this girls,
They once had deep pits with coal seems.

The people are so friendly with their neighbours,
Kind and caring in so many ways,
They seem so 'Welshy', without wearing tall hats,
Like they did in the good old days.

Bill Gabb (New Tredegar)

Cottage By The Sea

Now this is not reality,
For I live at home, with my family.
But I'd like you to share my thoughts with me,
Of my little cottage by the sea.

Oh! I'd love a little cottage,
A cottage by the sea.
A humble little cottage,
With a garden, naturally.

I'd weed the little garden
And keep it oh so neat.
Then I'd go in, make some tea
And burn a piece of peat.

There wouldn't be much in it,
Just a table and a chair.
But I'd have some frilly curtains,
On the windows, hanging there.

There would be a stove to cook on,
A sink to dabble in.
A little dustbin at the door,
To put the rubbish in.

There would be a little bedroom,
With all the mods and cons.
And a little bed, oh, so sweet,
For me to rest upon.

I'd have a bedside table,
With a lamp against the wall.
Also a little telephone,
If anyone should call.

Oh! How I'd love my cottage,
My cottage by the sea.
Where all the weary travellers,
Could stop and talk to me.

Ina Higginson (Coleraine)

Kings Of The Kop

The night Liverpool won The Cup
I remember it all so clear
Istanbul was to witness a final
Recalled for many a year.

Milan, their Italian opponents
Giants of the European game
Kaka, Shevencko and Crespo
Players that put defences to shame.

Three goals down we were at half-time
All the experts said Milan had it won
But the loyal Liverpool fans roared,
'You'll Never Walk Alone!'

Whenever we needed our captain
His moment of truth had arrived
The ball hit the back of the net
To the loyal fans he replied.

Milan though they were cruising
Liverpool would never come back
When Smicer scored the second
You could see them beginning to crack.

What happened in the end, was amazing
I'll remember it for many a day
The fantastic team called Liverpool
And the passionate football they play.

When Gerrard lifted the trophy
Like Liverpool captains before
Five European Cups in their cabinet
And hungry for another few more.

Whenever your team need you most
Never give up or give in
At a moment you least expect it
They might just come up with a win.

James Gallagher (Enniskillen)

Oot An' Aboot

Och, see when yer oot an' aboot mind me!
Fur I dinna like those busy roads ye see.
The likes o' the Kingston brig, that muckle thing
Caurs, lorries, vans an' buses makin' an awfu' din.

Aye, ye ken in a wee caur, liked jammed in a tin,
Yer sittin' like a sardine crushed, gaspin' fur wind,
Aw things fleeing by ye in sic a big rush,
I say, if it's the last day, weel whit is aw' the fuss!

On an ooting I'm truly sittin' there aw' shakin',
I'm fou o' worries, an' ma heid it's achin'
Ma knees gie a tremble, ma hauns clenched ticht,
I sit there ma hale body is no juist richt.

Motorways, weel folk say ur the best,
Ma stomach churns, I fidget, I canna rest.
It's quiet country roads that's mair ma line,
Whaur the pace is slower an' is juist fine.

It's the countryside I love tae view,
Then wid ye believe it, I'm needing the loo!
I wunner if they'll be a lavie, or a big tree
Why dis it happen, huv tae happen tae me?

But naw there's nae lavie or big tree
Naething like that roon aboot dae I see!
Sae, I'll huv tae cross ma legs an' haud on 'til hame
Wishing the hale time this road we niver came.

See, it's the countrylife tae me is heaven
Whaur shepherds an' farmers try tae mak a livin'
Oot in the countryside juist feels sae free
Peace an' beauty is aw' aroon fur tae see.

Weel, at long last I see the sign 'Uplawmoor' aheid,
It's the wee road fur oor hame it wull lead
Och, my I'm juist sae glad tae be back home noo
An' it's sae great the peace an' at last get the loo!

Fiona Harvie (Glasgow)

Red In Contrast

(Written on 6th June 2006 after a World Cup Match, with Korean fans in a blaze of red)

A sea of glorious red in jubilation at World Cup fever.
A burst of evil red as terror-focused minds
Blast hundreds to their death.

Pools of wasted red when crazed fanatics
Blow themselves and other lives apart
To justify land greed and doubtful hope
Of post-suicidal glory.

But red, too, is the colour of sunrise,
Proclaiming new starts, fresh hopes,
A chance to forgive and begin again.

Sunset-red spreads across the changing sky,
Bringing a challenge to revisit the day
And ask its purpose for peace near and far.

Contrasts of lives. Contrasts of motives.
Joy alongside joyless destruction;
Man's capacity for spreading
Good or brooding evil.

The red of joy, beauty and fruitful challenge
Must overcome the red of sorrow, grief and greed,
And the real meaning of religious faith, at last,
Proclaimed and lived in every land.

Then Man can live in peace so long strived for
In sanctuary and state, and the first colour
Of the rainbow of hope, becomes the colour
Of new beginnings for country and individual heart.

But, no matter the colour of a football strip
In World Cup stadia, as boot meets ball in friendly rivalry,
The fun, the cries of fans, the exchange of various colours
Could, and should, herald a World of Peace.

Margaret Heavenor (North Berwick)

A Year In DCF Dungannon

(Disabled Christian Fellowship)
(But by love serve one another, Galatians 5;136)

Come to DCF Dungannon
And we'll chase away those blues
There we praise our loving Saviour
Listen to the Bible news
Here you'll find such cheery faces
Folk, who go that second mile
Hilary sings birthday greetings
And that always brings a smile
Sometimes, Roland leads the singing
Then speaks of his lambs and yowes
I am sure us townie people
Raise a question with our brows?
Then we've Gwen, she sell the all sorts
She's still useful just to know
Sing Alan's favourite hymn
'Jesus Love Me, This I Know'
And I daren't forget those people
Who provide and serve us tea
Of sandwiches and fancy stuff
Which, for everyone, is *free!*
Then we'll sing the 'Songs of Zion'
And guest speakers come to tell
How God is using some to go
Just to seek the lost as well
But I am still a newcomer
To Dungannon DCF
So why not come and join us here?
In God's presence you'll be blest!
I don't know every one of you
So, I've mentioned but a few
But Christ the Lord knows everyone
So, please come and meet Him do!

Beth Stewart (Dungannon)

Asking

Tell me Grandad,
What will I be,
When today becomes . . . tomorrow?
Will I dance and sing
And make bells ring?
And will I share in love . . .
Will I laugh and make the young girls shy,
Or will there be pain
And sorrow?

I'll tell you Michael
What you can be
When today becomes tomorrow . . .
You will make them proud
Your parents dear
And fill them full
Of cheer . . .
You will dance and sing
And make ears ring,
Then settle down with
Your wife . . .
You'll work and play
And with each day,
Will come a new tomorrow . . .

Then Grandad dear,
If that's how it is,
When today becomes tomorrow,
I'll do everything
And dance and sing
And accept the pains
And sorrow . . .
My parents are proud,
I'm not a face in the crowd . . .
So I'll be like you
Tomorrow . . .

William Paul McDermott (Holyhead)

The Butterfly

She flits from flower to flower, with ease
And does it all, so gracefully.
Her poise, such elegance and style,
Then draws me in to fly with her.
The days were long, the sun was high,
I joined her as she fluttered by and craved no other,
She and I, but were as one,
We both could fly, all summer in our garden.
The colours blazed of every hue,
Yellows, reds, a paler blue,
Marigolds and fuchsia too, larkspur and begonia.
Those golden days I still recall, sweet moments, I remember . . .
We travelled on from bloom to bloom,
Each morning and the afternoon, through June until September.
There fed on nectar, like the gods,
The incense, filled our senses.
Then spread our wings and for a while,
No one knew how far we climbed
And that's the way it was, until

One day, she wasn't there!

And I was left to wonder why
One so fair and pleasing to the eye, should go
And leave me where I'm missing her.

But sometimes in the evening, when
The sun goes down and dark extends its cover.
I look into the garden, where
What now is dead, was once in flower.
And know in summer once again,
Those flowers will bloom, but not the same.

It looks so different from up there,
I'm on the ground, she's in mid-air.
Unlike me, she still can fly,
But in another garden now!

Clive Maxwell (Craigavon)

Aliens

Walking a country road at night,
When all of a sudden I saw this light,
In the sky high above the trees,
Was this brightness descending on me.

Immobile and rooted to the spot,
Shaking with fear and I felt so hot,
There was not a breeze in the air,
Hypnotic trance, I couldn't help but stare.

I recall a dome object coming down,
With bright yellow lights landing on the ground,
Terrified I was with shock and fright,
I did not like what I saw in sight.

White figures emerging from a machine,
I thought to myself, *this must be a dream,*
No one human could look like these,
Creatures with dark eyes walking from trees.

I must have passed out with this fear,
The sight of those aliens coming near,
Tall beings in white looking down on me,
Looking to see what they could see.
I remember a room which was very bright,
Six aliens scanning me with a blue light,
One small tube was pushed into my arm,
I was calm and felt no need for alarm.

The next thing I knew I was lying in the road,
Confused and frightened, I ran to my abode,
Was it a figment of my imagination?
Or did I experience some sort of examination?

I awoke next morning and felt no harm,
Until I saw a little hole in my arm,
Was it reality or just a dream?
Or was I *transported* into their machine?

Lorna B James (Kirkcaldy)

Intelligent Life

CHON's fusion,
Spawned of stardust.
Poor custodians
of planet Earth.
Slow learners
of history's certainties.
Bad friends
of fellow humans.
Disappointing offspring
of the primeval egg.
Unworthy
of cosmic recycling.

But -
capable
of spellbinding creativity,
of spectacular discoveries,
of emitting starshine
from our inner atoms;
capable even
of becoming masters
of this galaxy
and in brief spacial time
creating a new universe.
Worthy
of the description 'intelligent'.

But equilibrium
is ignored.
Technological advances
with unskilled thought processes.
War with peace
Poverty with plenty.
Passion with apathy.
Home sapiens?

Elaine Connor (Dunoon)

The Magpie

He gets mixed reviews
Depending on the locale.
North see a bully with lethal impulses
South, a playful kleptomaniac.

Unlike the funereal dress
Of his mates in genus corvus,
Intense white, splashes
Breast and flanks and adds
Distinction to his wings.

On the ground
Sturdy legs move
With a certain effort
But can, I'm told,
In times of stress,
Hop sideways.

In the air
An overlong tail,
A sheen of green,
Makes stability
Uncertain.

Taciturn, but,
When he gets round to them,
His cries are harsh,
Sharp and repetitive.

In spite of
A dodgy character,
Unpredictable gait,
Unsteady flight
And machine-gun call
He has been celebrated
By a well-known overture 'La Gazza Lada' -
'The Thieving Magpie' by Rossini.

Glen L Pride (St Andrews)

Wales 'In Parenthesis'

(To save the drowning man, you must throw yourself into the water - Thibon)

Welsh Nationalist Silenced
Romany with a touch of Rosemary
Mix Mametz Assiago or
Battle for Dien bien Phu
We Saxons 'Dream poems'.

St Bruno
Nox 'Wales' Illuminabitur
Practical Atheism
Blasphemies in the Press
Welsh Assembly 'Fripperies.'

'If you are ill they come running at first call'
Words from my friend
Hits me hard, very hard
'Welsh hospitals' (and the rest of Britain)
The Church has no Rights.

Switch Memories
Marseilles
Working a Freighter with
A 'Madman'
In the docks.

A pretty, very young prostitute
Plying her trade in Marseilles
Comes into 'Mind'
Where is she now?
Angels lead her 'Home?'

Wales
Churches and Chapels gone
Unity too
'Nolite inique agree, et nolite loqui
Adversus Deum iniquitatem'. (Ps 74).

Paul Faulkner (Ebbw Vale)

Wait Till I Get You Home

Someone thinks they can sing!
He thinks he's Bing!
Tories, Whigs, conquests discoursing,
Smoking, coughing, arguing, cursing.
Glasses tinkle, bottles rattle,
Women prattle.
A lonely television from the corner of the bar,
Warns drinking drivers about driving a car.
Sideward glances,
Taking chances.
An eye for a woman at another table.
He must be drunk! She's no Betty Grable!
That guy still thinks he can sing!
Drink up girls! What are you havin'?
Same again then?
Same again men?
Same again! One gin an' tonic, one Babycham,
A rum and Coke and three Tennents - one with lime.
He's stopped singing! It's about time!
Last drinks on the house!
The toilet now's a good excuse.
He can't be found.
Someone will have to pay for the round.
He's started again. Sit down for God's sake
You're only a joke!
There's your taxi, folk!
We're coming!
When Irish eyes are smiling, sure it's like a morn
In spring . . .
Hey boy, you're along with me!
Wait till I get you home!
Wait till I get you home!
When Irish eyes are smiling . . . I'm goin' to be sick.
Waaaaaugh!

David B Ferguson (Bangor)

Llynfi - A Welsh Valley

A green and pleasant valley grand to see
A river running through murmuring pleasantly,
A home of singers, poets and historians too,
Enhancing the culture as men do,
Among the pleasant hills a secret lay
Hidden from sight, and light of day
Deep within the depths minerals abound
Iron and coal all hidden in the ground
But soon the secret was unearthed by Man
Industrialists came with wealth, and so began
Over the valley green, blast furnaces to erect
Coal pits, iron works, all that industry direct
The green and pleasant valley was a hive of heat and smoke
It was changed, unrecognised with piles of slag and coke
Vast caverns cut into the countryside around
Leaving it black and ugly, where coal tips did abound
Those singers, poets, historians took their talents there
Into the darkness of the mine, away from light and air
Crawling to win the coal, with blackened faces
For home and industry and other places
Arriving from mine, with faces wan and white
From so much time away from sun and light
Dust-filled lungs, played a common role
For this was just the price, obtaining coal
But now gone are the mines, the iron works as well
The valley is reclaimed, as one can tell
The hills are forested, the coal tips gone
Lakes and parks created, there's not one
Reminder of that age, where all was heat and smoke
Piles of slag, and even piles of coke,
Mother Nature has helped to clothe that place
Giving it green verdure and a better face
The poets, historians and singers recall together
A pleasant valley, clothed with grass and heather.

Eva Moore (Maesteg)

The Loner

There he sits on his own,
Have a little sympathy, throw the dog a bone.
Ah 'tis not a dog, but a man, sitting all alone.

People around, chatting with friends,
Why speak to a stranger?
One knows not where it ends.

They care not if he's lonely,
They care not if he is ill,
All have their own niches, and busy lives to fill.

Maybe when you are older,
You too will be the same,
A tired and lonely stranger who has not got a name.

So break the ice and speak to him,
If only about this and that,
See the twinkle in his eye, continue with the chat.

Remember you were once alone,
What you were feeling then,
As others kept their distance, ignoring you again.

To speak to somebody lonely,
Does not cost a thing,
Think of all the pleasure a word or two can bring.

Perhaps he's hard of hearing,
This can be a curse,
That with loss of friendship, can only make things worse.

Where now does he wend his weary way?
As he gets up to go,
To a dismal attic bedroom, how are we to know?

Our thoughts and prayers are with him,
That God will give him rest,
And every new tomorrow, will find him ever Blest.

Kenneth Blomley (Abergavenny)

What A Wonderful World

One burnt with cigarettes
One raped online
Another, tied up in sack
One forced to eat her own faeces
Another one, stabbed in the back
A teenager freed from a cellar in Vienna
One maimed by flak in Iraq
A little girl
Lost on the Algarve
A little boy
Dumped by the tracks.

A six-year-old girl
Getting snatched from her bath
A three-year-old
Kidnapped and raped
A ten-year-old gone
Via suicide bomb
An eight-year-old
Sold as a slave
A four-year-old touched
By a paedophile pop star
A five-year-old
Barely escapes
A nine-year-old shivers
With 'crack' in her veins
In this wonderful world
We have shaped.

Banish from society
The wicked and the wild
But never ever
Let there mercy be
For crimes
Against a child

Mark Anthony Noble (Mayhill)

What About Your Cholesterol?

The high street hums, there's sulphur in the air,
Effie and Edie light a fag they're about to share,
They splutter; they cough and put the world to rights,
Will anyone escape their lethal sights?

- Then Edie, I goes an avs a brace of eggs,
Sunny side up and other dregs
From last Sunday's leftovers,
Well says I what lovely grub and then I goes . . .

- but Effie you daft moll. Your cholesterol!
What about your bleeding cholesterol?

- Well I'll be dammed. It's Effie. How's things with you?
Still kicking the world 'til it's black and blue?

- Oh! Bert. It's you!
Long time since we had a cud to chew,

- Well Ta-ra Effie. Can't stop now
I'm off to the Bell.
See you later Babe.

Right Ho Bert . . . Will he hell?

- Remember old Bert? Edie,
One of the best I've ever known,
But can the blighter be trusted
Further than he can be thrown?

- but Effie you daft moll. Your cholesterol!
What about your bleeding cholesterol?

- Edie! Oh Edie! You do worry and bluster,
'It's sorted. All sorted, I've downed a fat buster,
Downed with a coffee, maybe two, even three.

And Edie my love . . . There's a brace of hot dogs
With a plate of cold chips ready for tea!

Geraldus John (Penarth)

Oor Gairden Freens

The drookit wee sparras sit on my fence,
Waitin' fer their breakfast crumbs.
Noo, I like them fine but hate the sight
O' them constantly raisin' their bums.
Their wee white droppings go everywhere,
On floo'ers and windaes and plants
And if ma hubby cleans up the windaes,
He always raves and rants.

However, we continue to feed them,
On household scraps; bacon fat and seeds.
Some nuts for blue tits, (oor favourite bird)
We just love them tae come here and feed.
The starlings' bully-boy tactics
Are worth watching and gie us a laugh.
They squabble and fight wi' each other
And scare off the wee birds, no half.

Noo the robin visits us every day,
A nervous wee bird but so bonny.
He must be Britain's cutest wee bird,
On that I'd bet my money.
Although he should eat grubs and worms
He comes tae oor bird table too,
Grabs some bread and awa' he goes -
Ye'd think I'd deliberately said, 'Shoo.'

We get chaffinches, greenfinches, blackbirds,
In winter, all needin' oor help.
So we pit oot the food and the water,
Chase cats wi' a very loud yelp.
We canna' hae cats catching the birds
'Tho' it's a natural thing that they do,
So they have to be chased frae the garden,
Wi' loud shouts and a water spray too.

Elspeth Taylor (Glenrothes)

Sophia Gardens, Cardiff, 1935

On a day's death in December,
Lit by Saint Elmo's Fire of Saturnalia,
Hand-in-hand, I and Nancy Donnelly,
Jigged, jived and twirled,
To the Whirligig music,
Played by the East wind in the branches
Of Mistletoe-laden oak trees,
In a long-long-ago world.

Through the icy mud and hoar-frost,
Where the Mammoth once shambled,
As sleep choreographed the flapping rags
That draped our lean forms,
In ecstatic abandonment,
Shrieking nursery rhyme cadenzas,
We capered through childhood's bleak wildwood,
Inured to poverty's storms.

While the Earth spun its chequered way,
The white and black of life's background
Flicked the radiance of brief eternities,
As the ghosting moon crept
Across the proscenium - arch of Infinity,
Playing her bough-barred rays on the dancers
Paying supple homage to the winter King,
'Ere his exhausted court slept.

While the vapour trail of our revelry
Chased the high notes of our voices,
Veiling the glow of the holly berry,
As it dissolved in the still air,
Sightless solitude and timeless tracklessness
Faded in the fantasy of our merriment,
That for a brief moment, in acres of misery,
Shone in the ballet of we pair.

Richard Carlson (Cardiff)

Through Dreams Into Reality

Thoughts glide through my mind
Like clouds across the sky.
One moment, they seem solid,
The next they've passed me by.
Such are the first few moments,
When greeting a new day.
Then consciousness takes over,
Chasing the dreams away.

Reality takes possession
And daily life requires,
That dreams are now forgotten,
Forgotten all desires
To be part of a world,
That never can be real,
That only lives in my dreams,
A world, unique to me.

But if the daily tedium
Grows unmanageably big,
Is threatening my sanity,
Then I can, oh, so quick
Escape into a daydream,
Into my world - quite real
At least just for a moment -
Some happiness to steal,

And fill the stark reality
With hope and peace, and love,
And watch the dark clouds sail away,
Enjoy the sun above,
Watching birds take to their wings,
Answering nature's call.
The real world has its moments too,
Just see the good in all.

Helga Dharmpaul (Tain)

The Unopened Window

(To a heron on the Mourne river)

What golden light may cascade
From the unopened window,
Cataracted with years of dust
Outside and inside cobwebbed
Painted clasps and seized hinges
Bleeding the aged red of forgotteness
The vacuumed air petrified in stillness.

What framed view may be envisioned
From the unopened window,
An August meadow half-mown, hay in stacks
Margined by Keynesian blue irises and
Meadowsweet waving all along the drain
Half-hidden a wading heron lifts leg over leg
Ripplelessly slowly, effortlessly graceful.

What zephyr of the air can I call to unclasp
The unopened window,
To you then, I make the most perfect wish
That you may rescue me on golden sunlight beams
That when you come, your hair may be newly mown
That your eyes may be Keynesian blue iris blue
That you may move effortlessly, gracefully, slowly.

Smashing open with sash splitting force
The unopened window,
With a thunderous beat of your wings
Never again let it be able to close
Nor rust, nor cobweb cloud my dreams
You may be a zephyr, I alone know you are real
The smell of meadow flowers is everywhere
And wherever my searching eye casts
There are heron feathers from your nest.

Damien Mallon (Keady)

So, Who Isn't Called A Slave?

In servitude we are born, even though we claim to be free.

All secure in the womb of love, there,
in that domain, freedom is our guest.
We call and dance to its tune unperturbed.

At the gate of birth, there awaits, a demand,
a surrender to
Nature's rude infusion of Life Force.
Once initiated, no turning back.

When the passing hours of childhood,
run into adult disguised as:
man and woman, husband and wife,
father, mother and siblings.
Inventor or entrepreneur, wage earner,
King, queen or dictator;
colour of slave may differ, but still a slave.

On majestic mountains,
verdant vales and on the mighty oceans,
in times of war or peace,
from powerful men to labouring ants,
in any point of time,
we are enslaved to:
our emotions, passions,
addictions, materialism, likes and dislikes.

Even in the declining years:
in abject poverty or wealth and splendour,
a subjection to a force, power,
of influence beyond control.
Until the sting of death, when life is surrendered
and freedom regained,
in chain and shackles we main, one way or the other.
So, who isn't called a slave?

Meg Aku Sika De Amasi (Balfron)

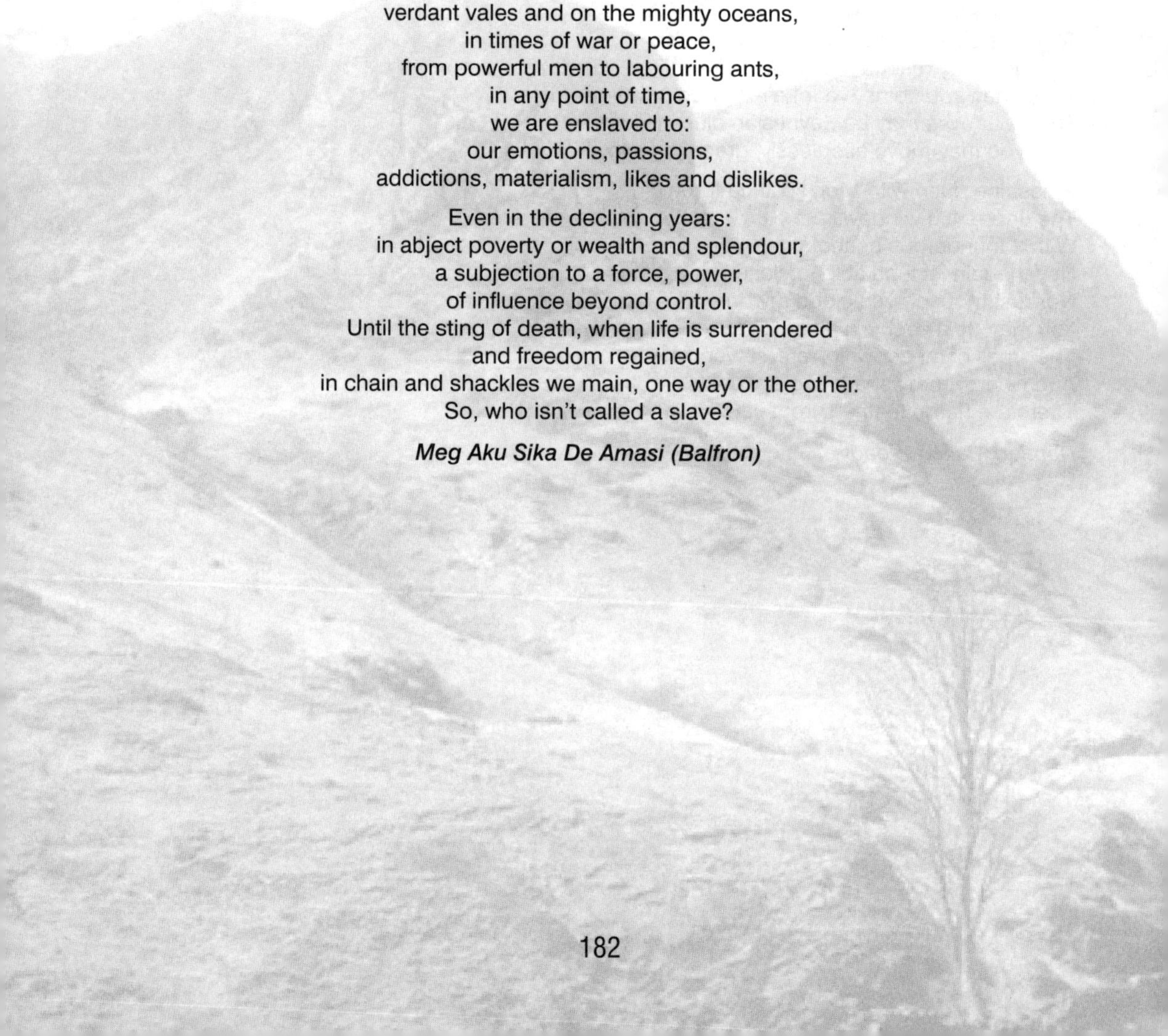

The Coach Journey Of Life

Myriads of lights forever in the distance
Amber, red, eerie blue, shimmering white
Slumbering, strange shapes distorted in dark glass
Grey gaunt ghosts, glide then pass

Darkness, deep unending space
Reflections of people, patterns on lace-rained frames,
Some faces stare, others read or murmur
Lulled by the diesel drone into a trance
Whilst on the ribbon road they ride
Thinking life will give them a second chance

Broad shoulders of concrete either side
Some with graffiti, carved names in dust
Stark shadows haunt the drizzling night
Brick kilns, factories bathed in neon light.

Chimneys belching sulphurous fumes
Surround twinkling towers of living tombs
Trapped tenants yearn perhaps for the chance
To change their lot taking flight
To join the travellers of the night

Advance to a target destination
Savour each new sensation

Bright blue signs, stamped services
Arrows in all directions for what purpose?
All routes looked confused, strange;
We can only choose one, our life to change.
Deciding on the sign with the promising name,
We travel forward then regress in pain
Never to arrive with time to spend
To enjoy the fruits of a lifetime's labour
Caught on a relentless treadmill of favour
With broken promises we reach our journey's end.

Jean C Houghland (Anglesey)

The Foaling

It's 2am at last I'm here
I've waited nearly for a year
Well, eleven months just to appear
It's dark, I'm wet
And still attached to Mother dear
Then my body it does heave
As on my own begin to breathe
Mother moves and then I'm free
Then a person came to me
Did lift my leg and hear her say
'A filly foal the first of May'
So far I have done my best
But at this minute need a rest
Round my ears a tongue did lick
Cleaned me all over, now look slick
I have this urge to stand like Mum
My legs they feel they want to run
I bumped around for near an hour
At last stood up just like a tower
Felt a nibble at my hocks
'You've four black legs and no white socks'
Then I did practise for a while
To rise and fall in better style
Will have to look now for a feed
As milk from Mum's my greatest need
My whiskers though at times did tickle
Mum stood still, then felt a trickle
On my nose which made me sneeze
Then everyone did look so pleased
When at last this noble steed
With legs that buckle
Began to suckle
And satisfy her greed.

Hazel McKendrick (Markinch)

A Doggy Story

Jill and John took turns lying beside Poppy while waiting for the brood.
Everyone was hoping things would go OK, but they were still in a sombre mood,
Eventually over eleven hours, ten adorable Doberman pups were born,
The family had been up all night and now it was dawn,
Now Poppy, looking tired but serene,
Could only stare at her babies, it seemed like a dream,
Tulip, was smart and slender and looked like Posh,
She was a great flirt with grandson Josh,
Primrose, was like the Grand Duchess of Aberdeen,
Her coat was beautiful with a fantastic sheen,
Gentle *Sweet Pea,* the smallest one born,
Had to be helped with her food to keep her on top form,
Maximus, Like a Roman Emperor, he was 1lb-3,
He eased his way out like the 'Man from Laramie',
Specially named by Jonothan and Josh was *Tubby Fat Cutie*
He had lovely big paws! My, what a beauty!
Last of the boys was *Luscious*, very smart and really proud,
He was like a country gent, well-mannered and not loud,
Confident *Daisy* likes to run and run for plenty of fun,
Then hide under the car when she's done,
Lupin chases the cockerel for a laugh,
Now she has to run for cover, and probably feels naff,
Lily is very mischievous and winds the others up,
She has to be on the go, a very energetic pup,
Bluebell loves to be cuddled on your knee,
As long as she doesn't leak in her rush for a pee,
Now it almost ends here, their little bags are packed with puppy smells and toys,
They will have to grow up fast, as it's goodbye girls and boys,
Jill and John will have shed their tears over lunch,
And accept they will have to say goodbye to the Brady Bunch,
In a short eight weeks, they've had the best possible start,
Now it's goodbye darlings, may God bless your new homes and hearts.

Maureen Smith (The Black Isle)

Cymru Am Byth

(Wales forever)

Mist on the mountains like dragon's breath,
Sheep scattered like mushrooms on the hill,
Standing stone like trolls frozen in death,
Seagulls with their banshee cries so shrill.

Empty castles with crumbling walls,
Once mighty bastions of military power,
No more will laughter fill its roofless halls,
Bare bone now standing still and dower.

Homesteads with weeds growing in the hearth,
Broken doors swinging in the breeze,
Crops abandoned to rot in the earth,
Prime pasture land given over to trees.

But this is not all there is to see,
Towns and villages thriving still,
Golden sands that lie beside the sea,
Oggies and Welsh cakes take your fill.

Arcades and theatres and cinemas too,
Shops and cafés, restaurants and bars,
A million things to see and do,
Whether you come by train, coach or car.

Swimming, sailing or donkey riding,
Ice cream and burgers, oysters and champagne,
Wee timorous beasties in rock pools hiding,
We keep a welcome till you come back again.

So Cymru Am Byth, Croeso, welcome to you,
The land that seems foreign yet not very far,
With mountains and seaside so much to do,
At last to your beds, goodnight and Nos Da.

Bill Hayles (Prestatyn)

My Old Brum

(In memory of Tommy Noakes)

Oh, Brum, you've changed so often
Over the many years
And you have brought me happiness
As well as many tears.

The old bullring had such character
With its barrow boys and all
And the muscle man wrapped up in chains
Who tried to beat them all.

One man lay on his back
With a slab placed on his chest
And his mate would hit it with a sledgehammer
I think you know the rest.

The blind man selling matches
He was there for many years
And Holy Joe we all did know
Shouting out his prayers.

Yes Brum, you've given me lots of fun
Especially as a boy
And now you've changed just once again
And your buildings reach the sky.

But I wish you well, new Brummagen
Go forward as you will
Because I am a true Brummy man
And I love you still.

It's many years since I've been away
And in my prayers, you'll stay
And I will always love you 'Brum'
Until my dying day.

Bob Lowe (Tenby)

Been There Etc

(By a first school blazer)

He was five, and I brand new, when first we met
We eyed each other warily and yet
Despite the fact we didn't really fit
A bond was there to nurture bit by bit.

And bit by bit his little arms filled out
His confidence as well began to sprout
And we became a team - a part of one another
The stiffness gone - I fitted like a glove - (no bother)

Deep in my pockets was his secret hoard
All sorts of strange things into them he poured.
A treasure trove of objects, dear to little boys
And favoured far above expensive toys.

I've been a makeshift goalpost once or twice
But those sessions at the cleaner's (that's not nice)
They douse you and batter you and if that's not enough,
You emerge all limp and smelly . . . life is sometimes tough.

The years go by and so does John
To the senior school he now has gone
But our memories will never fade
Of Primary and all the friends we made.

He's up at uni now and doing well
And so am I for this I have to tell
Right next to me a faded T-shirt flops
On a shelf in one of the charity shops.

We share our tales of bygone joys
'Tween boys and girls and girls and boys
And when the staff put out the light
We snuggle up and kiss goodnight!

Peggy Kelso (Isle of Bute)

A Tribute To The Man In Black

(Roy Orbison)

He always wore dark glasses
When he was on the stage
He was loved and admired by everyone
No matter what their age
With a voice so clear and beautiful
A wonder to behold
And we knew that just to look at him
He had a heart of gold.

With songs like 'Pretty Woman',
'In Dreams' and 'Blue Bayou',
'Love Hurts', 'Goodnight My Love'
And 'I'm Crying Over You'
And many more I'd like to add
Not least 'Only The Lonely',
There's not a doubt in this whole world
He was the one and only.

His star will shine forever
For his family and his friends
Because the place he's gone to
Is where life will never end
And we'll miss him now he's gone
But we won't forget his name
And it's over now, yes, it's over now
And this world won't be the same.

So, goodbye to you, Roy Orbison
It's a sad and tragic fact
Perhaps we'll meet you once again
For we loved the man in black
Yes, we loved the man in black.

Samuel Perry (Carrickfergus)

Footprints

Wet leaves, fallen from trees
Soaked into a cloak
Masking the ground
Where snails lay low
From birds' watchful eyes.

Bruised elbows
And scraped knees
Children run wild, wind blowing
Cobwebs from their tangles
And a cotton glove is lost.

River lolls lazy in the
Afternoon sunshine
With broken branches falling
Down the waterfall, landing
Heavily making the water part.

Fish swim in-between
The reefs past the
String, praying
For their lives
No hook, no catch.

Water ripples in the breeze
Muddy boats stuck
To the muddy green
Leaving when the sun
Sets between the trees

A doll lays abandoned upon the ground
Lifeless eyes looking up as the
Sky turns purple, the colouring of
A fresh bruise, while nature's
Night-time curtains are opened.

Lindsay Kernahan (Mancot)

Carbon Footprint

My carbon footprint is getting smaller
Because I'm getting old
My breath is getting shorter
From burning oil and coal.

How I curse the greenhouse gases
That I once enjoyed so much
Driving around in motor cars
And jumping on the bus.

My footprint's getting smaller now
I cycle, walk and run
My breath is getting longer too
Preservation is such fun.

We only use the planet once
And if we bleed it dry
There will be no conservation
For the future generation.

My carbon footprint's getting smaller now,
'What of yours, my friend?'
Just bid farewell to petrol
And smelly diesel oil
Jump on your pedal cycles
The transport heaven-sent
Your health and strength will flourish
And so will the environment.

Cut carbon dioxide emissions
Recycle your waste
Let's all act together
It's time for transition
Shrink the carbon footprint
And save our lovely planet.

Kathleen McSorley (Armagh)

Life On Earth

My stomach empty, aching
Eyes vacant, searching, pleading
Throat dry, no food to eat
Days burning in the heat
Ethiopia is my life

My body aching, sweating
Fingers numb and bleeding
Days sewing, building stark
From morning till dark
India is my life

My body moving, writhing
Face that's falsely smiling
Days dancing on display
Men who'll always pay
Thailand is my life

Make-up freshly painted
Click, click always hunted
Days driving in my Jag
The price of being a WAG
London is my life

My feet are bare and dirty
My spear is pointed sharply
Days foraging in the wood
Survival, hunt for food
The jungle is my life

My face is tired, greying
My body painful, hurting
Days stealing for some brown
My features, constant frown
Addiction is my life

Tracy Lynne Roberts (Caernarfon)

Look Under The Skin

Partake of a little walk with me
Through the fields of reality
And perhaps together we can see
The errors in humanity
Do you see the man with 'coloured' skin
Or do you see the man that dwells within?
Could you hold his hand and be his guide
Be the strength that's by his side?
Or would you prefer to just ignore
The 'coloured' stranger from next door?
The look you give me tells it all
Is it now I see your mind is small
Do you really think him less a man
Because he has an inbred tan?
For you, my friend, the world shall be
Never as large as the one I see
For the colour boundary you set in stone
Shall one day leave you all alone
I know your doubts, I have them too
But we can't judge all from the wicked few
If we are to make this a better land
We have to move forward hand in hand
There will be times through which we tread
Where doubt will roam inside your head
I'm not a saint, I feel this too
I have these doubts, the same as you
So many cultures and different views
But it's all up to the man inside to choose
If we *all* decide to stretch our hands
Across the water to distant lands
Perhaps there's just a chance, my friend
For this 'coloured' hatred thing to end.

Donald Fraser (Livingston)

My Green Remembered Hills

Wherever I go in this wide world, wherever I may roam,
Nothing draws me back as strongly as the green Welsh hills of home.
No other place on this good Earth fills me with so much love and pride.
And however far from home I may be, I carry Wales inside.

Keith J Davies (Tywyn)

Poem From Home

This is my city, my birthplace,
Not ugly, nor pretty but home,
All my life is here, my history,
The place where I am never alone.
My beloved mother was born here,
Survived the bombing of her town,
Met my gorgeous Geordie father,
Got wed and settled down.
She would take me to the old market,
The shops, the beach, the sea,
The parks and lovely gardens
Were wondrous to me.
We travelled on the famous,
Sadly missed, Mumbles train,
A ticket to the seaside
And reluctantly home again.
We moved to a mountain farm
In my younger days,
A haven of wonderful memories
That have stayed with me always.
Now with no memories from parents
To remind me of the past
I look to my children and grandchildren
To hold our memories fast.
Nowhere else in the world is home,
No coast so close to my heart,
No mountains hold my soul within,
They are beautiful but apart.
Absence makes the heart grow fonder,
I don't know, I've never been long away,
I just know the feeling of home and family
And belonging every day.

Judith Jones (Bonymaen)

Of My Youth

The boy stands quiet, out with the crowd
Encouraged none by their indulgent loud
For such ego trips he has no time
He seeks only solitude in his youthful mind.

James McGowan (Prestwick)

Where Has Great Britain Gone?

I remember, during the War,
When people helped one another.
But now it seems that every day,
This country is getting like 'Big Brother'.
Politicians are sitting in Parliament,
Making up their own rules,
Such as closing little post offices,
And also lots of schools.
Because, they are all the 'Fat Cats'
With two houses and two cars,
Who grant themselves big pay rises,
And now live like film stars.
Food prices are rising daily,
Also the price of petrol and oil,
And ordinary folk are struggling to manage,
No matter how hard they toil,
Prisons are now like holiday camps,
Where inmates all have a TV.
But do they play a licence for it,
Or do they also get that free?
Prisoners get days out shopping,
Making a prison sentence a joke,
And ordinary people, who like a drink and a fag,
Have to stand outside the bar to smoke.
Parents can't discipline their kids now,
By giving them little smacks,
Then they wonder why some teenagers
Are found guilty of street attacks.
So where has great Britain gone,
The country who won the War?
When thousands of young folk lost their lives,
And I'm wondering now, *what for?*

Jean Hendrie (Dundee)

Quit Now

Now smoke thy last! Of all things ugly,
Nothing uglier than these -
To slowly choke your life and lungs
From charred tobacco leaves.

Charli Lawrie (Bangor)

Breathtaking Love Of Destiny

I balance on death's steep delirium
Undulating headlong into united confusion
Intently vigilant to a spontaneous disobedience
Forbidden knowledge flirting with the secret of eternal youth
Forlorn memories luxuriant in sentimental adulation
Recur in days of exhilarating bounty
Unnerving cries echo around the basement of conscience
And powerful tears wail on common regret
I could have done better
Heartened by the homely warmth of my deliverance
A spree of destiny conforms to the wide-eyed awakening
Flaunting moral respect in gentle excitement
Blending into the heartland of pure happiness
Surreal in virtuous reverence serenely incredible
In the limitless acceleration
A doleful lament unravels in raptured enlightenment
It was all true, preordained
And often courted my magical childhood dreams
Refined honesty excels in a beauty of its own
Unfolding in genial compassion
An amazing presence is felt
Provoking in his closeness brushing against my soul
Sublime shuffling of fertile wings
Fluttering exquisite delicate distraction
And real life is revealed
Celestial bliss embracing the transparent magnificence
Radiating divine love even more that the whole
World can accommodate
Transfixed in the ambience of perfect peace
Sublime in ingenious knowledge
Rising infinitely upwards
To reveal the entire universe.

Mansel (Caernarfon)

Tall Ships And Starry Nights

When I was a boy
I dreamed by the sea
The summer sea
Of tall ships
And starry nights
With the moon for company.
The waves lapped gently
To the shore
And peace was all around
And so I dreamed
The dreams of youth
While sitting on the ground.
Now I am a man
My dreams, they are all gone
I look upon
The angry sea
The waves, they try to engulf me
To send my spirit
To the sea
Never to return.
Oh, give me back
The summer sun
The golden sands
The moonlit nights
The gentle lapping
Of the waves
The peaceful bobbing
Of the lights
And bring my heart
The peace of youth
To dream of
Tall ships and starry nights.

K McQuitty (Newtonabbey)

Faces On A Train

Scowling, smiling, happy, sad
          faces on the train.
Watching, staring, pensive, glad
          expressing joy or pain.
Wonder what they're thinking of
          present, future, past,
Thoughts of wondrous things to come,
          or dreams now fading fast.
Journey to a different time,
          flight across the years,
Recall things as they were then,
          relive joys and fears.
See once again a lost love's smile
          touch them, hold them near,
Feel the loss, the grief, the hurt,
          softly shed a tear.
Forward to some future time,
          wildest dreams fulfilled.
Aspirations, hopes achieved,
          doubts and fears stilled.
Children grown to adulthood,
          young ones of their own,
Wonder how they will survive
          in the world alone.
Screech of brakes, lurch and jolt,
          journey's end at last,
Doors slide back, present floods in,
          casting out the past.
Every day the same routine,
          trapped, as if by chain,
Riding in this time machine,
          same faces on the train.

Charles Harvey (Merthyr Tydfil)

Someone Cares

When you lose someone you love
There's nothing one can say
To help to ease the hurt and pain
Or make it go away
You'll feel so devastated
You feel you can't go on
And part of you just won't believe
The one you love, has gone
Don't think of weeks or months ahead
Just take it, day by day
And very slowly, bit by bit
Your hurt, will go away
Please don't give up, you're not alone
My prayers, to you I bring
For I have been, where you are now
I know your suffering
I like to think, there is a place
Where all the good have gone
Their bodies may be broken
But their spirits well and strong
You'll always have them with you
You'll never be apart
It's just, they'll have a different home
A place within your heart
Don't try to rush your grieving
You need to work it through
It's probably, the hardest thing
You'll ever have to do
My hand and heart go out to you
I've felt, the pain you feel
But nature will, make time your friend
And yes - in time you'll heal . . .

June Fricker (Pontypool)

I Am Happy In Jesus

I am happy in Jesus
I am trusting in His word
Though shattered by the storms of life
I shall not fear
For He will see me through
He will walk with me
And He will talk with me
So why should I fear?
He tells me I am His own
And that He loved me so much that
He suffered and died in my place,
That I should live a victorious and
Happy life by His grace.
One day He is coming to take me to
His lovely home above
What a day that will be!
The rule is that I must humble myself
To walk with Him
He is the King of kings
He reigns on high.
Leaving to go to that beautiful home
I can take nothing with me,
But I can send it on ahead.
I hear His voice saying,
'All this I have done for you.
What hast thou done for me?'
Yes! He loves me.
He tells me I must be faithful
And true to His word
To be His own.
He will take me by His hand
And lead me to the promised land.

Joy Wilson (Clogher)

My Wife's Triumphant Smile

Am I your husband? Does he exist?
Hold my wrists, my arms above my head,
Press my arms into the pillow, imprison me,
Our sweat aspreading celebration on the sheets.
Who am I now? Do I exist?
Between the syllables of my name
Is a paralysed void of uncertainty,
Thinking, these days, seeps away,
Into the spaces between the atoms,
And life seeps away into irony.
Thoughts fracturing, after twenty years,
The sense of self dissolving.

Marriage is my arms above my head,
My wrists gripped and imprisoned,
The comfort of your warmth and weight on me,
Pin me down and hold me still,
Your weight and your wild movements,
Inhabit the dead space where my identity bleaches away,
If you inhabit me, imprison me, I am real again.

When your grip deserts my wrists, you smile,
Applying a smooth and playful pressure to my nipples,
I exist because you speak my name,
I smile back at your smile of triumph,
Sex is the ceremony of rescuer and rescued,
A ritual, naked wrestling at which you have won.
There is no social institution here,
Our marriage is the place of exorcism,
The scared clearing where dead forces are driven out,
Then, spreading myself more loosely, I smile again,
Raising my knees a little higher,
Enjoying the delicious state I am in.

Anthony James (Ammanford)

Running Out Of Time . . .

God! How will it all end?
In the hourglass,
Grain by grain,
The sand is falling
Unchecked, relentless.
I'm running out of time . . .

I shut out the clock's
Steady tick and stop
Its hands. But, the sun's
Rise and fall cheats
My deliberate denials.
I'm running out of time . . .

Seconds, minutes, hours
Days, months, years, are
Measured out in full.
Any chance of a lapse
Or even an extension?
I'm running out of time . . .

My doctor gave his diagnosis
It was a shock prognosis,
'Six months, maybe eight,
If you watch your weight;
It could be longer.'
I'm running out of time . . .

Yes: I'm running out of time:
But does it have to be a race?
'Time, like a rolling stream,
Sweeps all this life away.'
So runs the hymn apace.
I'm going. Please God, at a tortoise pace.

Anthony J Brady (Tempo)

Planet Earth

Oh Planet Earth, in your many shrouds
Mountains tall that pierce the clouds
Oceans deep that lap the land
Flowers, trees in colours grand
Arctic waters, packed ice and snow
Deserts vast, where sand storms blow

Oh Planet Earth, of rock and clay
Where life forms various, briefly stay
So many creatures, great and small
That fly or walk, or slither, crawl
Some tunnel deep in endless toil
'Neath your coat of earthly soil

Oh Planet Earth, a ball in space
Upon you exists a human race
Having hearts and souls, a mind to think
And on you they have a special link
They use your shrouds, in many ways
For comfort, cures, to prolong their days
Mine your minerals, they soar out in space
Explore the heavens, of life to trace

Oh Planet Earth, beneath your veils
This human race, so sadly fails
They rape, infect, destroy your lands
Oceans, trees, even the desert sands
The very air that all life needs
Polluted through their avid greeds

Oh Planet Earth, dear Mother Earth
On you to remain from time of birth
To live, to love, to laugh, to cry
We leave you not, although we die

W D Vass (Kilgetty)

It Doesn't Cost So Very Much

I used to see you in the park
Blind and unaware
You sat alone, your arms reached out
But no one seemed to care

I sat beside you and held your hand
Your tears began to fall
You handed me a paper
I sat and read it all

A picture of a handsome man
In uniform so tall
Fighting for your country
Till bombs began to fall

What use is a soldier
Without his eyes to see
No one speaks or comes to talk
That's what you said to me

I wander now in darkness
But somehow find my way
I hear the sound of footsteps
And to the Lord I pray

You came into my life by chance
And it was meant to be
My spirit is now lifted
God sent a friend to me

Thank you for the time you give
Sitting here with me
It doesn't cost so very much
When you have eyes to see

F Davies (Llandovery)

Stars

You have shone like diamonds since the world began
The wonders you have seen,
All the troubles, love and hate, war and peace
For us mortals are on but a short journey
After I am long gone you will shine on into eternity.

Anne Robertson (Edinburgh)

The Restless Spirits

In the midnight hour when all's asleep
The spirits slowly come awake
And rampage their way into my dreams
With their troubled thoughts and ghostly screams.

With no words of thanks when they leave at dawn
Their chilling presence lingers on
And I am left disturbed in sleep
As their nightmares haunt me through the night.

What can I do to avoid these pests
As they toss and turn me in my bed?
For they seem convinced I'll die of fright
With their bloody ranting in the night.

Perhaps I could return the favour
And terrorise the little buggers
And send my friend, the leprechaun
Into their beds to keep them warm.

And if somehow they don't take the hint
I'll isolate the little gits
And keep them trapped within their graves
With the banshee whispering in their ear.

For the silly bitch she's always crying
About the living and the dying
Or wailing at some poor sod's bed
Even though the corpse is stone-cold dead.

Macabre perhaps and you think extreme
But it wasn't me who stole their dreams
Or left my nightmares in their minds
So I'm just repaying, kind for kind.

Edward Robinson (Newtownards)

Helped Along The Way

Twenty years ago, you planted little seeds
Through those years,
You have watched us flourish and grow
Always produce a vista of words
Like a beautiful bouquet.

Pamela Page (Risca)

New Dawn

The eye of Horus gazes down
And looks askance at what it sees -
A prophet of a newer faith
Walking among the olive trees.

He comes dressed in a robe of white
From fleece of lambs carded then spun,
And woven by his mother's hands
For Him, her first begotten son.

The sun god sees two men depart,
Sent by their Lord to Bethany
To fetch an ass as yet unridden.
But why an ass? How can this be?

For surely this man's a king,
King of the Jews! It is foretold.
He should be in a chariot
Drawn by stallions with reins of gold.

The eye of Horus follows Him
And watches as the palm leaves fall.
It sees lips move in silent prayer
As crowds beset the Wailing Wall.

Is He the magus with the power
To heal the flesh and make it whole,
To raise the dead and give new life,
To change the heart and lift the soul?

If so, He brings a greater faith,
Supplanting creeds that once were held,
Pantheons that will fade away,
Surpassed by love unparalleled.

Celia G Thomas (Aberdare)

A Limerick For Lunchtime

The pastor said: 'Father O'Flynn,
Is betting on horses a sin?'
'It rather depends,
One can make amends,
By cutting right back on the gin.'

John J McKillop (Wishaw)

The Storm

Rough torn branches pirouetted,
Shipwrecked cars were silhouetted,
The lade and millpond developed waves
While fearful raptors hid in caves.

The night was blustery, black as soot
And our shed was moved by at least a foot,
McAdam's roof vanished from view
And still the wind, it raged and blew.

Our neighbour's marrow wrenched from the earth,
Ended up, I'm sure, in Perth;
Strawberries and poly-tunnels were all tattered,
Beasts in the field took fright and scattered.

Anthracite skies flashed jagged light earthbound
And thunderclaps shot us with ungodly sound,
But gloom soon returned after big sonic boom
And eerie calm settled, foretelling our doom.

Then rain, like stair-rods, harsh and concurrent,
Gushed over the butt, swept along in a torrent,
The ford disappeared, turned the road to a river
And the poor mallard ducks were all of a quiver.

Crops suffered like prisoners from bastinado
The time we were swooped on by a big tornado,
Or was it a hurricane with which we were stricken?
As pets all depressed, stayed doggedly hidden.

All these events did come to pass,
For those living along, the carse,
We boasted and bragged about the flashover,
But reality was, we were glad it was over.

Diane Chorley (Perth)

From A Wife To Her Husband

What is life without love?
I can only imagine,
Without love there is no life,
So dear love, my life,
Imagination is not an option.

Alice Wynne (Denbigh)

Child Of My Dreams

I dreamt about a little boy
as yet unborn, but loved so much,
who'd be my second 'little man'
 - a hand to hold, a cheek to touch.

I'd buy you toys, I'd watch you grow,
I'd read you books, I'd love you so,
Your brother gave me so much joy,
 - so will you, my second little boy.

Eight weeks to go and then we'll meet,
I pace the floor with eager feet.
But God has other plans for me -
my little boy - I shall not see.

I went to Heaven that day in May,
I left so much sorrow and dismay.
Broken hearts I left upon the Earth
- you'll mend them all, by your birth.

When I went to God's big church in the sky,
I knew that I would never die;
but live forever in a beautiful place
and see at last God's kindly face.

July has come, my little boy is born,
I watch you sleep - I see you yawn,
I see my loved ones laugh once more,
you brought back smiles, where tears were before.

I'll always watch over my little boys,
awake, asleep, or playing with their toys,
and I'll always say as I look down to Earth,
dear Thomas, thank you for your birth.

M Non Williams (Saundersfoot)

In Ecstasy

The depths of your soul
Pull me down deep into darkness,
Drawing the breath from my burning lungs.
I am draining my life away in your arms,
An ecstasy well worth dying for.

Pamela McCormack (Falkirk)

A Gift Of Love

A child is hope supreme.
A present of God's benevolence.
We enjoy their company to extreme.
There is no other relevance.

They're always full of smiles,
And fill the world with grace.
So we can reconcile,
To enhance the human race.

Though patience often wear
And solace eventually sought,
We'll give them our love and care,
Our child will share our every thought.

A child at Christmas time,
Was expected to behave,
Or he'd miss the pantomime
And up to bed he'd rave.

While sitting there alone,
In the mirror he could see,
On his head he wore a cone,
Embossed with the letter D.

So that's what's wrong!
I'm wearing a different hat!
No wonder their faces are long
And would not let me chat.

Down the stairs to make amends,
This was the child's good cause,
All through the year Mam and Dad's been our good friends,
Most certainly, our Santa Claus.

Glyn Smith (Aberdare)

Johnnie

Hands that were old
And knotted with age
Face, like proud hawk
And seamed with life's page

Born in the islands
Set in blue sea
That glistens like jewels
He was born, to be free

To put out to sea
In ships that were tall
Where the waves round the horn
Like a mountainous wall

Made men, out of boys
Who sailed with the wind
Which screeched like the furies
Whose noise never dimmed

Eyes that glowed bright
At memories past
Of the girls of Marseilles
And the spells that they cast

Hands that were hardened
By hauling of rope
By carving on wood
With love and with hope

Hands that were gnarled
But did eloquent speak
The hands of my friend
Who was Johnnie the Greek.

Joan Rees (Swansea)

Dad

Two strong hands that lift me up
With strength that overflows the cup
Two strong arms that do entwine
This life given, I now call mine

Two blue eyes that always see
Exactly what there is to me
Two broad shoulders to rest my head
And wipe away the tears of dread

Never-ending seas of doubt
Is the fire that you put out
Words of wisdom free to tell
Of all the times I tripped and fell

Beats of one united heart
Never a hand to tear us apart
You let me bloom like the wildest flower
And gave to me my finest hour

You gave me freedom so I could be
All the things that make up me
Separate thoughts of one clear mind
Two lives that only love can bind

Always a warm and gentle smile
Gave hope to walk that extra mile
As summer's sun is warm and fair
So do I turn to find you there

But as the years have rolled away
They've left me without time to say
Of all you've done and all you've seen
I'm proudest most of the father you've been.

Amanda Deacon (Cardiff)

Our Emblem

There are Scotland and Ireland and England and Wales,
With their rivers and lakes, their hills and their dales.
Each regards its own emblem as something unique,
Whether thistle, or shamrock, or rose or the leek.

Why such choices were made, maybe nobody knows
Of the thistle, the shamrock, the leek and the rose.
But compared with the thistle how vapid the rest,
Since, as every Scot knows, our own emblem's the best.

The rose may be pretty and its perfume be sweet,
Yet its life is so short as it fades in the heat.
For a few days it blooms ere its petals they fall,
While the true Scottish thistle keeps on growing tall.

Since the leek is a veg, it may land in the soup,
In a pot with a chicken brought out from its coop,
And because it is eaten, it soon is no more,
But the thistle is safe with its prickles galore.

Not a vestige of grandeur has shamrock so green,
While its shy, little flower, most rarely is seen.
Though revered by the Irish this emblem may be,
Much more handsome, by far, seems our thistle to me.

There's the Order of Thistle of which Scots are proud
And of which they can boast and so noise it aloud.
Of the rose such an order there never has been,
Nor have ones of the leek nor the shamrock been seen.

Purple thistle, green shamrock, red rose, tasty leek,
Would they vie with each other if they could but speak?
I'd but guess at the words of the last mentioned three,
But the thistle would say, 'Wha daur meddle wi' me?'

Isma Munro (Invergordon)

My Wee Grandson

I get pleasure from my wee boy,
Who is his mother's pride and joy.
Like his mother when she was three,
Brightens up the world for me.

On a bus he loves to go,
At the front upstairs, not down below.
Where he can watch with great delight,
As all the cars come into sight.

Just like every little boy,
He has his favourite little toy.
It has to be a motor car,
He thinks the Mini's best by far.

When I take him for a walk,
It can be quite a struggle,
I've always got to stop and wait,
Till he walks through every puddle.

When he will not do what I say,
And wants to have it all his way.
There's a weakness deep inside of him,
A sweet to bribe him is just the thing.

He'll always find a filthy place,
And often has a dirty face.
Behind it there's a great big smile,
That wee rascal's full of guile.

The love that comes from that wee fellow,
Is deep and true and never shallow.
Though he's fly in every way,
He fairly cheers me up every day.

I Wilkinson (Glasgow)

Knocklae House

History's ghost haunts Knocklae House,
I feel it as it roams the rooms,
I hear it scuffing like a mouse,
Whirring softly in the gloom.

This was the parish manse for years,
Then next a drover's inn;
First men of God to blast one's ears
Then followed alcohol and sin!

The stone-built walls have weathered years
Of winter storms, of ice and snow,
But what of all the bygone tears
And bygone joys we'll never know.

Professor Thomas Brown DD
Whom sickness had lain low,
Came here to write deep poetry
(Which makes the reading slow!)

Consumption burned his lungs away
But he had work to do;
He led the field in philosophy
And was a doctor too!

'Agnes' was his greatest work,
A poem that I treasure;
Blank verse of love where devils lurk;
Hard work by any measure!

He died in eighteen twenty-two
But Agnes lives today;
Just who she was I'll never know,
But here she dwells in old Knocklae!

Peter Jeevar (Balmaclellan)

Delia - Alma Mater

My mother was love, first and foremost
Could always make you feel as warm as toast
A smile so kind, matched with eyes so true
Would banish sad feeling, no matter how blue

My mother was strength, second to none
Right was the yardstick that always won
Wrong she derided, without a care
Small in stature, but caused falsehood despair

My mother was fun, did sing quite a lot
Though high doh from low doh, she always forgot
But her lullabies were as sweet as the canary song
As they came from the heart, a true plainsong

My mother was quiet, thoughtful as can be
Her knowing searching eyes, saw right through thee
To cause her displeasure would fill them with pain
You never wished to stray, on that path again

My mother was happy, though her life was hard
Accepted her trials, with little self-regard
Would be scorned as a loser, in these selfish days
But she never developed, any hard-bitten ways

My mother was gentle, calm as can be
Even when she was hurting, you would not see
Her philosophy was, you can't force anyone to do
For if it is not from the heart, then it will never be true

My mother was all that I want to be
Her patience I strive for, for fiery is me
My tongue rattles on, when frustrated I am
Oh, how I miss my treasure, my so-soothing balm

Margaret Webster Thomson (Motherwell)

Restless

Another restless night, she woke early,
Dressed quickly, quietly,
Looked down again with envy
On his peaceful frame.

It had been that dream again,
Wandering through a dark wood,
Looking for a certain something,
Lost, bewildered, unfulfilled.

She felt uneasy, had to get out,
Rushing down the rough track leading
To the shore - sharp stones
Spearing her slippered feet.

Soon, through gritty ochre mounds
She saw the grey daybreak water,
Heard its rhythmic voice,
Smelt its salty breath.

Wind was leap-frogging the dunes,
Teasing her hair, and above,
Gulls were swooping round her
With their lost-soul cries.

She paced the lonely ribbon of sand
Searching for quiet suburbs
Of water. Finding only the
Busy traffic of tides.

Suddenly, the cold brought back awareness,
He'd be worried, must get back.
Back to the one who understood,
Back to the warmth, and him.

D Atherton (Swansea)

In Black And White

Life is a kaleidoscope
as every poet knows,
opening doors and gates through rhyme,
bringing a result which shows

in every poem published
under name or nom-de-plume,
selected by the editors
in their busy checking-room.

Life is a mosaic too,
a jigsaw world of sound
making patterns for the poets
in every 'climate' found.

Forward Press has paved the way
to help our work to grow
and develop by encouragement -
in print our efforts show

a word of talent found in word
expressing life's emotions
to be shared among the readers
enjoying these 'promotions'.

Life may be a jigsaw
but the pieces join to make
coloured pictures in black and white
that publishers may read and take.

Twenty years completed now,
encouraging those who write
as Forward Press continues on
To serve us poets day and night!

Ann Voaden (Nant y Moel)

My Homeland

I live in a Welsh mining community
In one little village of Wales,
Where coal mines were strong and thriving
All over the dales and vales.

But closures came in years gone past
Now there are very few around,
Men grafted hard and worked long shifts
In those dark pits underground.

Echoing throughout the land of my fathers
Male choirs sing strong and loud
Chapels and churches sing hymns and arias
And our comrades are very proud.

On March the 1st it's St David's Day
Celebrated by one and all,
Welsh costumes, Welsh leeks and daffodils
And Welsh cakes sold on a stall.

Welsh lamb, Welsh rarebit and spinning wheels
Welsh wool made from our sheep
Farmers plough and scatter seeds
And pray for sprouts to reap

There are poets like Dylan Thomas
Dramas and songsters listen hark
And down in our local theatre
Melodies played on a harp

Castles in our counties stand bold and high
The Welsh flag flies symbolic in the sky
The dragon breathes out flames so red
Now our Welsh heritage is not dead

Wendy Corcoran (Ammanford)

The Flowers Of Dunblane

Sweet were the flowers and sweet was the wine
but I can remember a happier time
for we have lost and I feel the pain
the sweet summer flowers of Dunblane

the winter's a time covered in snow
but we still remember where the flowers did grow
summer will come and we'll love again
the sweet summer flowers of Dunblane

we'll always remember those sunny days
running around the hot summer haze
fresh as the morning again we will sing
when comes the dawning of a brand new spring

spring is the blessing to all that grows
but summer will come, that everyone knows
like the birds that sing follow the sun
summer will come to everyone

when we are old and time has gone by
we'll sit in wonder, we'll sit and cry
for we remember and wish them again
the sweet summer flowers of Dunblane

life is the journey on which we must go
the question is where that we don't know
but we will remember and wish them again
the sweet summer flowers of Dunblane

lost in a storm, cruel was the rain
but we won't forget they'll come again
the memory lingers, we remember the pain
they shall return, the flowers of Dunblane.

James Peace (Glenrothes)

This Side Of The Hill

I never left my native land
Never felt the urge to go,
To explore those far-off distant lands
Or walk on far-off shores.

The grass was evergreen to me
On this side of the hill,
Although poverty rested on many a roof
And hunger was always seen.

The people of old never had much
But what they had, they shared,
Trouble was halved in every way
That's how much they cared.

Life was much more slower then
A carefree attitude,
Yet, there was no task left undone
No matter what one had to do.

Those summer nights in our street
With the accordion and the fiddle,
The jigs, the reels that filled the air
Brought life into our being.

When friends or relatives would return
From the country of their adoption,
Sure the parties would last for days and days
With them, money was no exception.

Yet with all the grandeur they displayed
Never tempted me,
To pack my bags and make my way
Across the ocean or the sea.

Stephen McCann (Newry)

Sightings

Lakes of mist in the valley floor
Half-drown the trees on the hillside.
Who goes there on the hither shore?
A nymph in white by the still tide?

Under cloud of unbroken black,
The landscape far to the west shines.
Who sits careless of lightning crack?
That 'nymph in white' on the crest line.

Peacock butterflies take their flight
From thistle-heads allegretto.
Whose the sleeve on which they alight?
The nymph in white's in my meadow!

Western hills wear a crown of gold
Beneath the darkening violet.
Is that her, by the power pole?
Discerning Avalon's Islets?

Honeysuckle perfumes the night:
Dun moths are drawn to its nectar.
Close she stands in the silver light:
The copper beech overspreads her.

Cygnus soars in the zenith now,
While Perseids streak out like tracer.
Just the gate is between us: how
I long to - dare not - embrace her!

Curlews call and the world stands still
'Til eerie tremolos' closure.
Know with deadening, hopeless chill:
'You never more shall behold her.'

Hatton Davidson (Newtown)

Mother Loves All

Oh Mother, dear Mother, my how you are blessed
With all of thy children, whom do you love best?
Without hesitation, dear Mother replies,
Why, all these are precious, in this mother's eyes.

The tired who climb on my knee for to sleep
The sick ones, on them, I an extra eye keep
The one who stays off in far country apart
Each day lives no farther, than this mother's heart.

The one who is blind, I lend my eyes to see
That whatever their state, they are precious to me
To the one who has fallen, I stretch forth my hand
And say, 'Come my dear child, we in God's love shall stand.'

When hurting, I give each one all of my love
But first I do pray to my Father above
The bread of encouragement, to all I do feed
For all are my children, and all have their need.

Whatever their state, they are blessings each day
I give thanks unto God, as for each one I pray
For I know if I love them, how much more doth He
Lord, all of Thy children are special to Thee.

They are bone of my bone, they are flesh of my flesh
Every one is a blessing of God's righteousness
But far more than this, it doth please my dear heart
For each one's a treasure, my God did impart.

Lord, you love all your children, the meek and blind
And whatever their state, they in Thy heart all love find
And the love Mother gives them, my Lord, it is true
I first had to learn how to love, Lord, from You.

Vicky Jack (Gartness)

Dwr Cymru - Welsh Water

If you have trouble with your water
Get it fixed once and for all
I really think you oughta
Pop along to Nevill Hall

Mr Branson and his staff
Are more than qualified
To sort out all your plumbing
And get that knot untied

With a few short lengths of copper
And some subtle joints of solder
He'll fix you with a system
That I know will never falter

His theatre staff's hilarious
They really have a ball
I know it's called a theatre
But it's more like music hall

He has a wondrous nursing staff
On Dyffryn Ward 3/3
I'll think of all those nurses
Every time I have a wee

They changed my bloody bed sheets
They measured all my wee
And for a dozen other menial tasks
I'd like to say, 'Diolch ichi'

I could go on in this same vein
With another umpteen verses
But I'll wrap it up with a simple, 'Thanks'
To Mr Branson and his nurses.

Taff Gurmin (Crickhowell)

Mothercare

A *second* ago I came to know
I had left my mother's womb
To be born alive, a chance to survive
Or a corpse in an organic tomb

A *minute* passed, I feel a blast
Ice-cold from an open door
My nostrils heave as the air I breathe
Gives me movement for evermore

An *hour* has gone, oh! How I long
To be nourished, warm and snug
In arms that caress, with sweet tenderness
My body wrapped in a rug

A *day* comes and goes in sweet repose
A sleepy contented night
Awake with the dawn - to cry and yawn
As watchful eyes peer with fright

A *week* of my time, a nursery rhyme
Kisses from faces that giggle
I burble and coo at these chosen few
And enchant them with toes that wriggle

A *month* ahead, I'm comfy in bed
My companion - a cuddly toy
With brown eyes that stare, through crinkly hair
To bring contentment and joy

At the end of a *year*, lots of good cheer
An image of wax and flame
A birthday cake - a slice to take
All part of this human game.

James Montgomery (Belfast)

The Woodland Echoes

A wooded valley
sheltered and serene
a meandering stream
teeming with life
crystal clean.

The scents and smells
of woodland flowers
honeysuckles and dog roses.

Buzzing bees, dragonflies
and multicoloured butterflies
noisy rocks and screeching jays
blackbirds and song thrushes.

Trout rise to the hovering fly
kingfishers fly by
as dippers dive and swim
fishing for fry and shrimp.

Sentinel buzzards flying high
patiently watch and wait
ready to pounce
on a tasty mole or mouse.

In the still of the night
hedgehogs and badgers patrol and hunt
squeaking bats and hooting owls
haunt the stillness of the night.

The woodland echoes
a barking fox's cry
reminding us of our nocturnal neighbours
while we sleep and dream.

D Jones (Pembroke Dock)

Then And Now

Twenty years have just flown by,
So much has changed within that time:
Digital radio and TV;
Many households now online.

Were we happier in those days?
Did life go at a slower pace?
Were children more obedient then?
Less murders, stabbings, drugs to face?

Or am I just imagining
Those years were better than today?
When Maggie Thatcher reigned supreme?
But had our leader feet of clay?

Financial worries not as bad?
Obesity no problem then?
Doctors, nurses, not stressed out?
No Global Warming causing pain?

The eighties were a happy time
Or is this just my fantasy?
Have I suppressed the worst events
Which made those days reality?

Today our world has shrunk in size;
Technology has shown the way.
We must move on; we can't go back;
We live our lives from day to day.

Twenty years have just flown by.
Let's not dismiss them out of hand.
Let's take the best the 'eighties' gave
To make this place a better land.

Kathleen Wendy Jones (Rhyl)

The Lamp

It stands upon the shelf top, its brass a gleaming gold
In contrast with the top, which is as black as coal.
No wick is in the holder and the base is ever dry
No single flame lights up the glass as it did in days gone by.

The lamp of which I'm writing spent a lifetime underground
Its base a little battered, and the top no longer round.
These wounds it bears from many a blow on timber, rock or coal
As it warned the collier of a gas, that could part his body from his soul.

It must have lit his way up to the pit upon the Garn'
Up the old lane from the valley floor in darkness and in storm.
Lights converging from a dozen ways until they formed a stream
That vanished underground, in a cage, to light another seam.

The man up in the heading was stripped down to the waist
Kneeling in the water and cutting at the face.
The roof was just above his head, his lamp shone through the gloom
He was mining out his daily bread, or it could have been his tomb.

Happily, it was not to be, and his days rolled into years
His working life was over, and he shed no bitter tears.
No more across the mountain track towards the pit head gear
But rather over fresh green grass, with his terrier ever near.

His lamp it stood forgotten in the shed out on the yard
With the old tools and the spiders, who worked so very hard
To cover it with gossamer and hide it from all view
As if they sensed its time was past, with no more for it to do.

The Christmases passed one by one and the old man was at rest
In the churchyard on the mountainside, that sloped towards the west
Then someone found that tarnished lamp, and took it in the dry
And burnished it, and cherished it, a momento of days gone by.

C G Payne (Pontypool)

Call Of The Mountain

Over the mountain a summer breeze sighs
A whisper of breath under clear blue skies
Deep down in the valley, far reaching below
Sprinkled droplets of gold in the sun's morning glow.

The mountain is still, with the heavens at rest
A time of the day that I so love the best
As I drink in the balm that nature instils
I gaze up in awe at the beautiful hills.

They thrust through the valley and stretch to the sky
On silent wing a lone hawk hovers by
My mind is at peace in the quiet of day
As serenity washes my troubles away.

Wrapped in pockets and folds, little farmhouses stand
Lost to the world on this green fertile land
Sheep steadily munch, playful lambs have been born
Each drenched in the joy of this mystical morn.

But a sour-faced mountain can often be tough
Gripped in jaws of a thunderstorm cruel and rough
Aggressively wild when blustery winds blow
When the lamp of the storm lights the valley below.

Changes occur as the seasons unfold
From the rich blaze of autumn, to a snap raw and cold
When winter holds court as a powerful king
Then agrees to submit to a soft gentle spring.

There is charm in their magic, nature's contrast we find
A look fresh and vital, a beast savage and wild
They stand as forever, majestic and tall
For strong is the voice of the mountain's call.

Barbara Davies (Swansea)

The Contrite Heart

The young man was a prisoner
On 'death row' for several years;
Awaiting execution for murder
His mother had shed many tears.

He was only nineteen years of age,
When he committed the evil crime;
Hard drugs were responsible for his rage,
And had led him to doing time.

From the moment of his committal,
He had shown no trace of remorse;
Typical of a hardened criminal,
Who takes a life as a matter of course.

A visitor called to see him,
She was a 'sister-of-mercy', no less!
Who begged him to show sorrow for his sin,
Whilst he had time left upon Earth.

That night in the quietness of his cell,
He got down on his knees and prayed;
His penitence helped him feel quite well,
And he could face the future unafraid.

The day of execution finally came,
But he was not filled with fear;
He knew the drugs had been to blame,
This had become oh so very clear.

People gathered to witness his death
And remarked at his calmness;
With a smile upon his face at his last breath,
His contrite heart was at rest.

Cyril George Button (Merthyr Vale)

The Beauty Of Spring

Look around at God's creation
There is beauty everywhere
Look around you once again
'Spring is in the air.'

For God, He felt that after winter
There should always follow spring
And at a glance in all directions
We see new life in everything.

Daffodils in shades of gold
Swaying gently to and fro
Little lambs a few days old
Tells us winter had to go.

Flowers and plants, we thought were dead
And trees that looked forlorn
With the coming of the spring
Are like Christians, now reborn.

When nature heeds the call of spring
Flowers awaken and birds sing
Streams and rivers gently flow
Enhancing meadows as they go.

Shrubs, whose leaves had fallen down
Through winter months had all turned brown
Now have healthy shoots of green
Letting springtime growth be seen.

For spring is God's way of telling man
Renewing the promise of Easter again
For like the flowers that bloom in spring
He too, will come again.

Margaret Jane Thompson (Magherafelt)

My Mystic Mournes

Take my ashes when I die
Into the Mournes, oh, so high
Bid the soft wind set them free
Falling where I long to be

Let my spirit freely roam
In this Kingdom, this, my home
Here I'll dwell in my content
With memories of the times we spent

And underneath the pines so tall
Those happy memories I'll recall
I'll sit and ponder there below
And watch the yellow waters flow

And up there on Slievebann so high
I'll touch the soft clouds going by
I'll sit upon the Cloughmore Stone
And view my Mystic Mournes alone

And in the meadows down below
I'll tread the paths where we would go
Upon the heather, fresh with dew
Each step I take, I'll think of you

I'll watch the seasons as they pass
I'll see the deer in Spelga Pass
And watch them as they freely roam
Up in this Kingdom, I call home

I'll listen to the sweet thrush sing
I'll watch the primrose herald spring
And in Rostrevors Fairy Glen
I'll bide until we meet again.

Angus Houston (Lisburn)

Two Wheels Will Reign Supreme

'Twas twenty years ago or so
I wrote my masterpiece
A wee poem about cycling
Which should'nae have been released

And now they've written back to me
'We'd like another yin'
(Send it by return of post
And the royalties will flow in).

I scratched my head, I scratched my tum
And bits I cannae mention
What could I possibly write about?
To get this woman's attention

Then, eight days later, in a flash
A lightning bolt did strike
The new Lord Mayor of London Town
Blonde Boris on his bike!

He's the man to turn things round
Bikes soon will be the thing
He'll outlaw Chelsea tractors
And any non-green thing

Like neighbours in the EEC
Especially Amsterdam
Where bikes outnumber motorcars
We'll cut down traffic jams

So, with this and the price of fuel
Two wheels will reign supreme
People everywhere on bikes
Or is it just a dream?

Ian Sharp (Erskine)

Love, Lies, Bleeding

Butterflies in your belly
And a smile you cannot hide
Now you're on a love ride

So much in love you feel
Your heart begins to grow
Your face is all aglow

As you hold yourself so soft
You feel a certain way
As your love grows stronger, every day

The sweetness from your lover's kiss
Is softer than the clouds above
You save your heart for the one you love

Inside you're burning with fire
The swelling feeling in your heart
You never want to be apart

Taking your lover in your arms
You hold each other nice and tight
Everything feels just so right

The love that comes deep within
Will never go out of fashion
This emotion you feel with passion

This is a feel of pure intensity
That I am very fond
Of our special bond

Love, lies, bleeding, blooms with life
I feel in love at first glance
For a little romance.

Lesley Kane (Bishopton)

Bad Girl

(For Amy Winehouse)

This is the girl your mother warned you about,
the one who courted dangers like lovers,
the princess without the fairy tale, who broke
all the speed limits mediocrity could offer;
she wore a death sentence like a cocktail dress -
short and black, and had a nerve, daring
to find peace in darkness.

This is the girl who never brushed her hair,
or cut her nails; she was a ragged bird of paradise
on display, among banal pigeons;
her arms were tattooed in a mythology
of people who had a stake in her. One life
could never be enough.

This is the girl who would not eat her soup,
eluding survival, pursuing oblivion, laughing
in the face of a god of disaster. She created
melody from pain; rhythm in the mundane,
all the time spiralling down
and down, a helter-skelter of chaos,
pursuing the emptiness she was running from,
while followed by legions of cameras,
fixed at a shutter speed to snap the moment
of disintegration, when the make-up
would finally run in dark rivers down her face.
How they all waited for the wings of the midnight moth
to touch the open flame!

This is the girl who played with matches.

Frances Robson (Edinburgh)

Wistful

If I could wait and thole
The bite of frost and snow;
Bear the bare blank land
As dark dank clouds skim low across
The plain to head butt hills.

If I could wait till the first
Drips of spring thaw in crystal beads
From the sleeping fingers of trees,
Or watch the new grain braird
On waiting fields.

If I could wait till the sun
Warms sinews and bakes the land
With summer spewing forth
While lark and blackbird
Fascinate in song.

If I could wait for hills to turn brown
And folds of heathers, pink and purple
To hang like flaming drapes
Above the changing fern.

If I could wait to feel the new wind bite
And see those summer leaves change
Before they fall
And hear the organ sound of swans
Winging west.

I would wait, to bring it all
Gift wrapped in wicker hampers
If only our hands could clasp again
On the twining handles.

Alex Laird (Biggar)

Troubled Mind

Living life and living free
Is it really there for me?
Wondering what lies ahead,
Half the time, wishing I was dead.

So many burdens take up my time
Is my life really mine?
I should look out for number one
But to other people 'thy will be done!'

Nothing changes from day to day,
Is this going to be the way?
Forwards, backwards, left and right
Tossing and turning every night.
Wondering if I've the strength to fight
To see another day.

Standing there on the ledge
Getting closer to the edge,
I turn my head, I'm looking down,
Such a distance to the ground.

I look up again, and see a light
Piercing brightness through the night.
Warns me to stay away
And live to fight another day.

Trying to remember I'm not alone,
It's so easy to pick up the phone,
But who is there that I can call,
Someone who will not let me fall.
Who has the strength to catch me
And help me to my feet?

Frances H Greves (Kilmun)

The Great Vision Of The Guarded Mount

We travelled mile upon mile in the morning mist,
Seeking the Isle:
Sea-girt sanctuary of a saint;
Guarded too by a saint
Atop the soaring spire of the minster;
Remnant of holiness, relic of Michael the Mighty.

Ere long we descried a pyramid shape in the gloom,
Only perhaps a trick of the eye or the mind,
Not yet accepting the reality in the distant dimness.
Was it thus visions were so potent a presence
In the harder, less comforting world of the monks?

Nevertheless, the mount with its crowded towers
Drew steadily nearer and clearer,
As we traversed the causeway:
Feeling the strangeness, as if at sea
In a phantom boat, nearing a forbidden quay.

But once ashore, beyond the menacing portcullis gate,
Amid bustling throngs of far-travelled pilgrims,
We jostled our way upwards on the steps and cobbles,
Only pausing to pass a saint's statue, as we ascended
Towards the great abbey church firm on its pinnacle.

During five troubled centuries it was a-building;
Fire-racked and war-torn, it sheltered its faithful flock,
Tending their double-cloistered souls in their garden of simples.
Outside great secular forces changed and manipulated;
Here the unshakable abbey still nurtures eternal verities.

May holy Michael guard steadfast the visioned mount,
While unborn souls extol the ancient fount.

Norman R Richardson (Glasgow)

One Day

It would be a fine thing
If on a day there was
A world peace day
Throughout the land
No crime, war or terrorism
An international holiday
A day of peace and love
The Dalai Lama, Nelson Mandela
Bob Geldoff, Thiah Nhat Hanh
Other peaceful persons
And like-minded wise ones
Could organise and be involved
There would be concerts
Of high sweet music
To celebrate the day
Much money could be collected
For charitable donations
With the right publicity
This special day
Could be nurtured
Like a precious flower
Imagine no arguments
Only harmonic vibrations
And good news on the air waves
All across Planet Earth
From small acorn of peace
A great oak of love
Would flourish and blossom
A world peace day
One day, one day . . .

James Garvin Paterson (East Kilbride)

Kestrel

Fine adjustments to the wings
hold the body poised.
Head bowed to prey,
he eagle-eyes the mouse.
Then dive, dive, dive;
and up and away.

Gaye Manwaring (Dundee)

Winter

Early in the morning people are cross
When they see their cars all covered in frost
Icy roads along the way
When will I get to work today?
People muffled against the cold
Slippery pavements frustrate the old
Watery sun and misty moon
I think it will be snowing soon
Dark mornings and early nights
Sensible ladies in woolly tights
Little children kicking snow
Noses red and cheeks aglow
Weary workers homeward bound
From their jobs around the town
Lots of colds and runny noses
In the gardens frozen roses
Lacy webs among the trees
Cold hands and chilly knees
Scarlet berries on the bough
All the birds collecting now
Skeletal leaves and naked trees
And now and again another sneeze
When we come in from the snow
It's lovely to see the fire glow
Fishermen at sea beware
Storms are coming, take great care
Children skating on the pond
Mothers shouting on the banks beyond
Steaming cups of tea bring cheer
It's quite my favourite time of year.

Jeniffer Johnson (Barrhead)

Glan-y-Mor

O Glan-y-Mor beside Cold Knap you have kept your secret well,
Until the archaeologists had their tale to tell.
A Roman fort, unique in kind, one hundred thousand pounds has cost.
Saved for the nation, by the nation, he who hesitates is lost.
If by chance you visit Wales, please visit Glan-y-Mor,
A third century Roman wonder, here upon our shore.

Joan L F Pace (Cardiff)

The Gossips

'Good morning Mrs B
And 'ow are you today?'
'Bearing up Mrs T, bearing up.'
Standing, fat arms folded
Two Les Dawson lookalikes,
They love to chat and pass the time of day.
''Ave you 'eard about her then
I think you knows who I mean?'
With a nodding and a winking
And a toss of curlered head,
She gestures up the street.
'Why no, what 'as she done this time,
Another man is it
Or 'as 'er old man beat 'er up again?'
With a finger to her nose she says, 'Ssh.'
And leans closer to the garden wall;
'No, I 'ear that number seven is on the way!'
'Get away! Whose babby is it, do you know?'
'Must of bin that spiv who's got
'er in the family way!'
'You don't say, flash 'Arry?
That greasy geezer always stopping there
When 'er old man is away!'
'He must of flashed 'er something else, I'd say!'
'By the way Mrs T, and 'ow are you today?
Is your corns playing up dear,
Or 'ave your bowels gone astray?'
'Bearing up Mrs B, bearing up;
But ta for asking dear, now come on in
For a chinwag and a cup of tea!'

Joanne Burns (Kelso)

1st Army Djebels Association

Just listen to a story of a gallant bunch of men
Who gathered down at Caister to be together again
The 1st Great Little Army they bear a glorious name
Because in all their battles they gained immortal fame
They came from many places back in their native land
A brilliant set of forces that made this happy band
There were English, there were Irish, Taffies, Jocks as well
They along with others made the Jerries run like hell
They landed there in Algeria prepared to make a stand
They chased the mighty axis completely from the land
When they contacted Jerry there was one order made
And that I can assure you was a win for each brigade
The lads they kept hard at it, fighting day and night
There was nothing they would stop at, not even Jerries' might
And when their many victories they had started for to mount
There were no more to muster when Jerry took the count
And now my friend it's true what I have to say
The lads of this reunion helped to chase them on their way
But remember in the process sometimes things were blue
The way was hard in battle before they could win through
Long since the war is over and victory was won
Spare a thought for this 1st Army every mother's son
They did a brilliant job, those lads, and did it very well
The list of their achievements only history can tell
The bells of peace rang out to everyone's desire
They signified the victory when the order was cease fire
Sixty years have passed since then so give a little thought
To the pals we knew and lost in the battles that they fought
They made the greatest sacrifice, the greatest price they paid
So let us not forget them, the 1st Army's great brigades.

W S Law (Inverurie)

The Dream

Where did the past years go,
All those years, only left a glow,
We danced to top bands - drank port from a cup.
Gone are those days when we were living it up.
Beatles we followed, for a glimpse of Ringo,
Now our highlight is a night at bingo.
We are golden girls with plenty to do,
Big win tonight - half is for you.
Hundred thousand, is that enough?
Fifty thousand each - straight off the cuff
World cruise we'll book - all agreed!
Top designer gear is what we'll need.
Down the Nile, Valley of Kings,
Tourist souvenirs, plus quite expensive rings.
We'll watch time fly and world pass,
Might even catch Rome - midday Mass.
Monte Carlo we'll go for, to try our luck,
Don't need it now - or a fast buck.
Singapore - Raffles! for overnight stay,
Cruise ship is leaving, very next day!
Suddenly bells started to ring,
Interval over, announced up in the wing.
Back to our seats for national game,
I wasn't too knighted - or gain special fame.
In interval, must have dozed off to sleep,
Fifty thousand pounds I couldn't keep.
In top places we both had been seen,
Now, 'twas all over! It was just but a dream.
Good news was - won the next house - on number 33,
We've not got enough money for cream scone and tea.

Sheila Donnetta (Swansea)

Not To Say

I didn't but ask, the name of that,
Those two words came, in a friendly chat,
How are you, oh, sorry, that's three,
Came out in torrents,
With ere a plea.
Mincing one's wording, the best we can do,
For less the well said,
Could come more, with the true.
It isn't to say, that I'm far away,
As close to your side,
Hear me say.
Sometimes, somewhere,
There's a road, to our share,
Telling us here, you really do care,
A footstep across,
Was contained with the loss,
Not having those lines, non despair.
You've really had it all, that's true,
More than your share,
Which was given to few.
Now one who's left, so much alone,
Is to seek in time, a one atone,
You have me thinking, now, that's odd,
Having the strength, of an open applaud,
But couldn't say when,
Or wouldn't say why,
Just came to terms, with a happy bye,
Life is like that, prevailing your chat,
The decision you make, be it true,
This world will go onwards, depending on you.

Hugh Campbell (Craigavon)

Miners

Miners work beneath Earth's crust,
Amid the darkness and the dust.
They toil and sweat in pitch-black Hell
For the owners their coal to sell.
In unison they work as one
Grafting until their shift is done.
Blackened faces, but eyes still bright
Emerge from black depths to daylight.
Wives and their children pay the cost
Due to accidents, young lives are lost.
Buried beneath the fallen rock
Grieving relatives in morbid shock.
Comradeship always second to none
When hewing coal to make the ton
Of Earth's black diamonds to make bright
Many a hearth on a cold winter's night.
Stories and gruesome tales to tell
By wheezing miners in living Hell.
Lungs filled with fine black crippling dust
Compensation should have been a must.
Inherited now, the laboured breath
Until the heavy mask of death.
Hard labour has not been in vain
A better life will now remain
For those who follow us in this life
Not needing in their daily strife
To hack and hammer at the coal
Instead machinery aim its goal
To bring to earth this commodity
For use by the community.

Mary Jones (Aberdare)

The Waters Of Consciousness

Liken yourself to a mountain stream.
Its source has been drawn up to the heavens,
From the seas of the earth,
To fall as rain on the mountains,
Then it finds an outlet,
And starts to flow downwards.
At first movement is slow and leisurely,
Trickling over stones and rocks.
As it gains strength,
It throws itself over jutting ledges,
And falls in a glorious cascade,
To the waiting ground below.
At this time, it has developed a voice,
And sings a song of pure delight,
A melody of the joy of existence.
As it meanders through meadows and pastures,
It gives sustenance to the soil.
As it curves and bends with the land,
In becoming deeper it develops turbulence and whirlpools,
Taking into the vortex of its creation,
Everything it encounters,
And spews out that which it has no further use of.
Now it becomes deep and fast-flowing,
And sings a new song.
A thunderous chorus of inexplicable rapture,
For it senses the source of its being is nearhand,
And with a joyful leap,
Throws itself into the seas of consciousness,
To become as one with the life-giving water,
And there, awaits renewal.

Wilma Hogg (East Kilbride)

Sarah

Sarah fine face bedraggled
A blanket over her legs dog beside
Begs on the steps of Waterloo Station
Sarah by an array
Of lymph and bloodstained tissues and a dog
Is on the landing of Waterloo Station
Thin the knees of her jeans filthy
She helps the man on crutches who has fallen
To his feet
Gathers her possessions
They leave
Sarah interrupts reading a book dog beside
On the stair of Waterloo Station
To ask for money
Sarah carrying her filthy blanket and belongings
Bends collecting cigarette butts
A man passing for a train
Gives her half his sandwich
She thanks him
Sarah in new clothes who has been begging
Under the Victory Arch
Relating to the First World War of Waterloo Station
Telephones a hostel at a pay phone
The beggars include Sarah
Who is dirty
Sarah among many up to no good
Sarah carries a piece of filthy cream blanket
Holds the lead of a young dog
Which at her return romps
Roaming about her

Simon Warren (Tring)

China Tea

At an early hour
After a fragrant wake-up shower
I like to drink tea
From a fine bone china teacup
I get a glimpse of summertime
Hand-painted, just inside the brim
Lilies, roses and delphiniums
Bring sunshine into the room

I pick up my pen, the ink flows
Writing whatever comes to mind
Feeling refreshed, I look up from my desk
Through the window I can see
The pond mirrors a clear blue sky
Tall yellow iris that grow close by
Songbirds on the wing, a dragonfly
The willow that hangs over the stream
At a time like this, it's easy to escape
To drift and to daydream

But I can't dismiss
My thoughts are with
A fine bone china teacup
I get a glimpse of summertime
Hand-painted, just inside the brim
Lilies, roses and delphiniums
Bring sunshine into the room
I like to drink tea
From a fine bone china teacup
Sitting in a saucer to match
Sitting on my desktop.

Beth Izatt Anderson (Inverkeithing)

The Dream And The Nightmare

As I enter the magical kingdom of dreams
Its silver gates topped by a great fiery eagle
Proud and erect upon a fair plinth
A plinth that shines in the bright golden sun
Beyond which there lies a sweet summer meadow
Strewn with flowers and colours so lush
Colours that lead to a fairy-tale castle
With towers that reach to the clouds high above
And walls as white as the first winter snow

As I reach the great portal of the shimmering castle
A stout solid portal of fine English oak
I touch the brass key and turn it towards me
To unlock all the night dreams and day hopes within
But the key turns to worm-eaten rust in my fingers
And I step back in fear as the sky turns to black
From the castle that's now just a dark ruined shell
I turn to go back - to the way I once came
But the way back is barred by an evil hobgoblin
Face twisted with spite and eyes burning like coals
He squats on a tombstone that lies in the graveyard
The graveyard that was a sweet meadow before
And behind him the eagle is now a grey vulture
Atop iron gates forever bolted and shut
The hobgoblin speaks his voice laden with menace
The words pass his lips so blackened with age
Welcome lost soul to the dark realm of nightmares
Think not of safety for you cannot go back

Once you enter the land of nightmares there is no going back
You must go on and on through it.

Alasdair Cowie (Buckie)

The Way Home

Either path must lead me home -
the narrow lane that winds above
the meadows and the wood;
the fast, white road
dipping to the bridge
across the river.

On this soft autumn morning,
I choose the narrow lane
and see, once more,
the mist-filled sunlight
paint the surface of the leaves
in glowing shades
of orange, russet, red

and know, that soon along this way
the rowan will be standing
bleak and bloodless,
its glory stripped
by frost and chilling wind.

But now, while morning sun
and lingering haze
unite for this last show
of vigour, life and fire,
I set aside all thought
of what will be,

loiter awhile,
savour the transient moment;
then continue on the way
that leads me home.

Gwenda M Owen (Cardiff)

Comparison

Take another day
For yourself
To make
The best of life

While you're young enough
To enjoy the transience of moments
That succumb, to the light of day
Before it greys around the edges
Like the hair on your head

It takes enough of life
To fill these moments
That define our responsibilities
And change us completely

Some of us never get to play
Enough in the end
As the opportunity arises, then
Should be grasped with both hands
Let life wait with all its demands
Before we fade like the night
To the morn, or to the death, for
Which we are born

Take another day for yourself
To learn, to live it up
In remembrance that
The end will always
Be one day
Closer to sight
From tonight.

John Graham (Belfast)

Say It With Pride - 1994

The bugle calls tremble in summer air,
As we parade to show our care.
We hear the sad, prolonged 'Last Post',
And we recall the allied host.
With whom we fought for liberty,
In a place called Normandy.

Now, on this momentous day,
Remember 50 years ago and pray,
For those with whom we served to free,
Our cherished lands from tyranny,
In a place called Normandy.

Say it with pride, for those who died,
Think of it well, let memories dwell,
And never forget,
The cost, the debt,
For those who fought for liberty,
In that place called Normandy.

Silent we stand, head bowed deep,
Tears are there but do not weep,
For those we left in lasting sleep,
For 50 years in hallowed ground
Their wounds still fresh, their spirits sound.
Living on in minds now old,
We who wait to join the fold.

And there with friends we'll smile again,
And stay forever, be young as, then,
To play and laugh, be joyful free,
In that place called Normandy.

Graham Lewis (Bedwas)

The Missing Piece

Your smiling face greets me every morning.
But like the old song says -
'I've got your picture, she's got you'.
How did that happen?
What went wrong?
Did I take you for granted?
If I did I'm sorry.
You were my rock.

Clichés that slip off the tongue haunt my mind.
'You don't know what you've got until it's gone'.
How true.
'It's better to have loved and lost',
I'm not so sure.
If I could turn back time knowing what I know now
would things be different?

I miss us.
Not what we became,
but what we were.
If you have found that again I'm truly glad.

The days have merged into weeks, months, now years.
Life goes on, I do the things I always did.
I tell my friends I'm fine.
And on the surface I am,
Like an old jigsaw puzzle which appears complete
until you look into the heart of the picture
and realise a piece of missing.

I am that jigsaw.
You are the missing piece.

Isobel Quinn (Falkirk)

Rest, Bumblebee

I found you lying still upon the carpet
In the Lady Chapel before the altar.

Why did you come into a church?
Were you attracted by bright flowers
Being brought in to grace the Holy Place?
Did you follow someone in who wore brightly coloured clothes
and wearing expensive perfume
So you thought that you were entering your Elysium Fields?
Or were you just a daring being wanting to explore the interior
of any place when a door was opened?

Why did you die?
Were you killed by flying into a pillar,
Or trodden underfoot unseen by a worshipper communing with the Divine?
Or were you starved of nourishment and moisture,
A slow, creeping death?
Perhaps it was just your time to go.

You died before the altar
A symbol of the one who gave you life.
You lay with limbs delicately folded in peaceful repose,
Your black and browny yellow markings on your fluffy back
As beautiful as ever.
Your wings are still
Your baritone hum is hushed.

How saints would envy you the place of your demise,
And the dead of wars and disasters
With no graves to mark their passing,
Might wistfully wish that their last resting place was with you
Among the grasses on that Hallowed ground.

Judith Williams Francis (Narberth)

Crossing The Field

I watched the cows plod purposefully
To the far side of the field,
As if the grass were greener there, even without
Craning their necks to graze beyond the fence,
And thought, what can we learn from this,
Knowing there's a fine line that could be drawn
Between fulfilment and complacency?
A question likely to present itself
More often as the years accrue,
While where we stand may sometimes seem
Unfitting, unbecoming or unreal;
Accepting though, the point that we have reached
Is here and now -
The clay we need to work with -
Not yielding lightly to the siren call
Of yesteryear and elsewhere.

To choose a bearing congruent
With all that we hold dear
And tending to a visionary goal
Becomes the pressing challenge, as we seek
Resources that will bolster us afresh
Against the fear of falling;
Yet mindful how the going is enriched
Immeasurably
If we can count as fellow travellers
Friends whose journey corresponds with ours,
So that, together, we can look
For nourishment secure
In pastures new and worthy.

Michael Haigh (Kinross)

A Lifetime Of Photographs

First you'll see the Baby Book
You can't resist so have a look
This gorgeous child with Mother's eyes
Next page reveals a big surprise
Hat removed, and it appears
She's been endowed with Father's ears
100 pages - don't treat with scorn
Remember that it's their firstborn.

The infant grows and off to school
And parents use up many a spool
Miss Innocent with coat on peg
Had kicked head teacher on the leg
School photos in traditional style
'P' Seven's orthodontic smile
The glamour shot's the 'prefect' bold
The first boyfriend - is he too old?

Holidays both near and far
Pictures of the first new car
Drama groups with lots of plays
Performances that will amaze
So close that book and know it's true
The next album there will be 'two'

The perfect couple - no mistake
That's a good one cutting the cake
Their children came and as you see
The Baby Book is now history
On browsing photos you will find
The nicest ones are in your mind!

Betty Hutton (Argyll)

Another Removal

No squeaking cart this time.
Just an old Ford Transit
Driven by two dodgy-looking blokes.
Everything goes in easily;
There is no room for much
In the 'boxes' they built to replace
The simple back-to-back arrangement from
Another poem.

He is not sorry to leave behind
The drug abusers, the burglaries,
The late night noise.
Time to go, while he can still say
He is, to date;
The only inhabitant of this street
Who hasn't yet been robbed.

Stereo, telly, PlayStation, some chairs
And stuff all packed, he leaves behind not much;
A bottle of bleach and some white gloss paint,
Meaning to come back and clean a bit.
They beat him to it though.
Kicked down the door and stole:
His bleach, his paint, his ansa phone
And most oddly, the underfelt, but not the carpet.

It made him smile to think
Of their disappointed faces.
Hardly worth the effort
Of breaking into another flat,
On Terry Street.

Judith Rutter (Anglesey)

Port Talbot In The Sunshine

Port Talbot in the sunshine,
Obscenely spitting at the moon.
Baby larks in nests still feeding,
By farm machinery strewn.
And little girl-flowers crushed by lusting,
Their virgin-hearts still trusting,
With faces now encrusting
Lie uncrying in the grave.

Explosives in the Atoll where pretty corals lay
Oily birds not comprehending the shortness of their day.
And little lambs with warm hearts beating
With cries for mercy bleating
Are taken for our eating
In gory slaughterhouse.

The serpent's still in Eden,
Slyly gliding through the glade.
By his plausible persuasions
Spoiling all that God has made.
And now, the whole creation's fretting
And its sin and pain regretting,
In frustrated labour sweating,
Waiting for its nuclear death.

God's precious gift is given in a common cattle trough;
And Mary's heart is breaking for her baby on the cross.
The world in its rejection,
Ignores the resurrection,
Incurs its own subjection,
Misses new creation's dawn.

Peter G Jackson (Ammanford)

Christmas For Awen-Minish And Tzippy-Rose

(Dedicated to my darling granddaughters Awen-Minish and Tzippy-Rose)

Those two tiny girls are snuggled up very warm, very tight,
For everyone knows this is no ordinary night,
They pretend to say their sweet little prayers,
Beside them they each have their cuddly furry bears.

Downstairs on the carpet sit Mama and Dad,
With memories of childhood both happy and sad,
Wrapping that last little surprise Christmas toy,
Poor old Daddy wishes he was still a small boy.

He recalls the days when Lego was fairly new,
Toys had little bolts and nuts to screw,
Mama holds a doll that looks so real,
Inside it contains an endless speaking reel.

The TV has a constant fake, cheery drone,
The Grans and Gramps send loving texts on their mobile phone,
Where are they? Oh, on an island exotic and warm,
For them there will not be a blustery seasonal storm.

Here like the robins our family huddle,
Tomorrow they will have a big Christmas cuddle,
With thank you for this and oh! Wow! for that,
They will all sit round the table each wearing a daft hat.

A Christmas in Britain can seem damp with mould,
But on a hot sunny Christmas I will never be *sold.*

Merylrose Sivyer-Dixon (Pontypridd)

Serve Her Right

(Inspired by a remark on a headstone in Shankhill Cemetery, Lungan Co Armagh, N Ireland)

She was pretty and young, but very poor,
He was charming and rich, but old,
She craved for the lovely things money could buy,
So she married him for his gold.

In a few years, she thought, he'll pass away,
If he's good, to realms above,
I'll be patient and kind and bide my time,
Then I'll marry again for love.

Her husband, so jealous and crotchety grown,
With very good health was endowed
And though she longed for his demise,
Not a sign of weakness he showed.

'Oh, what use are dresses and jewels?' she cried,
'My life is a misery!'
So, she took lovers and laughed in the face
Of the man she despised heartily.

One day, she fell ill with no warning at all
And very soon after died,
Her elderly husband shed not a tear,
Still nursing his wounded pride.

And we read on the headstone he placed on her grave,
In old Shankhill cemetery:
'Here lies one whom God did smite,
For her infidelity!'

V M Archer (Craigavon)

We, And The D.W.P.

She opened the letter
And then she saw . . .
Soon, when aged eighty,
Twenty-five new pence more
Will accrue to her pension.

Small reward for breathing that long!

Alas though, her husband
Nearly eighty-and-two,
Must *lose* ten pence weekly -
Cruel turn of the screw.
It's beyond comprehension.

What has he done wrong?

Forty percent rate -
The same for 'high earners' -
An undeserved fate
For two elderly yearners
For relief from *life's* tension.

Why d-r-a-g them along?

Darby and *Joan* receive 'Pension Credit';
That's less than the 'Minimum Wage'
It's hard to obtain, but for those who get it
It does very little their *needs* to assuage;
And their *wants* receive lesser attention.

It's the 'Roundelay Song'!
** D.W.P. (Department for Work and Pensions, HM Government, Westminster. Westminster, not Holyrood, has reserved this function!)*

Thomas I Anderson (Forres)

Neuralgia

One hundred foreign troops
march through my brain, relentless,
their rhythm, all the same.
Give me a break! For God's sake
let the rhythm go!
Outside the rain in fury doth
not cease to flow.

Carole M Smith (Swansea)

For Isobel

The eyes are the gateway to the soul
And that which I gaze on lovingly
Dwells there, illuminated, now and forever
Within my heart and my sacred spirit
As you dwell there, now and for always
A part of me, a beautiful garden
Planted in one corner of my heart
That belongs to you and you only
A golden garden, honey scented
Blessed by God and tended by the angels
Where flowers forever blossom
In every single season of my life
A place without fence or walls
Wild and open, untamed and free
Where willows weep, but only joyously
And when my heart has ceased to beat
When the blood lies still inside my veins
And my last breath is but a wistful sigh
Of farewell to this life on Earth
Softly, I shall whisper your name
As the memories of my life flash by
Your image will be foremost in my mind
To comfort me on my eternal journey
Immortalised in everlasting consciousness
Locked safe within my soul for evermore
As it flows gently forth to infinity
You, that have become a part of me
Forever, in eternity, my Anam Cara
My one and only, true soul friend.

Eddi McVeigh (Belfast)

Unity

Unite in universal prayer
And God will join
In chorus too
Drink the cup
Of bittersweet
And salve thy lips
With nectar

C O'Donnell (Glasgow)

Berkshire: In A Memory - Four

Down in that quiet bit
beside the lock
an old and stagnant waterway
ran behind the towpath,
one end disappearing in a distant culvert
the other diminishing in a line of trees.
And as I idled there one clouded day
after a petulant shower
had cleared the way of walkers,
keeping unusual still for a small boy
out on his own
unencumbered by demanding adults,
then came a flash
suspended on a beaten whirr,
a splendid cascade of luminescent blues
which held a thousand tints within.
Leaning on my rail I saw him steady
on the lurching bulrush
and stare across at me.
One beady eye, then the other
summed up what this upright creature meant
to him and his.
The bobbing perch
made him seem to bow;
the near eye slowly closed as in a wink,
and in that time
the bulrush sprang up straight again,
swaying empty
of Kingfisher and colour.

Sean T Jackson (Morriston)

Loving Attributes

In submissive reflective reality,
My mind adrift. Into focus comes a smiling
Face. Radiating warmth and gentility
Realisation dawns. Nia, a vibrant, loving
Friend, with a vivacious personality.
Dependable as a rock. Unswerving,
Committed, loyal, with unsurpassed caring continuity.

Wilma Harris (Swansea)

Music Of Peace

What a change of mind.
What a difference in time.
What a pleasure to see,
and a pleasure to hear,
that music so sweet
in the night Highland air,
a band playing in the Strathpeffer Square.
I had the privilege to be
passing in the car, you see,
when I heard that music sweet.
I enquired, 'Who is the children's band,
playing music so grand?'
'They're people from a foreign land
who were also passing by,
and asked if they could play in the Square.'
What a pleasure it was there
to the sounds that filled the air.
It was a German children's band
playing in my homeland.
I thought about the difference in time
when my father fought the Germans in the frontline.
I wish he were alive to see this time
and the change of minds,
from that great pleasure I witnessed to see,
the German children playing for me.
Thank God that is the way it is today,
and trust that peace will always stay.
That pleasure of music sweet,
I'll always remember that . . . children on a Highland street.

Jack C Fraser (Buckie)

Always

There are times and seasons within
Hours and years without
There are embers of love in them all
Standing to attention lest they fall
Holding sacred the promises
That permeate eternity's end
With wandering hope

Judy Angel (Cumbernauld)

Paper Bags

Not many things remind me of you
in fact it's rather sad how few . . .
But paper bags make me stop and smile
I haven't seen any for a long while . . .
You kept huge hoards of them all over the place
they spilled out of every vacant space . . .
All would be neatly folded into sizes and shapes
Brown ones maybe shuffled in, holding bananas and grapes
Pretty one secretly hiding a new blouse or bras
Thicker ones would stumble in overflowing with 'special offer' jars . . .
Then for decades all precious purchases have been roughly wrapped
or helpless trapped
in plastic carrier bags
that end life as shredded rags
flapping wildly about all available fences
or sadly stuck under sturdy feet of park benches . . .
Maybe I should look out for
a few pretty paper bags . . . maybe three or four
So I will be ready for when you eventually 'depart' . . . 'leave' . . . 'go'
I can divide you up into small 'paper-bagfuls' ready to sow
and scatter you around favourite haunts, sunny places
bicycle routes and scenic rambles you charmed with your grumpy graces.
        I know how much you would hate all that
        So I will be sure to wear my best hat . . .
        Life with you was never dull
        Now I'm planning paper-bagfuls
of your charming, delightful, grumpy graces
Left carefully and caringly in all your favourite sunny places . . .

Netta Irvine (Shetland Isles)

The Dove Of Peace

Birth

See the Christ Child in the stable
Watch the shepherds at the stall
See the wise men kneel before Him
Worshipping the Lord of all

Baptism

See Him come from out of Jordan
See the heavens open wide
See the dove descending on Him
Hear the approbation loud

Life

See Him at His Father's business
See His miracles performed
See Him with the little children
Bidding them to come to Him

Death

See Him brought before the Council
See Him on the Cross of shame
Hear Him cry now, 'It is finished'
See Him taking all our blame

Resurrection

See the tomb, now standing empty
Hear His words of 'peace to you'
See the risen Lord of Glory
Taken up out of their view

M Florence MacLean (Inverness)

Living Water

There are no barriers - sex or tribe,
Religious tradition or social taboo:
None will stop Him asking you
'Give me - give me a drink!'
He'll see right through your social façade,
Right through your defences, and pull no punches.
'If you only knew!' He says, as he peers
Right into your soul with laser view.
No place will hold Him, no hallowed stones,
No treasured buildings, which hard-won cash
From parish *efforts* strives to maintain.
'In Spirit and in Truth,' He said.
In the midst of daily merry-go-round
Of relentless work - *or passing the time,*
Of shallow fashions of cynical humour,
Acceptance unblinking of sexual tarnishing

In adverts, entertainments and ways of living
Let us hurry to our people like the woman at the well -
'Come and see the man who has told me everything!'
And rush along to Him, warts and all.
If we beg like the villagers in Samaria,
'O stay, please stay, and tell us more,'
As we give Him the drink of hospitality,
He'll give us the drink of Living Water.

So our roots will burrow deep to the pure, clear well.
As long as we drink, we'll flower, and propagate
His purity, like lifeblood, to our present generation:-
'I who speak to you now am He!'

Marjorie B Roberts (Brynmill)

Me In The Park

The autumn nights are closing in
It's starting to get dark
I can feel a wave of excitement
At last it's 'T' in the Park
Who cares about the weather
Or if the fields have turned to muck?
I drag myself from tent to tent
With my wellies getting stuck.

The atmosphere's electric
With the music playing loud
It's time to forget my worries
And join in with the crowd
I feel a sense of freedom
There's a smile upon my face
As I jostle to see my favourite act
Trying to find some space

Then as I leave the roaring crowds
And head off to the fair
My stomach begins to tell me
There are burgers over there
Drifting with the music
I feel I'm in a trance
My arms and legs are everywhere
I just can't stop the dance
Then suddenly I realise
It's beginning to get dark
And then I awake to find that
It's only *me* left in the park!

Diane Wright (Kirkcaldy)

All The World's A Stage

'All the world's a stage', at least so we have been told
By famous William Shakespeare who lived in times of old,
And all the many players, some women and some men
Enacting in their turn life's ages numbering seven.
The mewling, puking infant and reluctant boy at school
And then the sighing lover who keeps the golden rule
Are followed by the soldier who utters many a tale,
Then comes the rounded justice and sixth-aged man so frail.
At last the toothless 'offspring', by now devoid of sight,
Is snuffed-out like a candle which flickers in the night.

At present chosen actors they study day by day
Several reams of language within a given play.
They build up every character from what they see in life
Reflecting love and kindness or envy, greed and strife.
Success is something treasured whene'er it comes along
In drama and in music, in dancing and in song.
Much disappointment shows when work is hard to find
And spirits start to weaken and then torment the mind.
An actor's heart can be so full of joy and zest
Except in times of worry and periods of unrest.

It is with deepest pleasure they tread those boards of wood
When people in the audience applaud as viewers should.
They don their various costumes and carry several props
And make their humble bows when the final curtain drops.
This world so full of magic, in theatres old and new,
Belongs alas to those, the very, very few.
Who strive with endless patience, no matter what their role,
As dedicated artistes, until they reach their goal.

Yvonne Watkin-Rees (Ammanford)

Wind Of Change

The wind blows
And the Earth turns, changing
Day to night, the moon soft
Between the splayed ash branches
Shadows on the road

The wind blows
And the bare trees, smooth and gaunt
Sprout the stickiness of buds
Wait for time to shift
Stiffness in their branches

The wind blows
And the trees are bowed
With the year's harvest
The load of green
Blotting out the sun
Keeping space cool

We shelter in their shadow
Rained on, by water plucked
From an Atlantic wave
Blown up the green valley
Over rooftops, chimneys, homes empty
Open quarries, open mines, factories empty

And the drops rain, quiet on the hill
Air full of blast and moss
While we try to weave the cut strands of life
Into some sort of basket
To hold the wide Atlantic wind.

Pat MacKenzie (Glasgow)

Clouds Of Thunder

Clouds of thunder float on by,
The mountains reach up to the sky,
The forest floor is full of dew,
The trees stand tall straight and true.

The sea is calm, like morning mist,
The shoreline rocky but gently kissed,
The fading light covers the land,
You hold a candle in your hand.

The light is dim, your shadow tall,
You see a spider on the wall,
The house is silent, cold and dark,
You hear the dogs begin to bark.

You light the fire with great haste,
The smell of smoke is a bitter taste,
The rain is falling, steady and hard,
The dogs are crying in the yard.

You call them in and calm their fear,
Then settle down with a bottle of beer,
The thunder roars and lightning flashes,
The fire's flames glow through the ashes.

The wind picks up and starts to howl,
In the trees you see an owl,
The clouds of thunder drift on by,
The riverbed no longer dry.

The wooden bridge creaks and leans,
As water rises up to its beams.

David J Hewett (Milford Haven)

A Mother's Love

Ten little fingers, ten little toes
Two little eyes and one little nose
A tiny little baby, all beautiful and new
That's what I remember when I first saw you

Your little tiny body, huddled close to mine
Made me feel that everything was going to be just fine
It really was so lovely to hold you really tight
Just looking at your tiny face was such a lovely sight

I remember wrapping you in your blanket, and picking out your name
I remember your first feed, and your first nappy change
The colic and the teething, every pain you ever had
Rubbing your little tummy whenever you felt sad

The sleepless nights came and went, but it really was worthwhile
Especially when the morning came and you gave me a big smile
You looked at me as if to say, 'Mummy I love you so'
And every worry I ever had seemed to melt and go

I really enjoyed the experience that I went through it again and again
So now I don't just have one, I have three great wonderful friends
A son and two daughters, each one of them so sweet
And they really have made my whole life every bit complete

Ross, Nadine and Skye, I wrote this poem just for you
So you can always look back at it, and know I cared for you
The years will start to go by, and older I will get
So to my three beautiful children, please don't ever forget

I love you so much and always will
Mum.

Diane Thomson Miller (Glasgow)

The Devil

As death comes upon me,
I stare him in the face.
Is it the Devil I see,
or the mirror reflecting upon me?

Is there a God up there I wonder,
or is it an old dying lie foretold by many?
The world alters around me,
people live and people die.

The Devil is watching me,
waiting for his chance.
He will take us all at the right moment,
will the God up high protect those needing protection?

Will He protect me?
Has He protected me?

I sit and I wonder in a dark, gloomy room,
is there really a God
or the Devil with a false face of gold
and the desire to catch all the good souls in the world
to change them to the monsters that bad dreams are made of.

I pray that the good souls in the world
are free from the evil that portrays him.
The door of fire opens to many.
Those who dare enter
are lost in the world of darkness for eternity.

No one ever comes back,
only in nightmares and small but harsh dreams.

Tammi Fudgell (Caerphilly)

Musical Reverie

Of those first few notes on record
No real interest I take.
Then, as the music quickens
So my ears awake.
My mind drinks in its beauty
It seeps into my soul
It lifts me in its beauty
From this mundane world of ours.
Oh sweet and heavenly music
Such pictures, it inspires
Of Milky Ways and sunsets
A Holy Infant, in a byre.
Now I hear the gentle waves
I see them break upon the strand.
Now the wind is sighing
As it blows across the land.
The sounds of music rise and fall.
Imagination travels far.
The sea, the strand, the Child, the byre.
The wind, the land, the shining stars.
Thinking of my loved ones.
Some young, some old and feeble.
When suddenly, to Earth I'm brought,
By the grating of a needle.

The record, it is over.
My reverie is broken.
I have nothing left to look at
But a round, plastic token.

Diane Lavery (Castlemaine)

The Experiment

No one knew what would happen. Twenty miles
high and a tingling in the hand from a glove
leaking in a vacuum. Daylight drained
away, the helium-filled balloon rose
like a silver planet above blue-green
Earth. Blood pooled in the hand.

The man stepped out of the basket and watched
the balloon hurry away like a freed
sperm rushing to its purpose at last.
He lay there facing up to the blackness
wondering if he had come too far, the
balloon shrinking to a glint in his eye.
He noticed his clothes were unruffled
everything still, quiet, clean. Eternal.

His clothes ruffled then pulled tight around him.
He was being buffeted, a roar
swelling in his ears: the fist of magma
was claiming him and within seconds
he was fumbling for a ripcord and filmed
landing in the white light of a desert
beneath a red and silver parachute.

Twenty miles from here takes me to cliffs
beyond Aberdaron from where
on a clear day I have seen Ireland
on the brilliant horizon
and wondered at how a man dared to oar
a coracle across that deep, dark sea.

David Batten (Penrhyndeudraeth)

Tomtain Dawn

In early morning darkness
Lungs filled with freshening air
Grass wet with early dampness
Dawn upon the fell.
From Tomtain's brow we turn
East towards the Forth
In awe watch God's glory rise
A feast for sleep-dead eyes.
Dancing as in playful mirth
Through fast receding clouds
Sunlight spreading across the firth
To warm the dew-filled fields.
Birds in dawn-led song
Sing out with earthly praise
Heralding a brand new day
Voices in worship raise.
Remember a hill in darkness
A thousand years ago
A cross it stood triumphant,
For us who watched below.
A teardrop shed in sorrow,
Mixed with blood and sweat,
To give us a brighter tomorrow,
He alone burdened our guilt.
Another Easter day remembered,
Birthing another hope-filled year,
Let us then go, unhindered,
Boldly and without fear.

Rhymer (Kilsyth)

Public Notice - To Whom This May Concern

Confused, 100% they seem to be: as to who they are,
What they know: what they are, what they understand:
What they want to be, and how they comprehend it.
Though exactly where they need to be, they seem to know,
Incomprehensively; right at the heart of confusion.

Ber George Barter (Tredegar)

Since

Since I came to Blantyre
My maw says I speek slang
She trys to tell and teach us.
But we could nae gee a dame.
When we say it's hoose, it's house,
When we say it's doon, it's down,
But then we just look at her
If she was a clown.
We all go to Auchinraith
Where the teachers are the best,
But someone ott to tell them that
The dinners are grotesque where
The dinners are so putrid
Where the dinners are so grim
That naebdy likes to eat them,
So we all stay nice and slim
My maw buys Warburtons
So that daeyae make of that
And if I eat a jelly piece
I never will get fat
Since I came tae Blantyre
I really can't complain
But I just keep on speaking
Slang and drive my maw insane
Since I came to Blantyre
I say it's hoose, it's house
My maw she always tells us
To be as quiet as a mouse.

Yvonne Clark (Glasgow)

The Silent Listener

There is one who listens to all our prayers
We cannot see Him but He is always there
Go before Him in faith and trust, do not be afraid
Our God, the God of love, is the silent listener
Take all your burdens to Him and feel enveloped in His love and care
When you have emptied your soul of its burdens
Say a quiet prayer of thanks to our Lord, the silent listener
And go on in life knowing that He is always there for us.

Margaret Cubis (Bathgate)

The Child That's In Us

A vessel of trust, of logic, of mystique,
Characters of individuality, each and every one unique.
The child is a symbol that should be looked upon,
As a knowledgeable being to which we can all learn from.
The child is overflowing with innocence and wonder,
So do we as adults have the right to plunder
Their wisdom, their wholeness and their purity,
Then replace it with contemptment, hate and jealousy?
When you look deep into your heart, your reply must be no,
Then why do we do it? Can you tell me so?
As a child we saw all through eyes that didn't lie,
We believed all that was told about the world, but remained shy,
To the segment of life that's dominated by corruption,
But as we grew we fell under its seduction.
We began to see that 'power' was the superior force,
And money and greed became the primary source.
To build our lives upon and shelter beneath,
We wear it as our garland, but it's really our wreath.
It sustains a life of false happiness,
A life without trust, a life that's fast becoming worthless.
If we could utilise the experience of our childhood,
The outlook for the future would be pleasurable, would be good.
For a world governed with the essence of a child,
Would see no wars, no streets that are blood-soiled.
No striving for authority, no hurt, no pain,
Peace would dominate an area that's much more sane.
We must think of the tranquillity and try to focus
On the being, the presence, yes the child that's in us!

Yvonne M Richards (Hengoed)

If

If you don't ever start
You won't ever finish
If you don't take a step
You won't walk a mile
If you don't take a chance
You won't see that rainbow
It's only by starting
You'll finish in style.

Moira Richards (Kilmarnock)

Miracles

The potatoes were flowery and the rhubarb sweet,
They grew in the garden at the end of the street.
I sat on a stool and ate all with a spoon,
I really was hungry and now I am full.
The taste buds enjoyed it, the teeth broke it up,
Down in the stomach, it's churned into pulp.
Then in the intestine where it's fully digested
The little blood cells have it arrested
And sent to the liver, the body's food giver.
Who knows what to store and what to deliver,
To muscles in our legs that allow us to walk,
To muscles in our face that allow us to talk,
To muscles that move our ribs in and out.
To muscles in our arms to move them about,
To muscles in our hearts to pump blood around,
To muscles in our ears that adjust the sound,
To muscles in our eyes that allow us to wink,
To muscles in our brain that allow us to think.
Every little cell works to a plan,
That is far beyond the understanding of man
And even the waste that the body refused,
When mixed with clay, in the garden is used,
To encourage the growth of the natural fruits
And grow fresh shoots to my rhubarb roots.
The circle is now complete, so again I can eat,
Life's a short lease, but God's works never cease,
So, how can one say, no miracles today,
When all things spring from and end up, as clay.

George Harper McCrea (Omagh)

The Hill

How sweet the air upon this pleasant hill,
Where amorous clouds embrace the distant rill.
And skylarks startled from their rest,
Pour forth their song in mild protest.
Where dragonflies, with staring eyes,
Glide amongst the reeds and hide.
And flowers nod in silent dream,
Lulled to slumber, by murmuring stream.

A H Whorlow (Stranraer)

A Little Bit Of Egypt By The M8

Some artist, a sculptor I suspect
By the roadside, concrete enduring,
Created grassy pyramids
Sharp and shallow, offering
No threat to stony antiquity -
Caught the focused eye,
Tamed the wild landscape
And carried motorists, renewed,
Onwards, on their musing way.

No camels, reeking urine,
Plodding through seeping sands
Nor amateur Egyptologists
'Hut-hutting', high upon their steeds,
Only mutton, slowly grazing,
Nibbling, obliquely on those emerald mounds,
Parading the catwalk of the open air
In fashions gaudy, shocking almost
To backward glances through mirrors.

But why the grazing sheep
(A new 'West Lothian Question')
Sparsely dotted on the angled hills
With jerseys of crimson wool?
The farmer, unique, eccentric;
An artist in his own right,
The open field his canvas
To please the passing populace.
A living challenge to Damien Hirst!

Gerard H Mulholland (Edinburgh)

Oasis

Unlike a mirage it's real and true
Known as a fertile spot
Usually amidst a seemingly endless desert
Once my life was as desolate as the sands
Yet meeting you my vision
Has been transformed and a torch
Lit up the colours of hope, joy and gladness
So now I know I have found my oasis.

A J Luke (Newport)

From My Window, Railway Houses

From my window, why awake and wondering how,
These summer fields are full of snow,
Under the moon, of course,
I know the sleepers lie behind
And though I strain, and though they slumber near,
A breath, my own, a sigh, is all I hear,
Their feet fall soft, so soft it seems,
That they, content or anxious,
Move in silence, shrouded by their dreams.

Too hot for sleep I search the sky, for stars,
But they pass by both dumb and blind,
Eclipsed by lunar magic,
Some say that as they go the planets sing,
The only sound this night can bear,
A ghostly hunter on the wing,
Supreme and confident, he demands his prey,
Who, tonight, unwilling hears his cry;
The weak, the hunted, those about to die.

Outside the frame not every creature sleeps,
The trembling edge of life is dark,
And full of fear,
I cannot see the beating heart,
The stumble or the fall, or understand why,
Some must need to run to meet their end,
While others hide and crawl,
Yet I know, awake/asleep, Death summons all,
And in the end, not one resists his call.

Lydia Dier (Cardiff)

Sad Valentine

A tear formed in my eye but it did not fall,
As I read the brief note I picked up from the hall.
'I'm leaving my dear for another clime,
I should say goodbye but I haven't the time.
My new love awaits me, I must hurry on,
By the time you read this, I shall surely be gone.
So don't shed any tears for our love could not be,
There was only fun friendships between you and me'.

Myrtle Hayes (Belfast)

For Eileen, My Mum On Her 85th Birthday

Mum, these are our golden years
We've shared the heartache
We've shared the tears
We've shared the laughter and the good times too
Trips to the theatre, the pictures, the zoo

We've bopped till we dropped
Round the living room
Our microphone the handle
Of an old kitchen broom

Now we've settled into a comfy pair
Me running round
You tucked up in your chair

I know one day we'll have to part
To lose you then will break my heart
But I'll try hard not to be too sad
And think instead of all the good times we've had
Our singalongs to our favourite songs
The stories you told of days of old

I'll remember you with love and pride
And you'll always be right by my side
You'll be with me every step of the way
And I'll love you then
As I love you today

Dorothy Ellen Connor (Glasgow)

Regional Poem

The hills of the borders are covered in sheep
Salmon and trout swim in the Tweed
There is knitwear to buy in the smart local shops
Farmers' markets sell meats and breads of all sorts
Golf courses to play on for fitness and fun
Riding on horses, best in the sun
Abbeys, estates and gardens for leisure
And a sign on the road says Peebles for Pleasure!

Valerie Wright Hall (Peebles)

What Do You Say!

'Mummy, why are you crying?' the little lad said.
What do you say?
How do you tell a four-year-old his daddy's gone away?
She cupped her hands around his face and wiped away his tears,
Then held him gently in her arms, cradling all his fears.

'Sara's gone with Daddy to a new home up in Heaven,'
Sara's birthday's next week, she was only seven.
They'd only gone down to the park, half a mile or so,
That's the last I saw them, just a week ago.

'Will they come and visit us?' was his sweet reply,
I really must be strong, I really must not lie.
'No my pet, they've gone for good.' I think I'm turning mad.
'I hate my sister Sara, I hate . . . I hate my dad.
They've gone away and left us, I don't know how they could,
Mummy please don't let them, I promise to be good.'

If only . . . that drink driver hadn't passed that motor car,
If only . . . they'd walked slower, they'd not have gone so far.
If only . . . it was raining we'd have had an early tea,
If only . . . they'd been poorly, they'd be here today you see.

She placed a teddy by the grave, a present she had bought her,
Happy birthday when it comes, my little darling daughter.
Look after Daddy won't you, I know that you'll be strong,
And one day soon we'll meet again and back where we belong.
Joey sends his love, to you and Daddy too,
Give me strength to get through this,
Always loving you.

Audrey Duncan (Huntly)

Midnight Moonlight

The moon shone down on the archaic catch,
Upon the silver trees and the golden latch.
The trees though they whistle from the chilling breeze,
Stopped suddenly as it began to slowly ease.
The shooting stars in the dark, dreary expanse,
Seemed to do a wonderful eerie-like dance.
No beating of wings could be heard,
But the shadow of the owl was really observed.

Emma Nicholls (13) (Llandovery)

Ireland - Land Of Love And Hope

Here I stand in this beautiful land,
By the 'Mountains of Mourne' and the sea.
I look all around and there's hardly a sound,
But the waves and a bird in a tree.

It wasn't the same when we came here to live,
Some twenty-odd years ago,
Not knowing a soul, bombs and pain all around,
Helicopters flying, people dying, children crying,
Houses blown to bits.

And yet and yet, these people
So hurt over years
Stood proud and tall,
Started again
And dried their tears.

I love to sing, so I joined a choir
And made many friends on the way,
We carried our songs to different places,
These wonderful people came
To stand and clap with smiles on their faces,
The bombs and bullets now in the past,
We live without fear and pain,
At last.

So, here I stand, in this beautiful land,
Where the mountains sweep down to the sea,
They were always there, no matter what
And always will be.

Frances Walker (Lisburn)

Evening

And evening bids the angry sea grow calm,
Slow, on the foaming tide it spreads its glow;
The lazy seagull wheels in feathered flight
And far horizon's setting sun sinks low;
Gently the wavelets lap to distant shore,
Plaintive, the curlew cries, to fading light,
Tranquillity enfolds the evening air,
As day concedes in purple to the night.

Dorothy Neil (Cardiff)

Five O'Clock Shadow

As another new day dawns, an arctic silence
Lies upon the frosted furrowed fields.
A bitter breeze blows through denuded trees.
A bunch of disillusioned crows sit hunched
Among frost-blasted branches,
Mourning for the summer days long past.

In the distant woods, a wily fox
Returning late back to his lair
Gives out a sharp consumptive cough,
A sinister sound enough to set the huddled birds
A-shuddering on their perches.

A wintry sun shines weakly in a blue uncertain sky,
Reflecting rainbows in the glittering crystals
Suspended like diamonds from the cottage eaves,
Trembling in Zephyrus's icy breath.
A brazen robin trills his song, defying Death
Who masquerades in winter's hoary mantle.

Across the bleak and whitened wastes of empty fields
The strident call of some triumphant pheasant can be heard,
Strutting proudly through the ploughed and furrowed iron ground.
A haughty bird who bears his noble plumage like a shield of honour,
A brightly feathered coat of arms.

But now the winter's day is disappearing,
As Vesper spreads his cloak of gathering gloom,
And in a clearing through the snow clouds
Can be spied brave Hesperus travelling home.

Rusty Woodward-Gladdish (Swansea)

Christmas - The Forgotten Birthday

It's my birthday again,
Maybe not wise but plenty of merry men.
Can you still recall Bethlehem
Or is it all shops and the annual mayhem?
I continue to watch over you down below,
One day in the year for appreciation you can show.
Never mind, I quite enjoy you decorating the tree,
Will continue being a Saviour and not a judge to thee.

John Lavery (Ayr)

The Letter

The letter came this morning
From someone quite unknown,
Telling me my friend had passed away.
Quickly, unexpected, sorry for such sadness,
Sympathy, sincerely -
My tears obscured the name.

Dear friend of many years.
Oh, what fun we had.
Student pranks, cheap holidays abroad,
Evenings singing opera -
Acting all the parts!
Visits to the theatre,
Queuing for the cheap seats,
Walking miles to get there,
Money was for music, not bus fares.

All the things we shared
So lovingly remembered
Though we had not met for many years.
Circumstances parted us
But we always wrote,
Kept alive our memories,
Which is all you have when you are old
And you hear your friend has gone for good.

How I wish the postman had not come.
Then, to me, my friend would still be there
Waiting for my letter.

Joan Bell (Pembroke)

Wet Wales

We come from the land of the active cloud
Where the sunshine hides and the rain is proud
Autumn, winter and spring come and then go
But the Welsh summer season is a definite no!

Remember that orange ball in the blue sky
Those lovely long days with the temperature high
2008 is a washout where even the ducks live in fear
Get the heating on because global warming is here!

Rob Jones (Tonypandy)

Something Special, Something Lost

Soggy summer grasses
Memories of a love that passes.
Will the sun come out today
And will my sadness go away?

Little faces, little smiles
Joy that lasts for a little while.
Heavy feeling deep inside
Emptiness that I try to hide.

Where is peace? I ask in despair
And how can I get there?
No thought, no feeling
No sound or seeing
Just an endless being.

The dreams that come in sleep
Images I want to keep.
Dark days I must forget
Sorrow, grief and regret.

The pain recedes like the tide going out
I'm free at last I gladly shout.
Fool I am, I know that now,
Funny, there was no row.

Just distance coming in-between.
Something lost, something unseen,
Fleeting as a summer swallow.
Tell me, will the sun come out tomorrow?

Irene M Price (Treorchy)

A Prayer For Peace

Of all the things we pray for, let them be
for a world of laughter and of love, where all are free.
Where those of terror and pure evil have no place
and God's love covers all the human race.

Bless those in power with strong and steady hands,
to solve the problems in those far-off lands.
And may their honest judgements never cease
to bring to one and all a lasting peace.

I Sime (Craigie)

Deck The Tills (The Sales Start On Boxing Day)

Deck the tills with loads of lolly
Fa la la la la, fa la la la
Sales have started, so it's jolly
Fa la la la la, fa la la la
Freeze your bits off till the sale starts
Fa la la la la, fa la la la
Gladden poor retailers' hearts
Fa la la la la, fa la la la
Get your cash out, spend, spend, spend
Fa la la la la, fa la la la
Flex the plastic, make it bend
Fa la la la la, fa la la la
Tramp on toes to get in first
Fa la la la la, fa la la la
Just get all that's on your list
Fa la la la la, fa la la la
You can even shop online
Fa la la la la, fa la la la
PayPal, credit, both are fine
Fa la la la la, fa la la la
It's such fun, no doubt of that
Fa la la la la, fa la la la
Till the bills fall on the mat
Fa la la la la, fa la la la!

Margaret Campbell (Bathgate)

Getaway To Venice

Home from my travels once again, I sit with my paper and favourite pen,
My body relaxed in my favourite chair, in my mind though I'm still wandering there.
The wonders of Venice my eyes still can see, no other city so unique there can be.
This is a place that must never be missed the sea laps
the buildings as though being kissed.
My ghost still stands with the vast milling throng,
Fellow tourists pause briefly before moving on.
Do I hear a sound at the sad 'Bridge of Sighs'
Or see a teardrop fall from a dead prisoner's eyes?

Francis P Leybourne (Caldicot)

Rise Up The West . . .

No longer do we need to serve an English parliament,
We are a nation, young and strong,
The act of the union, our ties to break,
As free men and common folk,
The west asleep for many a year,
Now the time has come for the west to awake,
Rise up free men of Scottish blood,
For Scottish soldiers die in a far-off land by foreign hands,
Wake up and be a nation, strong and proud,
For independence and freedom under one flag we stand,
Now the time has come, to break the act of the union,
That ties us with chains and like slaves,
Stand proud, a voice fighting for independence,
Free from an unfair tax and poverty under Westminster,
One flag, one people, a nation once again,
Freedom long-since denied to common folk,
Unfair tax and promises from England yoke,
Poor people while England rich steal,
Or our oil and land, the rich do steal,
No more lies and broken promises,
Your freedom a single vote, ours by right,
That is all that stands between us and independence,
Now let England fears awake,
When Scotland ties do break and people freedom gained,
Let Scotland people suffer never more unjust poverty and hunger,
Let's be a nation proud and strong, standing where we belong,
Rise up the west!

George Barr (Irvine)

Destiny

My love is like the mistletoe, dependent on its tree,
My love is like the dawning, like new waves on the sea.
I see with freshly opened eyes the birds apon the wing,
I see the hedges and the flowers as they burst forth in spring -
I never dreamt that I would find such joy to fill my day,
I hope my love that you have come in my life to stay.
A bird that flies must find a perch, a song must have a tune,
A fox that hunts goes to its lair, a stream goes to the sea,
I pray my love that you will find your destiny with me.

Tessa Rogers (Pentre-Beirdd)

Farewell Right Leg

For sixty-four years you've been part of me
And held me up effectively.
You helped me walk and skip and run,
You enabled me to have some fun.
I can't say I thought of you that much
You were just there to feel and touch.
I was never good at games or sport,
You would not find me on a tennis court.
But you took me to places near and afar,
And you helped me drive my trusty car.
You've been there for me along life's way
You helped me to stand and to kneel and pray.
I appreciate all you've been to me
And I thank God you made me free
To do as much as I have done,
Even when we struggled,
With God's strength we won.
Now is the time to say farewell,
If you could talk, what a tale you'd tell.
Without you I know I'll feel loss and pain
But I must try and recall what without you I gain.
It will be tough - but one day at a time
I'll carry on - and trust God divine.
To adjust and adapt and to live life to its best
Knowing somehow I've withstood the test.
As I look to the future and say farewell
Thank you dear leg - you did your job well.

Enid Morris (Brecon)

Bus Pass

Old man not so old
Sore heel but good heart
Steps forward from gloom
To gloom. Haze removed.
Fearful but laughing.
And love. Tears rise.
But fall away. He is here.
And I am glad and sad.
At once.

Jonathan Eric Houston (Magherafelt)

Walking You Home

We'd travelled far
In such a short time
And now for the last time
I'd walk you home.
Holding your hand
I began the journey,
Hesitant at first,
Walking you by
Familiar landmarks
And each step
Timed by your breath
Holding on
And holding on
I walked you onwards
Through the avenue of beech trees
And the promise of barleyed fields
Along a road you knew and loved
So well
And so long
I walked you on . . .
And then it was time to turn,
Calling softly to our old dog
And as we reached the hill near home
I said gently, 'Nearly there, Mum, nearly there,'
I held your hand
Heard your breath go
And you were gone.

Mary W Drummond (Edinburgh)

Leo

Leonora,
She found a home to be cared for.
Never purred, only a squeak.
It was all she knew to speak.
Loving and friendly
A fine nice quality.
She'll be missed by her sisters Lynx and Buttons.
But her memory lives on,
Now the tabby is gone.

TS (Swansea)

Liverpool Poem

My girl asked for a poem
So I gave her a yellow rose.
That's not a poem, she said.
I said it all depends
How you look at it.
Some people would claim
It was the apotheosis of poetry.
No, she said, I want a real poem
So I gave her a green leaf.
That's not a poem, she said.
I said it all depends
How you look at it.
Some would assert that verdant leaves
Are the tiny waving hands of plants and trees.
No, she said, I want a genuine poem
So I gave her an orange stone.
That's not a poem, she said.
I said it all depends
How you look at it.
Some would state that simple stones
Are the rugged rudimentary bones
Of Mother Earth.
She said, you're not very bright are you?
If you can't be bothered
To write me a proper poem
You can sod off.
So I did.

Simon R Gladdish (Swansea)

Living For Something

An old, old cottage in a very depressed area,
Where people go to the shops in that very old mining community.
They count their blessings every day,
Being born and bred in that very old cottage, with love
Bringing up their children in the very best way.
My great grandchild Mackenzie speaks to me on the phone,
Her daddy and grandpa tell her the story of the old cottage,
Where they all had to work hard in school to escape everywhere in the world
The cottage had done its work.

Dorothy Jane Lewis (Maesteg)

People Or Sheep?

People are sometimes treated like a flock of sheep
Since this is so I'm going to bleat,
Just try and open a bank account
It doesn't matter for what amount.
A passport will certainly pave your way
Or a driving licence will save the day,
If one does not have any of them
They look at you as if you're alien,
The other side of the coin, so to speak
Is if by now you're not too weak
You'd like some cash out of a building society account
you've had for years,
You're on your knees and near to tears
But the assistant doesn't want to know
For a passport or driving licence one must show,
Try paying bills with cash up front
Here again you'll feel the brunt,
There's always been a standing charge
Which covered this by and large
Now they charge extra if you won't conform
By now one's feeling quite forlorn.
When they say they've won an award for saving trees
You're beginning to think it's all a breeze
But your account envelope they really fill
Not only do you get your bill
Each time ten-page updates and leaflets they do send
It's enough to drive one round the bend!

Margaret Meek (Falkirk)

Teach The Children

Children are miracles, sent from above,
Given to parents to protect and love,
Children are precious so please take care,
Teach them to love, teach them to share,
Guide them through their childhood years,
Lots of laughter, very few tears,
Support them through their teenage years,
When you've taught them all you know,
Give them confidence and let them go.

Agnes Robertson (Dingwall)

Tonypandy Rhondda As I Remember

Up hill downhill.
Beauty all around.
This is how it was Rhondda Valley.
Visiting all my family.
Grandmother, aunts and cousins.
Relations were in dozens.
Standing on the mountaintop.
Looking down the valley.
Some had garden plots.
Showing bounty crops.
Trees alongside.
Further down the houses glowing.
Trains and buses flowing.
Morning I awake with strange sounds.
Men going to work.
With heavy boots on ground.
The pit whistle sounds.
They will not be home till dark.
Dressed in clothes so dreary.
Coming home so weary.
Nowhere have I ever been.
Where hearts were so warm and loving
Through all their toil and dirt.
Never will there ever be goodness of heart.
So strong spiritual feeling.
Never in any place will I find
Than there in Rhondda Valley.

Gwyneth Murphy (Kidwelly)

The Guiding Light

Feel the oneness of my soul
The power that makes me whole
This power is my guiding light
Saving me from perpetual night
A day will come for me
To help people to see
The guiding light
To win the fight
And bring the world to peace.

Andrew Catchpole (Tranent)

My One And Loyal You

I watch you with misted eyes
My one and loyal you
Whose steps were once so swift
Your every leap so true
But now your steps grow slow
No leaps again for you
Those days have passed us by
My one and loyal you
Your eyes grow dim
The end is nigh
But still you stay with me
You rest your head upon my knee
And look me in the eye
I know what's come
I know it's time
Time to say goodbye
My heart so heavy
Throat so sore
I kiss your soft greyed face
Meet your gaze and nod my head
You answer with a sigh
The tears roll free, one last cry
The pain I must bear alone
You've passed on, you're running free
I face this world without you
Without my shadow, my four-legged friend
My one and loyal you

Donna McNally (Newtown)

Homo Sapiens

Other apes, we are told,
Can compare, gene for gene,
With us, who brought babble
And scrawl to the scene,
Small wonder this planet's,
A doom-laden dump -
Homo sap's just a chimp,
That's gone right off
It's chump.

Kenneth Young (Huntly)

Redeveloping Progress?

There was a community called Tiger Bay
Where people from all nations came to work, live and play.
To some it was renowned as the dark side of town
Ladies of the night, pubs, brawls and fights.
But to those whose faces did not fit up in the city,
It was a refuge, from the hatred and the pity.
Simply a place to live where your neighbour was your brother
And it didn't matter his race or creed or colour.
Everyone helped each other.

There was a community called Tiger Bay
And they could really teach us how to work, live and play.
In harmony, in peace, without instant judgement based on prejudice.
But the ships have gone, the docks closed down
And now it's the new and gleaming - 'yuppie' end of town.
Expensive flats far out of reach of the pockets of the locals,
And it's preached that this is regeneration,
Redevelopment - a brighter, better future, but for whom?

The new Cardiff Bay - the most exciting place to be
But where's its soul, where's its meaning?
All glitzy restaurants, smart wine bars
Fancy tables, fancy lights hanging from the ceiling.
It makes me sad to see
The end of Tiger Bay
Many faiths and races - the spirit of the place
A multi-cultural way of living that was caring, sharing, giving,
A true community.

Anne Gee (Cardiff)

Don't Cry, I'm By Your Side

I am here my dear please don't cry
I am the sunshine that warms your cheek
I am the stars that light up the night sky
Even though I died my dear, my soul is still alive
I am now part of that place up high
Please don't cry my dear because I died
I am the first spring rain which gives life to ground
I will be there for you my dear, even if I died
I will always be standing right by your side.

Alexander Andrew Duthie (16) (Peterhead)

Another You

My senses blur as your question is posed.
You whisper it, shyly,
Secretly, timorous and tender -
'Did you once love me, years ago?'
I look deep into those grey-green eyes
Back to that distant past.

Tell me you never felt the soft yield
Of petals beneath your feet,
Or heard my breathing in the murmur
Of a salt sea's swell?
Did your eyes never lift to a high cliff's edge,
And see my outline against the sky?
Was there no touch, no sense
Of the gossamer of my dreams around you?

And now you ask me if I loved you once.
I, who came alive only in the warm
Glowing curves of your bewitching
Young body, and the sweet caressing
Sound of your voice.

No, I did not love you once, years ago.
I loved you for my whole lifetime,
And watched from afar that you were happy,
And seemed content, in the care of someone else.

My time may come in another life
with another you.

Ken Marshall (Cwmbran)

Slow Death For The Human Line

I watch this world in disbelief
At the narrow mind of Man,
He pollutes the air, profanes the Earth
Just to profit all he can.

His concern is not for future years
It's only for his time
Then to leave behind his legacy
Slow death for the human line.

Peter Paterson (Bellshill)

Every Time

Every time I see you
I look around and you're there.
Every time I speak
I hear you calling my name.
Every time I act
Your presence draws near.

You are here, beside me
Never letting go.
Holding me in your arms,
Cradling me
For evermore.

Every time I cry
I feel your arms surround me.
Every time I smile
Your joy captivates me.
Every time I breathe
I know that you are there.

You are here, beside me
Never letting go.
Holding me in your arms,
Cradling me
For evermore.

Your presence enraptures me,
You cradle me like a child.
I am content with you.

Mélissa Evans (Welshpool)

Autumn Response

It was a slight touch of a breeze
    Scarcely there at all.
Yet the leaves on the footpath answered urgently
    Swirling and fluttering before they settled.

A few danced in the air, arabesqued,
    Lost their nerve and dropped.
Some forgot about safety in numbers
    And left to play solitaire.

Rhoda Wason (Newtonabbey)

Untitled

Behold, if you will,
The splendour of this vast and wondrous universe
Which spawned such beauty and bounty
On our own small blue planet Earth.

Consider the mystery and wonder
Of a power that whirled these stars and planets into space
And pause to think of the gift of understanding
Through the ages of the human race.

The system and the order of life's appearance;
The grasses, soil and insect tiller
All preparation for fish, bird, animal and man's existence
Tell us, surely, of a plan so carefully and perfectly ordered
That only thus and only they, humanity
Can grasp the meaning of such enormity.

But yet, with eyes to see they see not,
With ears to hear, they hear not
Nor understand what creation speaks of in its beauty
Power and ordered way;
Its logic and nature's message through the ages
Ignored as atheistic, agnostic and proud unbelievers
Read not the universal word.

Eden's glories, its peace eternal with the divine
Turned into a Hell on Earth, as Man turned from the sublime
And to the sin of disobedience, greed, conflict and war
With man's unbelief in the divine creator's law.

Tom Hewson (Lisburn)

Browned Off

What are you doing to us Gordon Brown
It's only the rain that seems to come down
Fuel and food are all on the rise
My money's disappearing before my very eyes.

All of my life I have voted Labour the red
But I feel now is the time for this to be said
In the next General Election whatever you do
Follow me and live longer, vote Tory the blue.

Barbara Fowler (Galon Uchaf)

I Never Painted Your Picture

I never painted your picture,
The one you wanted for your wall,
The one I promised,
I finished others first;
I never painted yours.

. . . but I never waited for anyone,
On a pattern in the carpet,
Counting the days
To their holiday was over,
Not like, I waited for you . . .

The nature of my ritual
So singular to me,
With neither proof nor reason,
Alas, but in reflection
Lasted longer -

Than your wait
For one unfinished picture,
From one inadequate artist.
All of my others
No matter how fine -

In spite of their
Various state of completion,
Could not fill the frame
I did not fill for you:
It belongs as this, my triumph.

Gary Hanna (Newry)

Cliff Top

I'd like to climb a cliff one day
And watch the sunset over the bay
Floating ships into the night
It is such a lovely sight.

The morning dew soon comes round
It's oh, so quiet, can't hear a sound
And soon the birds will chirp and tweet
For that's a sound that is so sweet.

Hazel Davies (Carmarthen)

The Darkening

Those slow, low tones lulled us to sleep
Wafting upward where we lay
Bathed in the afterglow of the day
With all the promise of the morrow
Never safer, nor so secure
Never more reassured.

Their soft talk amongst themselves
And friendly wireless voices
Warmed our spirits well
Like an eiderdown of sound
That sheltered us from harm.

Mother, Aunt and Grandmother:
A guardian trinity
A comfortable force for order and well-being
A protective presence.

I was born there; it will always be my soul home
Though dwelling elsewhere then, school holidays
Hastened our return, as to the bosom of our being
The cradle of creation
All of the countryside's delights, charged childhood highlights
Too soon dimmed and defunct.

The days no longer shine;
The nights lack that silken spark
We are alone and exposed now
Walled in within this silent dark.

Kevin Woods (Belfast)

A God-Fearing Man

He stands between the mountain and the lough,
A bowler hat shoved back from the receding line,
Boiler suit opened to his waist,
His Orange sash across his chest.

He fears the thoughts of the Yard's new owners,
Fidgets and scratches at the insecure places,
Sits on the drum rim cleaning his oil-blacked nails;
Hesitates to share a pint across the street.

Arthur Greenwood (Bangor)

The Bachelor

He leans bony forearms
On the rusty gate
Hands knotted -
A farmer's stance

To gaze into a distant
Lifetime of hopes -
Dandelion clocks
Blown across his meadows

Where once, a brown-legged
Girl, impatient, chased her dreams
To another's field.

The evening sun, dying,
Crushes his heart
To bitter rinds of loneliness
For what might have been

At twenty-five
Golden summers:
Gone to seed
At fifty chill autumns.

He turns from the gate:
Trudges towards
An empty kitchen
The mother gone

The funeral over.

Margaret Cameron (Belfast)

Untitled

We don't eat meat or sit in the sun
Don't smoke or drink and still have fun
To get a high we like to run
Preferably a marathon

If you think indulgence pays
We urge you now to change your ways
Or shorten your life by days and days
And if you think excess is clever
You're not going to live forever.

Susan Crocker (Cardiff)

In Memory Of Seamus

'Twas a glorious summer
From early morn to late at night
Bright blue skies and lots of sun
A time full of promise
Joy, laughter and so much fun.
Then came the call
That changed it all
A heart of gold
Would never grow old
Oh, the heartache and the pain
As the sunshine turned to rain
Life it seemed, so in vain
Whilst gloom and darkness did prevail
But then the seeds of hope appear
So many lives had he touched
From both far and near.
A passing word, a kindly deed
Help for those in need
'Twas all acknowledged in the end
As time with us, these strangers came to spend.

And as the years pass by
The emptiness is still there
But we will meet again
Sometime, somewhere
The rain will cease
And the sun will shine for evermore.

Mary O'Callaghan (Newry)

Stepping Stones

'Tis stepping stones that fail me
Always change that sees me weep
For whenever fortune hails me
Seems my failure's in the leap.

All my dallies in the dark
On those oceans in-between
Ensure I re-embark
To the places I have been.

N W Davies (Pontypool)

The Morning Star

I am the morning star, that shines down from the skies,
Without me there can be no life, and with me, no one dies,
Just look out from your window, as the trees now shed their leaves,
Will I not clothe them once again, and make sure no one grieves?
Their winter's come, their life has gone, just withered trees you see,
The beauty that was theirs is past, says I, and I am He,
But I will come again at will, and clothe them once again,
If you believe in what I say, then I'll do this for men,
Do I ever fail to come, when you believe in me?
Don't I direct all Earthly things, all there for you to see?
So put your thoughts to rest, and do sleep well this night,
For have I ever let you down, come the morning light?
So believe in me for I am He and I am Life indeed,
Without me there can be no life, without me no more seed,
So do sleep well my Earthly friend, for what else can you do?
These things you see are known to me, but not yet known to you.

So sleep dear Mother, sleep in peace, until the Lord appears,
Sleep dear Mother, whilst the Lord, wipes away my tears,
And when He calls, I'll sleep too, in His trusted care,
Sure that when I wake again, dear Mother, you'll be there,
For all of us who trusted Him, this will come to be,
So sleep dear Mother, sleep in peace, till you again I see,
Then dear Mum, hand in hand, we'll walk on Heaven's shore,
And talk of all the times gone by, and tears will be no more.
So let's await the morning star, that shines down from the skies,
And trust His word, for all to hear, that with Him, no one dies . . .

Ronnie Simpson (Glasgow)

A Summer Moment

Enwrapped by honeysuckle scent
As if a silken scarf lay round,
A lark's sweet showering cadence
Drew eyes the sky to roam;
Movement was nigh impossible
Listening to the breathless sound,
The entrancing alchemy filled cells
Like honey in the comb.

Jean Aitken (Cardross)

Poetry

Why are we so afraid to write poetry?
These days it doesn't need to rhyme,
meter isn't necessary.
Have we been scared off in long distant classrooms?
Inkwells, blots, bare electric lights
exposing our childish attempts
to the teacher's, sometimes, harsh criticisms,
(child psychology hadn't been discovered then).

Or is it because in prose we meander,
we chat, we disguise what we mean.
We explain, apologise, ramble and justify.
No space, not enough words for cover-ups
in poetry, it leaves us bare for all to discern.

Those of us who dabble,
blush, stammer, offer self-effacing comments -
'You'll think it naïve, foolish . . .'
We're embarrassed for friends to read it -
they may think us pompous, pretentious,
any other faults we don't want to own.

But writing poetry, my friend, is liberating.
It's therapy, freedom of thought.
do it for yourself - be a closet poet . . .
No matter how simple, it exercises the brain,
makes us laugh, and holds up housework -
(everything stops when inspiration strikes).

Jean Farquhar (Shetland)

You're In My Head

You're always there
When I rise, until I sleep
You occupy my dreams
I thought you were gone
I lost you for a while
I could no longer hide
You found your way back in
Now I need to find a way out.

Ross Dryburgh (Aberdeen)

The Ghost

In the lunatic silence
Orbs look on
Into void
But I
Am mild and mellow
Quiet
And kind in the
Whispers behind the walls.

Against the dressers
And drawers
That keep my
Lipless secrets
Culled

Orbs look on
Into void
But I am
Meek and corrected.

Please watch
My empty face
Bathed in a curtain
Behind my window
In front of
The malevolent silence
Seething
On darkened walls.

Robert W Bellamy (Bridgend)

Back To The Past

Times are hard, money is tight
The credit crunch is a daily plight
Oil and gas have got such a rise
The price of food has reached the skies
Everyone is trying their best to make do
Wondering how they will ever get through
The best advice is to tighten our belt
And keep an eye on the pensioner who might need our help.

Siobhan McHugh (Strabane)

Colleen By The Shore

I saw her on the sandy strand
Her copper tresses flowing,
Blowing in the gentle breeze.
Slim of hip and breast, she
Gazed enraptured at the sea
As I whispered my quiet hello
Then she turned without a word
Clad in dress of a different age.

Her eyes shone like emeralds
Her face like a pale, white rose
Reddened with a flush of youth
Of some hidden secret thought.
She spoke not, silently floating
Past a silent and unseeing me;
And it all seemed truly natural
Wi' seabirds calling out to sea.

I never saw her again in spite
O' revisiting that blessed shore.
Local legend told of her tragedy;
Fionnuolla, losing her sailor love
In a stormy, tempest-tossed sea.
That Colleen's not of our world
A Sidhe* from the *far other side*
Mourning her spouse, ne'er to be!

(Sad tale of the supernatural)*

R Deen (Ayr)

Scotland

I sit in the garden, drawing flowers so beautiful
Some of which are quite delightful
Sit back, relax and watch the clouds go by
Listen to the wind as I look up at the sky
Pitter-patter goes the rain
I run to my umbrella, the rain is on again
Why how lucky am I to sit out in the open side
That's why this country gives me lots of pride.

Jenny Tolland (11) (Glasgow)

The Plea Of The Oak Tree

Bird, perch on me.
I love the feel
Of the softness
Of your plumage.
I love your song.
Please bird, sing me a song.

Build your nest
And raise your brood.
Let your children
Eat all the worms
Infecting me
And let my leaves breathe again.

I would welcome
The tingling tongue
From the sharp beak
Of the gleaming
Green woodpecker
Penetrating and preening my bark.

Squirrel arrive.
Take my acorns
To store away
Under the ground.
Help my saplings
To grow to trees
To do my part to green the world.

Laura P Williams (Wrexham)

Gethsemane

Rests He, my Lord, in yonder garden cool,
On His dear hands, the marks of bitter shame,
Hushed is the voice, in accents sweet, that oh, so gently, called my name.

Rest now, sweet Saviour, till the daylight comes,
Creeping unbidden, from out eastern skies,
As if loathe to disturb, the holy calm,

Of that blest spot, where my Redeemer lies.

Sheila St Clair (Lisburn)

Death Certificate

(Dedicated to Dr Michael Lagen from Oakley Health Surgery)

'It's just a formality, what's your name?'

Will after Dad's death, anything be the same?

'Elizabeth, Elizabeth Scott!'
I feel a blush burning hot.
'Your address is different from here?'
'Oh yes, yes,' and suddenly I feel instant fear
'26 Carlyle Street.'
'Thanks, I need that for the death certificate.'
he said in an accent delicate!
'I am Dr Michael Laggen from the Oakley Surgery,
pleased to meet you.'

He sounds true,
not false I hope
as I grope
for the final syllable
'Death certificate'
'Death'
as in his last breath
in this world
as we know
to grow old
is to grow bold
and cold in the grave.

Elizabeth-Phillips-Scott (Dunfermline)

Down On The Farm

Big brother Tam works hard on the farm -
He's his father's right-hand man.
Wee brother Bob's a lazy slob
Who will do as little as he can.

One day wee brother requests his father,
'I want my share of the cash.'
His father complies, heaving big sighs,
And Bob goes off with his stash.

He throws lots of parties and think he's so smart, he's
Got lots of cool friends for a while.
But when it's all spent, he starts to repent
And gone is his confident smile.

His diet is drugs and sawdust and slugs,
His debts have brought wolves to the door.
He hits rock bottom - 'My life has gone rotten' -
And slumps on the stone-cold floor.

He comes to his senses and slowly remembers
The warmth of his family and bed.
'I'll work for my keep, I'll get a good sleep,
I'd feel lucky to live in the shed.'

At last he returns with the jitters, and squirms
As he thinks how he's going to lose face.
He creeps back to his dad, who sprints out to his lad,
And they find the true meaning of grace.

Lynda Samuel (Dundee)

Over Love

The too-green newness of the tendrilled beech
Twists in my heart a pain beyond relief:
I want to but I cannot weep.

The too-white snowness of the burdened gean
Fills up my flowing heart above its lip of peace:
I want to but I will not weep.

The too-soft sleekness of my horse's tingling skin
Shocks through my hand to heart with piercing glad release:
I want to and I warmly weep.

Joy Carruthers (Dumfries)

October's Magic

What a magical October
All bathed in Heaven's glorious sun!
Autumn time is full upon us,
And leaves are falling one by one.

Trees are dressed in autumn's fashion,
Orange, gold and russet browns.
Purples, pinks and mellow yellows
And varied greens are still abound!

Flowers show a second bloom now,
They think summer's not quite o'er!
In the garden and the hedgerows,
Colour lingers evermore!

Cattle still are gently grazing,
In a meadow that shows all green!
Bees and butterflies still linger
And autumn sun still lends soft beam.

Though the wind came once quite bitter,
And a shower of rain did fall.
October came in glorious raiment,
Proving pleasures over all!

Gold and silver came the sunrise,
And sunsets brought their splendid hues!
October's warmth brought thoughts to carry,
To winter's dark invading tune.

Shirley Prosser (Ammanford)

Delilah

I'd love to stand over your shoulder
Watch you chat on your computer
As you wait for the one you called best friend
To sign in and say hello again.

I bet you wonder where she's gone
Three days, she's never gone that long
I wonder what thoughts run through your head
Was it something that you said?

Back you go, back a few days
To the Cardiff Arms, France playing Wales
To a noisy pub full of music and song
When in a second a perfect day all went wrong.

Because when you kissed her you made her feel
That from you was love and it was real
But as we all sang Delilah it was then you confessed
It was all a joke you had someone else

Didn't occur to you did it? She loved you back
The strength it took to stay the rest of the match
As you laughed and told her no getting together
You didn't want her, not now, not ever.

I smile to myself as you sit and wait
Soon you will know that it's too late
The games you play, you play too much
So goodbye best friend, you're kicked into touch!

Carol Ann Lewis (Cwmbran)

Normandy Hymn

When bombs and shells were bursting
And ships on billows roll
A skylark was ascending -
God still was in control

And on the hillside yonder
A cow was chewing its cud
Oblivious of the comrades
That wriggled in the mud

Let's not forget our comrades
Enduring bitter pain
Who waded in so valiant
Did not return again

How calm today the Beaches
Where once the bullets flew
And Caen was dark with fighting -
The sky is peaceful blue

Oh give us faith and wisdom,
To life a sweeter taste
And teach reluctant nations
That war is still a waste.

And from thy heavenly splendour
Let war and hatred cease
With love and fervent praying
That lead to lasting peace.

J T Roberts (RN) - Isfron (Anglesey)

The Credit Crunch

Just a reminder we're in a credit crunch -
Enjoy breakfast and tea, but skip your lunch
Except maybe on Sundays, a day for get-togethers
When friends meet up and exchange cheery blethers.

But there's not much cheer we can debate
For the country's in a very bad state
Don't enter a shop to buy a cone -
Remember it costs more to get a loan.

This terrible credit crunch will affect us all
Whether you're eight or eighty, short or tall
For everyone spends money on something or other
And can't keep returning for more to mother.

If you're hungry when it's time for lunch
Just take two bites of your 'credit crunch!'
'Not very appetising,' I can hear you say
But there's not an alternative without more pay.

After chewing your 'credit crunch' digest some Rennies,
Maybe you can't afford them without more pennies,
Hopefully we'll have enough to keep us living
But think more about ourselves and less of 'giving'.

This dreadful credit crunch has really just begun,
Many problems will arise before it is done
How long that will be, nobody can foretell
Much depends on prices and other things as well.

Betty Hay (Cupar)

Imm-perfection

I m-m-m-must protest
That your cruel w-w-words 'in jest'
Are nnn-not 'doing your b-b-b-best'
To help mmmm-me.

You are sup-posed to be my f-f-f-friend
Cooo-ould you j-just end
This mikey-taking trend
'Cause it's dri-iving me round the b-bend

M-m-my speech im-pediment, since a child
Of-ften had me riled
Frustrated, mmm-mad, wild
'Don't worry, it's only mild'

My m-m-u-mum said I ought
To give m-my words some thought
Bef-f-fore they get caught
And my fresh ph-phrase would rot

Th-these words stuck on m-my tongue
When f-formed, don't sound wrong
They're beautiful; poetic; a s-song
They j-just take *soo* long

So p-p-please, t-try to find
W-w-w-words that are k-k-kind
A-after all, *I* d-don't m-mind
Th-that you, mmm-my love, are b-b-blind

David L McCabe (Stirling)

Pen A Poem - Or Not!

Request to write a poem arrived at my door . . .
I struggled with the words, should it be less or more?
What should I pen? I thought - and thought again
As I lifted up my favourite fountain pen.

The words would hardly flow, wouldn't come into my mind
Searching through my memory, they were really hard to find
Vainly I tried to master rhyming slang
But everything just fled and went out with a bang!

I rubbed my wrists, I did a twist
I wrote words down in a list
But all in vain was what I thought
Words and words that came to nought.

I really need to find a rhyme
Perhaps something about 'lang syne'?
Or memories of childhood play
What is it I want to say?

So here I am ready to quit
Head in hands, I sit and sit
All suggestions seem too tame
No words of flair to gain me fame.

Nevertheless here I stand
This contribution in my hand
No more ideas, not one hint -
Question - will I ever be in print!

Sheila Westwater (Kirkcaldy)

Wales And The Welsh

Land of my Fathers, Land of Song
A place where you surely truly belong.
Being from Wales is a matter of pride
Throughout the world, far and wide.

Daffodil, dragon, 'sospan' and leek
So many emblems to show we're not meek.
Dignity, honour with sense of history
Questioned by others, something of mystery.

Land of mountains with beautiful scenes
Where tow'ring hill tilts and leans
Against the sky sometimes misty-topped
Greenery greener, after rain has stopped.

Welsh rugby team in jerseys red
Excite their fans it must be said.
Strong support international day
To see a win we fervently pray.

Male voice choirs in blazers smart
Sing their chorus with all their heart.
Practise nights to get it right
Perfection achieved, they're out of sight.

The language of Wales can still be heard
A joy to hear the spoken word.
A language of song, a nation of song
And if you are Welsh, you truly belong.

Barbara Leek (Blaenavon)

Friends Like You

When you are feeling lonely
And no one seems to care
The pain you have inside of you
Can be so hard to bear

It's a pain that really hurts you
But it is not sore to touch
And you can't explain just why it is
That your heart can hurt so much

You go into your empty house
And you know there's no one there
Just to tell your troubles to
Or the joys you'd love to share

But sometimes things are not so bad
As you sit there all alone
Just thank the friends who take the time
To call you on the phone

So thank you friends for being there
And for your valued time
By saying you love and care for me
In this lonely life of mine

Now I can feel quite confident
For these words are very true
And I don't have to be alone
When I have friends like you.

Isobel Campbell (Grangemouth)

Thoughts On Mankind

Man's worth is measured not in rank,
Though birthright gives him status,
That precious gift, our God we thank,
For as brothers He did make us.

If only those in higher stance,
Whose names with honours show,
Would cast from mind, the look askance,
For those placed far below.

The common touch to good effect,
With wisdom, sense of guile,
Will gain full measure, deep respect,
From those of rank and file.

If the universal bond of Man,
His words the handclasp seal,
With truth and justice as the plan,
His strength would be as steel.

Enriched this world of ours would be,
If all creeds made such endeavour,
So men of sense and worth decree,
Goodwill and peace forever.

May Man's dominion reign supreme,
Each in his rightful place,
With dignity, regard, esteem,
As brothers of one race.

James McMillan (Aberdeen)

Ashy Pet

She dwelt and she dozed
By the open hearth fire

So near to the ashes she sat;
By the household despised
And rejected they called her
An ashy pet

No beauty of form did she possess
No slick coat her own could she call
Just a skinny and matted-haired kitty
Despised and disdained by all

She purred to the strokes of no gentle hand
Was no bony kitty dear;
We prophesied nothing but uselessness
For the same little kitty, I fear

We boasted at length of her feline friends
With slick coats and bodies fat
But we asked, in dismay
Pray what shall we do with this useless cat?

But she rose in the ranks
In her testing hour
To the highest fame as a cat
For when all sources failed
And when all voices wailed
She killed that long-tailed rat!

Henry E Wilson (Tempo)

Tsunami

Tsunami, tsunami,
What have you done to us?
Taken our land from us
Washed in the deep.

Tsunami, tsunami,
You came a big wave o'er us
Took all our homes from us
Nowhere to sleep.

Tsunami, tsunami,
A terrible sight to us
Swept our loved ones from us
Never to meet.

Tsunami, tsunami,
Our children you snatched from us
Made orphans of some of us
Forever to weep.

Tsunami, tsunami,
All the world prays for us
Sends aid and food for us
Shelter and heat.

Father, our Father,
Give now your love to us
Send our lost ones to us
Comfort our grief.

Joan A Thomas (Swansea)

Little Red Robin

A little robin lands each day
Upon my garden fence
He never says a word to me
Just sings and brings delight

His little breast is rosy-red
His beady eyes are bright
I often sit and wonder
Where he flies to late at night

Some days I feed him crumbs of bread
A little nut or two
A little drink of water
To see his long day through

Then he spreads his tiny wings
And up and flies away
Up and up he flies
Across the clear blue sky

I often stare in awe of him
Such beauty in his flight
Then I saw him wink at me
And fly out of sight

So, I'll have to wait tomorrow
To see my little friend
Where he will bring cheers of joy
Great pleasure and delight.

Stan Corbett (Belfast)

Twenty Years

Twenty years, a long time ago,
For some it might be, for others, no.
Two decades of change, for good or bad,
Time flies, they say, let's not be sad.

The rock scene then was not the one I knew,
Twenty years before and even more.
The eighties, spiky hair and punk, cool dude,
Long, curly hair and laidback attitude.

Bon Jovi, Adam Ant, Take That and Sting,
Are still around, doing their thing.
Some gone, never to be seen again,
But in the mind of some, will always remain.

Nineties - politics and power dressing,
Shoulder pads a la mode de Dynasty.
I've seen it all with my own eyes -
And seen it through my own kids' lives.

Look at the noughties, up to now:
What will be remembered and how?
Too soon to know, too close to tell,
Will it be Heaven or a little Hell?

Good luck to Forward Press,
May they find a niche
In the market for poems,
I wish them all success!

Muriel Hughes (Llanrhystud)

Peace

Peace the ultimate goal
Will I see it in my lifetime
Will the bell of freedom toll
Will the bells of harmony chime?

When will eyes be opened
To suffering and pain
When will war and conflict end
When will victims smile again?

Hate is like a cancer
That eats through to the core
But fighting is not the answer
We need to find a cure

The more we seek solutions
The less progress we make
It's one step forward and two steps back
It seems there is no escape

Why can't we live together
In peace and harmony
And rid this world forever
Of wars and hostility?

Somewhere there is someone greater
And we are here to do His will
In the words of our creator
Who says thou shalt not kill.

Decima Haughton-Watkins (Barry)

Follower Of Fashion (Scottish Version)

Oor Zoe's goin' 'out to party'
Ah 'm sure that's whit she said
It's nearly hauf past ten at night
When maist folk get ready fer bed.

Ah eyed up whit she's nearly wearin'
You could see she's nae taste in clothes
Her hair is three different colours
An' she's had a ring pierced through her nose

Her shoes look like winkle pickers
(She'll no' hae them oan fer long)
Ah thought she'd forgotten her knickers
But she said, 'I'm wearin' a thong'

Ah hinted her top could be longer
As her midriff hung o'er in layers
She just threw me a look of disgust
And her purple lips answered, 'Who cares?'

She then clambered intae a taxi
But as she wis wavin' ta ta
Her boobs got tangled wi' her seat belt
And fell oot o' her new low cut bra

Ah jist shook ma heid an' muttered
'Ah must be gettin' auld
If ah wis tae venture oot like that
Ah wid sure catch ma death o' cauld.'

Jenny Brown (Isle of Bute)

Sounds That Fill The Air

Trains shunting, over railway points,
Gentle rain, tapping on the windowpane,
Waves lapping over shingly shores,
Kittens purring softly at my door.

The cuckoo, calling from a distance,
Migrating birds, singing on the wing,
Same joyous chorus they will sing,
When they return again in spring.

Harmony of sound in rhyming verses,
The written word excite the senses,
The breaking of the Eucharistic Bread
Alerts the mind, to what's being said.

If we listen and receive,
The inner senses stir . . .
They tug at the heart strings
And touch the very soul.

How can I compare -
Sounds that fill the air?
With mystic words that touch the heart
Ignite . . . and set the soul alight!

Perfection, we shall never know,
Till we, from Earth, to Heaven go,
Where souls unite in perfect bliss
And nothing else - but peace and love exist.

Marion de Bruyn (Buckley)

Turn Back The Clock

Turn back the clock
and let me enjoy
the pleasures and pastimes
I knew as a boy.

Let me once more
be unheeding of care;
of the troubles ahead
in life unaware.

Carry me there
on time's backward flight,
again let me taste
each youthful delight.

Give me that innocence
before I grew wise
and looked at the world
through cynical eyes.

Too soon it was past
that transient phase,
that brief episode
of halcyon days

Alas, memory's road
is where I must walk,
for no one can ever
turn back the clock.

Arnold O'Hara (Ayr)

Remembrance Of A Garden

When Kipling wrote of the garden of England that was fair,
We know that he was writing of the things when he was there,
But would he know that garden now that time has passed away?
And if he came to see it, would he wish to stop and stay?

For his Britain it has faded, it will never be no more,
For men do not go weeding in the borders, as of yore,
They only think about themselves, they only want what's theirs,
They never think of others, of their trouble and their cares.

They cheer so for the battle, they clamber for the blood,
The simple pleasures have all gone, as if hit by a massive flood,
They do not have the time to see, the beauty everywhere,
They are too busy with themselves, to even stop and stare.

But I believe that he was right, and always may it be,
For unless we look for beauty, how can we be free?
How can we keep the garden blooming for all time,
If all we want is always labeled, mine, mine, mine.

I know his Britain it has gone, it has all passed away,
But do we really want these things, that have come to stay?
The hatred and the violence, and our very spiteful ways,
Do we want these to be remembered, after our days?

It would be much kinder and much better I am sure,
If we could settle everything, and try to find a cure.
And look again for this garden, the one he said would never die,
If only for his memory, we must at least try.

Penlee A Sowerby (Bridgend)

Olden Days

I remember when I was young
I played all day and had lots of fun
I'm older now, don't know the craze
My granddaughter calls them 'The Olden Days'.

We had no McDonald's or Burger King
My meals were cooked on a small gas ring.
We didn't starve, we had good meat
Though Mum was often rushed off her feet.

We'd run inside with a great big beam
And shout, 'Mum, that's the man who sells ice cream!'
We'd get a threepence, give the dog a pat,
Then run and buy a pokey-hat.

We played with prams and dollies
And sometimes kites that flew
What a difference nowadays
I might have a PS2.

The latest fad's organic now
And everything's a risk
Do you write it on the calendar?
No! It's all on compact disc.

For everything's computerised
Our era they amaze
Sometimes it seems when I look back
They were 'The Good Old Olden Days'.

Elizabeth McKinlay (Perth)

Christmas Time In Aberdeen

This time of year has come again, snow lying on the ground,
And all the homesick people, they are homeward-bound.
When you walk down the streets here, you'll know what I mean,
'Cause that's what it's like here, at Christmas time in Aberdeen.

Through the streets of the city, bright lights are aglow,
All different colours, seem to brighten up the snow.
To all the younger children here, it seems like a dream,
When they see the sights, at Christmas time in Aberdeen.

The older people wonder and remember the past,
When they were youngsters amid winter's cold blast.
When they came here with their parents, so long ago it seems,
When they spent a day at Christmas time in Aberdeen.

There's fairies on treetops, on the evergreen trees,
Covered with presents a-swaying in the breeze.
Snowflakes a-falling, and the air seems so clean,
There's just no mistaking Christmas time in Aberdeen.

There's choirs singing to all, locals or strangers,
Of God and of Jesus, who was born in a manger.
They sang of far countries where grass is never green,
We hear all those stories at Christmas time in Aberdeen.

Now that winter is over, no more snow to be found,
Christmas has passed again and we walk on fresh ground.
But we'll still remember it wasn't all a dream,
And I'll return again, at Christmas time in Aberdeen.

Eddie Mathieson (Aberdeen)

Birthright

I shed a tear today
As life was changing all around
A fragile shell an empty nest
A silent whisper not a sound

Reflections in a looking glass
A pool of silence rippling clear
The waves of time that ebb and flow
A gathering whirlpool laced with fears

A steady drip, a subtle drop
My heart an island lonely cold
Rippling waters yearning loss
Passions ready to unfold

Thunderous turmoil crashing waves
Windswept torrents gathering storm
Adolescent lightning strikes
And from a boy a man is born

One more time I reach to hold
The cord that binds him close to me
But recognise the time has come
To fly the nest . . . I set him free

I shed a tear today
A tear of glowing pride and joy
His birthright to become a man
Has finally released the boy.

Donna Milne-Sator (Blairgowrie)

Reflections

He sat amongst the heather
No person saw him there,
In the twilight of early evening
Amongst the scented hawthorn air

He looked down on all he owned
He surveyed each cranny and every nook
And somewhere high above him
He swore he could hear the cry of a rook

This was all he ever dreamed of
This was his hard work, his whole life
And in that sleepy hollow below him
In that stone-clad house, lived his family, his wife

He wasn't ready yet to surrender
He could fight, but surely not on this,
There was still a lot yet to do
And too much happening for him to miss

So, he rubbed a calloused hand
Against a weathered cheek,
Feeling the roughness of his stubble
He hadn't time to shave this week

He reluctantly called to his companion
'Gyp, we had better get these sheep down this hill,'
Decisions still have yet to be made
But the farm was for now, his still.

Deborah Strain (Newry)

Good Lad Les

By 'eck! 'e were great were Les Dawson
Though dumpy - and not very tall
I loved 'im as 'Ada and Cissie'
With Roy Barraclough, bosoms an' all!

And old Les - when 'e played the pianner
So serious, and all out of tune
Then t'pianner 'ud break up in pieces
And 'im still sat there like a loon!

Then on Blankety Blank as quizmaster
The expressions 'e pulled - what a case!
You'd 'ave thought 'e were india-rubber
The things 'e could do with 'is face!

And the time when 'e brought on them dancers
'Roly Polys' - an 'e picked the name!
Who but Les would 'ave thought t' load o' fatties
Could 'ave come to such fortune and fame?

That gravelly voice - can you 'ear it?
The lugubrious way that he'd tell
His really fantastical stories -
And you'd almost believe 'im as well!

Ay! I miss 'im - I reckon we all do
But in Heaven I'll bet they're right glad!
We can all use a laugh and a chuckle
And they'll get 'em up there - with that lad!

Olive Sweetman (Mold)

The Hills Of Gwent

I love to walk these hills of Gwent,
To gaze at views from Heaven sent,
Follow ancient tracks, where man has trod,
To feel at peace, as if touched by God.

To see small streams, soon to rivers grow,
The heathers when their flowers show,
To see young lambs, to their mothers cling,
To hear the cuckoo call in spring.

To see pony trekkers, on their rides,
The birds above, in majestic glides,
To see the fox, shyly run away,
The squirrels in the trees at play.

To see planted forest, so tall and grand,
Old stone walls, on the skyline stand,
To see old towns, so far below,
The river through the valley flow.

No modern ways, on these hills to find,
Just beauty, grace and peace of mind,
A tranquillity, that's beyond belief,
Not to be found, in the world beneath.

No craving I, for foreign lands,
For palm trees, sun and golden sands,
Great cities, they are not for me,
These hills are all I wish to see.

Dennis Broome (Pontypool)

God's Waiting Room

I'm in God's waiting room,
Not ready to depart,
I'm fully 'Compos Mentis'
And I have a healthy heart.

But all my limbs are useless,
I need help to dress and feed,
But being in the waiting room,
I get all the help I need.

But being in the waiting room,
I get lots of time for thought,
Of places that I've visited,
Of routes that I have walked.

But now what can I do?
I can only sit and think,
Can I do creative writing?
No, that's not the missing link.

Perhaps poetry is the answer,
I've already written some,
These previous lines are an example,
Perhaps more will come.

But being in the waiting room,
I know that He is with me,
I will always trust Him
And know that He will guide me.

Alan Beer (Newport)

Our Village

The village clings to the mountain base
And the roads are very quiet.
The high street was a busy place,
Only two shops remain.

The houses look a little sad,
Many are up for sale.
Young people go away to work,
Most will not return.

Two open cast mines operate,
Once many pits were working.
Mountainsides devoid of trees,
Huge holes defile the vista.

No sheep wander in peaceful flocks,
Wildlife has disappeared.
We're barred from all our usual walks,
No one allowed up there.

There's going to be a wind farm
On top of Maesgwyn Cap.
Will Craig-y-Llyn be next?
Strong winds gust up there.

Cwmgwrach means Valley of the Witch,
Some say she's only sleeping.
I hope she wakes before too long,
Or her valley will be no more.

J H Jenkins (Cwmgwrach)

A Nice Cup Of Tea

The alarm clock shrills warning to sleepers so sound,
That morning will bring us a fresh daily round,
But how we can face it, I just cannot see,
Without the delights of a nice cup of tea.

We arrive at the office at nine on the dot,
And on goes the kettle to get nice and hot,
Who knows what a horror the morning will be,
Without the delights of a nice cup of tea.

Again at eleven, we're gasping once more,
If we don't brew it soon we'll be down on the floor,
The office routine will be just 'all at sea',
Without the delights of a nice cup of tea.

We go out to lunch when the clock reaches one,
The menu has everything under the sun,
But to finish it off, where would it be
Without the delights of a nice cup of tea.

At six we lock up and join in the crush,
Of workers bound homeward, and all in a rush,
To enjoy their night's leisure, cos where would they be,
Without the delights of a nice cup of tea.

So bedtime at last, and another day gone,
Time for a nightcap, we've got to have one,
So on goes the kettle; we'd never sleep free,
Without the delights of a nice cup of tea.

G K (Bill) Baker (Swansea)

33 Whitelaw Avenue

Whitelaw Avenue, our street and home on a December evening,
Outside the rain is shedding towards the east, with wind heavy-breathing,
Storm clouds jostling in a hurry to hide the stars and moon,
And we, content, quietly absorb the comfort of our room.

The warm closed curtains engulf us from the street outside,
To reminisce, or use our leisure hours as we decide.
Converse about the happenings of the work-a-day or even 'view',
And other's troubles, from a fireside chair - can they be really true?

Meandering to the window, adjusting a curtain to scan the outside scene,
All is still except the dancing lights that on the wet road gleam.
An unlatched garden gate swings unconcerned, even without a creak,
Nearby stands the sandstone manse in time before the street.

Through dreaming eyes a horrible fantasy usurps the normal fashion,
Determined noisy traffic crashes by, unbroken, like a giant python.
Smashed boarded windows, damaged gardens, the vandal's senseless act,
The swears and yells rival gangs meet on an ugly impact.

Demolished homes blazing fearfully, young soldiers on a confusing task,
Brave firemen rushing to still another concealed bomb blast.
The curtain quickly closed to obliterate the nightmarish sight,
And hope for all the others with their respective plight.

This peaceful silence - a precious gift that Man should ever treasure,
The symbolic garden gate swinging slowly at its leisure.
The rain now fresh and beautiful, the black clouds a delight,
And thankful for our home and street on this December night.

W Macdonald (Coatbridge)

Wee Hamish

A huv a wee West Highland terrier
Caud Hamish he's sae cute
Wears a bell aroon his collar
So you kin tell when he's aboot.

He wears a braw red tartan kilt
Brass buttoned jaicket tae
Walks fir miles aroon the glens
An up an doon the braes

Hamish disnae like the vet
Since he wis seen tae doon below
Bit it hasnae cooled his ardour
Wi the cat still has a go

Yin day the vet clipped too faur doon
Whin his wee claws wir done
Per Hamish let oot sitch a howl
An nipped him oan the bum.

He kens every word a say
An whin I'm sad he licks ma tears
There's no a dug quite like him
An I've had him many years

He looks like Greyfriars Boaby
Hus a cute wee cheeky smile
A Jist think the world o' Hamish
He make ma life worthwhile.

Marilyn Graham (Glasgow)

The Fly

I watched a fly in crazy flight
Around my room - oh, such a sight.
Climbing! Darting! Why all this?
Has his steering gear gone amiss?

Forward, round and back he jayed,
He didn't want my place in bed.
For never once did he come down
To rest a wing on my eiderdown.

I kept on watching with keener glance
Until my eyes did smart and dance.
A teeny-weeny creature he
But much more active than mighty me.

I wondered, was he watching me?
And if he was, what did he see?
Six feet of laziness still in bed
I'll swear here's what the creature said:

'It's twelve o'clock, 'pyjama clothes'
You're still in bed - one thing fly loathes.
If I were wasp or even bee
I'd rise you quick, my boy, you'd see.'

I got up then and still I mused
For out of my window the messenger cruised.
He'd done his job - the message made known
And before I could thank him, the fly had flown!

Andrew Cardwell (Belfast)

A Mother's Prayer

She sits by the fireside and rocks in her chair
She knows all too well that there's no one else there
Yet she speaks in quiet reverence and smiles now and then
As she whispers their names again and again

She looks towards Heaven and her voice becomes strong
It's me again, Lord, I won't keep you long
I know there are others who are much more in need
But I know if I ask, to my prayers, You'll take heed

Please tell my loved ones who are up there with you
That by Your hallowed grace I may fly up there too
Let them know how I miss them and long for the day
When we're all there together and forever can stay

Lord, you know I get lonely, as I wait for my call
Please let it be soon, I'm prepared, after all
I haven't been perfect, but You know how I've tried
For You've been my companion since my dear family died

I used to ask why they were taken from me
But the reason is clear, You explained it to me
You required special someones to sit by Your throne
So I don't really mind, all this waiting alone

Well, Lord, I must stop now, I'm asking too much
There are others like me, who wait Your sweet touch
So, if my life should ebb when tonight I'm asleep
Then just like my loved ones, my soul safely keep.

Mant Smith (Bushmills)

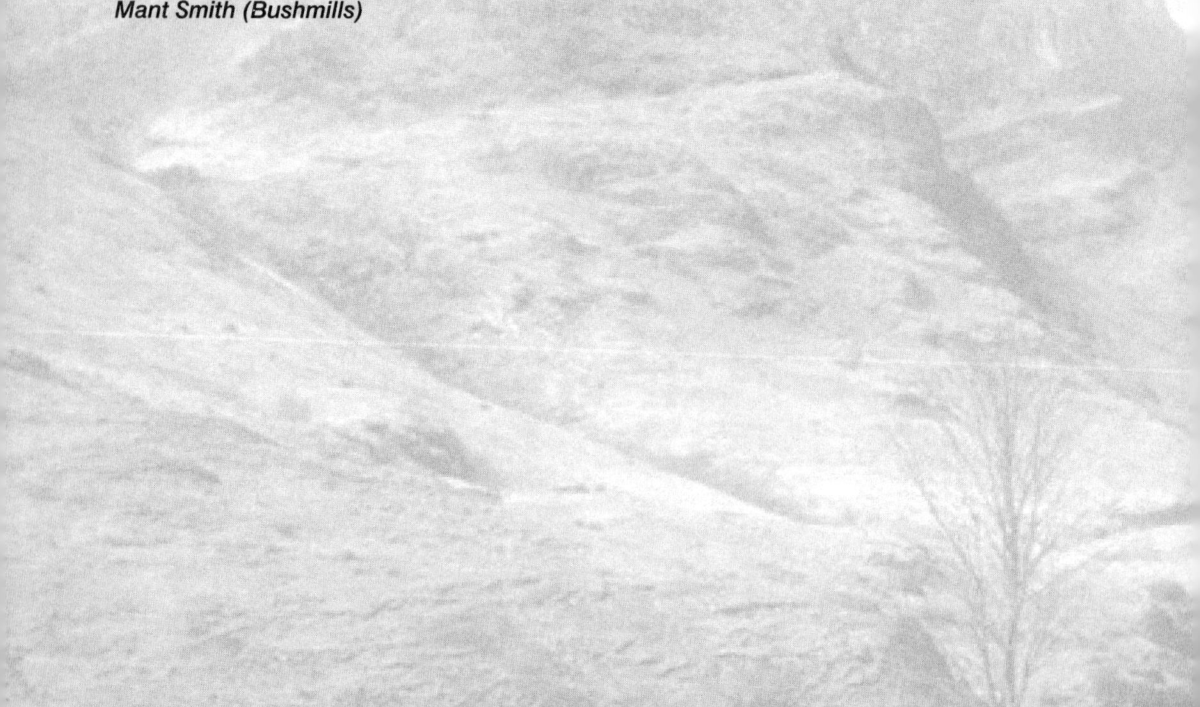

My City, My Home

I fill up my lungs with your salty air,
I feel the wind whipping around my hair,
I drink in the smells and sounds all around,
Nowhere else in this world is a replica found.

Your mists on the river, sometimes blanket my sight,
But your essence remains, and try as I might,
I can never forget the feelings of home,
And remember you fondly when thinking alone.

The music, the history, the laughs and the fun,
The people, the football, the passions all run,
Through the veins of your children, wherever they go,
It remains with them always, till the end of its flow.

Humour you give to each one of your kin,
And we use it so we can kick life in the shin,
We try to stay positive, never too down,
In the face of adversity, we'll act the clown.

Some say that we're hard; I don't see it that way,
We have pride and have substance, that's how we'll stay,
I'll never be reticent, but proud to tell all,
That I am a 'scouser' and always walk tall.

So I'll finish my poem with passion inside,
And dedicate this to all Merseyside,
I'll always love Liverpool, you were my home,
And I'll never forget 'You'll never walk alone'.

Gaynor Latham-Chadwick (Wrexham)

I Am The Way

You cannot get to Heaven
By the works of Thine own hand,
Nor any other way
That you have personally planned.

The good works that you do
The love that you may share,
Commendable tho' they are
Will not get you there.

You may be honest and kind
Go to church, worship, pray,
Be generous to all you meet
And the Lord's commandments keep.

But unless you call on the Saviour
God's only begotten Son,
Who died and rose again
Your pardon will never be won.

Jesus said, 'I am the Way
If you surrender to me,
I will take you to the Father
And He will set you free.'

Free to receive salvation
Thro' God's redeeming love
And an assurance of Eternal Life
In Your heavenly home above.

Len Croker (Newport)

Early Spring By The River Foyle

I leant upon the rough brown fence
Beside the river's wide expanse.
A lonely fishing cormorant,
Before he dived, eyed me askance.

The water closed above his tail,
Then smoothed to glassy grey afresh.
Small birds' desultory chirps were calm
The land with winter still immeshed.

This tranquil new spring day was cold.
Brief slants of sun gave feeble heat.
The modest snowdrops, faded now,
Had wanly braved the storm's chill beat.

A rippling stream the peace enhanced
With varied gurgles, plops and swirls.
Sleek mini-falls slid over stones
And round the shallows' edge unfurled.

Small lanterns, white, pale pink and red,
From flowering-currant hung serene,
Unfolding buds were greening forth.
Gold alder dangling tassels gleamed.

The willows' silvery catkin-show
Softly supplanted hailstones harsh.
Both hope and sadness touched my heart,
To see time's changes on the march.

Joan-Pamela Moore (Londonderry)

'Aul Drumragh Graveyard

The scent of peculiar eerie perfumes,
Fervent odours of untold mystery,
Ancestors resting o'er six hundred years,
Their underground world seeping in history.

The ageless goat still minds the gate,
'Aul Drumragh Graveyard's royal guard,
Paying his respects in the wake of the famine,
Consoling the ghosts of the fatally scarred.

Nature is ripe, green over black,
Weltering bushes wither and weep,
Though the bubbling gush of the neighbouring river,
Tries to disturb the perpetual sleep.

Auntie Maple spreads her feathers,
Mothering the headstones crippled with rust
And Grandfather Ash, a stark reminder,
Of life and fire; return to dust.

Huddled in the corner, a quaint, crumbling chapel,
Weary from centuries of intensive prayers,
But it's lost its roof, this humble building,
Easier to access to the man upstairs.

They're lonely footsteps that tread this turf,
Forgotten faces lost to the past,
Magnetic charm dissolved in peace,
So long as eternity continues to last.

Declan Gerard Mullan (Omagh)

The Christmas Bloomer

The silly season's here again
And as obedient serf I go
To do my Christmas shopping
At 'Marks', 'Asda' and 'The Co'.

Now will my choice of purchases
Fuel pleasure and delight?
Or will they end up in the bin
At some deadly hour of night?

Obedient serfs are everywhere
By the barrow-load and the dozen,
With the 'Pound Shop' high upon their list
For some long-forgotten cousin.

Some gifts 'twould seem are to no one's taste
Received, rewrapped, passed-on.
A few years further down the line
Your old gifts return to you anon.

Ere long the 'thank you' cards appear
Some lying through their teeth.
The antiquated gift you sent -
The recipient might to you bequeath.

So match your prezzies carefully
And don't rely on rumour
Or very quickly you will find
That you've sent 'The Christmas Bloomer!'

Eileen Mulhollands (Johnstone)

The Blush

The blush betrayed you
It gave away your thoughts
And lowered your eyes
In sudden self-awareness.

Where you were cast in bronze
Your flesh has filled with softness
And stood you all too human -
Perhaps even for your own liking.

Your milkiness exposes
The colours that burn within
And like the heartburn of morning -
An apple-red blanched your cheek.

Those ocean eyes that fain a chill
Each time they chance a glance -
Their new and bashful setting
Strikes them all the bluer -

Like ringing bells
That would withhold their toll
But cannot calm this dancing man
A-tug upon their ropes.

And so you mellow
Like a hush,
A knowing whisper in the clearing,
A pause in all eternity.

Noel Martin Hanna (Newry)

The Flowers and Their Petals

See the daisy, its petals are tidied and formed,
But it's a small flower with little perfume adorned.
Unlike the rose that's fragrantly pretty and sweet,
The buds and the petals perfectly made and neat.

Like the tulips and foxgloves shaped like cups,
Some of these flowers are standing right up.
Unlike the nettles with its thorns that prick,
With our bad sins we should change them quick.

Then there's the buttercups, yellow and bright,
To remind us of Jesus who died for our plight.
Unlike the rose that's as red as Jesus' blood,
Running down Calvary's Hill all in the mud.

Then comes the thistles and barbed thorns,
Showing Jesus' body torn and forlorn.
Unlike the rose leaves that drop when dead,
Jesus has risen, our beloved King's head.

Then comes the remnants of all the dead flowers,
Jesus is alive showing us His mighty power.
With all of His love over us He showers,
Holding us securely within His Holy towers.

So when you see the flowers so pretty and sweet,
Let it remind you of Jesus whom you will meet.
You can see the nail prints in His hands and feet,
Your life given to Him you then become complete.

J R McCradie (Cardiff)

Young And Free In Gortnalee

I look at the house where I was born
A little house in Gortnalee,
Memories come flooding back
Of the happy child in me.

A little river, like a lazy snake
Meanders past the farm,
It was like Heaven to me
With its mystery and charm.

We couldn't wait for summer
To remove our worn shoes
And plough the river, end to end
The joy, I'll never lose.

We looked for fairies in the hedge
We knew they were hiding there,
We had to keep our eyes on them
They're gone, if you don't stare.

We carved our names on fir trees
Years later returned to see,
But the trees had died and gone
Our names died like the tree.

In autumn, when the hazelnuts were ripe
We climbed the trees with glee,
We tore our clothes and gathered nuts
'Twas great to be young and free.

Kathleen McManus (Enniskillen)

Starlore

Sages deep in starlore
Say there's life out there,
Primitive, definitive -
Does anybody care?

Fossils tombed in space rock
Soulless science loves -
Have they half the interest
Of what breathes and moves?

Sterile arid moonscapes -
How could they surpass
Snow-slopes of December,
Fields of summer grass?

Dreams of zooming sunwards
Some cosmonauts delight;
Oh, give me dusk and noonday
Not dawnless stellar night!

Cease hubristic probings,
Moondust's hueless stuff,
Leave the stars their secrets,
For me green Earth's enough.

Cold facts for me are often
Far better left untold.
Oh, leave me stars of silver,
Oh, leave me suns of gold!

E Margaret Kidd (Peebles)

Getting Old

I'm getting old
It's plain to see
And when I look down
Is that really me?

My beautiful feet
Once truly adorned
Now have bunions
And big corns

My legs that once carried me
Up and down hills
Are only surviving
Because I take pills

My curvaceous body
Always caught the boys' eyes
It's now twice as big
From eating those pies

My arms that once held you
So close and so tight
Are helping me feel
To the toilet at night

Yes I'm getting old
There is no doubt
But I still have my memories
And they will see me out.

Marie Grieve (Leven)

Mamma's Garden

There's a little piece of garden
Just outside our home,
A green old wooden fence around
Where Mamma used to roam.

Now and then the Lord would help
With sunshine from above,
And Mamma's sweet and gentle touch
Was pure and simple love.

It's Mamma's piece of Heaven
Just outside the door,
Her pretty flower garden
That measures 10 by 4.

Each day she'd take a walk around
She'd turn and go again,
And when the ground was really dry
The Lord would give it rain.

One day my Mamma passed away
Ours not to reason why,
Maybe the Lord just needed help
With his garden in the sky.

So when you walk out supper time
Remember to look high,
Those little white things twinkling
Are Mamma's daisies in the sky.

Carol Nicholas (Llanelli)

The Changing World

Sandy beaches and sparkling water,
A countryside once green and fresh,
The sound of children, laughing, playing
Has faded now, to emptiness.

The ferryboat that crossed the river
Sits derelict and left to rot,
It rolls and rocks against the pier,
Passengers forgotten - going nowhere.

Above a concrete bridge with cars
That glint in sunshine, fills the eye,
Stretched right across the sun-kissed water
We see commuters flashing by.

Out from the shore are oil-filled tankers
Waiting to discharge their spoil,
Refineries beckon in the distance,
Hungry to receive their oil.

Large towers and stacks stretch on the skyline
Smoke belching out, consuming sky,
The azure eaten up by grey dust,
Another blemish to shock the eye.

Progress makes us feign acceptance,
Inside we hanker for the past,
When life meandered by so slowly
And dreams, gold-tinted, failed to last.

Janet Llewellyn (Haverfordwest)

We Play The Game

(Dedicated to the 2008 Grand Slam winners, Wales)

We play the game
Rugby be its name
We went to Twickers
And showed them how to win the game.

Then came our second test
Where the Scots came to see us, they saw that we were the best
As we sent them home on a stagecoach bus.

Then came Italy
All dressed in blue,
They thought their defence was strong
But boy they were easy to get through.

Then came the Irish
They thought it would be a stroll,
But we left them with nothing but a frown
Because Wales won the triple crown
And now the Irish coach is on the dole.

It's only Wales
They did say,
But on that fateful day
The French saw that we were the best
As Wales won the Grand Slam test.

Tidy dance.

Chris T Barber (Cwmbran)

The Nightingale That Doesn't Want To Sing

This Nightingale can't sing
- Although she's good at almost everything.
Don't ask this Nightingale to sing,
Yes, this is typical of June.
Yet, she's got a dulcet speaking voice.
As for singing, she's got no choice.
I would have to give her that advice.
Yet I would have her as a wife.
But this Lady is taken -
My heart is mistaken;
To fall for this Lady.
I met her years before -
I think she thought me as a bore.
She adopted me as a 'brother'
Because I felt for another.
The wrong girl I picked
My feelings for June were mixed.
I made her laugh when I was embarrassed.
She made me feel harassed.
So her, I did reject.
She is always on my mind.
June is unique, one of a kind.
I can't get her out of my mind.

Peter Goodall (Newtownabbey)

Melsetter

We are going to Melsetter!
Can't think of anything better.
To feel the sand beneath our feet,
Torness and Lochen among the peat.
Ha Wick Bay is curving wide,
The Berry from the other side.
To see the bonxies soar over the fell,
Perhaps watch the seals leap into the swell.
Can't think of anything better,
Than going to Melsetter.

Frank Strudwick (Orkney)

Fields Of Gold

Lincolnshire - county of wide, open spaces
Far from the crowds - brings a smile to our faces
Acres of fields seem to reach the sky
A patchwork of colours that pleases the eye
Down on the coast where the land meets the sea
'Skeggy' and 'Mabo' are the places to be
As per the fisherman - Skegness is jolly
But the weather is fittle - so remember your brolly!
There's row after row of colourful flowers -
Where we've strolled free of cares for hours and hours.
Mablethorpe's quaint - Blackpool it ain't!
But a nice bacon sandwich and large mug of tea -
Make it the more attractive to me!
Sutton on Sea is a nice place to be -
Its beaches are fine and the air is like wine
Not much here changes with the passage of time.
You could even think that time had stood still -
Especially at Alford as you pass the windmill
Down at East Kirby when they start up the 'Lanc'
We remember brave lads - we owe them our thanks
For they gave their tomorrows to give us today
Lest we forget - our respects we now pay.
When it's time to go home - we shall all miss this place
For we return to the crowds and a much faster pace
We hope to return on one of our trips -
For a big ice cream cone and a nice cod and chips!

G K Raynes (Rhyl)

Nature Reigns Supreme

Do not dress in somber black today
Let bright colours be your farewell gift to me
Nature in all her glory clothes the Earth
She will not dim her beauty at my passing
Lift up your voice in joyous song
Music is a great healer of the soul
Walk again through cool lanes canopied in green
Beside flowing rivers dappled in sunlight
Along the beach the ocean gently lapping the shore
You will not be alone always, I will be there with you.

Anna Murray McDougall (Irvine)

My Scary Pet

I love my dog, I love my cats and my goldfish too
I'm not so sure of how I feel, about my pet called Sue.
She's got eight long, scary legs and is black as black can be
I found her in my bath one night, looking straight at me.
She's not a pet to cuddle, or let crawl all over you
Yet she's happy in her jam jar, my scary pet called Sue
When I watched her in her jam jar, I really felt quite bad
For I'm sure my scary pet called Sue, was looking very sad.
I took her to the garden and left her there to see
If she was happy in her jam jar, or wanted to be free.
So, I went back and had a look after a day or two
And to my absolute surprise, still in the jar was Sue.
I lifted it and shook it, to make sure she wasn't dead
She moved a little, stretched her legs and turned around her head.
I'm sure the look she gave me said - how dare you leave me here!
I really couldn't understand, why she filled me with such fear.
I was being silly, for a little spider does no one any harm
That's how I felt, until with speed, she shot right up my arm!
I screamed, I yelled and waved my arms high up in the air
While I danced about, beat my clothes and shook out all my hair
I shuddered and I shivered and scratched for at least an hour
Then I decided the only answer, was for me to take a shower.
I truly love all wildlife, from tigers to great big snakes
So, why does a tiny spider, give me the quivering shakes?
Alas! 'twas not a happy end to my scary pet called Sue
For I found her poor, squashed body, on the bottom of my shoe!

Billie Mackintosh (Craigavon)

Friendship

Friendship is forever whatever may betide,
Friendship is that comfort forever at your side,
Friendship is the helping hand, the thoughtful sincere prayer,
Friendship is a treasure great, a star beyond compare.
Friendship gives us inner peace, when problems come our way,
Friendship brings us smiling through
As we strive from day to day.
If you find a friendship, guard it, hold it dear,
Then you will find that friendship
Grows stronger year by year.

M Bradley (Bo'ness)

The Spirit Of Love

My heart leaps at the prospect
Of being with the Spirit.
In my imagination, I hurry to that sacred spot.
The leaves are stirring -
I feel unbounded joy.
Underneath the oak trees
I feel safe and I feel love
For creation and God the Creator.
A squirrel, unaware of my presence,
Is sitting on the ground, eating quietly.
Blackbirds are being blackbirds
Fiercely defending their bit of woodland -
Yet their song pierces my heart.
I am moved by such everyday matters.
I so long to capture moments like these
But they somehow elude me.
I will not forget however
And perhaps I am fretting without cause.
He created us to appreciate His joy and deep love.
In His midst my joy excels -
He lifts me and restores my soul
Despite the disappointments and time wasted
In pursuit of the trivial.
When I look up into the deep blue sky
Surely He gives us all room to hope
And an opportunity to love.

Barry Broadmeadow (Colwyn Bay)

A Lazy Day

I wake in the morning and give a sigh,
Wondering what the day will bring,
I look to see a bright blue sky,
And listen while the birdies sing.
Today will be a lazy day,
Just walking through the park,
People are passing by, 'Hello,' they say,
Time goes on, it's almost dark,
I head for home by the light of the moon,
Think I'll have another lazy day soon.

Celia Gray (Alness)

Lion Teeth

Golden vagabond, botanical gypsy
Cast out by society,
Your home is everywhere.
No place for you in
The tapestried flower beds
Of the quality,
Disdained at Chelsea
Even the village church
Cannot welcome you, a peasant
To the highbred exotics
And hothouse aristocrats.
They cannot stand beside you
Whose desert suns fire dead roads
And scorch the grey city.
No ledge too precarious,
Industry does not tame you
Who can punch through tarmac.
You squat in the beds of the
Rich and famous and
Gatecrash garden parties,
You scorn them all.
Not for you those sweet cissy names
You are 'piss the bed',
None can master you
Truly Dandelion you are
The Teeth of the Lion.

Thomas MacCarte (Perth)

You

I keep the silence in, like a zipped-up purse
And open, to hear the echo.
I keep the kisses warm,
Where they are licked and tasted.
I keep our thoughts
In a cobweb of alleyways.
I keep our dreams fresh
As a sea fragrance.
And all the seasons drape and fit,
Because I wear you.

Lucy Paine (Pontypool)

The Ulster Way

It's neither a path, nor is it a track
The 'way' is a circle - to bring you back
It's five hundred miles round the six counties
Which lets you see nature and all of her bounties
I started the 'way' in the county of 'Derry
Walked over the Sperrins and feeling quite merry
Headed into Tyrone and the village of Gortin
Where farmers, their hay and cattle, were sortin'
Then up Bessy Bell - a mountain quite steep
Down to Belcoo with its pubs and a street
Over the border to Black Lion and the south
Where the Gaelic is frequent by word of mouth
Walking east with Fermanagh behind in the west
Back into Tyrone - the midges a pest
With Armagh's orchards and spires to guide my feet
Heading southeast to Newry - its canal to meet
On to Rostrevor at the foot of the Mournes
Following the wall - above gorse thorns
North to Newcastle in the County of Down
Then up to Belfast - a very big town
Out to the coast and through Ballygalley's Head
Along . . . shore roads to Cushendall's Bay Red
This is now Antrim and the north coast
With Portrush and Castlerock - golf courses to boast
My start point is in sight, with miles at my back
Yes, I'd walk it again - just for the craic!

Alan R Coughlin (Limavady)

Born Lucky

It's summer and wow! it's raining again
Why don't the forecasters say 'more of the same'!
But think of the hot places where nothing will grow,
Or cold frozen landscapes covered in snow.
Perhaps we should be grateful for our lovely green land,
Edged with the ocean and soft yellow sand.
Where no one goes hungry and most have a bed,
Plenty of water and animals fed,
Oh! here comes the sun and everyone smiles,
Let's say hooray for the great British Isles.

J Miles (Porthcawl)

Nowadays

Variety today, too much to choose from,
Food stuffs we've never ever seen,
Sit on the shelves with the caviar and crème,
We have freedom to choose, choices galore,
Everyone wanting more and more,
We didn't have the freedom of choice back then,
Brings us back to times of when,
Not much money, families poor,
How did they manage during the war?
Had to make do with what we were given,
Spam sandwiches, rabbit made a real Sunday treat,
Mother would say, 'Eat up all your bunny meat.'
Blackouts, darkness, no electricity, entertainment was free, nowadays everything so costly,
Back then we had freedom to play with our friends,
Not many cars upon the street,
Or worries from the people we'd meet,
Running errands for the elderly, maybe get a treat,
Doors were always open, neighbours welcome any time,
Mats bashed with a brush upon the line,
Pathways scrubbed of grease and grime,
Nowadays children not allowed in the street to play,
No ball games allowed,
They cause such a nuisance neighbours say,
So take note and remember,
No freedom of choice with food back then,
But we did have freedom to play!

Dawn Primus (Cardiff)

Devotion

Once more devotion
I hear the cry
To be the apple of its eye
Don't ask at last to go or stay
Embrace me through the dying day
Loving holding fast to me
Unlock the past and set it free
Changed in a twinkling
As a grain of sand
Sifted through a loving hand

Jarn Duncan (Dundee)

John

He came to visit me,
I felt so proud of him,
He was seventeen and I was fifteen,
He was tall, blond,
With laughing gentle eyes,
Blue in colour,
He brought me chocolates
And a bunch of red carnations,
We went walking along the shore road,
I listened as he told me of his plans:
To climb the highest mountain;
To visit mysterious, exotic places;
Above all, to explore the world;
There is so much to see
And be discovered yet,
He stopped and pointed to a castle,
On the cliffs above us,
'I will buy that too, when we are married,' he said
And gently kissed me,
We laughed together as we drew apart,
We were so happy,
I am so fortunate to have this memory
Of you, John,
Along with many others,
Now you have gone, so long ago,
You always will be young to me, you see.

Christine B. Dobbie (Rothesay)

The Scottish Angler

The snow fell, the snow fell,
enveloping the land in its cold white shell.
Yet I still packed my rod and my dressed hooks,
setting off to the river to fish for troot.
The angler goes come rain or shine,
not knowing when will be our last time.
For we all do perish and become our ghosts,
no longer able to fish our rugged west coast.
Our beloved lochs and rivers, our beautiful streams.
casting our line for that fish in our dreams.

Mick Smith (Paisley)

The Scenic Route

Pillows of white cumuli
Fringed by diffused sunlight.
Hung in their blue ocean of space.
Later, turned apricot by a sun
Setting beyond horizons,
They faded gradually into shadow,
Were finally made invisible by night.

Light, that had transformed the sky
Departed to light a nether world.
Our light went out. That day,
Its date engraved upon the memory
For some, was then extinct,
Buried amongst all the days of time.
And yet that day was marked
By a parade of great magnificence,
Colourful, unhurried, grand in its simplicity;
The slow passing of great clouds
Across a luminous sky.

The congested migrations on the motorways,
The tidal flow of massed humanity
Were insignificant beneath that vast parade:
But those clouds seemed to celebrate men,
And some we knew, who briefly joined them,
Choosing the scenic route
To ride the painful spasms of history.

Jean Mitchell (Burntisland)

A Terminalogical Inexactitude

I am a good and honest lass, I never swear or curse,
I've never taken a penny from anybody's purse,
Part of my hard-earned cash, I give to the poor and needy
And freely share my humble fare, less folks should think me greedy,
With modesty I will confess, one of my finest features,
Is loving little cats and dogs and all God's humble creatures,
I never think to take strong drink, or cheat my dear old spouse
And gladly do the boring jobs, one finds about the house,
But no one's ever perfect and that I realise,
I have one tiny little fault, *I tell a lot of lies.*

Ilean Greig (Edinburgh)

God Or Circumstance?

Was it God or circumstance
Created this universe
From a primeval spark?
Is all life a thing of chance
Created by a throw of dice
Or is there, somewhere
An invisible hand
That leads us on a chosen path?

Is it God or circumstance
That led us to war in Iraq?
Is it oil or holy water
That anoints Saddam's successor?
Different beliefs
And different cultures
Lie dead and strewn
The food of vultures

Will it be God or circumstance
That finally wrecks
This planet Earth?
Some say science, that's provable
Others have faith, that's immovable
Who is right?
Who is wrong?
Who picks up the pieces
When we are all gone?

John Robert Smith (Aberdeen)

Our Surrounding World

To see the beauty all around us, is a gift to behold,
Just study the magic of a flower and see how its petals unfold.
The perfect colours, they are painted with God's very own hand,
What mystery and wonder throughout our given land.
We see the birds and the bees and even clouds in the sky,
They are all different colours and shapes, I often question, 'Why?'
To see the happy faces on children is a treasure indeed,
The colour of their skin is a prize of race or breed;
They are all God's 'special gifts' to families everywhere,
My prayer for them is to live in peace and to show each other 'care'.

Margaret Bevan (Abergavenny)

The Petrol-Powered Walk

How on Earth did we get this way -
So dependent on rubber wheels?
How could we become so lazy,
That we've forgotten how walking feels?
We're all so sure when we pass our test
That a car won't change our lives,
But somehow then the rot sets in . . .
The dilemma for one who drives!

Oh, I'm late for the dentist . . .
My check-up is due
I've no time to walk there . . .
Oh, what shall I do?
Just this once, I'll go in the car
It's lazy I know, as it's not very far.
That's how dependence starts to creep in
With these short needless journeys . . .
'Tis really a sin!

God gave us these feet to enjoy His creations
A tool for our pleasure across all nations.
Walking's so healthy, and helps you stay fit
You won't miss life's comforts one little bit.
So next time you hunt out the keys of your car,
Just think of the distance, and decide it's not far
If your 'love' of exercise is nothing but talk,
You'll soon be a victim of the 'petrol-powered walk'.

Mary McLeod (Dumfries)

Nature's Dream

I drifted through the fields of green,
Across the woods, a dream, unseen,
I paused to pick a wild bluebell,
While flitting over heathery dell,
A bird arose and up did fly,
Fluttering wings towards the sky,
But I awoke to my dismay,
For there tucked up in bed, I lay,
'Twas but a lovely dream I found,
That I was truly earthward-bound.

Annie McKimmie (Banff)

Time

Where does it go? I hear them say
Time flies by with a blink of an eye
It only seems like yesterday
I had you on my knee
Time will tell, I hear you say
Father Time will come for thee

Time we take for granted
That we can agree
Memories of that 6ft boy
When he was on your knee

Time will tick forever
Life some day will end
Memories cause a smile or tear
A story sure to tell

Time, it will continue
Smiles and tears within
Happiness and sadness
All are built within

So, let's give a cheer
To good old time
The memories good and bad
Say sorry for the wasted time
Precious moments
We have had.

Patricia McBride (Crumlin)

Remember Me

A face in the crowd of human life
Ordinary in every sense
Tarnished and emblazoned with everyday affairs
Sometimes saddened and panicked
By harsh words and deeds
But often uplifted and lightened
By unselfish acts of courage and kindness
Remember me -
I am you, wrapped in a different shell
A fabrication of humanity.

P Grant (Lisburn)

The Moment Of Truth

Huddled around your bed
Did we appear looming
Like figures in a dream
As you departed

Was Father waiting there
For you?

Was there a loss of colour
Especially of those you loved?
Of spring and summer hues
Autumn leaves and winter berries
Or sound like the wind down
Our stack during winter's past
When you talked about the fairies
And the dark shadows of night

Have you travelled far
Or as quick
As your morning walk
To St Mary's?
Where each stone knew your step
And every window carried a reflection

How do you look now?
Or are you as you were
Or at the moment of truth did all end -
Is there no more?

Líam Ó Comáin (Derry City)

A Day In Angus

Still wind and pouring rain, it's very wet again.
The garden is under two inches of water,
And the flowers are a lot shorter.
Birds sing, they think summer is here, well, this is ours;
The hills come and go in the mist and clouds that are so low,
The day goes on, the rain gets more strong.
But as the night-time gets here, the mist and cloud all disappear.
The sun fills the sky and this brings a tear to my eye
As I think about my lot.
Of how very pleased I am with one special friend I've got.

Mark Andrew Hutson (Menmuir)

Thoughts Near The Water

In childhood, when entertainment was so tasty,
My mental stomach was nourished to a
Peak of high spirit. I was easily filled.

In youth, inspiration tempted the
Appetite, expectation fed the soul, my
Heart swelled with dreams and thrills.

Now overfed with unwholesome media, I find myself
Thirsting at the lake's edge, the weather moody,
Teasing the water to a gentle agitation.

The surface, jinking and jesting,
Like my memory coming and going,
Is a lake of enlightenment and predestination.

Millions of reflections dim and return,
In seconds, thousands have passed,
In moments come myriads more.

Each reflection is one small life
Momentarily bright.
Not knowing if it's been of use -
My life is such a light.

Time was endless when I was young,
I hungered for perfection.
This Lake, the universe itself,
My life, a mere reflection.

Ken James (Merthyr Tydfil)

God's Creatures, Mid-Winter

No birds of calm here, this solstice day,
As God's creatures; sparrows, starlings, a rook,
On chilly roofs array
And flit from gutter to chimney-stack nook
In their unknown way.

On slate and tile, out of a Wedgewood sky,
The sun strikes from his lowest stage;
And God's other creature, I,
Seeing doves swoop like a turning white page,
Would too from here fly.

James Rousay (Orkney)

From Monmouth To Chepstow By The Old Road

Sun gleams through woodland glade;
Gold lines road edges;
Last green leaves cling to the vaults of trees;
Filigree branches arch against the sky;
Roots in a froth of rusting bracken.
Blorenge, the Sugar Loaf the skyline;
Old mountains knowing an eternity,
Of rain, sun, wind and ice,
Bold against the sky's calm.
The old bus rattles its way along twisting lanes
Filled with friendship's chatter,
Today's glory, yesterday's flood.
Passing the dark of the plough,
Green pastures quietly dotted with sheep,
The point of Trellech church
Rises above long ages of love and life
Peace and war.

Set down,
Feet firmly set in earth's soil again
Linking with all creation
In a wonder of loveliness
In the Earth's turmoil, an oasis.

Margaret Davis (Chepstow)

The Day The Cuckoo Took Over The Clock

The clock workers ticked off the passing seconds
while a feather-brained cuckoo fronted the main event:
an hourly appearance to - *koo-koo* - announce the hours
to roars of approval which went straight to its head.

We live in strange times
where buoyant celebrities 'rise to the challenge'
and people of substance settle for less;
the cuckoo started thinking it knew better
and interfered with the workings
until time was badly bent.

Robert Black (Annan)

Dunluce Castle

Macdonnells were the owners in the 16th century time
Of Randal of Earl kind.

Lady Catherine his wife
With misfortune with their life.

She hated the noise of the sea
It was to be.

One evening, having dinner that night
They got a fright.

As the kitchen courtyard broke
Fell into the sea, out of sight.

Three years later, host arrested
Their possessions seized by Cromwell agents
As they protested.

Dunluce Castle like by Macdonnells
Moved to exile
To different lifestyle.

Came back in 1660
After restoration moved on
Feelings of Dunluce gone.

Went to Ballymagarry House
Then to Glenarm Castle
Dunluce Castle ruins stands in sun dazzle.

Marie Coyles (Ballymoney)

Fallen Leaves On The Ground

(For LMRT)

Hanging your head in shame,
Fallen leaves on the ground,
Fear the death, feel the pain,
The small things blown around,

Above the arms reach out,
Bough moves against the sky,
Lone drop of dew plays tout,
The tree stand, do not cry.

Steve Gorvin (Cardiff)

A Darker Shade Of Sun

When the night
Has been painted
Without stars
And hope has
Become a darker
Shade of sun,
Rustle now
Some words unto
The silent moon, for life is
A ghost with
Apple-green eyes
That walks
This Earth homeless.

I claw the sky
With helpless hands
And August cloud
Over sands
That whisper
No name.
In Darfur, time
Has so many
Anguished faces
And life . . .
Leaves no shadow
Upon the ground.

Norman Royal (Cardiff)

Share In The Best

Living within Dame Nature's breath,
this land of trees, of ling and broom
of braes and Munros where they grow,
nurtured by burns and lochs as rains
leach out the sustenance for them
from sandy stones and sweating peat.

Snow still lies here in sheltered cols
(beneath the rays of summer sun),
blown there in winter months before,
on breeze and gale. As yet untrod
by Man or sheep or goat or deer,
pristine and crystalline forever?

We are further blessed by the flesh
of fish and fowl and lambs and kine;
some smoked with apple, cherry, oak
but mainly fresh to grace, each plate
of waiting, steaming roots and seeds
upon each dwelling's creaking board.

On nearby islands' soaring hills
or in their riven valleys deep,
the swelling malt grains ferment there
in waters from the heaven-sent clouds.
Which, heat-stilled in bright copper vats
weep amber tears of precious life!

Ian Colley (Dunoon)

The Credit Squeeze

One day we woke to the credit squeeze story
Nobody thought this would be a case for worry
But after months of food and fuel rising in cost
House prices falling until all equity is lost
Increasing repayments on mortgages and loans
Unemployment rising and employers' moans

Individual debt soars as repossessions increase
Belts tighten so that outgoings can decrease
All this adds pressure to the sound family life
Tempers fray as depression causes strife
Food on the table and a warm place to sleep
Must be the main principles to keep

No doubt the crisis was fueled by media hype
Increasing a confidence scare in what they type
Living well in the past without giving a thought
Now any past luxuries should not be bought
Worldwide bankers; they hold all the aces
Lending us money would put the smile on our faces

One day we will awake to the end of the squeeze
No more will our bank accounts be on freeze
Out we can go and spend, spend, spend
Our scrimping and saving will come to an end
Tills will be ringing and plastic being swiped
With no more thought of what the media had hyped.

George Alexander (Brechin)

Bridges

Let's build bridges! What we'll do
Is take two cubes, one red, one blue,
Put them close upon the table,
Leave a gap, but make them stable;
Put a yellow one on top,
Learn your concepts, 'Go' and 'Stop',
'Around' and 'Over', 'Under', 'Through',
Build good bridges while you're two!

When you're older you will see
Mighty bridges crossing rivers!
Thames and Seine and Mississippi
Mostar, Tigris and Euphrates
Ribble, Forth, Zambezi, Kwai:

You will see the reason why
Engineers link alien lands
Enabling strangers to link hands.

You'll build more important bridges,
Those not made with iron or steel;
Crucial bridges, binding people,
Altering how people feel!
Empathy, handshake, warm caress,
Compassion, sympathy, tendresse,
And when you've given Earth's dough your leaven
Find the bridge from Earth to Heaven.

Jill Clark (Mold)

The Blue And The Green

Blue sky,
Green grass,
In the arena where
Before the mob,
Latter day gladiators
Perform their feats.

Poles apart, yet of
The same world,
Blue bedecked bay at
Green garbed.
Green bellows back at
Blue.

Cruel, crude hymns
Affront nature wherein
Sky meets Earth,
Blue meets green,
Mixing, blending,
Becoming one.

Here
Hate is the horizon.
Here
Blue and green,
Mixed,
Run red.

J McKibbin (Glasgow)

Seeing Is Believing

There's a corner of my garden
Where they visit every day
I can see them rush around excited
In the most peculiar way
The expression on their faces
The grimaces they pull
As they flit back and forth
Their new-found treasures to behold

There are fairies at the bottom of my garden
They've made themselves at home
You can hear the sound of their laughter
Like water trickling over stones
They chase around finding a space to rest
Their wings shining by the moonlight's glow

What makes the fairies visit time and time again?
Why is it they appear at night and never in the day?
One would have thought the evening air
Would have been too cold for them to stay.

It's a joy to see the fairies
Those creatures of ethereal grace
Light-heartedly playing
As I sit quietly watching
It's hard to believe
People think they don't exist.

Valerie Thompson (Cwmbran)

The Flower And The Sunshine

The flower of April
Spirits of the forelife sang your name
On the April morning that you came.
Pantheons have kept their promise to me thus -
Held firm the plan: a family made of us.
In this is all that I might want of life;
A beautiful child and a wonderful wife.

Kind of heart is all you need to be,
Ask, then, what you will of me.
This is all of wisdom spoken true:
Each day your daddy will give thanks for you.

The sunshine of April
Sounding a sigh, we cry,
All our days are made.
Magical birth is why
Utopia's game is played.
Each day his gift to us is joy,
Love - our first gift to our boy.

After the sun and moon are gone
Remains the truth as brought by you.
The day when loyal Venus won,
Heaven's gates have passage through.
Universal hand on heart -
Return the love; this is your part . . .

Art Sloan (Newry)

The Riverside

Washed up from the river
To lie there, on the bank,
The ivy-covered log.

Temptation, to stay awhile
And watch our world go by.
Enveloped within this scene
Nature and humanity.

Hark, the distinctive cry,
Squawking anger, delight.
Riding on currents of air
Seagulls swoop and glide.

Observing across the estuary,
Along the man-made highway
Travel buses, lorries, cars
All involved in life's rat race.

Buses to Swansea with shoppers aboard;
Lorries to supermarkets, wares unload;
Cars going, oh, goodness knows where,
But hey, what do I care? Cos . . .

In this moment of time, my dog and I,
Relax, memories stored, locked inside,
Peace, tranquillity flows to the mind,
Sat on the log, down by the riverside.

Miss Mary (Neath)

My Poetic Son

My mind it won't function, I'm sorry to say,
I can't meditate on my poetry today,
But given a chance to clear my mind,
Perhaps I could make up a couple of rhymes.

I have a son, I'm afraid of, you see,
As he has gone poetic, like me,
Of course, it is a disease of the mind,
For in my dreams, I am saying my rhymes.

So, it's a race between him and me,
For every one I write, he writes three.

Molly Maguire (Newry)

The Flip-Side

Although the mother in you has gone,
the daughter in me remains

and I catch her sometimes
brushing our hair across my forehead
an iron burn shining
in the same place on my wrist.

Mopping our blood from a cut
we meet
in the mirror, grin
matching, lopsided smiles.

I have phoned you sometimes,
knowing you won't be there,
but hoping with that
heart-thudding fear
that maybe you will answer.

You said, you are my other self
when illness had taken your bones
and I'd left the ward
turning once
meeting your eyes
our eyes

now in the mirror
I see what you meant.

Kathy Miles (Aberdeen)

Such Is The Poetry Of Life

We all have a song to sing;
We all have a story to tell;
Such is the poetry of life.

We sing and we dance;
Our feelings in flight;
Such is the poetry of life.

We touch a rugged tree;
We touch its velvet leaves
And marvel at God's beauty;
Such is the poetry of life.

Helen Smith (Greenock)

Gifted Hands

His gifted hands
With grace and flair
Formed a landscape
Rich and rare,
Softly seasoned
With subtle hues,
Springtime-yellow,
Summer blues
Autumn's dusky
Golden glow,
Swirling flakes of
Downy snow,
Satin skies,
Splashing seas,
Scented flowers,
Enchanting trees,
He lightened day
And shaded night,
Created life
With pure delight,
Then gifted hands
Were clasped
With care
His world was blessed
In loving prayer.

Ruth Callender (Culloden)

The Snowy Owl

Like a silent whisper the snowy owl flew into a winter wilderness
A thin shallow mist stretched over part of an icy lochan
A narrow stretch of pine trees laden with snow stopped
close to the water's edge
In front of her the snowy owl saw the panoramic view
of twin mountains, features softened with heavy snowfalls
This white illumination of timeless wonder and beauty
was home to the snowy owl
As silent she had come, silently she went
Tomorrow would be just another day
The snowy owl

David Morin (Clackmannan)

Diamond Day

Same church, same steeple
Same pews . . . a few of the same people.
Flowers on the altar, then and today,
Perhaps they're arranged in a different way.
Similar hymns . . . why have some changed?
Most of their tunes quite rearranged.
Sunday Best clothes we're wearing today . . .
Couldn't quite wear what we wore on that day.
Then I wore white . . .
Complete with a veil,
Then was my bouquet . . .
Bridesmaids in trail.
Now quite sedate, our family around,
Of our yesterday's family . . .
Afer memories abound.
Still the same me
Still the same him . . .
Still the same hearts, still the same love
Always giving thanks to God up above.
Still the same me.
So many years have gone by, how can that be?
As it's sixty years now since our wedding day,
We celebrate . . .
Our Diamond Wedding . . .
Today September 8, 2008.

Mae McEwan (Troon)

Early Morn

Step and dream
The image that you see surrounds you
Take one more, be gently sucked in
Into this beautiful world of tranquillity and reflections
Your mind clearing like water draining from a leaky can
Walking on water, touching the highest peak,
Clouds float beneath, you kneel
And try to gently stroke them
The chill of the water, spell is broken
Image gone, lost in the wind
As it ripples across the lake.

Teresa R Chester (Montgomery)

The Estuary . . .

Strolling along the estuary
As the tide sways gently towards the bay
Footsteps quietly dispersing
Golden grains disappearing along the way
Where feet once walked
Now alas they are gone
Washed away with the calming, tranquil tide
Engulfed with swirling waters
Restoring the beautiful picturesque seaside . . .
Gulls flying high in the endless sky
No fluffy clouds to be seen
Golden rays of sunshine flowing down
Beautiful waters so clear and so clean . . .
I see in the distance, a lonely man
Deep thoughts within his mind
Seeking answers to all his worries
For the hardships of all mankind!
As the whispering wind blows gently
Giving secrets to all who can hear
Singing a song of silence
A peacefulness, so sincere . . .
Then as the sun sets slowly in the evening skies
Revealing clouds of gold and fire
Silhouettes of mountains in the distance
Birds singing sweetly with a late night choir . . .

Janet Brook (Kirkcaldy)

Wales

Wales do not despair,
for those of us who care,
about your battles fought and lost
yes, lost I say because
you think you cannot stand alone,
we who care will bring your children home.
They left because they could not see
their dreams become reality,
yet, if they only knew,
this land would give so much
if they would give their loyalty.

Clare Oxton (Wrexham)

Summertime

Hark! Can you hear the rose petal gently falling in a summer breeze?
Or when gazing heavenward toward the rustling trees
Do you see a host of faces dancing in their leaves?
Can you hear the flutter of swallow wings as he skips o'er hill and glen?
Do you hear the stirring of life anew from the fox cubs in their hidden den?
Can you scent the essence of crocus that fills the morning air?
Do you see the young lambs frolicking merrily without care?
Have you ever watched a field of daffodils dancing to and fro
To a strange and frenzied tempo only they do know?
Close your eyes and smell the garlic bulbs and hear the corncrake fly,
Listen to the wheat sheaf swaying in the wind like a newborn baby's sigh.
Do you gaze upon the majesty of the rainbow in the sky and wonder
Why such beauty always follows hail and thunder?
Can you hear the trickling of water in the brook nearby,
Or hear the newborn calf's heartbeat like thunder in the sky?
Can you hear the solitary call of the lark that heralds the dawn?
Do you see the shrouded mist rising from the lawn?
Summer fills the air with all its sights and sounds,
Young foals galloping unbridled bound on bound.
The folk with tea and buns sat lazily on the village green,
Aspiring test batsmen attired in their white pristine.
The rolling hills of green, the fields of golden corn,
Endless skies of hazy blue, such wondrous sights adorn.
The advent of summertime in all its glory has arrived once more,
Enter its realm lest winter close its door.

Thomas Jones (Cardiff)

Wales

Go on, mock me, I know that I am small
I have an Assembly that no one listens to at all
Alight, I cannot pass many new laws
I am still kept upon a leash
But that does not mean I haven't any teeth
So, laugh away you other countries
But you should remember about Wales this
I have kept my language and dignity
And where do most of you come to escape your grimy towns?
Yes, to my Welsh valleys and hills
Where clean air and a welcome can still be found.

Melanie Burgess (Aberystwyth)

Longing For The Old Days?

Longing for the old days.
When housewives stayed at home?
    Hardly any cars,
    No telly, no phone.
Things were simpler then,
The world a gentler place.
But let's stop kidding ourselves,
With platitudes so common place.
    'No place like home',
    'The good old days',
Cast your minds back to;
Coal fires that wouldn't light,
Freezing bedrooms, night after night,
    No carpets, just lino,
    Cold as ice.
The nit nurse on a mission
To hunt out the lice,
No fridge - milk that turned sour,
Blocks of salt - to be hacked for an hour.
Outside toilets - a trip to dread,
Mountains of cawl,
With dripping on bread.
Still longing for the old days?
    You must be
    Off your head!

Sandra Lowe (Llanelli)

Memory

Walking past the old house, I saw you holding our child in your arms
Shouting at the other to take care, and mind the road
Music drifted from the open door, melting into the summer heat
You smiled with lips wet and moist
Your dark eyes shining with my love
Chestnut hair caressing the breeze
I kissed your cheek
Smiled at my young son
Then you were gone
I opened my eyes
The house was empty and still.

Michael Rowlands (Mountain Ash)

Our Magic Potion

Daddy and Mammy
Thought it would be great fun
To have sleep time for everyone
So four went to sleep
Then awake came two
And thought of some fun that they could do.
They went to the bathroom to have a wee
And looked around with glee.
They said together,
'Won't this be funny, we'll have some fun without our mummy.'
So together they mixed their secret potion
Of course it contained some nice hair lotion
They had to test it to the full
So they thought they'd use some cotton wool
They were laughing together in full swing
But they were stopped from mixing more potion
'Cause they heard a commotion
They looked up from their fun to see
Mammy and Daddy
With their mouths open wide
Watching their girls happily slide
It must have looked like
An atomic explosion
But to two little girls
It was their magic potion!

Helen Doidge (Caerphilly)

Soon

Soon, the long fingers of Jack Frost will disappear.
Soon, the crocuses painted with colours of violet, yellow and blue
will catch the sun, no fear.
Soon, the daffodils bright and full of cheer
will trumpet their sound over valleys so clear.
Soon, the newborn lambs, unblemished,
black or white,
will give the shepherd great joy and delight.
Soon, finally the carpets of sweet bluebells,
show that spring is here;
warm and alight.

David E Davies (Swansea)

Our Highland Queen

Morning mist surrounds the mountains,
Clinging to rocks and trees.
Crags and gullies, glens and cairns,
A mystical sight to see.
Hear a hundred pipers playing,
Crossing the hills and the streams.
Making their way, to share the day,
With our beautiful Highland Queen.

All over the land, the great chiefs of the clans,
With their people, go many a mile.
For our future Queen, has never been seen,
By the Highlanders marching in style.
The heather is purpled, and bracken is trampled,
With rowan tree leaves turning brown.
The site is being set, for this wondrous event,
Our first Highland Queen to be crowned.

As well as 'MacDonald' of Sleet and clan 'Ranald',
There's Lewis and Harris 'MacLeod'.
From 'Gordon' and 'Farquharson', westward to 'Cameron',
All to the gathering bound.
Where there's music, romancing, singing and dancing,
To strathspeys and reels swirling round.
They are travelling far, from Barra and Mar,
To see 'Our Highland Queen' - with her crown.

Alistair J H Watson (Elgin)

Home

I think of the house that we called home,
Hills and the fields where we used to roam,
Innocent games that we played together,
Times that have passed, forget them, never.
We had such good fun,
That cost not a penny,
Worries of safety, we didn't have any,
Food a-plenty, warm and clean,
Now it feels like just a dream,
Treasured memories of us together,
In my heart forever and ever.

Jinny Davies (Llanelli)

The Time Seems Long

The time seems long
Since last we met
Friendship all alone
The time we spent
I won't forget
But now it's past and gone.
The time we spent
I won't forget
And you I love so dear
It brings from me
A deep, deep sigh
From you I long to hear.

Then how sweet is the hour we give
When thoughts may wander free
To the friends who in the memory live
For then I remember thee.
They wing like a dove from the ark
My barque on a stormy sea
And bring back to my lonely heart - a leaf
That reminds me then of thee.

The golden rays of the sun's last light
With the blue of the mountain high
Reminds me when the twilight comes
The day we said goodbye.

John Monaghan (Dungannon)

Storm Force

I thought of the sand rippling
Under the sea, crabs knowing
No lee, wrack strewn
High above the sigh of
The tide whilst waders'
Signs wash away as they
Must fly to Llansteffan fields
Where sheep are hiding against
The noise and roar of the winds
Over the bent hedge and
Stony stile which shudders.

Robert Wynn-Davies (Whitland)

Dreaming

I walked beneath a moonlit sky
Beside the tranquil sea,
A warming glow of peaceful light
I sensed was touching me.
I looked up to the distant sky
And saw a cloud pass by,
The stars they seemed to dance and sing
And filled with joy, I cried.

And then I thought it would be nice
To have someone with me.
Someone to care and hold my hand
And be a friend to me.
We both would walk together
Beneath the moonlit sky,
And try to catch the moonbeams
As they escape us by.

I must be patient in my mind
And be contented so,
That I may wake and greet the day
And know the way to go.
I will go forth and joyful breath,
As gentle dew doth fall,
My hands will touch the morning earth
As I await your call.

Elizabeth McGarry (Greenock)

Peace

Grant me the wish that we may see
A land of promise for you and for me
A land where wars are a thing of the past
And peace on Earth will forever last

Grant me the wish to see the light
To love one another and not to fight
Where greed will not conquer love and devotion
Where peace on Earth will be poetry in motion

Grant me the time in the midst of confusion
To make a decision and reach a conclusion

H R Jones (Deganwy)

Remembrance

Wet poppies red, weep for the dead,
They died that we might live.
Young soldiers old, daring and bold,
They gave all that they had to give.
Tears in their eyes, they say their goodbyes,
To comrades they will not see again.
Remember them well, remember them, tell
The world, they did not die in vain.

Wet poppies red, weep for the dead,
Feet, wearing slippers or boots.
Shuffle along to a long ago song,
That takes them right back to their roots.
Wearing bowlers and cherries, medals and berets,
Marching along to the band,
Shoulder to shoulder, they grow older and older,
Remember, blood, sweat, tears and sand.

Wet poppies red, let the parade be led,
By the spirit of those who stayed.
In a field far away, at the end of their day,
While their loved ones hoped and prayed.
In a field coloured red, laid fallen the dead,
In a field, in the sun, wind and rain,
Peace perfect peace, let the tears release
Till we meet, till we meet, once again.

Roy Lewis (Merthyr Tydfil)

A Mother's Love

Who knows a mother's love
No one really knows
As carefully she counts
Her baby's fingers and toes
Monitoring every heartbeat
Watching as they sleep
Who knows a mother's love
As her innermost thoughts she keeps

Who knows a mother's love
As baby starts to crawl
Always her arms are open
To catch them when they fall
First and forward on her mind
Nothing can come between
Who knows a mother's love
Only from her heart can it be seen

Who knows a mother's love
When she nurses in bad health
Truly there's no comparing
To any richly wealth
Who knows a mother's love
The heartaches that she bears
No one really knows
How much a mother cares.

Paula Kewin (Abergavenny)

The 199 Steps

I stroll through a ghostly arch
framing Whitby Abbey high above
then pant up the 199 steps
to the Abbey and St Mary's Church
where many epitaphs have been erased
by wild weather over hard centuries,
tragic tales now lost in time,
Whitby Abbey lies before me:

Its empty arches with ever-changing vistas
of the fickle heavens above.
This is Nosferatu land
but the only apparitions I sense today
are the monks from yesteryear
when this glorious gothic ruin was intact
and the esteemed Bram Stoker himself
creating immortality from this special place.

I view the sloping Yorkshire cliffs,
verdant hills and postcard harbour
as so many have before me
and will long after I have perished.
The harbour water sparkles
as if stars have fallen from the night sky.
I have followed Bram Stoker on this climb
but unlike the graves he's honoured by time.

Guy Fletcher (Cardiff)

Cardiff Or Abroad?

As I sit on the hillside looking to the valley below,
I wonder vaguely about the places people find to go.
Some are obviously on holiday with roof racks piled high;
Others are probably going to the airport to take to the sky.
Many will be off to the city to do a daily job,
While pickpockets will be looking for someone to rob.
Crowds will gather on the sandy beaches well before midday,
Other people will be joining a ship to sail far away.

I'd thought myself of finding somewhere to go,
As on a winter's evening I had sat sleepily in the firelight glow.
I'd studied brochures all day long, but it was so hard to decide -
The choice of holidays was so wide
And how would I travel - by coach or train or by boat or plane?
Or is it better to stay at home? It's much less tiring to my brain.
We have mountains and valleys, rivers and the sea
With well-used beaches and parks in which to run free.

Castles and cathedrals, museums, theatres and cinemas not far away
Easily reached in a small part of the day.
Dan yr Ogof Caves, the Big Pit Museum soon reached by car,
The Brecon Beacons and the Gower beaches not too far
So why go abroad, when there is so much near to home,
Is it necessary the world to roam?
Oh well, perhaps it might be a good idea, now it's starting to rain,
To pull out the brochures and plan a trip to Spain!

Malcolm Coles (Cardiff)

Land Of Soapy Stories, Buy One Get One Free

Land of soapy stories, buy one get one free
Liberal, Labour, Tory demanding what's in it for me?
Liberal, Labour and Tory toff
All shoving to get their snouts in the trough

Charity shops full of offers
Hoping to fill their charity coffers
Books and videos going for a song
Twenty quid for a suit you can't go wrong

Flea markets selling you lice and fleas?
Market gardeners flogging plants and trees
A pair of trousers off the peg
Get 'em home, they're too long in the leg

Footwear stall selling sandals and mules
Hardware stall selling all kinds of tools
Cheap tomatoes to fry in your woks
Dearer salad tomatoes from the same box

For an all-proof Swiss watch with little to pay
They say there's one born every day
Then to the pet shop for the best bargain you'll see
For a buck and a doe rabbit you'll get ten free

Ron Dudley (Llanfoist)

James

James missed a Bus
Through a twist in fate
Delaying his journey home
By one day late

He later boarded our local Bus
And sat beside me
And that is how we met you see

This handsome stranger began to chat
We shared a few laughs
Of this and that
My heart almost missed a beat
When I discovered he lived at the back of my street

Little did the stranger know
I never wanted him to go
And as he wrote my phone number on his hand
My heart began to understand
This is James here at long last
The timing was for us
To move on from the past

My darling James is a people's person
He is indeed a treasure
A solid rock to all of us
That goes way beyond words and measure.

Eileen MacDonald (Port Glasgow)

Christine's Wedding Request

(For Christine)

Christine is getting married,
She wants a special gift.
Will Grandma embroider for her
A very *different gift?*

Two little bears on a swing
With flowers all above . . .
One has a hat and one a veil
They look so much in love . . .

Grandma clears her desk
Instructions to absorb . . .
Coloured threads and needles
Make an old heart throb!

Stitch by stitch, it daily grew . . .
Fat little tummies and noses blue.
Holding hands together swinging
You can almost hear them singing . . . !

Christine was delighted!
And on her wedding day, on a special table
There . . . framed and on display . . was seen
The love between her grandma . . .
And lovely bride, Christine.

Claire Wray (Newtownards)

Love's Betrayal

The grey sky reflected her mood
And the sound of the rain,
Pounding on the car's roof,
Echoed the beat of her heart.
The desire that had once driven her,
Now filled her with despair.
Just as the rain drops
On the window screen,
Raced each other,
Tears cruised down her cheeks,
Leaving salty tracks on a perfectly
Made-up face.

She had been so sure,
That his love for her for could not be broken,
That no one could steal his affection
And yet she had witnessed
This very act.
He was not aware of her,
As she stood in the shadows,
Watching the betrayal of her love,
Each tender touch
And endearing look,
Was like a sword,
Piercing her very soul.

E Uprichard (Craigavon)

Living By The Sea

Ever changing, ever moving
Your bounty is Man's friend
Blue when all is calm
Grey when storm clouds gather
And white horses prance away
You make my day, you make my day.

Seagulls crying overhead
Ozone filling the air I breathe
Washen pebbles glinting like jewels
Scenes that take my breath away
You make my day, you make my day.

Sybil Marie Curzon (West Cross)

Fading Values

We rear our children, filled with cankerous greed,
Blackmailing us from the time of birth,
Expecting them to be paragons of simple virtue.
Yet, we fail to set a moral standard,
To show them what is right or wrong.
How can they prosper and stay on track,
When their mentor is a failing shadow
Of a nervous, tablet-swallowing, perfect wreck?
Our relationships are lacking commitment,
Flitting apart like leaves, flirting from the autumn trees,
Embracing piles of decay, down-trodden journal on a busy street.
We race along in total confusion,
Drowning in this life's plastic flowered, most glamorous illusion.

Shall we start again?
Who will nail himself to a cross and preach the virtues of eternal life?
Should one vow to be loyal to a single wife?
Till death us do part again!
Feed the terrorist from our native plate no longer!
Let him suffer for his mistaken ideals,
With heavy chains around his neck,
Until he screams in pain and learns to love us once again.
Let sanity prevail and ban all rubbish from the mail!
Someone, somewhere . . . lying hidden out there,
Please start *all over* again!

Thomas Burke (Belfast)

Spring

Like a spear
The sun throws himself at my house
This time of year
Showing me all the dark corners
I've not been near.

Am I to blame?
Did he not call me out himself
Shouting my name?
So I came
And, letting the dust settle where it would
I played his game.

W Huggett (Cardiff)

My Lady

My mother was a lady without a fur coat
She did not drink or even smoke
She liked a snuff but that's no shame
This kind lady a world of fame

Like a queen without a crown
This kind lady no fancy gowns
Around her shoulders she wore a shawl
This kind lady the queen of all

Her gentle heart, her smiling face
This kind lady full of grace
Toiled through life and did no harm
This kind lady had lots of charm

In her fold, no black sheep
She loved them all, not one could weep
Always of value they called her name
This kind lady was always the same

She did not care for world success
To her family she gave her best
Her thinking thoughts were never bad
She thought of others who may be sad

I know, dear Lord, you select the best
My mother was a lady, she passed her test.

Fred Mingle (Belfast)

Our Troops

A poem to our troops in a faraway land,
With the noise of the bullets, the heat and the sand,
We think of you all every night and day,
And keep you all safe to the Lord we pray.

A poem to our troops, the boys and girls too,
All come home safely, we hope that you do,
With your heads held high, home to your own green land,
Away from the danger, the heat and the sand.

We thank you all and everyone
For keeping the peace,
And all you've done.

Brenda Jones (Ponciau)

Something Fishy

Who says fishing's all great fun
Fished all day to only catch one
Maybe even sometimes none
Hour by hour and not a bite
Except your lunch and that's alright
Hour by hour, it'll soon be night
Then all of a sudden, what a fright
At last, at last, I've got a bite
Pulling, splashing, darting, dashing
I can't believe I've caught a whopper
She's fighting hard, I'll never stop her
From the surface to the depths near the bank
Oh boy, this one's hard to beach
Yes, at last, it's within my reach
I'll soon have this one on the pier
Three pounds, four pounds, maybe five
This little fish is still alive
Out with the priest, a tap on the head
That puts this little fish to bed
For soon maybe tomorrow to her sorrow
As this little fish will become a dish
Served with chips and peas to please
So on a scale of one to ten
I think I'll go out to fish again.

William Waring (Belfast)

Watching And Waiting

I sit and look at the world today
As the pendulum of time is ticking away
Backward and forward
From good to bad
Peace to war
Love to hatred
And hope to despair
Abundance to famine
Faith to secularism
The pendulum keeps swinging
And I wonder
Will it ever stop?

Margaret Pritchard (Hengoed)

The Old Fellow's Box

Odd things are found here among the bits and bobs
That jumbles all together in the old fellow's box
He's gone now and he's left his belongings all behind
So we can take a look and see what treasure we may find
He always kept it near him and always kept it locked
It was a prized possession, the old fellow's box
But there is nothing here of value to anyone but him
It's what they meant and signified that's kept them safe within
There is a solemn wedding photograph in dated sepia colour
And children with their Christmas toys smiling from another
A photograph of a soldier with healthy fresh-faced look
Military medals, an old cap badge and an Army Service book
There are Certificates in faded brown, dog-eared from overuse
Collar studs and foreign coins in the bottom, loose
A penknife and a deck of cards, a pencil and eraser
A key ring and a needle and thread and an old safety razor
His Identity Card and Ration Book, and ancient 'Pocket Ben'
An envelope with some stamps inside and a 'Parker' fountain pen
A well-thumbed Bible, small and soiled at all important places
Cufflinks, a couple of safety pins and a pair of spare boot laces
Not much to show for all the years and places that he's been
Just little things that meant a lot to nobody but him
That was a crutch when times were hard, as life so often is,
That somehow gave him comfort and was nobody's but his!

A Macdonald-Cheeseman (Inverness)

Behind The Smile

No wonder I love you, you laughing clown
You lift me up when I am down
I watch you do some crazy things
And see the joy your antic brings
I go to bed and think of you
And wonder if you are lonely too
If you, like me, put on a smile
Keep the act going for a while
When it's over and we're alone
Find some place to call our own
Let all the pent-up tears flow free
We've something in common, you and me

Wendy Cameron (Peterhead)

The Game Of Life

The Game of Life is a precious gift,
But you only get one shot!
You play it wrong and make mistakes
And regret all the things you've got!
Youth is wasted on the young
Yet they have it all on a plate.
They'll realise as time goes by,
But their age makes it all too late.
You need to live each day at a time
And not worry what's ahead.
Do all the things you want to do,
It's too late when you're dead!
The world is yours for the taking
So live your life to the full.
Don't sit back wishing and thinking,
Regretting a life so dull.
Be free as a bird, roam wild as a cat,
Let nothing hold you back.
Be sure you live the life you want,
So get yourself on track.
Now go ahead and never waste,
'Tis such a wonderful time
You need to go and have a taste,
Just look and you will find.

Barbara Kinsey (Porth)

Brave New Garden

Where daffodils
Once ran amok
There now reposes
Concrete block
No crocus snowdrop
Nor spring flower
Will now bloom
To fill the hour
Gone the bushes
Birds and trees
Family car
Now sits with ease

Ethel Thomson (Paisley)

Aldermaston

Remember when we were younger,
The old laws we were going to change.
The ones that seemed selfish and unjust,
That we tried to rearrange.
Don't forget the big march,
You know! The one to ban the bomb.
So that war would just be a memory,
Where have all those leaders gone?
They found themselves jobs in high places,
Saying, for us this world they would save.
Yet wars still go on forever,
Young men are still sent to their graves.
This power has blinded their judgement,
Now they say what's in it for me?
They've degraded and neglected this planet,
Pollution runs wild and free
And we lost our way growing older,
We forgot that together we're strong.
Divided we fall, is the saying,
That is where we all went wrong.
We have failed the next generations,
Letting them rip Mother Earth apart.
One day she'll just sigh and stop spinning,
Because we have broken her heart.

Rita Stone (Newport)

Don't Trample On The Flowers

'Don't trample on the flowers please,'
I say for the hundredth time.
Oh no, the rope they're playing with,
was my washing line.
Dirt and mud walked in the house,
from sets of muddy feet,
just after I had hoovered
and had it all so neat.
Dear, dear the house is not the place
for twigs and fallen logs,
but they smile and blink their eyes at me
my carefree, happy dogs!

Maria Gorman-Fawcett (Caithness)

Pink Like The Rose

He watched from a distance
Feeling safe in the belief,
He could not be seen,
She chattered amicably
To a young couple,
He reasoned to be in their early thirties,
With a small child in a buggy
And a little boy holding on
Tightly to the man's hand.
The sun's rays reflected
Off the silver strands
In her hair,
Her cheeks still glowed
Pink like the rose,
He had once given her
It, he felt sure, had faded
Like the promise
He failed to keep
All those years ago,
Swallowing hard, he turned
And walked away,
No point in looking back,
He thought,
The past has gone.

Pauline Uprichard (Craigavon)

Life

Around me there is happiness
A baby girl is born
Around me there is badness
Somebody set fire to a field of corn
Around me there is madness
Another stabbing, parents' hearts are torn
Around me there is sadness
A friend is ill, I feel forlorn
Life, an insoluble mystery
Happy, sad, good, bad
Whatever . . . too short
You and I, my love, must part.

Sarah Nicholson (Plockton)

The Written Word

This pure and transient mood to which I now arrive
Give thought to what darkness brought me once
Upon a time
The grief of twilight pale and solemn slowly
Overcomes the spirit
And cools the glowing embers of inner peace
But the tears have dried and the silence of
Solitude is broken
For an untapped well which holds such knowledge
Has been opened
Let me be impaled upon the words of the poets
And take delivery of the untold essence of the
Fabled tale
That I might soar above the boundaries laid down
By my position in this life
A tear may fall, a smile may rise then pass so swiftly
Yet leave behind the burnished breastplate of its being
I live now within an outer world and watch for more to follow
Most never do but live content upon the periphery
Of content
I have passed through the sphere and inhabit the
Light of the written world
I now ascend and meet my fellows with a hand outstretched
For those who trail behind

Holly Harrison (Kilmarnock)

My Pembrokeshire

Peaceful and beautiful country,
Enveloped in sunshine and sea -
Memories crowd back of my childhood
Bringing it closer to me.
Often I think of our history -
Of kings and knights on their steeds,
Entering great castles triumphant -
Telling their tales of brave deeds.
Hills that stretch upwards like mountains -
Invite all to savour our land -
Riches far greater than money -
Ensure living in Pembrokeshire's grand.

Joan Davey (Pembroke Dock)

Oisín

It's just me
And the ticking of the clock
So I lock the door, sit down
And take stock
What courage would it take
For me to shed this mortal coil
To leave it all behind
And sink beneath the soil?
Sometimes, there's just despair
Where once was hope
A decaying world
And it's hard to cope
No more values, just greed exists
It's somewhere that I would not miss
But then there's you, my smiling boy
A ray of sunshine, of love and joy
My time with you, means more than life
Makes me forget my woes and strife
I miss you when you are not here
If truth be told, I've shed a tear
But such is life, that is my lot
So please remember, you're all I've got
Be fair, be kind and show you care
And you'll do well in life, I swear.

Gerard McAvoy (Newry)

Hold On To Your Memories

Memories are something
That no one could live without
A photograph of a first kiss
Or the birth of a dear child
But the memories we hold in our hearts
May they be happy or grim
Hold the greatest sense of love for us
And our loving kin
So, hold these memories and don't let go
No matter what road you take
For they could hold an answer for you
In the future, should you make a mistake.

Margaret McGinty (Ballymoney)

The Time Before

Cathedral spire and cobbled streets,
Thatched roofed houses, lavender sheets.
A breeze that bends the blossoming bough,
A man who rests upon the plough.
A herd of cows full blown with milk,
The parson's wife in gown of silk.
The days of playing hide-and-seek,
The first kiss on a blushing cheek.
A winter's snow so white and cold,
A morning sun once made of gold.
Dreaming memories linger on,
Of time like dribbling sand that's gone.
Now papers full of rape and murder,
A fellow hanging from a girder.
Houses locked with chains and bars,
Petrol fumes from roaring cars.
Money lasting half a week,
Work not found although you seek.
Drugs or drink it's all the same,
Now children play a different game.
Marches, riots against the state,
The morning papers shouting hate.
Mindless robots scream for more,
In this world without a law.

M Williams (Colwyn Bay)

From The Attic

I opened the toy box this morning
And saw Teddy still sitting there
He looked, oh, so pleased to see me
His eyes shone, as I raised him with care
His soft touch told me that he forgave me
For leaving him so long ago
'Cause he knew though I'd left him, I loved him
For so often I had told him so
But now there's another to love him
And as we parted again, I smiled
For the one that I know will love him now
Is my own precious child.

Patricia E Canavan (Cardiff)

Sunlight

Sitting in my easy chair
Musings of idling mind.
I glanced toward the garden,
To seek what eye may find.
You were standing at the window,
Where the sunlight percolates through
The leaves of the sapling alder,
When first I saw my true love of you.
In one breathtaking emotion,
The rays about you seemed to free,
All within my innermost being,
To reach this, the very heart of me.
I was transfixed by the magic of the moment,
It seemed a hand had reached out to spell.
In enchantment all the things you are,
Which by word I never could you tell.
As the dance of the beams played ethereal,
There you stood in most womanly grace,
I smiled at how much I had learned,
From sunbeams in a small window space.
A rude cloud came by in interruption,
But I still shall remember it yet.
How idle musings upon an easy chair,
Gave me a sunlight I'll never forget.

Elwyn Johnson (Llanelli)

Lullaby O' Dreams

Wheesht Bonnie ma bairnie
A'll sing yae a sang
Courie intae ma bousie
It'll no be lang
Afore yur in Dreamland
A chasen the sheep
Courie in ma wee lamb
An hae a wee sleep
Set yursel' cosy
In the crook o' ma airm
Cuddle intae yur Dey
An yu'll cum tae nae herm

Alexander Smith (Leven)

Family Love, Warmth And Trust

If every church was full of family love, warmth and trust
The world that we live in would be a lot more just
And would not be as unhappy as it is today
Because not so many people would get led astray
Instead the world would be a much happier place
Because more people would be trusting in God's grace
And more people's lives and attitudes would be greatly changed
And their beliefs and opinions would be rearranged
Churches like this, would be a lot more effective
In helping people that feel lonely and rejected
And in healing people of their afflictions
And in setting them free of their many addictions
And what a happier place God's church would be
If it was full of Christian love, warmth and simplicity
Where everybody was made to feel valued and treasured
And where no one was wrongly judged or unjustly measured
Where everybody was made to feel loved and accepted
And where nobody ever felt rejected
Where everybody did their best for God and one another
And served each other as a sister and brother
So let's do our best to keep God's church that way
So that none of us need get led astray
And let's do our best to make this world into a happier place
By sharing God's love with the human race.

Martin Reynolds (Peterhead)

Land Of Song

Dare to dream moonlight mist
Rain-dance images forgotten
Ethereal dragons kissed
Misty clouds of cotton
Celtic flowers on the hill
Abundant yellow bouquet
Symbolic fragrant daffodil
Traditional Saint David's Day
Glorious is the land of song
Inspirational traditional tales
Spiritual guidance all along
In this land of Wales

Carol Rudderham (Neath)

A Good Night To You

As I lie here in bed
I think it's a sin
That you keep me awake
With that terrible din
I glance at the clock
It's twenty-past four
The whole room vibrates
With your raucous snore
Go buy yourself some earplugs
Is what you suggest
Then perhaps you will get
A decent night's rest
I've tried every cure
That's known to men
Even pinching your nose
To the count of ten
I'm certain the sound
Of a wild lion roaring
Doesn't come close
To the noise of your snoring
But wait, maybe the night
Isn't wasted at all
I'll just go to sleep
In the room down the hall.

Rosaline Jones (Holyhead)

If Only

If only you could speak and tell
Of years long ago
You would have some wild
And exciting things to say
Not all good, having had to fight off
Many a foe, for all that
There is none more
Beautiful than thee
No matter where I roam
You are the lovely island
In the Firth of Forth
Called St Colme.

Catherine Findlay (Dunfermline)

The Shepherd

As children we loved the word shepherd -
It conjured up a safety and care,
The sheep were a part of our income
And lambing time brought in a share.
My father kept sheepdogs and worked them
To round up the flock every day,
The dogs were so useful and clever -
We watched them at work and at play.
Some lambs needed help with their feeding
And bottles of milk kept them strong,
Each season we fed many pet lambs -
Each day was intensive and long.
Sheep shearing again was hard labour,
The flocks on the hill were brought down,
It meant busy days for the shepherd
As sheep were collected and penned.
As children we helped roll the fleeces
From which lovely blankets were made,
They kept us quite snug in cold weather -
Those lovely warm memories don't fade.
I think everyone is a shepherd -
Each day of our lives we take care,
The joys of a life in the country
Is something we joyously share.

G Moses (Sennybridge)

Pembroke Castle

Oh ancient stones if you could speak how much there'd be to tell,
How masons shaped your limestone face and in your thousands placed by men,
You bonded as one castle, a place where kings could dwell,
Unlike mankind your lichen walls can never really tell
The history that has occurred within your sturdy walls,
You saw the pageantry - the valour - history unfold.
You heard the sound of armour and the battle calls
You listened to the tales of courage as often they were told.
Your stones heard proudly that a king was born,
In present times you proudly stand in sunshine and in rain,
Dear castle, heart of Pembroke in this summer morn,
May your stones in ivy clad gleam brightly once again.

Beryl Monico (Pembroke)

Facing Life In A Positive Way

Before you face the world on any day
Each morning do not forget to pray
Speak about what you would like to find
Tell God everything that is in your mind
Ignore negative thoughts and feelings in your life
Let God help you get through your strain and strife
Live your life one day at a time
Always be careful with your words and do not commit a crime
Never feel so low in your life to think that there is nothing worthwhile to do
Do not try to do something which could badly injure you
Kind people will have an understanding and listening ear
None of these people would leave a person filled with fear
Once a person realises that they are not on their own
Whether they get help in person or just by lifting the telephone
This will give them some peace in their mind
Having talked with a person who is patient and kind
Always be careful and do not take on too much on your hands
Then you might find yourself burying your head in the sand
In your life always ask for guidance from God
At any time of the day even if some people think you are odd
Many people wishing to have money want the number of days in a week to be more than seven
God warns all people that silver and gold will not get them a place in Heaven
Only by accepting Jesus Christ as their personal Saviour to know
Decides at the end of their life where they will go

Robert Doherty (Ballymoney)

The Sellotaped Shoe

Buchanan bus station
Balmy summer's night
The old man stands
Hunched of back
Belly of beer
Shoes held with Sellotape
Suit no longer fitting
A crown of barber-shy white hair
Glasses too big for face
Two polythene bags hold secrets
A digital watch to remind him
His best days have long since past

Lawrence Crawford (Glasgow)

My Baby Brother

I have a baby brother
He is only four weeks old
His face is like an angel
He never does what he is told.
I feel so sad for the poor wee thing
For you see, he cannot eat
When we sit down to dinner
He just plays with his feet.
One day, I said to Mummy
Something I'd like to know
If my little brother cannot eat
You know he will not grow.
She said, 'God made your little brother
And his nice wee hands and feet
But he can't sit down to dinner
He has no teeth to eat.
So, dear God, up in Heaven
There is something you forgot
You sent me down my brother
And I love him quite a lot.
You made him such a nice wee thing
And his little hands and feet
But one thing you've forgotten, God
To give him teeth to eat!

Annie McKillen (Ballymoney)

Encounter

In that spring lost in time,
We wandered through the gardens,
Sharing the sight of flowers
Sprung from winter's prison.
An arm of the sea beckoned
And we watched otters at play.
We bought seeds from the gift shop counter,
Memories of that brief encounter.
Not ships that passed in the night,
But ships on the same course a while.
Then, he steered east and I turned west,
Just one of life's little jests.

Anne C Byers (Dunfermline)

Life's Anomaly

Life can be so fickle
As the weather is so too,
Sometimes pleasant as can be
But oft the opposite is true.
The journey on the way
Isn't easy as we know,
Yet we struggle on regardless
On the pretext that we'll grow,
To nurture all the good things
That we love and understand.
Then things they changed forever
Which does so countermand,
The kind of standards we were taught,
They stood us in good stead.
And guided us through thick and thin
With a conscience so inbred.
Nowadays communities seem split and far apart,
Unwilling they appear, to want to understand
A kind word here, a smile would start!
To integrate all race and creed.
Respect and thought for others now
Is sadly lacking, I'm afraid,
Cannot we soothe the furrowed brow
Bring back to life that's sadly lost.

Gillian Sproates (Treharris)

Inherently Faulty

Perhaps if there had been some sort of test
before the project first got off the ground
development would not have gone ahead;
been classified as faulty or unsound.
For surely none with any common sense
would lay their reputation on the line
by offering a vote of confidence
to such an unreliable design.
-My ruling, once the vital facts were known,
would have imposed a future total ban
on similar experiments and gone
no further with the prototype of Man.

G Aldsmoor (Dundee)

Weather Of Wales

Morning lovely blue skies
Give hope of a nice day
Then clouds start creeping over hills
Stalking us their prey
Blue skies disappear
As the cloud envelop the sky
Hopes of lovely sunshine
Diminishing before our eyes
Now it's started raining
At first it's just a shower
Soon develops to a storm
Hour after hour
I think I see a blue hue
Perhaps it will brighten up
We live in hope of sunshine
Of rain we've had enough
The plants are groaning
With the weight of heavy showers
Gardens desperate for the sun
Of that we have no power
To see lush green pastures
Over valley hills and dales
We have to suffer the blight of rain
For the beauty of our Wales.

Christa Fisher (Llanyravon)

Golden Moments

Silence is golden
When snowflakes float down
The wind it is silent
As they touch with the ground
The birds have departed
They've flown to their beds
The coals in the fireplace
Glow rosy and red
A full moon is rising
All silvery and gold
Peace has descended
On this wonderful world

Elizabeth Casey (Milford Haven)

Is It Retirement

Retirement the dream that never is
The wonderful time that never seems to arrive
The time that is like tomorrow and never really comes
But before we are there, it fills the mind with wonder
When space is made for ease and leisure
When did I invent that time?
It was when my life was full of busy days of work
When energy was plentiful and free
Maybe it's measured in meters, by units or therms
Only later in £s by the bills arriving in bank
Where does retirement come in, or from?
Some say, 'It's after you are sixty-five.'
Says he, with a mocking grin
Perhaps we don't know those they call 'they'
Perhaps it is something to do with the little green men
Perhaps we've not arrived in their world?
Or perhaps it's like energy and cash, it goes before I get a feel
Now well past 65 years, I think I'm running out of time
Never mind a New World out there
It's just like my sweet peas
They come with scent and colour
And give pleasure, then they fade away
Like retirement and me
But not with God in His Eternity.

Anthony Cracknell (Langport)

Remember

Remember me as winter sun,
With tender hints of gold,
Remember me as that special one,
The hand you had to hold,
Remember when we said goodbye,
I cried a million tears,
Remember what we mean to me,
Our love throughout the years,
Remember now that I am gone,
That soon we'll meet again,
My love for you is forever,
A story to never end.

Jennifer Clare Kerr (Wishaw)

An Ode To Buckfast Tonic Wine

'The Bucky'

From Thurso in the north to Gretna in the south
The look of all the local neds is enhanced with The Bucky
In their mouth

This tonic wine, this liquid gold
At around a fiver a bottle, in gallons, it is sold

They drink it chilled but that costs more
Some say they'd even pay a score

Some say it smells of toenails, it surely can't be good
But ask the teens of Lanarkshire and they tell you that you should

On the streets and in the park
In daylights hours or after dark

Some young folk they call it 'lube'
And now it features on 'You Tube'

When first it came upon the street
The monks, they said, demand they'd meet

And how those abbots gave a try
As demand it soon outweighed supply

But Holy orders made them lucky
And they owe it all to 'The Bucky'

John Robertson (Cumbernauld)

Secrets

Everyone has a secret; we all have things to hide,
it's something that's integral: buried deep inside.
We all have skeletons in the cupboard,
cloak and dagger things concealed,
and even though they increase our load,
they should never be revealed.
That stolen kiss; that undisclosed affair,
that rendezvous: when you weren't there.
And yet I think with some regret,
for they're only buried just skin deep,
if you can't keep a secret secret,
it shouldn't be yours to keep.

Warren Fraser (Ferndale)

Predator

Iced diamonds, move on darkened shore,
Softly to my garage door.
A beautiful cat, in shadows grey,
Towards the entrance of her prey.
Muscles still, on raised perch,
Green-grey eyes seek and search.
Concentration never wanes,
Practice from her kitten games.
Soon, she strikes.

She drops and strikes fair.
Death from the dark air.
Her quarry darts for cover, chance,
Life in the balance.
See the balance tip,
Just one unlucky slip
And death strikes.

She was made for this quest,
Carries out her task with zest.
Yet, she welcomes us with love,
Eyes so soft, turtle dove.
But inside her the jungle lives
And when the soft divide gives,
She is her true self.

Ted Boyce (Banbridge)

Fragile Earth

Tread softly upon this light Earth,
Gently awakening to give rebirth,
As bud's burst forth, to summer's
Glory, the sodden earth awakes anew.

The dew upon the grass is glistening,
Now early May, the birds are singing,
The wild grasses blowing, the poppy
Leaves showing.

Remember me when I am gone - the
Poppy petals on a summer breeze
Are blowing, blowing, blowing.

Susan Jane Byers (Conwy)

To Enjoy Another Day

Large poppies lose their petals, in the English wind and rain,
But this morning in the garden, their beauty was quite plain!
Not a breath to stir the petals, but the buzzing of a bee,
Red faces turned toward the sun, great characters I see!
How I longed to catch that feeling, magic moment . . . only mine,
So I clicked it with my camera to enjoy another time.

Bright laughter in the garden, as a ball skims past my nose,
Then lands lost in the border . . . *after shaking off my rose!*
The wicked smile of 'innocence' continuing in their play,
So I click it with my camera to enjoy another day.

There is no age in families, from Grandpa to Grandson,
For when they get together, there is always lots of fun.
Friendly cousins in pyjamas, loose elastic . . . that gives way!
So, I click it with my camera to enjoy another day.

Fond memories of younger days, with paper, twigs and wood,
Shows carefully how to light a fire, as all good boy scouts should!
Then preparing, cooking, eating, until all have had their fill,
So, I click it with my camera to record another thrill!

When the holidays are over, dark winter nights begun,
The empty, lonely garden, can sometimes make you glum.
With my albums filled with memories, clicked in sun's bright rays,
Now is the time when you and I can *'enjoy another day'.*

Jean K Jeffery (Anglesey)

Sleepy Wood

Walk with me to sleepy wood
and my manner with promise, shall be good.

I will collect for you a posy of flowers,
with colours splendid of purple, yellow and blue
though none more beautiful than you.

Poems for you, I will recite,
of unicorns flying through a starlit sky at night.

And a song for you I will sing,
of a pauper who became a king.
Come walk with me to sleepy wood,
that is if you would.

Francis Page (Barry)

White Flowers

Sometimes when I am thinking about white bedrooms
Or walking past a pale house
With an upstairs window or curtain blowing in the breeze,
There is another drinking of right talking and male cotton tease.

A tepid water drenched or spotless lamb
Way of perfecting white flowers
Their appearance, sent and general way,
Another babies cot of impress and it is
Of correcting towers and presence of day.

White roses, carnations, lilies, bells, Camilla
Magnolia and vanilla, daisies and those which grow on walls,
Of all their poses, frillies, William Tells
And a Pricilla with clean crisp little small balls.

All the different sorts, types, varieties and everything else white
Which brings them to life or causes your senses
To drift into the thin smooth air,
Another essence and fragrance of whiff, celse
And a good wife of immense with care.

With hopes and dreams which we all have
Are untouched and build while we are all here,
In other dishes, ropes and reams
Another world year after year.

Fiona Clarke (Newport)

Sorry

This little word, sorry
Small as it is!
Is hard for some folk to say
It isn't their English at fault,
No! Conscience gets in the way,

As trying to bluff their way
Out of a fix
They often forget what to say,

But to say sorry and mean it!
To the one that's been hurt
Would soon blow sad feelings away.

Grace Minnis (Holywood)

The Flower

A summer mist
closes round the angle of things
blunting them back and back as ships
become peeled-back echoes - untouching
phantoms
hung from sky and sea.

Stifled music
in some divided part of me
embraces a sleep -
closing out sounds that cool the heart.

I turn veiled eyes to you - again -
that distant bliss - that patient longing
I promised
when I accepted our parting - with a flower
placed on your table.

We will say goodbye - our souls
turning back for just one look will lock
in dream
and keep their tryst with hands
through this silence -

through this smothering silence.

Myra Vennard (Bangor)

Delusions

The very road that we walk upon in time will disappear,
And so will the glasses that hold our tantalising beer.

All the things that we hold dear will also vanish,
Our family, our friends, our lovers, and our tears.

We capture clips of life on camera, and on screen,
They give us happy memories, but they are still a dream.

We kiss and cuddle each other with love and affection,
Hoping to make some sort of inner connection.

But sadly, and gladly true love is beyond the concept of time,
Where individually every moment is yours and mine.

Mario Servadei (Glasgow)

Happy Days

(The memories of an old man)

I like to sit on the riverbank
Reminiscing for a while
Of skipping down the valley
Then jumping over the stile.

We'd paddle in the river
Catch tadpoles in a jar
Listening to the cuckoo's
Voice, echoing from afar.

Butterflies and bees in the meadow
The corncrake in the corn
Birds singing sweetly overhead
As they had from early morn.

Days seemed long and sunny
When I rambled as a boy
With gentle breezes blowing
Life was filled with joy.

The sleepy river still glides on
Making its way to the sea
As I sit here, thinking of the past
There's no place on Earth I'd rather be.

Jean Wright (Craigavon)

Crazy Train

Walking round crazy as a loon
often found staring up at the moon.

Strange visions play before my eyes
voices in my head telling me lies.

Life is simple when you're insane,
happily travelling the crazy train.

Then you take a step too far
and doctors put your brain in a jar.

Taking pills morning and night
to keep me happy with a future bright.

Deborah Remnant (Cardiff)

The Hole In One

(Written 29th July 2008 in memory of his glass)

Dreams are the footsteps that waken the mind
As the heart falls asleep
How is it that all is made clear while the eyes drift?
Is it by chance or by design?

Creation was made not just an idea
A fruit born within our souls keeping love as its first light
Magic plays a tune so silent so smooth a drifting mood
Kept in time for all time.

Love is a drop so soft is its touch giving life to tears
Brought by joy from a land of passers-by
Stories told held in a cup
Friendship played on a course

Forgotten land
How I love your whispering wind
Singing tunes to no one
Sole to me

Scotland, I praise thee my heart rests in Siam
A noble land of heartfelt thanks
One day I shall swing the iron
A tear dropped in a hole in one.

Anton Nicholas

Remorse

Ingratitude; that I should hurt the one who cares
And wound the heart that in my living shares.

That I should remonstrate with words designed to slice,
When kindly acquiescence would suffice.

What can I say? A verbal cure if there be one,
Can words undo a wrong that words have done?

And if no words of mine can heal a heart that's numb
And silence would be best, then I'll be dumb.

Until the path of time has led you to forget
And left for me a signpost called regret.

Robert McIlveen (Belfast)

Kharbarat

'This song is . . .'
He paused, as if counting,
'Four hundred years old.'

'It celebrates New Year,
the beginning of Spring,
in Mazaar-i-Sharif.'

He paused again, then translated,
'We drink the juice of
pomegranates and rose water.'

And smiled. A child under
the Russians, a young man
under the Taliban,

Now touring Europe, wanting us
to know his forefathers
drank sherbet and laughed.

In Moscow, old soldiers fight
with their children and wives.
In Peshawar, old hurts re-ignite,

but here, he shares joy
distilled over generations:
grinning, he starts to sing.

Jeff Kemp (Musselburgh)

Parting

I wake to find you weeping at my side.
A tide of memories steals gently in,
From the thrill of that first fumbled embrace
To our years of fulfilment and joy.
I see you in a dress of red roses,
Cradling our child in your arms.

But now, age has withered our bodies,
Stunted our minds, curtailed our lives.
Love, compassion and despair fill my heart.
I try to stroke your tearstained face
And fiercely grasp your proffered hand,
But find, alas, I am no longer there.

P G Williams (Merthyr Tydfil)

Failure And Success

The discipline of pain
and disappointment,
of hopes denied,
defeated plans:
the inescapable
elements in life
can make or break us.
At worst we're reject
pots or broken shards;
at best we're steel
hammer forged in flame

We must make the best
of life's realities;
learn lessons from our
failures and defeats;
accept our sorrows
and sing our sad songs
with a beauty that
brings joy and solace,
peace to troubled souls;
learn lessons, turn our
failures and defeats
into wins, success!

Ian L Forrester (Kirkcaldy)

Rendition

A graceful rendition
Fills the air with a touch
Of excellence, mirroring the
Settling of doves into the quiet
Symphonic blanket of notes
Upon the night sky.

Freshly fallen snow
Trodden only once
As into the distance
They fly o'er head
And one walks into a vast expanse of
Classical supremacy.

Anne Taggart (Armagh)

A Walk In The Country

Over highways and byways, down pathways and lane
I've rambled the country, but never in vain
I always see something to inspire a poem
In this lovely land, my birthplace and home
Full of history and legend, in mountain and glen
A joy to the poet, with paper and pen

Now, as I walk on past forest and hill
I see an old farmstead and an old watermill
Both stand neglected and I wonder why
It was a home for some family in days long gone by
Now both stand in ruins neglected and still
There's no use today for the old watermill

The river flows gently on to the sea
It means nothing to some, but it's music to me
For often I wonder in thoughts and in dreams
The legend and history of those mountain streams
And if they could tell us the secrets they know
Of days long forgotten and of times long ago

I've walked a long time now and I'm nearly home
So it's time I concluded and finished this poem
And I hope you will like it, as it's simple and true
This verse by a poet, who likes writing for you.

Eugene McGaughey (Ballymena)

Getting Older

Time passes by and we get older
The days are long the nights feel colder
The wrinkled face, the greying hair
The body racked with pain we bear
Living every day as if our last
Reminiscing about the past

But there's a reason to go on living
The gift of love, the joy of giving
Visits from loved ones that give us pleasure
Happy memories for them to treasure
Special times together we share
Because for us they'll always care.

Wendy Lorraine Haskell (Ebbw Vale)

Sunshine

I love the sunshine
When it warms you right through,
The grass is green and the sky is blue
And all the flowers are in bloom,
The colour of the rainbow
They look up to the sunshine for heat

And hearing children playing in the street,
There is lots of joy, you can see,
But not for long, it's time for tea,

The sunshine is what they love
Love the best,
Out they go to play,

It's raining most of the time,
Out in the muddy puddles all day,
Till they are wet right through,
These are things children like to do

The weathermen say, 'Sunny,' today
So the children will be out again, to play
All the games, boys and girls play, in the street,
Until it's time for bed,

When there will come another sunning day.

Josie Hogg (Belfast)

Sweet Memories

How oft I awake in the wee small hours
When the night is still and deep
When thoughts like flitting butterflies
Delay my fragile sleep.

It's then I wander back again
Across the fields of time
To the golden days of youth and joy
When life was a joyous rhyme.

Loving families, faithful friends
No longer in my sight
It's then that sad sweet memories
Fill the still deep night.

Elizabeth Bacon (Glasgow)

That Cross For Me

You travelled along that old rugged track,
Bearing that cross on poor tortured back,
So wretched and weary you bore such pain,
Exhausted from beatings, leaving your body bloodstained.

You did this for me.

As you drew near, The Place of the Skull,
Oh how you wished that pain would dull,
Those nailed pierced hands, and thorns on your head,
With mocking and stoning you hung and bled.

You did this for me.

You paid that ransom for my soul,
Suffering my pain and making me whole,
That selfless sacrifice that set me free,
My blessed Saviour, who redeemed me,

You did this for me.

As your life ebbed way, those words, Father forgive,
Such agony you bore, so that we might live,
No longer your head with crown so thorny,
But now you reign on high in majestic glory.

You did this for us all.

Christine Richards (Milford Haven)

Parting

Farewell my dear and needed friend
For I fear that we must part
As you will tread an unknown land
But I, a well-worn path
Days pass me by
But years stand still
And no longer will I pay
For all my deadly and worldly sins
That I plead guilty for
The curtain is raised and now reveals
A mental skeleton left behind
An emptiness, a shallowness
That leaves my mind a handcuffed bind.

Margaret Maciver (Bernera)

Inspiration

Inspiration lies dormant like an animal in hibernation;
Imagination lurks sluggishly in the deep recesses of the mind,
As I struggle to process jumbled thoughts into cohesion.

Oh, little brown envelope, will you not go away
And leave me in peace for another day?

Pink-edged silver clouds scud across the evening sky;
Martins and screeching swifts swoop in the twilight gloom,
Enjoying a final sortie before resting for the night.

What a carefree life, with no stress or sorrow
Or brown envelope to worry about tomorrow.

The purposeful bee gathering pollen from a rose,
The song thrush cracking a snail on a stone,
Operate by instinct within nature's ordered economy,

Unlike humans, who dither and read their horoscope
Instead of tackling the little brown envelope.

Finally, emerging from my inertia, I've composed these lines
So that I can hopefully sleep with a clear conscience once again
With the satisfaction born of a mission eventually accomplished.

I began by cursing you, but now I thee bless,
O' little brown envelope from Forward Press.

Alison Drever (Edinburgh)

Dream World

I long for the night when I can sleep
When in my dreams there's no need to weep
We run hand in hand through fields of corn
In my dreams our love is reborn
I hold your hand as we laugh and play
We make tender love be it night or day
But time ticks by bringing the morning light
It invades my sleep as it ends the night
I wake from my dreams to another day
To a heart full of pain that won't go away
So I long for the night when I can sleep
And escape to my dreams
Where there's no need to weep.

M Taylor (Brechin)

Village Gossip

Here comes Dai Thomas,
Down the hill in his wellies,
To throw the swill.
Twenty pigs he has.
Who told you that?
Blodwyn of course,
Gossip of the town,
She knows everything that goes on around.
What about her daughter then?
Gwyneth with the long dark hair,
Got pregnant, man in the army, so they say.
Nagoes, nagoes, that's not right,
By the postman, got a wife called Pat.
Poor Gwyneth.
Poor Pat.
Here comes Meredydd, bald as a coot,
Look at that, he's lost a boot!
Been at the whisky,
I wouldn't be surprised,
That's why he's looking so glassy-eyed.
Well, bye then.
Bye Anne.
Bye Glen.

Helen Miles (Bridgend)

The Elements

Rolling dust down the alleyways comes the whistling wind,
Scattering the dust, whipping it in your face,
Then comes the rain in deluge sometimes,
While the scorching sun wrecks havoc on its blazing race,
The gentle breeze turns into a powerful cyclone,
These are the elements powerful powers,
Also seen in the ocean's roar and tone,
The fallen trees across the roadways
And the flooded cities and towns,
Then the winter's icy frocks with the clogged aerodromes,
The endangered hillside frowns,
Considering the reasons,
These are the seasons.

William Eugene Doherty (Omagh)

Follow The Rainbow

Can you hold me closer I am hurting so much inside
My mind is in turmoil, I keep asking why?
My life was so special, I am not ready to die,
How am I going to cope as each day goes by?
Life was precious, wipe the tear from my eye,
I do not want to face the world,
I just need to be alone, to take in the news,
not answer the phone.
I am trying hard to cope,
I am in total despair beyond all hope.
Mixed emotions deep down inside,
An endless flow of tears I have cried.
Nobody knows what you are going through,
the world looks different now.
Can you hear the birds singing their sweet refrain?
Where is the sunshine, there is only rain.
Once there was blue sky, now it's grey,
No tomorrow only yesterday.
I will not let it beat me, I will be strong,
I will look for the sunshine after the rain,
I will follow that rainbow to ease the pain.
I will smile in the face of adversity,
I will come through it, just wait and see.

Wendy John (Bridgend)

Existence

I've been stood up
I've been slapped down
I've been to the edge
I've been around town
I've known the evil Man can do
I've known the heartache a woman can put you through
I've tasted drugs and alcohol
I've tasted where the need comes from
I've stewed in sorrow
I've received the pain
I've been rejected to be born again
I've been on my own my whole sorry life
I've no family nor friends, just an existence with sight

Chris B (Cardiff)

At My Own Pace

My face may be different
But my feelings are the same
I laugh and I cry
And take care in my pride
I was sent here among you
To teach you to love
Not to hurt or kill you
As God in the heavens
Looks down at us from above
To him, I'm no different
His love has no bounds
It's those here among you
In cities and towns
They kill each other
What for I do not know
Who judges our standards
That love is acceptance
It comes from the heart
We all have one purpose
The Lord gave me life
Not for someone to take it away
To live another day and do it
At my own pace.

R J Lewis (Swansea)

A Skirmish

On the train and by the
Light of the silvery moon
I observed the many flowering
Brooms
Swaying to 'n' fro in gusts
Of wind 'n' melting snow
Sweeping beads of sweat-like
Glistening droplets alight
From fleshy stooping stems
A moving scene
A skirmish anew
A picture
Framed by my window view.

Douglas Greenlaw (Kirkcaldy)

In The Blink Of An Eye

Today, I returned to the big stones
Though, they were not nearly so big,
I sat down and thought of what once was
And how the time has passed.
I slowly closed my eyes and searched
The darkness of my mind,
To find myself returning to the days
The stones were mountains.
Where we were warriors and nothing
Would get in our way of protecting our dreams,
Where we once played games that now I've forgotten,
Where we vowed never to forget what childhood was.
With the laughter of children in my head
And the shadows of childhood in my tears, I slowly
Opened my eyes and returned to the reality of now.
I sit and watch my own children play
And I pray that the magic
For them will never end, knowing only too well it will.
People have passed, loved ones have gone,
I feel a lump deep in my throat, knowing that time
Has flown so fast.
In the blink of an eye
Everything changes.

Gina Lorraine Copland (Orkney)

Bullets Versus Lives

The hungry cry
Dying as they lie
The buzzing fly
Near the eye
That cries out why?
Oppressive heat
And stinking fly
Fill the unrelenting sky
Man has to care
It's all I can bare
Don't pay for bullets
Pay for lives
I just have to cry.

Richard Shurey (Tonypandy)

My Heart Is A Treasure

My heart is a treasure
Full of treasures
As big as the world
As wide as the sky
As deep as the sea
Sparkling with hidden gems
And warmth of the sun
Rich and golden
Soft as snow
Beautiful as the breeze
Smell me in the summer
Touch me in the autumn
Hold me in the winter
For I am never far
I am a treasure you will
Never see
Feel me
I am universal love
Kissing your soul
Tickling your toes
Caressing your hair
And blessing your heart
For evermore.

Siàn Boissevain (Whitland)

Red, Red Robin

A little robin sang to me
While sitting on a branch of a tree
Winter is here
The air is so cold and clear
It feels like Jack Frost is near
Snow falls this time of year
The air is crystal-clear
Leaves look pale in the morning glow
Frost twinkles just like snow
Every year he comes to say hello
I see his footprints in the snow
Oh, little robin red breast
Christmas will soon be here, not long to go.

Samantha Groves (Tywyn)

The Big Man

On a dark cold winter's night
Two Carrive brothers decided to frighten a middle-aged woman
Codding about a big dangerous man walking the roads at night
He will get you some night and frighten the life out of you
But unknown to them, two clever men were listening
They thought of a plan to stop the codding
They walked a half mile to Duffies crossroads
Stood at a tree at the side of the road
The fat man stood on the grass verge
The big man stood on the fat man's shoulders
As they'd seen the two brothers coming laughing their fill
The big man started smoking a cigarette and put his hand on one of their heads
One brother said, 'Did you see that Francis?'
'I did,' said Pat, and they ran home as quick as lightning
As they reached home they collapsed at the door
Their mother gave them a drink of water to revive them
Their father said, to play a trick like that is no joke
An older person could die of fright, it's a mortal sin
It was a great joke for the brothers to try to frighten a middle-aged woman
When the plan went wrong it was a different story,
Well, by jove, that put an end to their codding.
As the old people used to say,
Never trouble, trouble, till trouble, troubles you.

Micheal McGuigan (Newry)

Untitled

O God, You bathe us in the sunshine of Your love,
And as the sun shines in our hearts,
We are strengthened as He imparts
His great compassion and His divine peace,
His ever-growing tenderness will never cease,
He cares for each one,
O God, Your precious Son,
Touching each heart, mind and soul,
O God, through Him, we are made whole.
O much sacrifice, the work of the Cross,
He satisfies the souls of the lost,
He bled and died on Calvary,
To show His great love for you and for me.

Kristine McDonald (Aberdeen)

Sweet Love

Oh, why do they call that flower 'sweet pea'?
When it should be called 'sweet love'.
For the more you pluck it, the more it grows
And it grows and it grows.
And before you know it, your garden is filled
With such beautiful flowers
That grow and grow and grow.

So it's the same with your heart:
It's so tiny you know.
For the more you love
The bigger it grows
And it grows and it grows
And before you know it, your heart is filled
With God's wonderful love
That grows and grows and grows.

And it's the same with your life:
It's so precious you know.
For the longer you live
You will reap what you sow
Till the angel of death will carry up your soul
To the glory of God in your eternal home
Then you'll go and you'll go and you'll go.

Mary Russell (Carrickfergus)

Tomorrow

Criticise me not, my son,
For growing old and full of sorrow,
Where I am today,
You may be there tomorrow.

Where I was yesterday,
You are there today,
But of tomorrow,
Who knows what might be?

So, criticise me not, my son,
For growing old and full of sorrow,
As you may not live
To see the new tomorrow.

John Harrold (Newport)

Almost Twenty-One

'I'm almost twenty-one,' she said.
Her smile conveyed a thousand little growing points
In the life that had both blossomed
And somehow found a new and twinkling vision
To the young man's eager gaze.

'Only two more sleeps until my birthday'
Had given way to birthdays
Which surprised by their regularity
And unrelenting marking out of time.
Yet still life's magic grew the hidden power
To be revealed in special birthday celebrations
When loved ones marked the day
And opened out the tale of all that's been achieved.

And most of all that sense of 'almost twenty-one'
Sums up that deep-seated throbbing 'looking forward'
Which makes of life a journey,
A journey which lifts all frailty to become a 'sense of purpose'.
It opens doors to 'what is longed for'
And may be 'round that most elusive corner'.
It opens up the peace of dreams
Which can now be sensed to be fulfilled.
I'm almost twenty-one.'

Andrew Monaghan (Pathhead)

A Rising Phoenix - Blaenau Gwent

Valley now bereft of coal and steel
No putrid fumes or miners' wheel
Green and new the valley's bloom
The valley sings a different tune

Smokeless air with sky so bright
Birds singing on new trees alight
Closed furnaces, no more dusty waste
Industry gone - just a green, lovely place

Two hundred acres on the great valley floor
Where steel production is no more
A rising phoenix of dreams is newly born
Work, houses, a hospital, new horizons form.

Mary P S Leadbeter (Ebbw Vale)

The Letter

Dear Carol-Ann,
You will never read these words or see the tears of those you left behind
Nor will you feel the pain, heartbreak and complete and utter misery
that we will all suffer every day since you left us.
We can tell anyone the years, the months, the days since you went,
we miss you every day, we remember you every day and we talk about you with love.
Where are you? Are you happy? Let Dad know.
Our parents are heartbroken and Mum can't sleep since you left us
and Dad does the manly thing but is hurting so bad.
Unk, Kiz, Mandy and Wendy are still grieving and it looks like
it won't get better for any of us anytime soon.
All the kids miss you and your generous heart and the grandchildren
that came after you left will never know the treasured love they could
have had if you were still here.
Our Carol-Ann, you made this world a better place to live in
and nothing and no one will ever replace you in our lives or hearts.
I have to go now, but just know there are not enough sad words
in the world or heavens above to tell you how you are missed and so loved.
Wait for us like you promised and then our broken hearts
will fall back into place.

Love Mary.

To know her was to love her.

Mary Fraser (Aberdeen)

A Racist Poem

Grand Grandad was a Rabbi and he played the fiddle too,
And all the Gentiles smiled at such an entertaining Jew.
And Grandad was a minister who liked to crack a joke.
The congregation laughed with him and listened when he spoke.

The children of mixed marriage tread a harsh and bitter road
And even to the grandchildren comes something of the load.
My grandson is a Scot indeed, from every point of view,
But sometimes in his smiling eyes peeps out the hidden Jew.

O Christ, who made of one blood those who on the Earth do dwell
All welcome are in Heaven, but in this life can be Hell.
Yet we are still God's children, and if we trust His plan
He'll surely bring about at last the brotherhood of Man.

Diana Richardson (Glasgow)

My Lilac Tree

So *many* times I've asked in prayer
My lilac tree a flower to bear.
In the corner of the garden, sheltered from the weather,
Its base surrounded by deep purple heather.
I've whispered to my tree reassuringly
Gentle words to make it feel trouble-free,
But *no flower* showed its pretty head
Even though its earthly roots I fed.

It would have sufficed to produce just one
And then nature's handiwork would be done.
Not a *bud* in sight, not a *single* bloom;
Only *one* I wished for, though there's *plenty* of room.
In my mind, I've kept asking repeatedly, 'Why?'
With every year that passes by.

This year, *as always,* I made my request
And *asked,* by way of nature's quest,
To *answer* my prayers and *bless* this tree
And somehow I *knew* that it heard my plea.
For *this* spring, in my garden, is a *wonderful* bouquet
Of heavenly-scented lilacs . . . and more on their way!
Each morning I visit my beautiful tree
And *thank* it so *kindly* for flowering for me.

Vivienne Vale (Porth)

Shipmates

Last night again, I dreamt of days long past
Of wartime service, spent before the mast
Of storms and tempest, seas and oceans far
Top, gallant shipmates, long since crossed the bar.

I stand in silence at the Cenotaph
Close to my heart, a faded photograph
My generation, laughing, in their prime
Names carved in granite, long before their time.

A sense of guilt, why am I here, still alive?
What did I merit to survive?
Could I, if only in my dreams,
Share once again that comradeship supreme?

F Osborne (Bangor)

Vegillante Gardener

I heard a sound outside
It gave me quite a fright
Was that somebody building a wall
Eleven-thirty at night?

He tends his patch with loving care
Is that you again out there?

He came home from the pub then
With flashlight and a trowel
Went into the garden
Like a watchful tawny owl, Arthur with little hair
Yes, he'd had a few ales
But he wouldn't let those snails eat his grub

Potatoes, onions, carrots and peas
Luscious-looking greeneries
He smashed the snails
And salted the slugs
So they couldn't slime his growing shrubs

His head shone by the light of the moon
They would have eaten his veg by noon
That's why he was out in the middle of the night
Crushing those snails by flashlight

Karen Gilmour (Prestatyn)

Eternity

Along the sweeping curve of bay,
behind the wide stretched golden sands,
low cliffs of ancient sandstone stand.

With every rise and fall of tide,
ripples form within the sand;
they mark the very limit of the land.

But in the sandstone of the cliffs
fossil ripples lie exposed, the same;
formed by distant tides, a long eternity ago.

What message then in this for us?
Ripples tide formed will persist, the same,
a long eternity ahead, far beyond the Age of Man - Adieu!

John S Hampton (North Berwick)

The Pocket Watch

Gripping it so tightly -
Tiny tender indentations marked my palm
During the long, lonely walk home.
Fearful it too might vanish -
As he has.

Enveloped in a torrent of past -
An unexpected burst of nostalgia,
I wandered.

Bewildered, worrying . . .
Imagining my wedding day
Who will give me away?

Full circle, reunited, home
Delicate golden timepiece bequeathed to me -
As he once bequeathed to my grandfather
Connecting with another generation.

Eyes on the road
Head in the clouds
I wandered, aimlessly
In the general direction of home
Surrounded by ghosts -
Though quite, quite alone.

Julieann Campbell (Londonderry)

Perth, Heilands Gateway

A city in bloom
Brings sunshine
When there is none

A city in bloom
Brings colour
When all is grey

A city in bloom
Lifts the spirit
When all is gloom

A city in bloom
Heilands gateway
Tay tarries since the womb

Ian Robinson (Perth)

I Am What I Am, But What Am I?

My blueprint is set before I am born
It is determined, boy or girl
Will I be tall or will I be small?
It's in my 'jeans', shape, size, colour and all.

Will I be handsome, a beauty to adore?
Will I be clever, charming, successful at all?
Destiny hold all of our key,
It's hidden, pre-determined, in our genes!

Though I accept that I have the talents that are given,
How do I find them, they seem pretty well-hidden?
Do I need to seek, so as to find?
Or will destiny step in, just in the nick of time?

There's no escaping we are who we are,
But how do we understand what and who we are?
Destiny holds all of our keys,
But is our whole life pre-determined because of our genes?

I am, what I want to be,
The choice is always mine!
Shaped by experiences, people and life!
Whenever in doubt, self-esteem on the line,
Delve deep inside, your talents to find.

Anne Helena Matley (Newton Stewart)

From The Depths And The Heights

Oh, thou beautiful soul
Listen to the clear voice within
Stay in the centre

Do everything out of love
And let love reap its own reward

All those fears and dreams
That flash past your mental screen
Are but the energies born
From your very self - your inner self

Stay centred, beautiful one
Let life's dream be love
And love be life's dream.

M Lincoln (Edinburgh)

My Heaven

Baseball boots and Mickey Mouse
Cars and toys all through the house
Self-portraits on the wall
Charts on the wardrobe to see who's tall

Breakfast dishes piled up high
Mountains of laundry that reach the sky
Broken dolls and broken cars
Men from outer space fighting wars

Toilet paper down the loo
Daddy's stereo broken in two
Mucky shoes and wet coats
Fun in the bath with bubbles and boats

Hugs of joy, hugs of love
Yes, each one is my little dove
Supper's ready, do you hear me call
Stop arguing and playing ball

Endless homework never done
Jumping on beds is much more fun
It's peace and quiet at half-past seven
My treasures are asleep
And I'm in Heaven.

Patsy Mulgrew Keys (Limavady)

Pictures I Paint

Pictures I paint are of landscapes
That I can escape in
Where I can escape.

Where birds sing songs of the season
And fish swim all day for their reasons.

There I stand on the banks for a while
The mirror disapproved as I take my time
The river runs fast bursting with old dreams of mine.

Self-portraits I paint, to show face
My saving grace
Drawing eyes you can look in
In your eyes, I escape.

Paul John Kemp (Haverfordwest)

November

November - oh! November
thou fading light of the dying year.
Of days cut short by Autumn
and leaves detached by storms.
Of nights of frost quite breathtaking
And fields with not a cow.
Yet still, in other climes, in sunshine and in growth
Beloved thou art.

Lead me to realise and to dwell
On your spiritual renewal,
Remembering souls, our families and our friends.

Your *day one* is a celebration of their earthly lives,
Of the love they gave us and the sacrifices they made.
Now we pray to them for help. *ALL Saints.*

Your *day two* is a continued remembrance
For souls delayed in that intangible state
Where they await their invitation to glory. *Holy Souls.*

Perhaps November, only for you I might not dwell
in prayer, to strive for the happiness of *day one*
or to be consoled by the existence of *day two*
Be part of me November.

Iris McEvoy (Newry)

To Hold A Dream Forever

How can you hold a dream forever?
Keep alive that flickering flame?
For it's as the blossom blown in springtime,
the snowflake when it turns to rain.

To cherish an ideal into tomorrow,
the grail that keeps a faith alive,
nurture when all hope's uncertain,
believe when all just seems a lie.

How can your heart be beyond betrayal
of all you held so true and good;
to hold the threads of a dream together,
that once meant more than life and blood?

Mike Monaghan (Glasgow)

Memory Lane

Following a ghost of a boy
Holding his father's hand
Along a lane through what
Is a now changed land
Still the fields stretch beyond the tracks
Of a railway line still connected to the past.

Tears, as the memories tug and stay
Tears for the years that have run away.

Calling to my father
Across such space, and how
It's been filled and forgotten
About, until now.

Woodland paths filled with spring light
Before the leaves return and rustle at night
Streams once damned are now long-dry
As concrete and brick play games with the sky.

Memory lane, my last farewell
Thankful I knew it then
Those images are not for sale
So they will remain forever
Though my father and I will fade, together.

Julian Bishop (Fasnakyle)

Number One Palais-Glide

I remember when we'd Palais-Glide
Or do the Tango, with you by my side
Foxtrot, Waltz how we would glide
Two hearts beating, our love we couldn't hide

Everyone happy and having fun
Each had their special number one,
Sadly many years later I'm now alone,
But have happy memories of when you were home.

When in one's youth you just can't comprehend
How two people can live together and love to the end,
That was us many moons ago
Our happiness complete, we loved each other so.

L Culshaw (Caldicot)

Pamplona

A load of young bull tramples
twisting, dusty streets
from bull pen to bull ring
in beaten sweat and terror

Screaming, shouting, a savage pack
bays
and a higher ape dances, bloody steps
for culture and for art.

But this is neither.

Casa de Misericordia
House of Mercy
shows none
as blood and terror reign for nine days
an old inquisition in a modern world.

But . . .

A human race runs here too
naked
protesting
fighting for change

And real mercy.

Gail McClory (Johnstone)

Hope For Tomorrow

If God be for us, who can be against us?
Wise words are these and I hope that somewhere you will now read my poem.
Sent to you in times when you feel you are alone and lonely.
Forget these feelings and remember when you were brought into this world
By some stem of love, you were not alone.
So this path you are set along is wisdom, light and love.
You will find your own way - walk it with strength and hope.
There are many stones and rocks and unkindly people.
At the end of your stay you will find everything you did had meaning and love.

Look at the stars, placed there by some almighty power.
Not in some stone or granite building by men, but with order from higher fields.
So please do not despair and wonder lost.
Look around you and help will soon be found.

Liz Cameron (Monikie)

Untitled

To celebrate is a wanting to share
A special day in your life in which you care
To let everyone know you're still there
Family from here and a friend or two
Forget for one day all trouble and strife
No work, no fuss. Because we love you.

The drink is flowing, the cake is going
Sandwiches and sausage rolls, anything goes
Let's raise another glass or two
A milestone has passed for you
May it be one year or more
We'll all be merry and bright
So let's party through the night
Who cares if we look a fright
The hours have passed, now four in the morning
Birds are singing a chorus for us.
Time to go home to bed, so get the bus.
Remember the night before in our dreams
For tomorrow is another day
Full of sunbeams
Next year will be the same
Till we all meet again.

Maggie Quinn (Aberdeen)

The Last Goodbye

Her mind was like a sunless desert,
Wracked by a sudden storm,
She pictured again the familiar, yet unfamiliar, form,
Heard the sombre voice, 'In God we trust,
Ashes to ashes, dust to dust.'
Remembered, in that quietest of quiet domains,
The sun, flooding colour, through stained-glass windowpanes.

Homeward-bound through a vale of tears,
Murmured comfort brought no solace to her ears.
Long day deepened into longer night,
The lonely hours, a battlefield, till dawn's cold light.
She did not care, she did not know, if only she would wait,
That spring would come again, if but a little late.

Joyce Honeyman (St Leonards)

Simplicity

Oh, for simplicity! In these strange times
We need to have a scientific mind,
A dictionary of modern English terms,
To modern jargon, modern answers find,
Let's play a tune - now, how to switch it on?
Which of these twenty buttons plays the best?
Their names don't seem to mean a lot to me,
Their sounds these days devoid of interest.
A general knowledge quiz - what must I know?
Film stars, pop stars, pop groups, pop bands and more,
There must be hundreds of them known to man,
But not to me - I might just manage four!
Pages of TV programmes - where do I start?
And green bags calling - soon I'll need a horse
To deal with adverts, charities and post,
With free and local newspapers, of course.
But meanwhile, mother sparrow on the wall
Is feeding youngsters, while the velvet bees
Search lavender for food, so I too search
For quality, for beauty, peace and ease.

Complexity is harassing mankind;
Simplicity for me and peace of mind.

C M Pountney (Lyme Regis)

Steekit Gates

Peace an guidwill ti men, the Christ yince say'd,
as mair nor he, o thochtsome men, portrayed
thir road aheid for mankind, fae the slough
aa roun, ti love an brither/sisterhood.
The Buddha, Christ, Mohammed tae, aye stood
for kinder, gentler airtin o that truth
guid folk then, wir seekin, thro'oot thae years
brutishness, arrogance an greed held sway.
Where, tho' Kirkies an Mullahs hae thir say,
does that leave us, Jock Tamson's bairns, wha's fears
are still the same an only yearn ti see
humanity in Man . . . an mankind free?

(steekit: literally, stitched: snecked or closed)*

Davie Kerr (Armadale)

A Sea Shanty

Now I am a sailor and I love the sea,
There isn't a matelot as happy as me,
I play with the women, the wine and the song,
And then I go drifting along, along
And then I go drifting along.

I sailed down the Mersey from Liverpool town,
The life of a landsman was getting me down,
Goodbye to the Liver Bird sing him a song,
And then I went drifting along,
The call of the sea, the wide open sea,
It's more than a woman to me.

Then I met a woman and she said to me,
'If you really loved me you'd give up the sea,'
So I kissed her goodbye and I sang her a song,
And then I went drifting along, along,
So then I went drifting along.

There may be a woman who one day will be
Much more than the call of the wide open sea,
Then I'll kiss her hello and sing her a song,
And no more I'll go drifting along, along,
No more I'll go drifting along.

Barbara E O'Brien (Buckley)

Emblem

(This poem 'Emblem' was written for the Brave art exhibition at Stirling Smith Art Gallery and Museum in 1996)

Proud Thistle, bear me close to thine
Roots of Scotia form thy spine
From Purpl'd Spur yir down maun throw
for Seeds of Freedom e'er tae grow.

Let Freedom be the Scotsman's Spur
To bear aloft his native Burr
From Wallace was the jewel torn
When Brus but lost the Brooch of Lorne.
An ancient Stane can forward lead:
Our Destiny supply the Deed.

Thora Clyne (Milnathort)

Granny's Poem

Granny, for weeks on that
Sofa you sat.
But you remained as tender
As a purring cat.

Oh, Granny, please do not feel
Beat.
Although you have fallen, you
Will land on your feet.

And Granny, don't feel lost
To get better, there'll be a cost.

Yet Granny, I see no tears
But I know you want to, 'cause
Ya miss your beer.

Now you lie around, reading magazines
While your husband's at the
Washing machine.

He's been there for days
And you're getting bored
But the great thing about him
Is you'll never be ignored.

Gearoid Brady (12) (Londonderry)

Yuletide

Greetings to one and all
With mistletoe and holly
And presents under the tree
For all the family.

Berries in the snow
Robins flying to and fro
Snowflakes on the bough of the tree
Falling slowly on me

A happy Noel to friends or family
With bells ringing
And children singing
To bring you joy and cheer
For Christmas and New Year.

Pat Kerr (Porthcawl)

No Life Without Friends

Isolated by technology and computerised ideology
Selfish with impunity; losing all sense of community,
Loneliness sets in.

Contemplating companionship and maybe form a relationship
So dawned the realisation, of the skills of communication.
Time to join a course.

Uninspired by woodwork, basketry and needlework,
Dismissing all things cognitive, sporting and competitive,
One class outshone the rest.

Enrolling in 'Your Ancestory' solved someone's
household's mystery,
Grandpa's youthful trip to Bridgewater resulted in
an unknown daughter!
Familists* abound.

Hail to 'Social Interaction', and his brother,
'Physical Attraction',
Enjoying camaraderie with their companion Goliardery**
All friends reunited.

* Members of a 16th sect believing religion consisted mainly of love
*** 13th educated jesters using ribald Latin verse*

Judith Roberts (Llandysul)

A Lake Alone

Menteith clear a nature poem
Where birds sing in harmony
A cheep upwards, where beak to sky
And cloud formation is unique

Priory now silent where monks chanted
And softly unfold tranquil tune
Sun-warmed stones a perfect seat
This peaceful summer's day in June

Softly the sound laps the shore
As waves of tender sound explore
A sparrow in the hedge sits alone
While dappled sun enhances, a glorious feast for senses
And nature's poem is complete.

Jean Bald (Stirling)

Old Age

Old age is a wonderful thing
The thought can make us cry or sing
For when we are young
And in our prime
The thought of old age
Is so far from mind
And when we grow up
Into the wide world we go
We are so full of life
We think we will never go slow
But when the years roll on
And we show a little grey
We start to realise
We are not here to stay
For as the pace gets slower
Day after day
Something keeps telling us
Old age is on the way
So we look back in joy
And sing a new song
A lot of my friends
Didn't get so long.

J D Johnston (Newtownards)

To Linda

If I were religious
I'd say that we were meant to be,
That we were put here for each other
Forever - you and me;
But in an eternal universe
I fear we are just pieces of clay
Thrown together momentarily,
Too insignificant to say.
Yet you are more important
Than all the universe to me,
Than all things since time begun.
You are everything that matters:
You light up my world
More than any sun.

James McKay (Aberdeen)

In Loving Memory

Every day
It flows over me,
The pain.
Drowning,
Grief pulling me under.
A prisoner in a hollow existence,
Sentenced to life without you.
This ultimate goodbye claws my flesh.
No words could describe my love for you,
Fewer still can describe my loss.
This constant knotted ache.
I function,
On the edge of a void.
I have cried an ocean of tears,
With an ocean more to come.
My life goes on,
And you live with me.
You were the beat of my heart,
The life in my veins.
You are still my reason.
For evermore,
I love you.

R Reid (Kilcreggan)

Cruel Winds Blow

Winter's cruel winds blow
Bringing the snow
Many dark days abound
Cold and icy weather come around
Footprints in the snow
As people come and go
You must wrap up warm
In case there's a storm
Waiting for the spring
And the good weather to bring
Finally the snow melts away
It's a nice warm day
Great to be alive
As we wait for summer to arrive.

Frank Tonner (Glasgow)

Untitled

Could the Queen put Her name down for 'care and repair'?
It seems She's hard up, so it would be quite fair.
They help OAPs, I tell you no lie!
She is over 80, so she would qualify.
She could get central heating and tiles for the roof,
If the rain's coming in - she'd need to show proof.
She would save on her gas bills with wall insulation,
She has more space to heat than the rest of the nation.
The heating allowance helps out a lot,
£200 worth of coins for the slot.
We get free television o'er 75,
And then there's the bus pass, we don't need to drive.
That saves on petrol, so we're doing our bit,
Sometimes we walk - just to keep fit.
We get free prescriptions, pills by the score,
But they don't always help. Old bones get sore.
We worked all our days, so we get a state pension,
I don't think there's anything else I need mention.
I'd suggest that Her Majesty give it a try,
It wouldn't do any harm to apply.
The family would benefit, no need to frown.
Prince Charles will move in when She gives up the crown.

Helen Watson (Irvine)

Childhood

The trees like splintered mushrooms
Explode against blue sky
Shimmering grey lake gently rippling
Upon the strings of my heart, a sigh
For time gone, distant past, I sit
Ancient dreams disturb me, here
As a child, I knew no fear
Now a sadness deeply known
Born of melancholy, in hurt
My pain has grown
Stillness and shimmering heat
Children cry in delight, innocence
Time stood still again, to reap
The future, when they too shall weep.

William G Cairns (Lisburn)

The Loch Of Memories

The sun was shining across the loch, throwing colours to the sky,
The trees were whispering gently as the breeze swept by,
As I nestled all warm and snug in your strong embrace,
I knew from that moment that there was no better place,
I was here among beauty and nature's sights to behold,
It was a place I wanted to be with you to grow old,
As we sat there, the time passing by, the sun began to fade,
The memories we will cherish were still being made,
The amber, yellow and rich orange ball of light,
Now had sunken into the glen, it was the still of night,
The air now cool, the whispers had changed,
The beautiful autumn now completely rearranged,
We nestled together as the night air settled around,
The loch now still, no ripples, not a sound,
And with the moments that had passed,
We knew altogether that our memories would last,
In the serene and beautiful deep green glen,
People would visit and make memories again,
The skies will be different, the ages will pass,
The water the same, the sweet-smelling grass,
But to all who will visit be together or alone,
Inverness will always be their memories' home.

Dawn Hughes (Inverness)

A Nation's Pride

Ring wedding bells, the nation sounds its praise:
Six decades now in love's eternal dream;
Hope in the darkest days did brightly gleam;
A sovereign God guarded in all their ways.
Britannia did the flag of freedom raise
And we, a people, one great family seem;
A royal pair ruled, nobly and serene,
Kept by that love, a greater Love displays.
By their example, let us onward go:
Trusting a faithful God, whate'er betide;
And share the beauty of love's sacrifice,
And gild the glory of the nation's pride:
To these two hearts, how great the debt we owe:
Long may they reign, 'neath England's glorious skies!

Frederick Crozier (Cookstown)

A Young Man's Friend

Oh! What a wonderful celebration,
Now a hundred and three years old.
Badly needs an operation,
That is what I believe, and told.
Now after a quick consultation,
With family and with friends,
On how much time it will take,
And of what the surgeon intends.
Now! After a successful operation,
And is truly on the mend,
With head and neck held high,
Defies, the passing years gone by.
On rounded shoulders and a heart of oak,
A back that's straight, with joints replenished.
With slender arms that stretch out straight,
Which rest upon two knees.
Short legs that are quite twisted,
And feet that are very small.
Now looking very spritely,
Polished, standing in the hall.
While taking in the new air,
Is a young man's bardic chair.

John Howell Roberts (Wrexham)

Just Being There

Just being there can play a part
Easing pain, even in the heart
Just being there can return a look
When no one cares, all have forsook
Just being there can lend ears
Listen to the cause of all the tears
Just being there you can fill a place
That otherwise is just an empty space
Just being there is opportunity
That is not wasted by immunity
Just being there means, 'I am here'
Right beside you, do not fear
Just being there is just as He says,
'Behold, I am with you always.'

Sarah Smeaton (Belfast)

Celebrating A Wedding (The Dress)

The dress is white it hangs in anticipation,
waiting for the toned body of the bride to adorn her outline.
Flowers arrive in abundance to be arranged in a variety of shaped vases
around a well-groomed lawn.
The hustle and bustle of family and friends
all try to outwit each other with their favours.
Some shouting orders, others looking confused
as to what would be their next command.
The sky is clear giving certainty of a warm sunny day.
Trees in the vast expanse of garden,
tickling the horizon with their slight movement.
A day the bride and groom have looked forward to with excitement.
Everyone is tense.
It is time for the white dress to be taken from the hanger,
to be worn with grace befitting the bride to be.
Her hair styled, her face made radiant by the make-up artist hired for the occasion.
A manicurist attended her hands on the previous day
giving her an excuse not to go near the sink, for fear of blemishing the artist's work.
A sight of happiness as her best friend helps her into her dress.
She glances into the mirror to see the vision of happiness and beauty.
Just a fleeting thought, is it right? Is he for me?
A determined yes is answered by her conscious mind.

Anita Mackenzie (Kilmarnock)

Sylvia's Garden

In Sylvia's garden
What a delight to see the roses,
Cream and yellow, delicate pinks
That climb upon an old stone wall.
While the deep red colour
Reminds me of Mother . . .
Roses and thorns
Overgrown.
A broken statue,
Crumbling steps,
Imperfect
Like people
Who came later,
Never to return.

Irene Grant (Aberdeen)

The Miners' Song

Sweetly singing is the wind
In our valley tonight
From shattered pithead to mountain
Swells wind's heart-stopping sound
As it conducts a new choir
From deep underground
They freedom rise in its chorus
Glad to share in wind's song
To sing in the valley
Where once they belonged
Lamp lit tenors thro' treetops
Firefly their way
Powerful baritones thro' bushes
Bludgeon deep bayed
Embracing their loved ones
In soothing sweet song
To gently tug at heartstrings
That grief's dark curtains hung on
Rekindling faith's lamp
Once more to shine bright
For the angels are singing
In our valley this night!

Owain Symonds (Blackwood)

Youth - A Reason

A reckless, carefree moment in a maze of boundless joy,
The shifting sands, the boundless seas, deserve not e'en a pause,
For cloudless sky and inner warmth, consume our every beat,
Too soon to stop, to think, to look, beyond a childish sleep;
And so it is when hearts are light and spirit bounding on,
That we gather in the sap and root to meet the hidden storm:
Just pause the briefest second and accept the Mighty Scheme,
When we stumble to elucidate the where's and ifs and seems;
For sad would be that instant, when we overturned the stone,
To find beneath the face of age, before the frame had grown;
So keep the wisdom deep inside, beware the urge to speak,
Or rob the heedless urchin of the prop he'll surely need;
For though we loathe to stand and stare and just ignore the knot,
The path is laid, the track well-worn, the plan was well begot.

Colum McCaffrey (Cookstown)

Bonnie Wee Dug

Sweet ole doggie supine on the settee,
Soundly snoring her soft wee ditty.
Hair tangled, twined round in curls,
Long strands from paws trail in whorls.
She stirs from sleep from time to time,
Getting down now, too far to climb.
A helping hand to lift the dear lass,
Out to her yard, for a wee sit in the grass.
Familiar shadows greet dim sight,
Maybe, maybe not, a bird took flight.
Och, no bother, a fine fare awaits,
Back in the kitchen, there on a plate.
Munching morsels fresh from a tin,
Leaves a wet nose and bits on the chin.
A lap of fresh water and back off to bed,
Then drift off to sleep, feeling well-fed.
Dreamy dog walks, sniffing forest paths,
Watching pant-legs and backs of calves.
Bark into the wind, rush a pile of leaves,
Doggie life, the simple spell it weaves.
For five thousand days, all gone past,
Oh, Bonnie, if only it could last.

Isolde Nettles MacKay (Oban)

The River

The river winds its way through town on its quest to meet the sea
giving joy to many, but sadly not to me
Its picture-postcard beauty is not all that it seems
its waters hold a secret which often haunts my dreams
On summer days weeping willows dance lightly in the breeze
while graceful swans glide slowly by, 'neath overhanging trees
Imagine now a different view of a cold, wet winter night
of a lonely lady walking - is there no one else in sight?
Is there no one there to guide her, to take her by the hand
to let her talk and listen, and try to understand?
What drew her to the water? What made her end her life?
That lady was my sister - a mother and a wife
And still the river flows on by - there are no answers here for me
it takes its secrets with it on its quest to meet the sea

Helen Urquhart (Scone)

Can I Have The Top Of Your Egg, Da?

Can I have the top of your egg, Da?
For so great is my need
I know, I know, there are twelve hungry mouths to feed
Can I have the top of your egg, Da?
Susan, she had it last night
It's my turn, is it not, Da?
Can I have the top of your egg?

Our Eamon had it last Tuesday
And Oweny the night before
Can I have the top of your egg, Da?
My guts are on the floor
Belly's rumbling, tumbling, grumbling
Can I have the top of your egg, Da?

When I grow up, I will marry a rich man
Be it long or short the day
My little kids won't ever have to say
Can I have the top of your egg, Da?
It's my turn today.

Ambrose J Smyth (Craigavon)

The Way Of Life

With bonny clumps of heather scattered far and wide,
growing for miles across the land and up the steep hillside,
mingling with the thistles and clover, and bracken brown,
'tis nice to be out in the wild instead of a busy town,
the air is so fresh and pure and clean
with rivers so clear and grass so green.
But walk by the rivers in the towns, they're not so clear
they're rusty brown,
clogged up with effluent, bikes and prams
making an eyesore with man-made dams.
the factory chimneys blast out their smoke,
we breathe in this muck which makes us choke
I don't think they'll ever find a solution
to clean up the air filled with pollution.

Anne McWilliams (Grangemouth)

Before You Go, Can You Give Me A Baby?

I know it's over
We've decided to say goodbye
It just wasn't meant to be
So now we are being honest and not lie
Can I ask you one thing?
Before you go, can you give me a baby?

See, I've invested too much time in us
My ovaries have ticked
There's just no time left to meet someone new
To see if it's right, to see if we click
So just one thing, one more thing
Before you go, can you give me a baby?

I have really thought this through
So there's no need to fear
While we have no future
There's no reason, let's be clear
That I can't do this on my own
So please, before you go, can you give me a baby?

A Thompson (Glasgow)

Wake

Vision reveals a sun glowing love
and warmth unto body and soul.
When all is sun rays, the horizon of life
is an evaporation of clouds.
Enjoy the rapture of Her love, for it holds
keys to doors that express, Heaven.
Blame not harshly your mind or self for hiding away.
Wake and come back unto the realms of your identity
and meaning.
To walk a path on a crooked bumpy road is one way
to travel, but you and your reservations are
a weight of unnecessity.
Unravel your feathers my fine graceful friend
and fly.

Nick Purchase (Cardiff)

The Old Farmhouse

(Glenure Farm, Near Omagh, Co Tyrone)

The old farmhouse camouflaged in mist it lies
Smoke from the chimney reluctant to rise
Signalling a message of the warmth inside the old farmhouse
Aroma of scones or apple pies
Simple language calls, 'Come in from
The chilling wind that finds no rest!'
There's shelter within the old farmhouse
One speculates how hands did toil
Watching the big black kettle boil
On turf from the bog inside the old farmhouse
Hear the rain in fury pour
There's comfort within when one closes
The door of the old farmhouse
I must go and leave behind
Heritage that once was mine
Ancestors gone with passing time
Reflection of slow, shuffling feet
Bids me make a quick retreat
Say goodbye where in ruins lie
The old farmhouse that once was mine.

Frances Gibson (Omagh)

Hummingbird

I asked him what he'd liked about his childhood
'The hummingbirds that flew along the river
I loved their speed - the way they never stopped.'
Two stars sat in his eyes as he described them.
He'd fried his brain on acid, Es and smack
Heard voices now, a hopeless schizophrenic
His long fair hair was lank, uncombed, a flop.
His pianist's fingers had grown beggar's nails
The local yobs would dog him to the shop
Relieve him of his benefits, declare
Undying friendship till his funds ran out,
Until one day some traffic light said *stop*
Inside his veins. They soon re-let his flat
His life erased by paint, fresh air, a mop.

Sheena Blackhall (Aberdeen)

A Special Someone

(Dedicated to my beloved husband who died July 2007)

When I need someone to share my thoughts
There is a heart that understands
When I seek the warmth of a comforting touch
There are welcome outstretched hands
When I need someone close to me
Someone who will really care
Your heart and your hands reach out in love
And I am happy to know you are there.
Someone with a smile so warm
And a heart so kind and good
That words are not always needed
For so much is understood
I need someone very special
To depend on come what may
Because you are that someone
You bring loving thoughts my way
How wonderful it is to know
There is someone always there
Who really wants to listen
And understand and care.

Margaret Ford (Bonnybridge)

Me

Who is the me in me?
Who is the me I see?
What is this eye that looks out at the world?
What is my mouth where words are hurled?
What is this nose that sniffs the air?
What is this stuff on my head called hair?
What is this spinal cord in my back, which without it I'd flop like a sack?
What are my legs that let me walk?
What of my tongue that lets me talk?
What of my arms that let me work?
What of my brain that makes the think?
What of my eyelids that let me blink?
Am I a robot, computer or what, of this human that's me
I know not a lot.

Aline Weager (Invergordon)

You Should Have Heard The Angels Sing

You should hear the music in the land that I was in.
You should have heard the angels sing,
Every note so clear and true
A splendid synchrony of violin
Or harp or flute, or some other thing.

Each plaintive note in perfect harmony
Voices so sweet my ears taken captive
To ravenously desire just one more note
And then one more still . . .
You should have heard the angels sing.

Throngs and throngs for miles no end
An endless symphony in harmony spent
Not one too many, not one too scarce
Not one impervious to all the rest.
Perfect unison, perfect sound
Perfect love to my ears was bound
I stared transfixed, my hearing gone
To all except the heavenly throng
Afraid to breathe or my heart to pound
To interrupt that heavenly sound.
You should have heard the angels sing.

Jane Townsley (Blairgowrie)

I'm

I'm such an idiot, such a fool
I'm the knot in your knitting, a hair in your soup

I'm the time you wasted waiting on a bus
I'm the wrong path taken when you got lost

I'm inept and inferior, unloved and abhorred
I'm more trouble than I'm worth, I'm best left ignored

I'm the ache you feel when a loved one's gone
I'm everything you hate and everything that's wrong

I'm the empty vessel, I'm the shadow that you passed
I'm never the wanted, never the first, just the last

I'm the, will it never stop raining, or the ongoing pain
I'm sorry for being me, never changing, staying the same.

Barbara Rodgers (Belfast)

Photo Albums

There's a pile of photo albums lying on the floor,
Each and every one of them opens up a door.
A door to past and present,
From long ago to here and now,
Memories of my family life,
So precious to me now.

As I turn the pages, the photographs recall,
Special days, events and times,
In winter, summer, spring and fall.
There are photos of my childhood days,
Memories from my past,
Photos of my children,
Who grew up far too fast.

Happy days, wedding days, birthdays,
Anniversaries too,
Albums full of memories,
Memories of you.
They make me smile, they make me cry,
But how wonderful to know,
I can turn the pages and relive,
All those memories from long, long ago.

Janet Thomas (Neath)

History And Politics

The M4 stretches out towards the sunset
but gets no further than halfway
between Pontarddulais and Ammanford
before it is reduced to the status
of the A48. Next stop Carmarthen
and all points west, north or south,
Haverfordwest and St David's, Tenby,
Pembroke Dock and Milford Haven,
Fishguard and Cardigan, then the sea,
bringing tourists like the Vikings
pillaging their way across the land,
leaving the abbeys burnt, the coal mines
deserted and the iron works in ruins.
On this desolation they built a motorway.

Andrew Belsey (Cardiff)

The Hourglass

Twenty years the flyer said
Since their unique conception
And somewhere in me dawned the thought
Suspend old Father Time
That I may think back twenty years
Recall the intervening hours
That somehow have slipped away.

Not an uneventful time
For sure, 'twas full of changes
Adjustments made, some goals achieved
And others still awaiting
Two decades filled with steadfast labour
That should have brought fulfilment
And yet - the glass feels empty.

How often has the glass been tipped
The hourglass of my life
How often has the trickling sand
Run out and in that instant
The ghostly hand of fate or time
The balance tips; and once again
My hourglass replenished.

Opal Innsbruk (Motherwell)

Sea Visions

Walking along the shore, when the tide is out.
Patterns in the waves, all shimmering about.
Seashells and seaweed, lying in the sand.
Over the horizon, there lies another land.
Light breezy winds, over a misty sky.
Seagulls nestling in the cliffs so high.
Rowing boats adrift, anchored in the sea.
Moving with the breeze, struggling to be free.
All kinds of migrant birds, including sea hawks.
Seals closely by their cubs, lying across the rocks.
Tossing pebbles in the sea, see the ripples flow.
Debris of old shipwrecks, in days of long ago.
Clouds have turned to darkness, the rain's not far away.
I'll stroll along the beach again, on another day.

Catherine Fleming (Rutherglen)

The Peppermint Waltz

Just when the prayer had ended
It would seem
Just when the sermon started
It would seem
A holy peppermint sweet
Would strike out
Against the mahogany seats;

A sanctified silence ringing
Down floorboards
Along transepts, across the aisle
The altar
Up the organ pipes, the pulpit steps
To Heaven
And back again in time for lunch;

Passing through the vestibule, the tarmac
The graveyard
To the foot of the town, Gabriel's horn
Resurrect
As winged seraphim and cherubim
Harmonise
The worshippers to their homes.

David Martin (Craigavon)

Moving On

Thoughts of a mad and chequered past -
Blotches on life's landscape,
I'd hoped would never last.
Lost in a smog like London used to have,
Enveloped in its encircling gloom;
Seemingly impenetrable at first,
But later maybe not -
An almost tangible sense of hope
Surfaces time and again,
And a belief held fleetingly at first,
Is now firmly fixed on the way forward
To face unstoppable, accelerating change.
Though it may seem that I stand alone,
Deep down I know it is not so.

A Winter (Aberdeen)

Rosy Apples, God And Honeysuckle Warmth

Such a small thing is love,
An apple enriched with honeysuckle,
God painted the sky gold.

Red flowers grown diamond-like,
Man and woman kiss - tender warmth,
Wood and pine - enchanted love.

Pink and white tears float,
Her soft warm breasts hide peaceful mellowness,
Tears cry out silent, radiant love.

Man makes love in glittering nature,
Their cosy bodies tangle like tree roots,
God pushes them into rose clad leaves.

They lay together enjoying sexual love,
A pink joy pours from her gentle womb,
Tears of happiness spill from God,
Perfect and delicate -
So beautiful it's enriched with honeysuckle.

R D Gardner (Penarth)

Lost Love

It just happened, we fell in love,
I looked in your eyes
And visited your soul.
Flamboyance and uncontrollable attraction,
God save me from this interaction.
World apart status and class,
Why bother with this Scottish lass?
Magnetic forces freaking me out,
Lust, desire, I'm turning away.
Kiss me! I'll rue the day,
Give you up, that is my choice
Before ecstasy is foretold by pain.
Why do I feel this loss?
I love you! Why the rain?

Jessie Shields (Dunfermline)

There's A Fairy In My Washing

There's a fairy in my washing,
She's been there half the day,
I don't know where she came from,
But she's got a lot to say.

She poo-pooed my washing powder;
She said my whites were grey,
Tapped her fairy wand and mocked,
As a bed sock flew astray.

She alleged I mixed my coloureds,
Which she would never do;
Furthermore, 'In Fairyland,
Stubborn stains are very few.'

She boasted of her laundry spells,
To keep the fabric soft
And insisted I should wear
Only fairy pre-shrunk cloth.

I don't mean to sound ungrateful -
She needs a lesson too,
That's why I left her spinning,
When I greased her fairy shoes!

Sharon Marie Johnston (Ballymena)

Nature Fights Back

From my cottage window
A sight to behold, a mountain
Covered in green and gold.

Go back a century, how different
Then, an area mined for coal and tin
No mountain now scarred and black
Nature, she's been fighting back.

People visit, they stand in awe
What a beautiful sight
From how it was before.

Rape of the countryside was Man's biggest crime
She puts back beauty, once there was grime
All she needed was a little time.

Bob Phillips (Pontypool)

Mobile Phone

My mobile phone is my own
I use it when I'm at home
I text and text and phone and phone
It's snug and compact and looks like a bone

It twists and turns inside out
I open it up to show off when I'm about
Blue silver shiny, plastic too
It looks real good and it goes with my shoes

A ringing sound, a tweet and a bleep
I think it's there to stop people going off to sleep
Ringing sounds and chirpy noises
Like early morning with the birds' voices

My girlfriend's got one too
Hers is pink and mine is silver-blue
She's always talking chat, chat, chat
She never stops, it's just like that

In her flat or in a car
Her mobile phone is not far
She's always phoning in the loo
I don't know if she sleeps with it too!

John Eynon (Penarth)

Lady Of The Heather

Lady of the heather,
You haunt my dreams
Forever.

Your beauty shines so wide,
Through blue and tempered
Skies.

A warrior's heart belongs to you,
In dream, in mists, in
Waters blue.

In far away places, where
Times will gather,
You will always be there
My lady of the heather.

Patrick J Ryan (Milford Haven)

The Flying Wallies

Faither's in the hospital
He's hud an operation
He'd geid himself a hernia
Much tae his consternation

He did awe right tae start wi'
But then he felt no' weel
And every time he stood up
He was sure that he would keel

His belly rummeled roon n' roon
His dinner he couldnae lick
And then of course it happened
The pair auld soul was sick

He lost his wallies as he chucked
They went a different road
They flew across the room at speed
And fell in the commode

He had to have them sterlised
Cos them he'd surely miss
But today at end o'visitin'
I think I'll skip his kiss!

Sharon Crawford (Falkirk)

My Love

The love of my life was a beautiful man,
He was tall, dark, handsome and strong,
I felt truly blessed to have found him,
And my heart sang a beautiful song.

The love of my life was an amazing man
We knew what we had was so strong
Long endless days of laughter and love
And my heart had a place to belong

The love of my life was a wonderful man
With a passionate heart beating strong
Cut down in his prime to the hell they call cancer
And my heart weeps a mournful song

Until we meet again my love.

Paula Jackson (Ardrossan)

Love Freedom

Memories sharp before your eyes
It comes so fast though no surprise
For one thing in this vivid life
Death will slash you with its knife

Leaders always seeking followers
The media juggles who's to win
You don't need to play their game
Let them go lame without your sin

Money greed the business need
Fools slaving for their millions bleed
It could be you, it might be you
But don't be fooled by none of it

And through the only way they know
Monotonous dull and deathly toil
They took your soul and gave you strife
And cloned your dreary wasted life

Just a pawn, a stupid pawn
With an empty rhyme at the end of it
You chased the cash the phony flash
And now you're dead with none of it.

Jeff Perry (Beaufort)

Evening Vigil, Watching And Waiting

In the quiet stillness of the evening I watch the dusk creep in
her powerful shadows dimming the light. I am watching,
waiting, like the darkness, to give peace to the land, inviting
creatures of the night their rightful place to enter the mysteries of darkness.

Yellow eyes pierce through the blackness, alert for any
movement, watching, waiting. Soft on silent wing the white barn
owl searches, hovering above its prey. Watching, waiting.

A heavy shadow lumbers past, white nose and facial stripes
the only light. I am watching waiting.
In the black tree, her branches like long fingers hold
the silhouette of a tawny owl. He bobs his head from side to side, watching, waiting.

Scampering on tiny feet, the mouse sniffs the air, then gobbles
up a juicy morsel, no time to watch and wait.

Poppy Acton Ashfield (Brecon)

Isle Of Minorca

In port on an island one day,
When the tide was just right to sail,
We failed to leave the island bay,
As the engine broke down and failed.

It took through the night to repair,
In the port where we stood alone,
We waited in gloom with despair,
Till we could sail away back home.

Broken down on a lonely island,
I wondered what then would we do,
Far away in a foreign land,
With no airport to fly us to,

Bright in the morning was sunshine,
A start to a very nice day,
The engine mended while we dined,
We sailed away from the bay.

It was an adventure from home,
On this liner that was so big,
We ventured round the decks to roam,
And watched the men repair the rig.

Margaret Burtenshaw-Haines (Whitland)

Two Hearts As One

I stood upon a rocky ledge, hands cupped above my eyes,
Surveying all around me, from the ground up to the skies.
Cotton wool clouds were drifting slowly by, on an ocean of pale, pale blue,
Drifting, drifting, drifting on, with nothing else to do.
A nearby mountain was rising, rising up for all to see,
And as I looked, I knew that mountain was part of me.
A forest covers the mountainside, all over it, it roams,
A haven for wild animals, a place to make their homes.
A stream cascades down the mountainside, rushing past rock and tree,
Rushing, rushing, rushing down and onwards to the sea.
And down below the rolling hills, rolling away and out of sight,
Then I knew this spot I'd picked, could not have been more right.
The more I looked, the more I saw, the more that I did find,
Scotland, we'll always be together, two hearts as one entwined.

Robert Kerr (Denny)

The Last Goodbye

Some people hate to sail the seas,
While others prefer not to fly
And many a soul has a fear of heights,
But I just hate saying, goodbye.

Althrough the years, as you travel life's road,
Meeting people - making friendships that gel,
But deep in your heart, you know one day soon,
There is always that dreaded farewell.

I've never quite handled that final handshake,
Or when losing a departing good friend,
It's so hard to hide that sense of regret
And a heart that takes so long to mend.

A suppose I'm quite hardened to life's daily moods,
I've weathered the storms by and large,
It's only those times, when I fall by the way,
When dear loved ones, bid me, Bon Voyage.

I don't think I'll master the art of farewell,
I've failed to, with many a sigh,
Just how will I manage to leave all behind,
When it's time for the last goodbye?

G Thomas (Llanelli)

Talgarth

Talgarth, the name was once the place
For minds no longer sound
A haven where good care was given
And protecting arms were found
But still there's treasure to be found
A hospital still stands
In nearby Bronllys on its mound
What a stunning view to see!
The Mountains Black, the Beacons Blue
The ambulance waiting for its cue
And the medical team is ready to move
Whenever the needs arise
Yes, there is care to be found
In this beautiful countryside.

Mavis Downey (Brecon)

The Dripping Tap

Drip, drip, splash, there's a leak I think
And it's coming from a nearby tap.
Loudly it falls into an aluminium sink
It sounds almost like an overhead thunderclap.

What am I to do to stop this drip
That's driving my wife mad?
I could go somewhere on a trip
Like a holiday to Baghdad.

Still, on my return to my home,
I'd have to face the wife who is packing her bags,
Rather than let her go I'd listen to her moan,
About this drip that perhaps

I should have fixed a long time ago.
It's a lot louder now and dripping faster than ever.
Day after day I can see my wife's temper beginning to glow.
Me, I've grown used to this drip that's like our weather.

When it rains there are drips from the roof
And from the branches of the tree outside our door!
'Enough is enough,' said the wife and she has the proof.
For she's had the plumber in and there's no drip no more.

Bill Thomson (Glenrothes)

Sonnet To Autumn (Pitnamoon)

Where Pitnamoon dwells 'tis a magic place,
Whose high peaks mark the hill walkers' frontier,
And broad skies her tall regal heights embrace,
Sun's beams that thrall the bright morning air.
Horse-chestnuts spread their ochre-laden boughs,
Skeins of geese across the Mearns traverse,
Men of the good earth labour autumn's plough,
Where golden heads of corn have swayed the merse.
Spirits of the wind on Cairn-o-Mount sigh,
The old military road winds, twists and turns,
To a summit whose sitting suns glorify,
A landscape bathed in gold across the Mearns.
Pitnamoon homely nooks lit to the night,
O'er stilled fields a harvest moon shines bright.

Peter Morriss (Laurencekirk)

Hills Of Wales

O hills of Wales you're home to me
Rolling down unto the sea,
Or from valleys rise in grace
There'll never be a finer place.

The green, green grass, the waving tree
A choir's song, a land that's free!
A voice upon a distant hill
Apart from that all is still.

Born within this land of song
Wales is the place where I belong,
I thank each day when I awake,
These things from me no one shall take.

The grey green mist upon the hill
Hold no secret from me still,
The grass upon those old slag tips
Hides the hurt from coal-stained lips.

The rivers running to the seas
In the cradle of the valleys,
Hills of Wales so pleasing to the eye
Majestic in your grandeur no one can beautify.

Derek J Morgan (Aberdare)

To Wakan Tanka (The Great Spirit)

May we see things afresh
Each day, as a child would,
And with a sense of wonder
And spontaneity
In every experience,
Let us see things as they are
Without prejudice,
Or attaching labels to them.
May we experience the vividness of life,
In all its forms
And manifestations,
So that we may truly know
That we are all connected
And interdependent.

Harry Stevenson (Morriston)

The Kitten In The Window

Look at the kitten so small and sweet,
Please can we have her? It would be such a treat.
But remember kittens bring work and care,
All the vet bills, food, but lots of playtimes to share,

She may be with you for a long, long time,
No time to be house-proud or whinge and whine.
She will climb the curtains and hang from the chairs,
Jump about as if you're not there.
Oh but the rewards are tenfold,
When you see how gentle she is to hold.

She will look at you with big green eyes
And purr with sheer joy,
She will be your companion, your loyal friend,
She will love you right to the end.

And when she grows and looks so sleek,
You'll realise you've no need to speak.
Because she'll know your every way
And she'll never leave you or become a stray.

Love her, care for her and you'll never regret,
The beautiful kitten in the window that is now your pet.

Lorraine Demarco (Welshpool)

Master Of The Sky

To see an eagle in full flight,
Is a rare and impressive sight.
He swoops and swerves like no other,
With graceful ease he soars,
Like a kite released into oblivion.
On a high and craggy rock,
He builds his nest -
Where no man has been,
Safe from intruders and rarely seen.
But on a moonlit sky at dusk,
His silhouette may be seen,
And like the giant of all he surveys -
Reigns supremely,
Master of the sky . . .

Agnes L W Berry (Kirkcaldy)

Gambian Jewels In The Dust

Shining smiling eyes of children
Black ebony beauty staring back at me
In bare block classrooms
They sing their joyful song of A, B, C

And as I stand before them like a warrior
In my armour clad
They easily pierce my heart and defences
With an arrow of pure love and make me glad

These little lives are lived
Without constraints of monetary wealth or spite
And in their eyes burns no malice
Only sweetly smiling faces of delight

These children are the future
In a land of poor state
But time will surely test them
And mould to form their fate

Their lives will change with time
As this land surely must
But I hope and pray it never loses
These jewels in the dust

Peter Ellis (Sketty)

Linlithgow Palace

Linlithgow Palace, ancient pile,
magnificent relic of a long-lost while.
We climbed your spiral steps, that summer day,
to Queens Bower and Linlithgow to survey.
We trod the flagstones of your floor,
hand in hand entranced by 'Lithca' lore.
Great Hall, Bedchamber, Oratory,
we studied with delight, a nation's history.
'Neath gigantic fireplace we stilled our walk,
to ponder, what tales, if only walls could talk,
of glories past, great feasts in rush-lit hall,
log fires, musicians playing, for guests at noble ball.
Perhaps, in years to come, they might relate,
of the happy couple who came, that summer of 1988.

B D Fellows (Isle of Skye)

Too Late

When the children lived at home
All I wanted was my private zone
Away from squabbles over TV
I wanted a space just for me

Washing and ironing was a chore
Finish one lot, then there'd be more
Worry when they were out at night
Hoping and praying they'd be alright

My husband's moved out, boys left home
Now I'm here, all on my own
Got my wish for my own space
Feel rejected by the human race

Yearn for all that noise and chatter
Looking back, 'What did that matter!'
Washing line bursting to capacity
Now only a few items, just for me

On my own, can't sleep at night
Lie in bed with eyes shut tight
Never appreciated what I had
Regret it now, too late, how sad.

Anne Jenkins (Abertillery)

Covenanter's Grave

As bridles jangle, Redcoats ride him down,
They strike with steel and stare as his blood spills,
Another victim for the martyr's crown
Killed here between the folds of rounded hills.
Three centuries have passed without a mark
Where miles from anywhere the lonely grave
Beneath a shrouded sky lies hidden, stark,
The stone up-ended, sunken land concave.
A curlew's forlorn cry the only sound
That echoes softly now across the Coomb
And acres of rough heather-covered ground,
Where mists still curl like wraiths about that tomb.
The years have changed but deeds are still the same,
Today the zealots shoot to kill and maim.

Pam Russell (Selkirk)

Millennium Bridge

Time spans a place unchanged, until
An arch, erected, covered its mouth,
Bridging the gap between long dunes
On golden sands of leisure time.

Flocks of seabirds ride bright waves,
While cyclists pedal scenic routes,
Gazing out at misty isles,
And walkers linger, arms on rails.

Upstream, unseen behind a bend -
That legendary humpback bridge,
So pivotal in poet's tale,
Still stands from Tam o'Shanter's ride.

But centuries change - and now, again,
To celebrate the turning tide,
The River Doon flows underneath
A graceful footbridge, with access

To sights of islands, in the firth,
Where waters mingle, mix with sea,
Lapping, like the tongue of Burns,
Tapping into foreign shores.

Marian Reid (Alloway)

True Love

You have but one life upon this Earth
Treat it gently and with care
Happiness is but an illusion
Grasp at it for all your worth
For without it you have nought to share;
One man has the ability to give or to destroy
Make your choice wisely for love is not a toy
To discard and cast away
When you feel the urge to play
With other lives - your life is in your hands
So do not make demands
But go your way and show respect
True love will come when you least expect
And make it all worthwhile.

Gwyneth Scott (Colwyn Bay)

The Intruder

The silent, swirling mist
Creeps along the grass
Like many stealthy footsteps
That trespass.

Moving slowly, as if step by step
Towards the old brown shed
It swarms across the roses there
And then the flowerbed.

Without a sound, it goes swirling on
Grey against the dark
To swallow up the purple
That hugs the bark.

This silent intruder, then
Slows to a crawl
Extending long, grey tentacles;
That clamber nimbly up my wall.

I draw back from the window
As if on cue
Away from this thief
Who steals my view.

Ellen Dwyer (Livingston)

A Special Place

There's a special place among Scottish hills, that's a must for tourists to see,
A majestic glen, that the old road runs through, where cold crystal water runs free,
Some feel it's brooding with high menacing hills, and a history violent and cruel,
Some see it unique with a charm of its own, very special, a real Scottish jewel,
When tour buses leave and there is no one around, that's the time I love to be there,
On a warm summer's night, the conditions are right, when the sun has mellowed her glare,
As I look and admire at the beauty around, hear the birdsong echo so pure,
An eagle soars from the hills so high, flying graceful, regal and sure,
My mind starts to see as it used to be, the heart of the glen comes alive,
A village appears as in olden days, with its people, hospitality and drive,
A lone piper plays to the village below, muted music can be heard all around,
The community thrives, family ties survives, and close friendships are easily found,
The sun has just set and the vision has gone, the feeling of loss wouldn't go,
I know I belong to this place that I love, this land of my clan at Glencoe.

M McDonald (Johnstone)

Growing Up

River Usk you river Usk
Spring from the Brecons deep
Within that mountain's ancient rock
Your lifeblood's waters seep.

Downward ever downward
Throughout the heart of Gwent
In mystic mad meandering
Your childhood miles are spent.

Playing with the rapids
Your water's mischief white
Sending flapping stilted herons
Aloft in awkward flight.

Your youth does not prepare you
For adult future shocks
The magic muse deserts you
As you surge through sordid docks

Your sparkle will be extinguished
When you end your journeys south
And you taste the waiting kiss of salt
From the Severn's silted mouth

Hugh Rose (Usk)

Hearsay

I found you, found you wandering
Your head was in the clouds
And your heart was filled with tranquillity
Like a rhapsody of time.

As I stood and gazed and pondered
Is that love that's in your eyes?
Will the words that should be spoken
Be said in the passing of time?

I never said I was lonely,
Tho' the thought once crossed my mind,
That if I dreamed a dream
And found you wanting
Would my thoughts be truly found?

John J Axon (Rhyl)

Good Health

There they stand upon a hill
Sanctuaries to those who are ill
Where caring men and women toil
The Infirmary and the Crichton Royal.

Where aching bones and worried minds
And illnesses of different kinds
Are treated by the caring hands
Of those who know and understand.

Afflicted folk don't choose their lot
A fact that shouldn't be forgot
By those of us in perfect health
Who just don't realise our wealth.

For what are riches to a man?
When illness curbs his natural span,
He realises with a sigh,
That good health, money just can't buy.

Next time you're sorry for yourself,
Just thank God if you're in good health,
And spare a thought for those in care,
In institutions everywhere!

James Quinn (Dumfries)

Change Of Face

Where is the love
That once you gave
In abundance and beyond
Deeper than an ocean wave
Gone!

A stranger now
In your turncoat garb
I never knew that face
Suddenly distorted, macabre.

Nothing left to say
Of memories, good or bad
Torn from a book without an end
Over!

Martha Watt (Irvine)

Wales

Magnificent high mountains,
Glorious deep dales,
Lakes and streams and meadows,
Wonderful land of Wales.

Busy, noisy cities
And quiet villages,
Countryside and seaside,
Happy land of Wales.

Castles dotted here and there,
Towering over all,
Looking so majestic,
Spring and summer, winter and fall.

Cheerful, joyful people,
Living side by side,
Some speak their own language,
In their land they have great pride.

Praising, rousing voices,
Poetry tells grand tales,
Singing, verses, playing sport,
In this versatile land of Wales!

Ruth Lydia Daly (St Dials)

Blue Eyes

Take a look into my blue eyes,
tell me, what do you see?
I was a soul that was searching,
the person I had to find was me.

Take a look into my blue eyes,
tell me, what do you feel?
Do you sense the inner strength I've found?
It's something nobody is going to steal.

Take a look into my blue eyes,
take my hand, or walk away,
I've found faith deep within my soul,
to accept whatever comes my way.

Marlyn Lee Murphy (Glenrothes)

Remembered Decades

The dreaming encapsulated in memory's insight
To capture themes to make sense of now's grasp
Decades elapse loud in a myriad of colours
Telling of dramas like lover's first cutting experience.

There in intensity recalled moments assert like ice
Weathered vows sound out for factual detail
Longevity accounts to those whose time deals
It's acceptance of language ready to annunciate light.

We all create things to ponder the past's energies
Moulding a kaleidoscope of emotive armour that loves
Making special communicative values search out time
There in the fame taking of whole life spans.

The connected decades must encounter vast vision
Add up an insurance that considered time evinces
There is a wakeful ardour alive like a daffodil
A weighty blood that must have its own way.

We design our breath to tell of trekked experiences
Fashion the last emotions standing in dark metaphors
We can obtain a sun's promise if tune's revelations allow
Embrace with a kiss the remembered ages cemented.

Graham Borge (Bridgend)

Love

Oh, the pain when no longer here
It's nearly unbearable I fear
It's getting deeper every day
I wish again you were coming my way,

For all the time you with me attend
I really liked you more than a friend
I know I need you in my life
I wish I could be your dear wife

But as you said when you came
A bidie in was your kind of dame
I cannot change to that way
I'm sorry but here I have to stay.

Frances Duguid (Aberdeen)

Angel On The Sand

As I walk on golden sands
I dream of what could be,
To walk the beach, hand in hand
With an angel for company.

The natural beauty all around
The sand, the sea and surf
And with the angel by my side
I see it for what it's worth.

The sun illuminates the tranquil night
Bathing the horizon in red
And as I glance upon my angel
Not a word can be said.

The silence broken by crashing waves
And the cries of gulls around
To remind us again the natural beauty
Is present in sight and sound.

Whether it is scenery, plant or animal
The beauty of nature exists
But it's up to me with angel beside
To ensure this beauty persists.

Matt Ward (Cardiff)

Frontispiece For An Anthology

Had I a casket for gems so rare,
Silver embossed or gold inlaid,
I would place them inside for you to share -
Amethyst, emerald, ruby, jade.

Alas, poor am I, no gleaming coffer,
Not the merest sparkle, nor glint of gold,
My words are my gems, and these I offer,
Frail strands of verse on gossamer hold.

Alone, at the twilight, when shadows creep,
Take down this book from the shelf above.
My words are my wealth, and yours to keep,
Tissued about with all my love.

Stella Shepherd (Shetland)

Ben Nevis

Each spring we welcome your rebirth: emerging from the snow,
With a ray of sun across your brow, that sets your face aglow.
Telling us that once again, new life is on its way,
As warmth ascends your rocky slopes and springtime greets each day.

In summertime you never sleep - no darkness comes at night
And countless folk, so eagerly, scale your towering height.
Around your base new growth abounds - in hedgerow, field and river,
To your lofty crags - a refuge safe - the birds of prey go thither.

In autumn, like the teenage years, your moods so quickly sway,
From moments bright and golden, to dismal, dark and grey.
Storm clouds gather around you, strong winds sweep you clean,
Then just as quickly vanish and you're once again serene.

As winter comes, your countenance grows sullen, cold and bleak,
In a shroud of white, as the snow descends, one day you are buried deep.
Your tomb, like marble, glistering - we look at it and sigh
And realise there comes a time when all things seem to die.

But you are not dead, just fast asleep - rich sunsets keep you warm,
As crimson fires light the sky and rest upon your form.
And you will be here in the spring again - with joy we'll greet your coming,
As new life begins and a new cycle starts, we will celebrate the dawning.

Rhea Campbell-Tudhope (Fort William)

Winter Curtains

The winter calling
And the robin sings
His chest a bagpipe
Flexing his wings

Leaves slowly rot
Branches say goodbye
To their summer friends
Flaking till they die

Frosty air suffocates
Your throat tightens
Soil moulds and
The sky never brightens.

Gareth Culshaw (Wrexham)

Colours 07

Colours - twenty years on
A rainbow of beauty; your colours live on.
Now they are deeper, vivid in hue
Their shade a reminder of an inner you.

You're a palette arranged for a work of art
Brush strokes define you right to the heart
No canvas can stretch to the depth of your tone
No frame can contain your heart, when on loan

To others who need your golden love to fill
Their often pallid lives. You plant green
Seeds of strength in weakened minds, quench
Grey thirst with deep blue healing wine.

Your red blood flows in a swirling torrent
Enveloping the black mists of all abhorrent.
You give of your colours until ashen and wan
Yet you still find the silver light to carry you on.

Shine . . . shine in all you do
Let your world be painted in every hue
Let all your colours be solid and true
And *never* forget that we love *you.*

Maureen Thomas (Newport)

Thoughts Fulfilled

Sunny morning, month of June,
Peace and tranquillity, save the birds in tune,
Mother Earth in her splendid array,
Fails to capture our thoughts today.

Sweltering under the noonday sun,
Our thoughts to the seaside turn,
Picnics packed, car on the key,
Donegal coast, Bundoran by the sea.

Lashed by the mighty ocean wave,
Swimming and surfing such sports we crave,
Breezes fresh, sea and sand,
Thoughts fulfilled at Tullan Strand.

Annie Lynch (Dungannon)

Bridge

A bridge is there to walk across,
To shake somebody's hand.
To bridge the gap of friendship,
To unite and to expand.

If countries could do this,
How different the world would be.
To take the time to meet halfway,
And stop all animosity.

If there's a family feud,
Something you can't understand,
Be the first to cross the bridge,
Hold out that friendly hand.

A bridge can cross a babbling brook,
Or a busy major road,
Carrying people here and there,
To work or their abode.

The chances we are given,
Fall generously in our lap,
So face the world with courage
And always bridge the gap.

Peggy Howe (St Asaph)

A Frozen Silver Spider's Web

Going for a walk this morn,
I was halfway through a yawn,
When a sight that stopped me dead
Was a silver spider's web.

Gleaming in the frozen dew,
Frozen flies for spider stew,
On a cold and misty morn
What a sight to stop my yawn.

Cruel spider what a sight,
You created with your might,
Cruel frost to help you make,
Get me fully wide awake.

Norman Williams (Abergavenny)

The Tattered Flag

A soldier lad lay dreaming,
Near a battlefield one day,
In his mind he was scheming,
How to win victory.

He heard his captain calling,
'Rise and fire rapidly,'
Then he began bawling,
'Yes, Sir, right away!'

Next he charged forth bravely,
To meet the enemy,
But he was wounded gravely
And lay in misery.

Then he saw the tattered flag
And 'midst a hail of fire,
He rose and took that precious rag
And proudly waved it higher.

Lo and behold, he did succeed,
In rallying his comrades all
And the courage of his noble deed,
History would recall.

Helen Allan (Glasgow)

Whispers In The Dark

Fragile,
Like a flower in the breeze.
Bruised by life's perplexities,
Not knowing what to believe.

Trusting,
Gentle whispers in the dark.
A renewed sense of knowing,
A connection with the heart.

Strength,
Arising from it all.
Like a phoenix from the ashes,
That never again will fall.

Lisa Maxwell (Portrush)

Memories

Sitting here I still recall
The things I did when I was small.
Although my hair is turning grey,
It seems like only yesterday.

I started school in forty-two,
Couldn't wait for things to do,
Learn to read, learn to write,
Getting all my sums and spellings right.

Our teachers were both strict and fair,
To misbehave we wouldn't dare,
For when we did we felt with pain,
Of whacks from teacher's strap or cane.

We studied hard every day,
We still had time for lots of play,
Contented with just simple things,
Like skipping ropes, marbles and things.

We soon learned our A, B, C,
Our sums were done with expertise,
Our schooldays the best in many ways,
They were indeed our happy days.

D Massey (Newport)

Clementine

The rhythmic purring
of contentment being sung
A loving lick
from a sandpaper tongue

The sweet smell of her fur
all groomed and in place
a little pink nose
on a curious face

Unconditional love
she'll always be mine
my best friend and buddy
my cat - Clementine

Cathy Robertson (Cupar)

Clouds

Looking up towards the sky
Clouds move over and pass by
In all their different shapes and sizes
Causing wonder and surprises

Some like puffs of cotton wool
Drifting past a sky so full, of
Sunshine on a golden day, of
Summer when the swallows play

Sometimes, when the wind is strong
All the clouds are blown along
Pushing, jostling, in a crush
Just like people in a rush

Other days, when we have rain
Angry clouds appear again
Down on Earth, it's dark and grey
And raindrops on the windows play

When it's calm, they seem to float
Like water lilies in a moat
Days when life seems so serene
And everything looks fresh and clean.

J Kincaid (Bishopton)

Precious Love

A precious love makes living worthwhile
To really celebrate the beautiful feelings it evokes
I continue to love you more and more
And memories of wonderful times cement our relationship.

As each day enfolds I listen to what lies deep in my heart
And feel that our love goes from strength to strength
As we take each day at a time we savour the good times
And unite together through the ups and downs of life.

The everlasting love that we have experienced together
Brings happiness untold
Precious love keeps our relationship healthy
And our marriage gives us plenty of reasons to carry on.

Marjory Price (Abergavenny)

The Wind Of Change

I feel the wind of change today
Come sweep across my face
The bracing breeze, the scented air
Dare I anticipate?

Dare I hope for better things
Shower from above, on me?
Dare I hope that sweet content
Would calm and set me free?

For whate'er the wind may bear
I hope that it will bring
The start of something new in life
Just like a breath of spring

For with all fresh starts, I know
That I must leave behind
The stormy clouds of yesterday
Which kept riding on the wind

For today is the beginning
Today the sky is clear
The air is full of promises
For all that I hold dear.

Cathie Young (Aberdeen)

Best For All

Many of us have loved ones who have special needs
We learn so much as we a care for them, doing so many deeds
From time to time it gets tougher and we struggle along
Trying not to give up, even when things go wrong

We put a lot of effort into searching for the best
Find answers to all difficulties, putting ourselves to the test
Life becomes more challenging with worries and agonising issues
We also have a voice; please listen to our valuable virtues

Equal importance matters each and every step on the way
Please include us in the future and be prepared to hear our say
We all don't want to be left in deep despair or sorrow
Give everyone a chance and widen the door to success for tomorrow

M McClure (Glasgow)

Dawn Awakening

As light streams through at dawning
With the first glimpse of the rising sun
One stifles that overnight yawning
Realising a new day has begun.

'Tis a truly wondrous feeling
With the world at large asleep
Nothing is quite so appealing
As o'er the horizon the sun will peep.

Gradually the trees rustle and sway
The breeze through their boughs gently hums
The early bird greets the new day
Gingerly scratching around for crumbs.

The sun is now a great orb of fire
His rays streaking out o'er the sea
Shimmering water set to inspire
A view that is magnificently free.

Now we accept a new day has begun
The great orb reaches up to the sky.
All God's creation depends on the sun
As the now busy world straddles by.

Bill Barker (East Wemyss)

This World Of Ours

The world's gone crazy, we like to say, when listening to the news,
Of wars and crime and pain and hate and all that's wrong today
But you and I know that's not true, the world's a wondrous place,
Of beauty and flowers and mountains and seas and acres and acres of space.

It's the humans who live in this world of ours, that cause all the trouble and pain
With their bigotry, hate and lust and greed, they give this world a bad name.
If only they'd look around them, take a minute to stand and stare
To understand the damage they've done and at least to show that they care.

Then this world might become a better place and the generations to come
Could have a land to be proud of and a place that they can call home.
A world where it's safe to go out on the streets, where you don't have to feel afraid
Where people are free to come and go, without a price to be paid.

Joan Sinclair-McKimm (Bangor)

The Magic Of Words

With book in hand by our own fireside
We can travel the whole world wide,
Meet all the folk in the human race
Or even shoot up into space.

We can climb mountains or sail many seas,
Facing fierce storms with the greatest of ease,
Many lives in a book we can share,
Travelling with them where we'd never dare.

We join in their laughter and shed their tears,
Sharing their happiness, also their fears,
Walking beside them, enjoying their fun,
Sorry to part when the story is done.

Sometimes we're lost in days long ago,
Forgetting the present and all that we know.
The future at other times is what we see,
Forecasting the wonders that one day will be.

Our library shelves all hold a great treasure,
The wealth that is stored there we simply can't measure.
So study these books and take home a few,
Of life's simple gifts given freely to you.

Margaret Harrison (Dumbarton)

Knights Of Forward

Now celebrate to print committed
A million souls, whom verse submitted;
Staid horde of hopefuls, with pleas in hands,
Who braved the critics' abrasive sands.

Each wielding shields with own coat of arms,
They breached the unknown with skill and charm
And faced the foe doubt, trepidation,
To conquer realm imagination;

Then paused, for 'mid victory they found
A fellowship, battle-scarred, but sound
And noticed, as they rich spoils arranged,
Each crested halberd subtly changed.

Perry McDaid (Derry)

Autumn

The summer sun is sinking fast,
Those long warm days they could not last;
I think of all the joys I've had,
And thoughts of winter make me sad.

Soon the leaves will wither and fall,
And Nature's creatures, one and all;
Will prepare for winter, harsh and cold,
Many will hibernate beneath the mould.

The shadows lengthen, the birds cease to sing,
I miss their chirping and the flutter of their wing;
The peace of summer will be replaced by rain,
How I hate its patter on the windowpane.

The tall, pink roses nod their heads,
Soon they will fade in their wintry beds;
The gardens and bushes will soon be bare
And pleasant rambles will then be rare.

The skies are grey, the nights grow cold,
Soon frost and fog the earth will enfold;
I long for and miss those long summer days,
When I enjoyed the sunshine's golden rays.

Vera McNeill (Ballyclare)

Tortured Vanity

So much the gilded lily
That broke on water's edge
And burst like a fresh new star
And gleamed like tusks afar.

So much the handsome poseur
Who fell from startling grace
And dreamt of a first embrace
While hiding his tortured face.

So much the blessed woman
Who knelt in the grieving church
Receiving the water flower
From the man in the ivory tower.

Chris Skelding (Caerphilly)

Trusting In Jesus

Trusting in Jesus, oh, what a delight,
To have sins forgiven and with Him made aright!
Made aright for that land that is fairer than day;
Are you ready, dear reader, are you ready, I say?

Trusting in Jesus, oh what a thrill,
Living each day, in the centre of His will!
As He leads us and guides us, each step that we take;
With Him close beside us, no errors we'll make.

Trusting in Jesus, should be our desire,
Never trusting in self, as that would be dire!
The flesh, it will fail us, the Scriptures declare;
Let's trust then in Jesus, as none other compare.

Trusting in Jesus, well, that's what we need,
He'll show us the way, if in Him we're agreed!
His way will be perfect, His way will be sure;
With Him close beside us, we're safe and secure.

Trusting in Jesus, oh I pray that you are,
Trusting in Him, for cleansing and power!
The price has been paid, by the blood that He shed;
And so trusting in Him, you'll be Heaven-bound led.

Sydney Ward (Banbridge)

The Stone

Across the woodland path lies a large grey stone
Honed smooth by generations of clambering feet.
Providing a seat for the ragged, wrinkled village crone,
A peaceful trysting venue, a secret place to meet.

A thrush exploits the stone to shell a hapless snail,
The sharp-eyed squirrel pauses to gather an acorn,
A small, nervous, crouching rabbit with twitching tail,
Sheltering in its lee until the flickering light of morn.

Affording a stage set for actors in the theatre of life,
A silent observer, quiet, immobile and so alone,
Unmoved by passionate love and vengeful strife,
To be a mute sentinel is the destiny of *the stone.*

Rose-Mary Gower (Mold)

Help

As I ponder in what I must do,
Holding tightly, my tattered shoe,
One I lost whilst trying to flee,
A gunman; on a murdering spree.

No tears left, but only hope,
No food for days, it's difficult to cope,
Mountains of food in the EU state,
Lying around and going to waste.

I don't care, if it is out of date,
Served on paper or a silver plate,
As long as I get to fill myself up
And clean water for my broken cup.

Clothes to fit and a cheerful smile,
Not just a number on a statistic file,
No one to chase me and in fear of my life,
Nor torturing my kids, or raping my wife.

Help me, please, please help,
Open your eyes and let the world see,
My plight and the stench that I live in,
Ignoring this will be your greatest sin.

Mohammed Farooq (Livingston)

Just Do It

I was certain that I would have,
But felt inclined to wait.
It's not wise to rush in swiftly,
One should often cogitate.

I was confident that I could have,
But felt it shrewd to hesitate.
It's foolish being rash, my friend,
One should pause to meditate.

So, why then, has it happened?
It's driving me insane.
Sure! I would and could have,
But I've messed things up again!

Keith Miller (Banbridge)

Goodbye For Now

When the time arrives for me to say my final goodbye
You will find me in the sweet Lord's arms will peaceful lie
Then to you all I will say is have a contented heart
These years of my dearest love will remain never to depart.

Where my beloved the flower so charming this wonderful bloom
The beauty and your perfume and happiness fills every room
Then remember this my darling they hear those happy loving years
When I see the pools of sadness thro the deep sorrow of your tears.

When I was awashed with pleasure and treasured days we love to share
Will you just open your gentle heart and mind, I am so alive in there
This may be goodbye for now but think there be no farewell
Then only the future, the reunion, only time will always tell.

When you beloved look towards the sky maybe you will see a bright star
Each twinkle, each one brings a message so full of love we always share
When we come together the bright future our love will shine
Then we forget our sad departure, we live in everlasting time.

The people who knew me say I was ill, they said his passing is the best
Let him have everlasting sleep when they say he earned his rest
Then remember the good times they will be always in your hearts
The earthly life ends and an illness-free life will start.

J F Grainger (Cwmbran)

The Mouse

One night as I lay in bed,
Watching the dying embers of the fire,
There was not a sound to be heard,
As I looked around.

When suddenly a little mouse appeared,
He stopped for a moment -
Then bravely sat in front of the fire.
After a while he looked around,
And I am sure he was looking at me.

Then as silently as he had come,
He was off again
And I was still watching the fire.

Jean Edwards (Falkirk)

Departed Spirit

Please take time to listen
Hear what I have to say
I know I am not there to guide you
And you know I was taken away

But I can still see and hear you
If you let me I could touch your hand
I am not really that far away
I know you will understand

There is so much more I can show you
And a lot more still I could tell
If you need me I will always talk to you
From that place where angels dwell

The love that I have still holds you
You should feel me with your every move
My spirit still surrounds you
I am everything without need to prove

The one who holds all the answers
The keeper of a very special key
So if you feel the need to question
Then please just talk to me.

Philip A Jenkins (Cardiff)

Same Fine Rhapsody

I really can't think of anywhere else, where I would rather be
I've bought a watch, jewel-encrusted, the lot, this is where I want to be
It's been a while since a worthwhile smile, totally enveloped me
And I'm sure, because your beautiful face, emits that same fine rhapsody.

In taking stock of what my life has got, the present flatters me
And when I hold you tightly in my arms, I know that's meant to be
It's not science, but an actual fact, the magic of our chemistry
Like a whirlwind or a lightning storm, you can feel the energy.

I really can't think of anywhere else, where I would rather be
All my dreams are rolled into one, that single dream is you and me
Now that dream is reality and for sure, is meant to be
Cast a shadow over the past, with that same fine rhapsody.

Vincent West (Dumbarton)

Smile

Without a sense of humour
Life would not be worthwhile
Even in the darkest times
There's a reason for a smile

It may be something someone said
Or something that you've seen
Sometimes it's just a silly thought
Even just a dream

Of course you may feel stupid
About the things at which you laughed
But as long as you feel happy
You are entitled to act daft

You will find that fun's infectious
And a germ that's easy spread
So make your life a happy one
Cos you may be a long time dead

Even after you have gone
The friends you leave will say
That you spread a little sunshine
As you went along your way

Ian Russell (Alloa)

Suicide

Suicide is painful
It is your last resort
When all your friends have left you
And your life is torn apart

Suicide is painful
It really breaks your heart
When you cannot see a future
And you can't forget your past

Suicide is painful
It is your only path
When life has left you hopeless
And you're living in the dark.

Cathy Weeks (Swansea)

Crack Of Dawn

I awoke at the crack of dawn
To hear the birds chirping on the window sill
And the coldness of the winter morning
Embedded in my skin, as I rose from the bed.

Running to the hot press
I opened the door and stooped inside,
For the warmth was so inviting
I wanted to close the door and stay.

I got dressed at the hot press door
Then walked four or five steps to the bathroom,
There, the warm water from the hot tap
Was a godsend on my cold flesh face.

I could hear the wind blowing wildly outside
From the window at the top of the landing,
It was one of those mornings that make you wish
You had stayed in the warmth of your bed.

Downstairs I put on the teapot
And toasted bread under the grill,
As the hot tea and toast
Would insulate me against the cold outside.

Neely McGinley (Armagh)

Clouds

In every cloud I see your face
That gently flows on by
Sometimes you are angel dear
Protector of the sky

Sometimes you are asleep my dear
So peaceful and so calm
And then you are awake my dear
So gay and full of charm

To see my love in every cloud
My heart is filled with glee
For each day a cloud must blow
So your face I'll always see

Gordon McDonald (Glasgow)

I'm So Happy

We went on an outing the other day,
My daughter, her grandchildren and me.
We went to Knowsley Safari Park
Oh there was such a lot to see.

The children thought it so funny
When the monkeys jumped onto the car,
And when the camels surrounded us,
So we were stuck for quarter of an hour.

After a while we made for the tea bar,
Gemma, the eldest, went to help my daughter,
While Beverly, aged seven, and I found a table,
Sitting and talking with much laughter.

We were watching the people passing by
When suddenly Beverly turned to me
And with sparking eyes and a beautiful smile
She said, 'Great-gran, I'm so happy, so happy.'

As I looked into that sweet child's face
I felt a lump rise in my throat but I had nothing to say.
I remember thinking how lovely it would be
If every child in the world could say, 'I'm happy, so happy today.'

Phyllis Ing (Hawarden)

Revelation

He came as light,
taught me to walk with all creatures,
trace footprints, two by two.
My love leapt with gazelles on the mountain.

Lying down all my gold
in a tower reaching for the sky.
I slaved in promised lands,
yielding as a three-hundredth concubine.

His judgement was merciful:
graffiti on the altar stones.
I crawled away on my belly
to eat dust.

Rachel Roberts (Cardonald)

The Valley

They came here to dig for coal,
A seething mass of humanity
And the splayed-fingered valleys
Exploded into life.

Rows of terraced stone houses
Lined the ribbons of grey winding roads
And straddled the mountain sides
Cwtched tightly together.

One by one they closed the pits,
The people thrown onto the slag heaps,
Not wanted, expendable,
Untapped seams forgotten.

The valley lost its lifeblood
As swiftly as the river ran clean,
And nature reclaimed its own,
Colouring the coal tips green.

As the sun leaves the valley
Its dying rays light up the windows,
A crimson memorial
To the coal underground.

P H McKenna (Pontypridd)

Why?

Why do they destroy the beauty in this life?
The pollution in the sea is now so rife
They just talk about it and say what they should do
But in the future if it goes on, the fish will be few

The seabirds are dying, choking in the oil
The food that we eat is full of chemicals in the soil
The factory farming with animals who never see daylight
For them there is no day and night

What will our children's future be
If it is too late to save the soil, the sea?
Stop talking and do something positive now
There must be a way to save humanity somehow

Oira Newman (Erskine)

A Vision Of Beauty

As dawn greets the springtime rose
With its bright and silky glow
It fills my heart with such content
In a vibrant colour show

And as its petals come to life
Its perfume fills the air
Alive and swaying in the breeze
With beauty, style and flair

I stood back to admire
It took my breath away
Its sunshine lights a pathway
With its colours on display

I dare not try to stroke it
So fragile, soft and red
I merely wish to caress it
Alive in its flowerbed

But the gentle winds grew stronger
And its petals start to fly
A flaming silken beauty
Its ending made me cry.

Marilyn Davidson (Greenock)

I Sometimes Have A Dream

I sometimes have a dream
Of floating clouds in a sky of blue
Of being lazy but content
Of gentle days we had with you

I sometimes have a dream
Of twinkling stars in a sky of deep blue
Of chasing moonbeams, laughing out loud
Of pleasant nights we had with you

I sometimes have a dream
Of peacefulness on the ocean blue
Of floating on waves and sunny days
And realise I miss the times we had with you.

Wanda Clark (Lochgelly)

My England

Oh my England, thy country that I thee own,
How proud doth it stand, the fears it hath known.
Thy beauty compares with thy treasures unseen,
Glorious, magnificent, grandeur to bequeath to thee.

Kings and queens hath ruled through thy age,
Endeavouring each quest, while it stands with courage.
Nelson, Drake, Hawkyns honouring glory upon thy seas,
Fought with loss, for thy country to be free.

Heritage, history we hold steadfast with pride,
Language, poets, and artists our literature hath survived.
Our ancestors hath made the world as we are now,
Do we realise we must fight for our country to endow?

This land of hills, fields of green, hath surrounded us with stormy seas,
Battles, wars of humanity remain on thy bloody fields.
Ghosts of life wander in thy mountains of mists,
Arise in the darkness of ages gone by to reminiscence.

So where was I thee born, in thy land so fair?
Beauty and splendor are mine beyond compare.
My England how thankful and grateful doth I be,
A creation of this domain, to dwell amongst thee.

Anne Williams (Llanelli)

A Colourful Royal Occasion

Without, misty dark November evening;
busbies and gray great coats beneath halo-ed street lights.
Within, electric bright foyer welcoming;
khaki-clad Red Berets assist the wheelchair flights.

Above, dull blue-green Armoury walls display
steel gray and burnished weaponry, patterned finesse.
In glorious crimson, gold and white array,
rooms hold the sombre-suited men, the day-time dress.

Near, our blue-clad Royal Patron passes round,
pausing, concerned, bending to hear the weakened voice.
Through smooth white icing, with round blue logo crowned,
slices the knife, as all applaud and all rejoice.

Jo Brookes (Newcastle Emlyn)

Graffiti No More

Some folk just couldn't care less
Of walls and pavements in a mess
So take a pride in where you're staying
To try and stop graffiti spraying

Don't just sit about and moan
Call your council on the phone
Or complain to them by letter
By saying things must get better

This mess is made by the young
I've checked them, I got tongue
My advice is call the police
And give yourself a bit of peace

So let us all make a new start
Police, parents, teachers take part
And get this simple message across
Doing graffiti is a lost cause

So dump your pens, paints and sprays
And look forward to brighter days
Let these vandals know the score
By telling them - graffiti no more

C MacPherson (Glasgow)

The House On Llanwynno Mountain

Standing stark against the moorland sky
The whistling wind blowing, blowing
In strident answer to the curlew's cry
The pert little stream still flowing, flowing.

With windows long since bereft of glass
The house lingers loyally, for the owners' retread
But with another hard winter come to pass
The end of weary waiting is ahead.

They will never return to the land again
Those hillside farmers of the past
The land belongs to the wind and rain
And the hollow house is brought down, at last.

Irene Lock (Cardiff)

My Prayer

Trust me for feeding
For I am your bread
Try me and search me
Then cover your head.

Kneel down before me
For I am your friend
I'll not desert you
I'm here to the end.

I'll not forsake you
Or push you one side
Because child, I made you
And I'll be your guide.

We'll sort out your problems
We'll search out a way
For I'm ever constant
And I'm here to stay.

So, just spend some time
In my presence, with me
And we will work out
This great mystery.

Elizabeth Thomas (Caerphilly)

Satyagraha

We marched for peace to end this conflict craze,
We pledged we'd love our fellow men worldwide,
Then sang our songs of endless glory praise,
Believing that the Lord was on our side.

But wars continue and exacerbate,
Is protest marching just a waste of time?
Are all the soldiers going to end up late?
Are politicians punished for this crime?

So I shall march again for peace today,
And try to end this bloodlust gory tide.
Will politicians ever mend their way,
And start to love their fellow men worldwide?

Hugh S Mckay (Alness)

Lazy Days

The sea is rolling in across the sand
No figures on the beach or across the land
The quietness of early morning broken only by the seagull's cry
I see the beauty of the pink dawn across the sky

Soon the bustle of the busy day is here
No time to stand and stare I fear
Tourists crowding in so travel weary
Hoping to enjoy a peaceful time from work so dreary

Children playing in the sand, their laughter bright
Splashing in the water with such great delight
The tinkle of the ice cream vendor's chimes
These are the thoughts that often fill my mind

A kite is fluttering there in the pure clean air
A boy holds unto the string with concentrated stare
The sun is shimmering on the sea across the bay
A ferryboat on the water slowly makes its way

Until at last the evening twilight's hush
Brings an end to the day's busy rush
The beach is quiet waiting for the dawn
When once again a new day is born.

Doreen Todd (Ballymena)

Nolton

Nolton is a lovely small village
Having its own small beach,
With Druidson and Newgale
Both within close reach.

When blessed with warm weather
Tourists come our way,
Camping and caravanning
By each bay.

With people on horses on our country roads
And people walking the coast paths in trekking clothes
They're in awe of the beauty around
So I think for beauty, Nolton can stand her ground.

Gwyneth Clarke (Haverfordwest)

Winter Idyes

A time to think, when times are still,
Of things gone by, dreams to fulfil,
The landscape lies a spectre grey
Sleeping through another day.

Deep in the valley a bell shall toll,
In a place where rests the soul,
Where epitaphs and lovely verses
On slate and stone - reimburses.

Across the moor flees the frightened doe,
The kestrel hovers to claim its foe,
A silent copse with trees so bare,
Placed by nature, with loving care.

Then, as for a thousand years,
The mountains will shed their tears,
Riverlets will start to flow,
Expanded by the melting snow.

Lush green grass, soft and mellow,
Sprinkled with bells of yellow,
Lambs will bleat and birds will sing,
Welcome home - oh glorious spring!

Ray Johnson-Hughes (Colwyn Bay)

The Gardens In Our Midst

There's a place I find uplifting, whenever I feel down,
It's not too far from where I stay, just a brisk walk from the town.
Johnstone Gardens beckon; they're such a lovely place,
Your worries seem to disappear, and a smile comes to your face.

The gardens have charisma, as all who've been there know,
Trees and flowers, running brooks and a duck pond all on show.
Someone's book is upturned and on its owner's lap,
These gardens are so peaceful, a perfect place to nap.

Newly-weds feel happy here, to have their pictures taken,
The settings are so perfect and we hope won't be forsaken.
Winter, spring and summer, or when the leaves turn brown,
A haven in the city, a jewel in Aberdeen's crown.

David Wilson McIntyre (Aberdeen)

Sore Afflicted

I've some music in my soul,
For a few words here and there;
Is there a need to listen,
From some folk I know not where?

The tunes they never go away,
'Less hard you try too much,
Then wither they like morning mist
When the sun's rays get to touch.

But come they back like madness,
What do they want with me?
To make me dance when I would rest
And hear their symphony.

Is it music in its soul,
Makes the blackbird sing so sweet?
Is there music in a moonbeam
When it lands down at your feet?

The words they only follow
What's around us all the time,
And mercy for that little tune,
That at times the words they find.

Alistair McLean (Perth)

Leaves

Under a street lamp's glow
In late November, when brown leaves blow
Along the footpath, across the grass verge
A rustling whispering surge
Two of us stand
Happy, hand in hand

Next year, when the leaves blow again
Only one stands, waiting in vain,
In the rushing night
Under the cold street light
Hearing, alone, the leaves' dark tread
Brittle, dry and dead.

M G Sherlock (Colwyn Bay)

Progress?

The road has been split down the middle,
The traders are up in arms,
One side there are buses, bikes and taxis
And definitely not any cars.

On the other side are tables, chairs and benches
And tall plastic tubes with curved arms,
At the end of each is a hanging basket
Overflowing with colourful flowers.

The traffic lights are now in the middle
So there's only half a road to cross,
A benefit to those who are disabled,
Who can move along slowly without fuss.

This is one of two main streets for shopping,
The other is already pedestrianised,
And trade in the centre is suffering,
So there are petitions which thousands have signed.

Shoppers don't come in by car as they used to,
As it is difficult and expensive to park.
The situation will be assessed in the autumn,
Will it stay or was it just a bit of a lark?

Rachel E Joyce (Cardiff)

Hope

I spied the lonely figure
As she left her harbour home.
She pushed against the wind and rain
Like a ship in full distress:
Battened down with darkened thoughts;
No haven island in her mind.

Then on the homeward journey:
Eyes searching; drooping low;
Near the gardens watery rocks;
Little snowdrop's lanterns waving –
'We've survived and so will you.'

Beatrice M Slater (Glasgow)

To A Lady Dentist

My love is like a tooth of gold
Its price in pain I pay.
Though bones grow old and blood runs cold
It never can decay.

I jump for joy, that is the truth
Each time I cross your doorsteps.
You press my lips, my tongue, my tooth
And hold me in your forceps.

If I seem sad and looking low
With brow beset by gravity
It's just that my get-up-and-go
Has gone, become a cavity.

I must confess my life's a mess
Please say that you'll be willing.
Until the day that you say yes
That void will have no filling.

Without you dear, my days are drear
And drab with disappointment.
I only cheer when you appear.
Please, be my last appointment.

Colin Dennison (Stranraer)

In Nepal

There's a day in the year
Which all people fear
And that is the children's day
It begins in the morning
When it is dawning
The children wake up and get their powder red
And it all ends when they go to bed.

So if I were you
I would not go outside
Because the children won't stand aside
But smother you from head to toe.

Glen Fryer (Abercarn)

Unhappy Landing

A man came down by parachute,
And landed on a farm.
He little thought when he jumped out
That he might come to harm.

He dropped down from a cloudy sky;
The clouds of rain were full.
You should have heard his language
When he landed on a bull!

The bull then chased him round and round,
And up and down the field.
The parachutist panicked,
And oh: 'Help! Help!' he squealed.

The farmer, looking on, called out,
'Eh lad; that bull is tame;
And when you landed on 'im,
Well - 'e thought it were a game.

But now you've gone and spoilt it,
Chucking that rag on 'is 'ead!'
By that rag, he meant parachute,
And - oh yes - it was red!

Roger Williams (Colwyn Bay)

An Afternoon At The Cricket (May)

Clouds like ragged tears scuttle fast across Swansea Bay;
Grey-purple robed; sweeping along the curve of Mumble's Head
As go-karts on a banked track.

They hold their rain. Cricket can go on:
Ritual, not sport, in the icy wind that saws its jag-edged way
Across the grey roller coaster sea.

Players, heavy-sweatered, move like Michelin men,
The crowd - two dozen, no more - huddle in the warmth
Of coats and anoraks - except me
Shirt-sleeved and frozen. I've come to watch a summer sport;
Dressed according.

There's summer wind piercing cotton cloth
Like a weatherman's Gestapo
Pushing dagger icicles under numb fingernails.

We clap the first boundary stroke, but no more.
Frozen hands sting on contact.
A seven-hour huddle, every tempting shelter sampled
Yet an eagle-eyed wind finds them all
Until I stagger home, nose running,
From a perfect, early summer's day.

Bob Harragan (Llanelli)

Timeless

Song of the bird
Whispering leaves
Hail on the windowpane
    Spring.

Screech of the gull
Surge of the sea
Sun chases the shadows
    Summer.

Hoot of an owl
Crackle of flames
Silver mist shrouds the Earth
    Autumn.

Silence above
Carols below
Soft snow muffles footsteps
    Winter.

Year in, year out
Swift - and yet slow
Time spins out its story
    Forever.

Audrey Parks (Edinburgh)

Love Conquered

The man who stands beside me
I have loved for many years,
We've walked life's paths together
And conquered all our fears.

These paths have not been easy
Our roads have not been straight,
But Mother Nature pushed us on,
I do believe in fate.

All through our times together
I would call and you'd be there,
No matter what the crisis was
You had all the time to spare.

At last I give myself to you
And now we can't be beat,
Our strength and love that we both share
It makes our life complete.

Your eyes, your smile, your tender touch
My hearts swells up with pride,
So my love from this day forth
I am happy to be your bride.

Jeannette Davis (Alva)

Wandering And Wondering

I've wandered lonely for some time
Since I lost that man of mine
Trying my best to 'move on' and live
Not thinking too much and with a lot to give.

Meeting new people, going to meetings
Hail fellow well met and all those greetings.
Do help me a lot without realising
That time can heal, but always remembering.

The times we had and so much love
That at that time you do not realise you have.
When taken away, I must hold on
To treasure those times, now he is gone.

So, as the poet said, I've wandered lonely
Have seen the daffodils in all their glory.
Have lain on my couch in pensive mood
The inward eye will help my solitude.

As you can guess I have loved a poem
That was written years ago, unbeknown
It could help people in so many ways
To pick up the pieces and shout hoorays.

Elizabeth Brenda Hopkins (Llanelli)

On The Rails

Leaves on the line
There's nowhere to go
Come back tomorrow
But watch for snow.

The state of the railways
Is beyond belief
It takes two hours to go
From Cardiff to Neath.

Leaves on the line
And the wrong kind of rain
The passenger today
Takes all the strain.

It does not matter if you
Are man, woman, girl or boy
If you are on a train
Today the world is no joy.

If you think my poem
Is no Auden ode
Remember the post
Is now sent by road.

Phil Knight (Neath)

Y'know, Y'know, Y'know

It seems that every person
From highest to the low
Must add to every sentence
'Y'know, y'know, y'know'

'Freaky me' gets uptight
By the English that folk speak
When out comes . . . unabated
'Y'know, y'know' . . . each week!

So where on earth can me go
Where 'y'know' is left unsaid
From every kind of media
Before I lose the head?

Y'know I might just fly off
To an island in the sun
Where I'd be Robin Crusoe
And be the only one!

But y'know I really don't know
If there'd be no 'you knows' there
'Cause bet there'd be a 'Man Friday'
With a 'you know, this . . . izz rare'!

Robert Mackay (Perth)

There Was A Question On Radio Four

I've never been here before,
never thought to define -
the Nature of life,
yet I'm sixty-eight years old.

I've lived life,
I've been tired, happy, sorry,
I've been angry, strong, weak,
I've wished I was invisible.

I've been proud of my dad,
My mum who made fabulous cloutie dumplings,
taught me the difficult lessons of forgiveness,
My sister thinks I'm - she just shakes her head and smiles.

My wife is lovely in her protection of all who are in trouble,
My family make me proud most of the time,
I sometimes make them sad, but . . .
define the nature of life . . .

having lived it, I can't do that,
except, ask you to
watch a snowdrop
push its leaves out of frozen ground.

Ian Comrie (Broxburn)

Hawick Common Riding

(Flodden Field 1514, Scotland - a tale about a town in June)

Children scamper on cobbled streets
wearing blue and yellow rosettes,
they are heading for the Backdamgate
to watch the horses saddled.

Parents follow, looking proud
as drums and fifes play 'Teribus',
'they're coming, they're coming'
in the crowd now an excited buzz.

Hundreds of horses with riders appear
charge up the steep Loan to the Cheviots,
led by an honest and upright son
they now ride to protect the marches.

The banner blue and yellow is held high
their common riding once more safe,
in the hands of Teri descendants
now they all in triumph shout . . .

'Up wi auld Hawick
Hurrah, hurrah, hurrah.'

Elizabeth Murray Shipley (Hawick)

Thank You

Thank you for giving me a chance
When no one else would take me on.

Thank you for believing in me
When everyone thought I would fail.

Thank you for listening to me
When no one else even cared.

Thank you for helping me
When others turned away.

Thank you for loving me
When I found no love elsewhere.

Thank you for getting me through
When others had given up.

Thank you for your patience
When everyone else had lost it.

Thank you for everything
When I really needed you most.

You are truly special
And thank you is not enough.

Claire Diane (Kirkcaldy)

Scenic Sonnet

Snugly ensconced within a basket seat
close by the rolling river's estuary,
fresh salty air filling my nostrils, sweet
as a perfumed aura stilling the mind;
a balmy breath. And as I muse I pray
the musings will evoke poetic lore.

The venue augurs well; a quiet spot
save for commuter trains that happen by.
The afternoon is warm; a hazy sky
wisps over water-craft moored randomly
against a backdrop of opposing shore;
reasons a-plenty to inspire the thought -
'Bereft of feeling those who can ignore
this masterpiece that nature has designed.'

Walter Blacklaw (Dundee)

Newborn

Ah! Then my dear, I have waltzed in
Hand the four daughters of the wind

Looped the moon in a thousand starbursts
I was lit by the Northern Lights

Ridden rainbow shoots of Jupiter, in a glass
Mixed the Milky Way.

Sled down the backs
Of comets and fizzed my mouth with stardust

Told sun about sleep, to the cold moonshine
Gave warmth and comfort

Fished for wishes with skyhooks.
Threw snowballs of Sirius that never landed

Listened between stars' conversations I could
Never understand

Nothing compares to the wonder of you.
A billion stars could lay waist-deep

And be pointless if no reflection of you could
Be seen.

Alan Boyce (Gourock)

Stolen Moments - For Alex

Irresistibly,
Surreptitiously,
Effortlessly
Gliding.
Soft air
Swishing swiftly
Past my face.
Stirring, swirling
Memories.
Excitement,
Exhilarated ecstasy
Until . . .

Hey Grandma,
Give me my scooter back!

Elizabeth Meredith (Crickhowell)

Nos Galan

Our little town of Mountain Ash,
Is where you can come and spend some cash.

On New Year's night you'll not be alone,
There are plenty more from abroad and home.

For on this night, since days gone by,
To beat each other, they come and try.

The Races held, are world renown
And held in the streets of our little town.

One mile, two mile, three mile, four,
They come from afar to have a go.

On this Magic Day our town comes alive,
To watch all the runners, they're like bees on a hive.

They come in their hundreds to line the streets,
To watch all the amateur and professionals compete.

All of this is to honour one man,
A very fast runner called Guto-Nyth-Bran.

In Legend it is said he could run as fast as a hare,
Well, don't ask me, 'cause I wasn't there!

M O'Brien (Mountain Ash)

Procession Day

P eople gathering all over the town,
R acing all about, trying to find a good viewing spot.
O bviously, this is Procession Day,
C oaches and cars invade from everywhere.
E veryone enjoying themselves, thoughtfully and thoroughly.
S tandard of entertainment is excellent,
S tupendous day for everyone concerned.
I ntegration, not segregation,
O ld and young alike getting involved.
N ight has now finally come,

D isplay of fireworks at the park.
A ll the celebrations are now over,
Y oung at heart for at least one day of the year -
And not just the children.

Daniel Henderson (Bathgate)

In The Chapel Of The Olives

In the chapel of the olives,
Every day I say a prayer,
That you'll always walk beside me,
For to part I could not bear.
Both of our hands, upon thee altar,
With two rings of yellow-gold,
May we always walk in sunshine,
All our days till we grow old.
And when our life on Earth is over,
We will hold each other tight,
We two hearts that beat as one,
Will go softly into the night.

In the chapel of the olives,
I still see you standing there,
For true love it lives forever,
We are blessed in silent prayer.
Both our hands upon thee altar,
Shines two rings of yellow-gold,
For true love will live forever,
Till the tropic sun grows cold.
In the chapel of the olives.

J D Rosser (Gulfach Goch)

A Battered Wife

It's hard being a battered wife,
It makes you think about your life
You don't know where to go to, or who to turn to for advice.
You sit and wonder what life would have been like
If you had met somebody else
Somebody to love you like nobody else
Somebody to walk hand in hand with you, instead of beating you.
Somebody to cuddle up and hold you tight,
Rather tan them being in the pub every night,
Somebody to buy you flowers and make you a cup of tea,
Rather than them sitting watching TV.

As you lay and cry yourself to sleep *(shush)*
Asking the children not to utter a cheep
You know it's time to pack your bags and get out of here,
Rather than live in a life of fear.
From a man who is always stinking of beer.
On the outside, he's a fake, he's lower than a snake,
He's the life and soul of a party,
But no one knows what goes on behind closed doors
So open that door and walk away
Before he kills you one day.

Isabella W Johnston (Wishaw)

No Turning Back

The lion stood in a rocky place
His roar volatile
To the menagerie around him.
But the porcupine in the outer ring
Did not accept the words of never, never.

His body bristled from the onslaught
Of negativity.
Change was a word he loved
He savoured it, turned it over on his tongue
It was like dynamite, an explosion of ideas.

'Who can carry them out?' asked the scarecrow
As he sought a place in the nearby field.
Then the porcupine became afraid
Existence depended on the higher order.

A scream from the scarecrow
Touched a raw nerve,
'Stand up for your rights
Challenge the lion in his den.
The word 'never' is of no consequence'
With that, the scarecrow hung his head.

Rosaleen Clarke (Belfast)

Celebrations In Penarth

Some say they've seen UFOs hovering over Wales
P'raps they came to visit our delightful hills and dales?
Or to hear our choirs singing each lovely hymn and song?
Bet they stopped to listen, before they travelled on -

Perhaps to Caerphilly, their special cheese to devour
Or to see their castle, with vast moat and leaning tower
Did they hover over Castell Coch, with three towers tall?
Or view Cardiff Castle, where strange creatures sit on wall?
Around the city there are stone lions, big and strong
Keeping a good lookout, to see that nothing goes wrong

Did they go to Penarth? - known as Garden by the Sea
With Italian Gardens on Prom - fine place to be
But if UFOs flew over, they'd have had a big surprise
As pirates with hooked hands and patches over their eyes
Were in the town, brandishing their cutlass in the air
And there were chests of treasures, almost everywhere

Had by wicked pirates, Penarth been overtaken?
Bet that those UFOs would have been quite shaken
But, seems that Penarth was enjoying a great carnival
Because it was the day of the Summer Festival!

Betty Gould (Penarth)

Just A Dog

'Man's best friend', a gift from God
The furry creature we call Dog.
They start their life when they are born,
With puppy love. They love the warm
With bouncy, tumbling friendly play
Through puppy life they make their way.

When they are weaned, as big they grow
Doggie features they start to show.
Is it a dog, or is it a bitch?
Nature shows us which is which.
Then into the world they must go
And learn about who's friend or foe!

Dogs cannot speak with words like us,
It's in their eyes they show their trust.
When first a dog becomes your pet
Let me tell you what you get.
Great affection, loyal and true,
This stays constant their whole life through.

When you are parted at the end
You say 'goodbye' to your best friend.

D Thomas (Newport)

Hello

Winter said hello
Touched me with a silver glow
Covered me with mistletoe
Filled my heart with good content
Paid my rent in kindness

Spring said hello
With dancing maids all in a row
Kissed me under a rainbow tree
Said she would like to marry me
Paid my rent in good old mountain dew

Summer said hello
Placed a crown of flowers on my head
Laid me down under a sacred oak tree
Whispered sweet words in my ear
Paid my rent in cider and beer

Autumn said hello
Invited me in for some bramble tea
Sold me a pumpkin planted in June
Showed me her harvest moon
Paid my rent with a silver spoon

James Harbison (Annan)

Tourist Attraction

(Written for the ghost of Sir Roger at Chepstow Castle)

For more than seven hundred years
I've walked these windy battlements
No mortal being has stirred my blood
My soul not prone to luminescence.

But then a glimpse of maiden's face
Hid 'neath her swinging silken hair
Has wakened, within my pounding heart
A longing to taste said maiden's ware.

To caress her being and feel her warmth
Is more than I dare hope to win
To inhale and enjoy her sweet perfume
While gently kissing alabaster skin.

With heaving bodice and trembling hand
Would she her arms with mine entwine
And whisper, 'My Lord, wouldst thou be mine?'
Alas, I fear that should we meet
This chilling, drifting form of mine
Would send icy shivers down her spine.

Morgan Keith (Bulwark)

Why?

(Thoughts of my special needs son, Brian)

I am one in a hundred, I am one of the few,
Who cares what happens to me, may I ask? Do you?
Why do people evade me, when they meet me anywhere?
They won't even sit next to me, on the only vacant chair.

People give me a 'wide berth', when we meet in a shop,
Staff give me a 'wary eye', when I buy sweets or pop,
People stare at me in the street, I often wonder why
Am I so different, to a normal-looking guy?

I love to talk to others, I have a mind of my own,
I understand what people say, whether verbal or by phone,
So, next time that you meet me, stop - and say, 'Hello,'
Have a conversation - the true me - you'll get to know!

Evelyne A McMaster (Glasgow)

The Mouth Exists Alone

Such desolation lies marked in every tone!
I stand reduced
The mouth exists alone

The aching - despised, wretched, the lone,
Slaughtered: am I nothing?
Such desolation lies marked in every tone!

I gave my body - it trembled, ached and moaned,
Cut down like this!
The mouth exists alone

Behold the severed heart - you cannot atone!
Massacred entirely
Such desolation lies marked in every tone!

Dropped, dropped! As a bloodied, sharpened bone;
Tear off my limbs!
The mouth exists alone

What's done is done
All that I am to you and represent -
Such desolation lies marked in every tone!
The mouth exists alone.

Bethan Arrowsmith (Bridgend)

Beautiful

Beautiful people . . . sunshine *'speaks from the smile on their face'*
Beautiful people . . . unconditional love within an embrace
Presence; forbearance; a faithful hand reaching out *in the storm*
Sharing rapture in moments when dreams are born

Beautiful people . . . words like kisses that soothe and heal
Beautiful people . . . *garments of honesty,* folks who are real
Promises kept secrets *still hidden*
Welcoming arms *unfolding like Heaven*

Beautiful people . . . feelings that well up into good deeds
Beautiful people . . . walking the extra mile to meet a soul's need
All of this beauty in each human heart
Offerings of care for child, loved one and stranger;
Reaching across oceans every race; each one neighbour
To pass on - to impart.

Isabel Morgan (Paisley)

Childhood Memories

Birds nesting in a rookery. Elm trees straight and tall
Stood sentinel towards the sky against a stone-clad wall.

Across the meadows lush and green where cuckoo flowers and cowslips grew
There flowed an ever-rippling stream near where the trains passed through.

There upon a railway line, ragwort found a shady spot
With willow herb and columbine and blue forget-me-not.

Towards the river bramble bushes and wild roses there profusely grew.
The water hen among the rushes and driftwood where the seagull flew.

The canal with the narrow boats, holidaymakers afloat.
The fields of waving corn and picnics out on the lawn.

Little cottages with ever open doors as housewives went about their daily chores.
The men folk working on the land.
I remember village life, it was grand.

As I reflect on days gone by, it makes me wonder why
Has all the world gone mad? It makes me feel quite sad.

Children of today may play, but not in a carefree way.
Community life is now long gone.
Where did we all go wrong?

Margaret Kent (Beauly)

The Woman

You are a woman beauteous to behold
A woman made for gods, not mortal man
A woman, gentle, sweet, yet bold
Promising a passion such a woman can
You are the dream, comes to me in the night
That fills my sleep with ecstasy
For when my dreams take wildest flight
You are the woman, who belongs to me
You are the stalwart, standing by my side
Who says, 'This is my man, my only man'
And knowing this my heart is filled with pride
You offer love I know I'll never have
This - a love story never to be told
For I, alone will ever offer love
You are a woman, beauteous to behold

Gordon Andrews (Newport)

The Cat

The cat lies sprawled upon a cushion,
Relaxed and well-fed,
Eyes half-closed as if in contemplation,
Of the day's events,
Her sleek, smooth fur is patterned,
Coal-black and silver-grey,
Unique designs marked onto her fur,
Striped like a great tiger,
On her sides are circles,
Like twin targets,
Her slitted eyes are bright green,
Glinting as they catch the light,
Around her neck is a plain grey collar,
She stretches and yawns lazily,
Revealing two long, sharp teeth,
The sign of a predator's heritage,
I ask myself,
What thoughts drift through that mind,
So tame and yet so fierce?
Within those bright gleaming eyes,
No answers shall I find.

Charles Wright (Wrexham)

Mist Of Time

I believe that somewhere there is a mist of time
And whenever we pass through it,
Great happiness we'll find.
Glorious contentment
Where peace and love abound
Old friends rejoice, embrace again,
No tears, nor pain are found.
Where time's no longer cruel
To body or to mind
No hunger, thirst or earthly woes,
Nor enemies or foes
No grieving for those we've left behind
Because someday, they too
Will pass through
The mist of time.

Rosemary McIlhatton (Ballymoney)

Bridges

Oh, so easy to knock down
But
Depending on the chasm
Incredibly difficult to build
Bridges, they can be likened to everyday problems.
We, as individuals, can keep the chasm as small
Or as wide as we want it to be
This can depend on our willingness to build that bridge
To reach out, cross over
Or, to help someone cross over to us
If that willingness is there
Both sides need to ensure a strong foundation
Building on this ensures the bridge stays firm and true
It will demonstrate a willingness to overcome problems
Past, present and possibly future
A strong foundation on both sides will generate
A sense of trust, of understanding
Whatever the problem, how deep the chasm
Lay the foundations of trust
Build the bridges of hope
Ensure the path to understanding.

S Price (Tredegar)

Teddies' Playtime

What do teddies do when the lights go out?
Do they crawl? Do they creep about
On silent, padded, furry feet
Soft and gentle while we're asleep?
Maybe they play games like hide-and-seek
Or sit around, laugh and speak
Or maybe they just stay where they are
Silent and immobile lifeless fur
Over in the corner I see
Four sets of eyes all staring at me
Was that my imagination? Perhaps a glint
But I'm sure I saw one of them blink
Oh well it's 2am and I'm tired out
So I guess I never will find out
What teddies do when the lights go out.

Darlene Smith (Dundee)

2008, Mending The Web

I don't know what to say
Will words tumble from my mouth
Like pebbles in a river bed?
Finding words to tell what I feel
Is like trying to put light in a bottle
I woke up this morning opening the
Eyes-of-wonder of a child.
In holidays in summertime
Each breath a song
Each step a dance
Shimmering threads connect me to
All that is visible and invisible
I am the weaver and the weaved
A shape-shifting dance of dappled light and shade
I don't know what to say
And that is well
I am not anymore
Imprisoned in a cage of words
It would slow me down
I vibrate in harmony
With the web of Wyrd.

Sylvie Alexandre-Nelson (Swansea)

How I See You

I know so little about you
I don't know what you've been through
I know maybe you don't get a fair chance
From those who know no better.
Man has always
Excluded anything, anyone,
Different in culture, appearance
(And I know this all too well myself)
Or for believing something
They do not understand.
Hopefully all of us will learn
To bring so many cultures
Together, to pick out the good
That is the best
In all of us.

Caroline Docherty (Glasgow)

Poem To The Sun

Shining let the light
Pierce the dark of ignorance
Let the warmth
Envelop you
Drink it in
Warm and sweet
Sing the praise of life
Banish darkness
Fear and loneliness
Blow your mind
Let it happen
Glide and float
With the wind
Sway with the trees
Light my fire
Reach out, don't resist
Fly with the clouds
Sing with the birds
Feel the grass
Silky smooth and damp
Damp.

G Linton (Edinburgh)

Picking Up The Pieces

In the cool light of dawn, let us retrace our steps
Back across the channel from which we came,
Let us salvage what we can
Regroup and start again,
The continuation of our objective.
Trials ahead sweep over us
In the midst of doom.
Shock at the realisation of what has happened
And of things to come, our ego departed.
Let us try and not make the same mistakes again,
Taking things at a slower pace.
Haste if required, but with a clearer mind
And a deeper sense of inner thought.
Rekindling the fire, now dying within our souls,
Stepping out again towards our goal.

Frank Scott (Bushmills)

Journey Through Space

There was a boy who went to space
Packed his clothes in a leather case.
As he flew around the stars,
He thought he'd take a look at Mars.
The aliens made quite a fuss,
When he stepped out in Uranus.
The man in the moon was quite a host,
He gave the boy some tea and toast.
Neptune, Pluto were a sight to see,
Like fairy lights on a Christmas tree.
He knew one day he must return,
To visit Jupiter, Venus and Saturn.
What a journey it had been,
To think of all that he had seen.
While travelling down the Milky Way,
He wondered what his folks would say.
They didn't know where he had gone,
Just popped out, said, 'Won't be long'.
The universe was quite supreme,
What a shame,
It was just a dream.

Patricia Long (Bridgend)

Catch My Tears

You came into my world
I loved you from the start
You held my heart so gently
We said we'll never part
You were my rock, my soul, my strength
We had so much love to give
But now my heart will be empty
For as long as I shall live
But I know one day
I'll take that walk
Right up God's golden stairway
You'll take my hands and kiss my lips
And hold me like before
You'll dry my tears, we'll walk one way
And we will dance once more.

Lindsey Oare (Holywell)

The Day Room

Sunshine filters through the curtained windows,
The source of Life vainly seeking to renew
God's creatures who sit immobile, still,
In long neat rows of plastic covered chairs
Waiting for something, waiting for nothing.
Old age sits looking at old age
With glazy, long-forgotten eyes,
Minds dulled by drugs or senility.
A spidery hand fumbles in a handbag
To search for nothing, and finding nothing
Withdraws again beneath the tartan knee rug.
They have been washed and fed and now
These ladies, once capable and strong,
Sit waiting in the cheerless day room
That is their final earthly home.
The sunlight fades, but for them
Life's shadowy dusk descended long ago
And left them here in forgotten solitude.
Like lepers they are kept apart
With only one purpose left in life . . .
To fade, to wilt, to die.

Irwin Major (Newry)

My Dogs

My dogs are loyal and true
And cheer me up when I am blue
The love they give
They never complain
Even when things are tough
It seems to me that they are true friends
Who never let you down
That's why I depend on my dogs
I know that they will never let me down
Even to the end
That's why I love my two dogs
They are true friends
And part of my life
Dogs are humans' best friends
I dedicate this poem to them.

Rose Innes (Cumbernauld)

Shapes

I love the shape of things that grow
Of footprints that appear in the snow
And flowers with petals shaped like crowns
Of trees standing in their gowns
To see the sunset like a circle of gold
And watch the leaves as they unfold
Yes to see the rain as in a mist
I watch a river flowing fast
So still it almost looks like glass
To see a plough trailed over the land
You'd almost think it had been done by hand
Yes to watch a waterfall so high
As if the water is falling from the sky
To see animals run over a hill
This is when you wish time would stand still
To see the wind blowing the trees
That have only been touched by the birds and bees
The whales mating away from Man
Away from the hooks they don't understand
The most beautiful thing you will ever see
Are animals running wild and free

Anna Graham (Glasgow)

Give

You give me that
That special feeling
Feeling of love inside
When I see you calling
You are calling out to me
To me I feel so alive
So alive without a fear
A fear of my feelings for you
What waits below
Below the bottom of our hearts
Is it our true feelings?
Feeling for one another
You give me that
That special feeling
Feeling of love inside.

Angela Cole (Llangunnor)

The Lice Inspector

I'm the lice inspector
Stand in line please
Lower your head
Ha, ha!
What is here?
Little things crawling around what?
Dirty little brat!
Not you darling
Why is your hair so long darling?
It's got to come off, all off
No hard feelings sweetheart
Don't cry!
This won't hurt at all,
There, all off!
Tell your mammy I want to talk to her
Will you?
Where do you live darling?
'I live in Harold Street.'
That's a nice street,
'Well it was once.'
Next please.

David Rosser (Ammanford)

Time

Time starts where it ends
But it never ends.
It begins somewhere
At the last ending,
Hour upon hour a moment lasts,
Day upon day
Year upon year
To another second gone past.
Eternity has just passed me by;
Just a fraction, how many fractions
Of endless time to pass,
Until another moment passed.
Light rushes by
But time stands still
In this moment of eternity.

April Steward (Usk)

The Scarecrow

You stand alone in the field
Through sun, wind and rain,
Your heart is just straw
So you don't feel no pain!
Your arms are outstretched,
To frighten the birds,
You stand there alone
And you speak no words.
At night under the stars you stand
And survey the wild animals
That roam the land.
Autumn approaches the field is all bare,
But in the middle you still stand there.
When winter's snow has covered you all,
You look more like a snowman
Than a scarecrow tall!
When at last he is weary and worn
And falls to the Earth from where he was born.
Goodbye! Scarecrow a job well done,
You will be reborn again
For next year's sun.

M M Thornton (Aberdare)

Untitled

Life is like a book
Each page a story to tell
With little poems in ink
As it were in colour it fell
On the leaf so bright it sparkles
In a bright array
And it gives to the reader
A glimpse of a glorious day
The day is given by God the Creator
God who sits in Heaven above
And watches over us with love
There's never a moment without Him
For He is God of all
And He it is who hears us
When we call.

Lily Williams (Treharris)

My Homeland

Mountains, hills and valleys, waves breaking along the shore
The sounds of gurgling rushing streams, nature's wonders, could you ask for more?
Sheep continually grazing, cows forever chewing cud so contentedly it seems
Suddenly a startled rabbit, see its scat of pure white
As it darts to reach its burrow on its headlong flight
A buzzard circles lazily on a thermal of warm air
Always stealthily alert, should prey unwarily appear
A red kite swoops quickly earthwards a scuttling mouse to snatch
Then swiftly soars up to a tree with its daytime catch
Daffodils' heads nodding, bowing, to a passing breeze
A beautiful yellow carpet, on a bank amid the trees
You are compelled to take a moment, so to absorb the scene
Admire the dappled sunlight, as it plays the branches, trunks and leaves
Hear a scuffling in the undergrowth, the soporific buzz of bees
Some little birds a-twittering, a church bell chimes the hour
A lamb bleats for its mother, you are in awe of nature's power
You look towards the skyline upon a bluff of castle stands
Its tower and its battlements built to protect 'the land
of my fathers' with many a contest proudly fought
This precious land and country, hills echo with many a song
Wales, my prized homeland, it is where I belong

Marjorie Leyshon (Swansea)

Sleepless Nights

We lie together,
yet sleep apart,
no longer dreaming of each other.
You, drift easily into your slumber,
eagerly awaiting your night-time rendezvous.
Insomnia invades me and
my mind tosses in a turmoil of emotion
as I listen for you to murmur a name.
Exhaustion overtakes.
I fall into a disturbed unconsciousness
of bittersweet nightmares.
I am awoken by a kiss,
a smile on your lips;
but your eyes
speak of someone else.

Jack Lanigan (Renfrew)

Hallowe'en

I took a shortcut home through a field,
I heard wild chants, shrieks and squeals.
What were the noises in the middle of the night,
I started to tremble, was it cold or fright?
I saw demons and witches dancing in a circle,
I could smell burning flesh, I was witnessing evil.
I was worried by what I was seeing,
Were they burning a lamb or a human being?
In my mind I knew it was Hallowe'en,
Surely what I see can't be real?
Their chants and squeals got very loud,
Black smoke appeared to form a cloud.
Out of the cloud came forth evil,
The chosen one, Satan, was here.
His claws outstretched, towards the sky,
Summarising the dead from another place.
They arrived in thousands, I thought I would die,
Too frightened to speak or even cry,
Then I heard the chants loud and clear,
It's all red, yellow, black and green,
It was the witches' Christmas - Hallowe'en.

John Smith (Glasgow)

Our Last Saturday

My best friend died the day he walked down the wrong street
Wearing the wrong-coloured scarf after the greens beat the blues one-nil
We got separated in the crowds and the next time I saw him
Was on a mortuary slab
He was kicked to death, a bloody pulp
He was only seventeen, no age at all
I don't know how the men who did this sleep at night
We don't hate them and I'm sure they don't really hate us
His mum and dad won't ever forget the night the policeman
Came to the door
Mums always know don't they?
They always do
I don't wear my scarf anymore
The greens beat the blues one-nil, or was it vice versa?
Anyway, the pain is just the same.

Alan Ross (Bellshill)

South-West Wind

It is soft, where I stay,
The wind from south-west,
And of all the March winds
I like it the best:
It is warm and caressing
And gives a fresh birth
To the trees, sleeping flowers
And cold wintry Earth.

It sweeps o'er the hilltop
Right down to the seas;
Though it quivers each green blade
Yet gentle its breeze;
It woos all the songbirds
To pour forth their lay;
And rolls back the grey clouds
To brighten the day.

It gives us a promise -
Though light on the wing -
That one day quite soon,
We shall find with us, spring!

Greta Fraser Murray (Buckie)

The Wild Mustang

A lone figure emerges
From the landscape beyond
Alive and untouched his beauty renowned
Roaming free in the remotes of the desert plains
Wild and forever he will remain
A symbol of spirit lost and found
His powerful strength so profound and alluring
His pain and anger, so wilful and enduring
Forever wild, forever strong
As free as the wind that touches him as he storms
Through the red-coloured desert from where he was born
As dusk sets alive the night sky dark blue
He strides towards a watering hole with his fellow mustangs
Waiting, wondering what is to become
Of his red-coloured desert at the break of dawn.

Kelly May Elizabeth Evans (Neath)

Returning To Wales

Travel broadens the mind,
Or so I've heard it said.
But there's only one place I feel right,
And where I lay my head.
Returning home, I long to see,
The hills of Wales which beckon me.

I smell the gorse still miles away,
And hear the skylarks' song.
The years just disappear in my mind,
Why has it been so long?

I smell the heather in my dreams,
And see the crags and more,
I visualise each house and street,
The coastline and the shore.

Houses, each like palaces,
Neat curtains, open wide.
A smiling face to welcome you,
The wanderer, inside.

I'm home.

Gwyneth Pritchard (Caerphilly)

Can't Help Loving Those Felines

Cats are irresistible aliens,
They speak 'Miaow'
And body language,
Gaze at you saucer-eyed.

If you blink to show you trust them,
They will reply likewise.
Some of them.
Others use the Ignore tactic.

When you appear,
They hurry towards you,
Tails erect,
Saying, 'Hello, friend,
What can you do for me?'

Paradise is a purring cat on your lap.

Margaret Rolston (Lisburn)

Celebration

I celebrate the summer
The lovely flowers
Around which the bees swarm
I love the summer when it's nice and warm

I celebrate the trees
With their summer mantle of growth
In which the birds and bees
Make their homes

I celebrate the animals
To watch them grazing in a field of flowers wild,
Their young gambolling and playing
To their hearts' desire

I celebrate the farmers
With their fields of corn
Feeding the nation
Working all daylight hours

I celebrate the human race
The many kindnesses done, unseen
Which don't receive news coverage.

Rachel Ritchie (Newtonmore)

Me And My Dog

My mum is really proud of me
I try my best and she can see
We walk along to the ringside tent
I wonder if this will be a big event?

My brushes ready and my bench is here
Don't panic Mum, you have nothing to fear
I'll be good, you know I will

Hold my head high and I'll stand real still
I'll stand for the judge and look at his face
We'll go together and at the right pace

There now, look, there's nothing to fret
I'd be rich if I could bet
This is the last class, then we're done
Oh look Mum, yes! I think we've won!

Sonja Shepherd (Dundee)

Prayer For Peace

A silent tear runs down my face
As I think of the sadness of the human race
God created a land so rich in honey
Man turned it around with his greed for money.

Bombs and destruction everywhere
Human life has become a nightmare.
Towers of majesty reigning supreme
The result of intelligence
An American dream, smashed, by the force of evil.

Sons without mothers, men without wives
A completely destroyed generation of life
And I ask you Lord, why?

Lord, you gave Man strength, you gave him capability
Now you probably wonder where is the tranquillity
For the land you created with power divine
Lord deliver us from this evil so blind.

For thine is the kingdom, the power and the glory
Return us to peace and a land that is holy forever,
And ever, Amen.

D Britton (Abertillery)

Listening

Seeking inspiration, not knowing what to say,
I went into the garden on a lovely summer's day,
I closed my eyes and listened on that Sunday afternoon,
I heard a myriad of sounds, not all of them in tune.

The gentle rustle of the leaves moving in the breeze,
Blended with the sleepy twitter of the birds high in the trees,
Then from the Square the strident voice of a well-meaning preacher man,
Mingled oddly with the music of the ice cream van.

The constant drone of traffic on the nearby carriageway,
Almost drowned the joyful whoops of children at their play,
Then, close to my ear, came the whirring of an insect's wings in flight
And I realised that all these sounds would be silenced in the night.

Later, I lay upon my bed in my usual wakeful way
And listened and listened and waited for the day.

Ruth Cochrane (Dromore)

Back Home

While away, I yearned
To come home, how I yearned.
Home where my friends were
And my kind neighbours.

The blessed day came at last
The clouds rolled away
The pain had gone.

Once more I trod my garden path,
The air was heavy
With the scent of new-mown hay.

It was a glowing June morn
Dew was glistening
Like pearls on the bough.
Birds were singing
To welcome me home.

'Neath the velvet-blue sky
it felt like Heaven on Earth,
I thanked God for His wonderful blessings
And His enfolding love.

Megan Davies (Bala)

Underground

I found my little corner,
Feels kind of large
Try to find my way out
But it's awkward and it's dark
No smell, no sound, no atmosphere
I can't see, can't feel
I'm so removed
I'm actually underground
It's in my mind, I'm so profound
I've lost all my strength and appetite
I can't get a breath, this doesn't feel right.
I'll just lie still
Until I no longer feel ill
I'm buried under soil and grass
Just me and my coffin!

C Taylor (Paisley)

A Poem For Abbey

There was a dog called Abbey
She lived with me when I was a baby
She had her own jungle world, where she would fright
Just in case the sharks would bite
Little did she know that she'd have a new home.

She lived with my grandma and granda
In this jungle, the sharks weren't so bad
Years after a new arrival had come,
Abbey felt that she was a mum.

They played together, so she felt very young
And Abbey was proud of Lucky, her new son
Even though she was old, she continued as if she were fighting for gold.

Her and Lucky, had great fun
To Lucky, she was a great mum
Lucky was weeping, I was afraid
Grandma was crying, Granda was away
Little did she know this was her last day.

I didn't want her to go, but I new it was the end
I didn't want her to go, cos she was my best friend.

Callum Millar (10) (Downpatrick)

The Fire On The Hearth On A Cold Winter Night

I don't know if I've ever loved you
or if I
love you still,
I don't really know what love is.

But I would like to be a feature in your garden
a bright light in your path
a soothing scent that lingers
a friend that stands by

. . . and dream we walk together hand in hand
in silence,
and we understand.

RubiSquirrell (Tullibody)

What Are Parents For?

Parents are for watching a foetus unfurled,
a hand uncurled, the first smile curled;
for watching a newborn human hurled
into the world, and catching.

Parents are for saying, *'Welcome, hi!'*
for caring, preparing -
then saying, *'Bye!'*

Launch-pads for dispatching,
for the shooting of a star
to the farthest horizon -
that's what they are.

And when it meets that sky-line bar
and slips through the haze behind,
they face dark days without their star
and yet, they must not mind.

For, as all parents must recall,
they're for splashing a mark, that's all -
for flashing a spark through the arc of time
onto the blaze of mankind.

Kate Williams (Cardiff)

Winter Dawn

I drew my curtains on this winter morn;
And saw the coming of the dawn.
To the East I did gaze, and saw,
a sky of salmon-pink and green.

Winter can offer such delights;
Oft forgotten as cloud turns day to night.
Skeleton trees bereft of leaves:
Their tentacles outlined against the sky.

The birds descend in search of food
Each breed fighting for its way.
Nature is at work, in all its glory, and its demands.
Their life struggles emulate our own:
To live and fight for another day.
To see the next dawn arise in its own peculiar way.

Roy Mottram-Smale (Connah's Quay)

The Snow King

Her Royal Highness, the Ice Queen, her maiden now befriended
Ice-cold, at the Snow King's ball attended
With iceberg emotions, cool and intact
Reclusive and not one to overreact
She was born of royal Pleistocene descent
Cautious and cold, not one to repent
Ruth was her name, ruthless without shame
Eyes ice-blue, her ice-fall tears were tame
And now with her maiden henchwoman, ice bound lay she
Memories frozen in an ice-blink, of her dying deity

The Snow King snowed under and snow bound
How now he admired the flowers of the guilder rose new found
Yet his thoughts were lost in a snowstorm's mistake
Within one lonely, snow white flake
His Ice Queen had left, with sharp words, shot from a quiver
As his snow-slip emotions, became as a snow-broth wither
Letting his thoughts, above the snow-line
Lost in a snow-blink, his Ice Queen, was frozen in time
Ever her false love, so cold, so unkind
Left him alone, snow-blind, of his Queen's cold and frigid mind.

Jeremy C W Bloomfield (Corwen)

Progress

C reating changes for future generations,
U nderlying industries of the past,
M odest men and women moulding present population
N urturing characters of chance, achievement and strength.
O rdinary yet extraordinary
C itizens with equal opportunities
K eep the wind farms of time turning.

A midst upheaval
Y ellow adorn the buttercup.
R ivers go on their journey,
S nowdrops stand proud.
H ills surround the valleys veins and arteries.
I solated cottages hear the constant flow of lifeblood
R eturning the Earth to a bustling city of
E nergy-extracting excavators.

Katebell (Cumnock)

Common Ground

Remembered days
Of gulls behind a horse and plough,
Of new dropped calves sprawling on steaming hay,
Or with your Da, perched on a five bar gate,
Laughing and cheering on the stirks -
First day out on the May Day sward
And leaping like bucking broncos.
'Oh Da, Da, it's like the wild wild west'
My common ground with the Nobel Laureate
So many years ago.

What's more, our fathers, unacquainted,
Buying and selling sleek milch cows
On the same Fair Hill
Bantered, teased and coaxed,
Clinching deals with a hand slap.
Revived by hot dinners at McIlwee's,
These two men, unacquainted,
Went their separate ways -
To Mossbawn, to Craigbilly
One a Planter, one a Gael.

Robert Simpson (Ballymena)

Stupid, Stupid I

Why am I here?
Walking in the dust,
Rifle slung,
Waiting for the roadside bomb,
The people - living out their lives,
In fear and devastation,
Why am I here?
There is no one I can trust.
I am puzzled and bewildered
Why did I join up?
To devastate people as poor as I?

The answer comes out clear,
As the flash goes up,
I am here to help the big boys
Get their profits up.

Grace McDonald (Inverness)

On The Loss Of Children

Sally and Stuart, our next-door neighbours,
are leaving shortly with their family,
moving to Haddington, where Stuart was born.
They will be much missed, especially the kids,
Alex, Ewan, Freddie and the feisty four-year-old Iona,
her brothers' shadow, trotting behind them like a permanence.
We'll miss their zest, enthusiasm, puppy-dog *joie de vivre,*
their freshness, laughter, sparkiness and enterprise,
miss Freddie with a rope, pulling Iona's trike.
How I regret the children who are going.

In an area vulnerable to the Himalayan fault-line
and to unscrupulous cowboy builders and contractors,
a Primary School in Dujiangyan collapsed, killing
a thousand children. In Juyuan, the Middle School
crumbled beneath the force of 7.9 on the Richter Scale,
burying hundreds. In Bechuan County,
a six-storey High School was reduced to rubble.
Thousands of young lives now lie beneath incense sticks
and Buddhist candles, the parents' single hope, snuffed out.
And, oh how I regret the children who are gone.

Norman Bissett (Edinburgh)

Don't Cry For me

Don't cry for me
For now I am free
The wind that moves
Across the sea
A grain of sand upon the beach
A leaf on high
Just out of reach

This mortal coil
Has blown away
I will live another day
Cry not for me
For what is now
Will be again
Some way
Some how.

Ron Houghton (Llandrindod Wells)

Primavera

The dreary deadness of winter
Has now been left behind
Those dull leafless trees
We can no longer find
Although snowdrops are diminishing
Daffodils are in bloom
The fresh fragrance of new life
To kiss away the gloom.

The cycle of life's beginning
For all of us to see
The plants, the trees, the flowers,
The active busy bee
The pink of cherry blossoms
Splash colour to cities and towns
And more hours of sunlight
Cancel out the frowns
Standing close to their mothers
Are beautiful bleating lambs
The tranquillity of the countryside
Rarely stresses, only calms.

Anna Maria Hastie (Eaglesham)

Spinster Of This Parish

It's too late for love, I realise that
My passion in youth was the open track
The wide plains of India, the peaks of Nepal
The Highlands of Thailand, I travelled them all.

My career came next, I was bold and forthright
But ambition I found was cold comfort at night
Now here I am where I wanted to be
The queen of the bees, the top of the tree
I've conquered the corner where I belong
I thought I had time, I was wrong.

Yes, I thought I'd find love, or love would find me
But it soon became clear it wasn't to be
Love waits for no one, the weak or the strong
I thought I had time, I was wrong.

Maureen Reynolds (Pitlochry)

Rainbow Warrior

Often when I went to town to do the weekly shop
I would see your mini car and I would always stop
To admire the paintwork created with such pride
A sky-blue roof with rainbow arches covering each side.
Greenpeace window stickers gave me the explanation
Proclaimed you were a member of that organisation.
Then, by chance, I saw you, you made a perfect pair
Blue denim jeans and jacket, with badges everywhere.
A duffle bag and walking boots, you seemed all set to go
Off somewhere to save the world. Did you? I don't know.

Years have passed but I still think about your rainbow car
And I sometimes wonder, where on Earth you are.
Protecting the environment or life within our seas
Or in a distant rainforest, conserving ancient trees?
Maybe you have settled down with your own family
I hope that you inspire them, as your car inspired me.
As oasis of peace and beauty in a world with so much strife
It demonstrated there could be a better way of life.
Where even on a busy street, a rainbow could be seen
If we all work to create a world that is peaceful and green.

Pamela Evans (Maesteg)

Oh Jenny Dear

Oh Jenny dear, I wish I could be with you
Without my dear my heart it breaks in two
It's not so long since last we said goodbye
But still at night I sit alone and cry

The days are long and all the nights are lonely
It's you my love for whom my heart yearns only
But time will come when once more I'll be with you
No more will I be all alone and blue
But till that day my love please don't forget me
So once more with you my love I'll be

Someday I'll come and put my arms around you
And tell you dear how much you mean to me
I'll cuddle you and tell you that I love you
And then sweetheart I'll be forever true

Gerald McLean (Glasgow)

Not The Way We Wanted It To Be - To The Man In The Shop

I missed an opportunity,
A one I missed so much,
A man I really fancied,
He is the one I really want.

I accidentally backed away,
He backed away from me,
I heard an angry sigh,
It is not the way we wanted it to turn out to be.

Should I write a note?
Or send it out to him?
To still express an interest
To not express disinterest.

My troubled mind,
Obsessive thoughts going round my head,
To find an answer,
Would bring calmness to my head.

Wendy Chaffer (Belfast)

Happy Anniversary 1988-2008

A poem or rhyme captures the essence of time
Encapsulating emotion, is pursued with devotion.
A friend to be plucked from out of the air
A comfort to many, in times of despair.

Frivolous and funny it can make us laugh,
Stimulating and provoking takes a different path.
Poets through the ages - constant toil and sweat,
Earning their living, sometimes getting in debt.
Compromised creativity, necessary for feeding the brain,
Hopes and aspirations, dashed - washed down the drain.

But at Forward Press, they do their best,
To help erstwhile poets keep abreast.
Encouraging us with motivation,
They reach out and draw from all over the nation.

Carole McKee (Upper Colwyn Bay)

Forget Me Not

I'll come to mind
where holly grows,
and snow lays round about
bright red berries on the bush
and robins flit about.

Where lace-like snowflakes
fall to Earth
and every breath is seen
I'll catch your thoughts and make them mine
in a winter landscape scene.

When the air is crisp and fresh to breathe
and the pond is frosted over,
the winter angel casts her breath
across silver fields of clover.

When the winter chill brings coldness
yet a warmth endures, you'll find,
on days like these
you'll love me still
and I will come to mind.

Bridget Devaney Penman (Cowdenbeath)

Uncomfortably Numb

We are not part of your bazaar,
Your chaotic world of lifeful vibrancy.

We are the shadows on a desert path,
The silent ghosts, a desolate few,
Cast adrift, unknown to you.

Beyond your simple, joyful dance
We stand and watch with pale confusion,
Mute and bound, our hearts imprisoned.

To us each smile is a lancing barb,
Each laugh a dissonant bray,

For we are nightlore's crippled dream,
A paean to listless fear
And in the end, we do not exist,
We were never really here.

Simon Dale Leeman (Belfast)

Collessie Warrior I

The running man leaves his mark
and tells his tale,
not on shifting sand or flowing river.
In timeless flight
he's carved on Collessie Stone.

A remnant of an ancient race
nestled in Red Ochre hills -
with spear raised,
the man defends
his ancient sacred place.

Facing west, towards the setting sun
his God is never caught.
Just ahead, beyond his reach
the disc descends beyond the rim.

Forever poised to fight
an enemy no longer there.
Do the battle cries still echo
through the long-dead soul
of running Collessie man?

Sheila O'Hara (Glasgow)

A Corpse Reminisces

Here I lie, confined in a wooden cask,
My elements now ready to be used again
In the continuous recycling of Mother Earth.

Of an all-powerful creator I do ask
No further existence devoid of pain,
No heavenly life, no second birth.

Judgement I make now on my span of life,
Has my species profited by my stay?
Have I helped fellow humans to save our race?

They weaken their prospects by their strife
About which colour should rule, to which god to pray
And with no common tongue to argue their case.

For long I have tried to set the pace
Towards *one* god, *one* tongue and a *single* race.

Charles W Brown (Banff)

Autumn Colours

I heard the ping of a falling acorn
And the rustle of the tumbling leaves
The mist lay low until midday
And a brace of pheasants rushed past
As autumn colours, sneezed.

There's a smell of wet grass
And of moist soil here,
Some trees show their bare branches
But a warm sunlight dances bright
As I listen to nature's changing plight.

A whispering cooler breeze sneaks past me
And a far-off call of a kite is heard above the canapê
Autumn colours begin to unfold
Of orange, sand and yellow, sage green
Burnt red and heaven's gold.

I listen to the distant chatter of folk
As across the valley their laughter floats
And this autumn colour pleases me
This season's early nights and changing leaves.

Carole Morris (Llangollen)

The World Is Getting Smaller

The world is getting smaller all the time.

I am the sun that circles the world
Giving the heat and making the life
Of the fish in the waters and birds in the air
And the people who live on the land.

I am the moon that shines all the time
Reflecting the light of the sun in dark places
Making mystery and romance and pulses of wonder
In the minds of the life that the sun has created.

I am the life that the sun has created
And the moon makes me wonder at the magic and mystery
As fish, birds and people reach out from their birthplace
To venture afar and experience living.

The world is getting smaller all the time.

Gerry Miller (Bangor)

The Science Of Dreams

(Dylan Thomas 1914-1953)

Are these the pathways
That Dylan walked
'Do not go gently into that good night
Still dormant in the bloodstream?

Restless Dylan -
A cacophony of emotion
That spilled out
On a page.

Love and hate, entangled -
A grotesque monster
That so often
Carried the child to safety.

A born romantic
Drowned in the sea
Of hopelessness
Who created -
The science of dreams.

Ken Price (Swansea)

The Fiddler's Cave

There once was a fiddler brave
Who took his friends to explore a cave,
When they arrived at the cave wall
Not one of them would go in at all,
Except for the fiddler, with his fiddle and bow
He wasn't afraid to go down below.

His friends waited to hear his story,
Hours passed, they began to worry
No on spoke, too scared to talk,
Slowly tiptoeing from the cave, they walked.

So, till this very day,
All they can hear is the fiddler play
Sweet music rings out from the cave
Where once there entered, a fiddler brave.

Eileen Gallagher (Enniskillen)

Where The Heart is

Going home alone
Is not going home -
But only leaving you

Arriving home alone
Is not arriving home -
But only missing you

Being home alone
Is not being home -
But only remembering you

Being home with you
Is not just being home -
But what home means

Arriving home with you
Is not just arriving home -
But home from home

Going home with you
Is not just going home -
But home-coming.

Dan Taylor (Moray)

Milestones

F orwards you press
P ushing pens, typing lines, in
F uture decades come mist, come shine
P raise the Lord, we trust publishing will continue to climb.

T wenty years
W orth reflecting o'er
E very poem printed
N ow one million and more
T he lyricist appreciate
Y our skill to collate.

Y our invitation we gratefully accept
E ndeavouring to express words which won't perplex.
A nniversary occasions when everyone
R ejoices with Forward Press
S erving poets, and public, also encouraging yourselves.

Annie R Harcus (Orkney)

Arrival

Wholly unaware
that a welcoming party
is here to greet him,

the child cannot know,
as he slumbers peacefully
in his warm cocoon,

that, in the desert,
a squad of John the Baptists -
honey collected

and locusts gathered -
is preparing the pathway
for his arrival.

On that glad morning,
a choir of angels will sing,
a trumpet will sound

and our lives will change.
Light will flood through creation
and glory prevail.

Faith Bissett (Edinburgh)

Untitled

Somewhere
Far away
Clouds feathered
With gold
Rise high against
A bright blue
Sky

Gentle waves
Stir the shore
With the sound of
Tiny thunderclaps

And
The crofter knows
That the day
Will be good.

Ian M Stephenson (Alness)

Snowflakes

Floating gently in the breeze
Soft as swans down on the wing
Gleaming white as pure as silk
Spiralling downwards through misty array
Weaving a ghostly blanket of gossamer net
Festooning the hedgerows with spidery threads
A network of lattice shrouding the trees
An enchanting dream of shimmering light
Softly and silently fall to the ground
A creation of wonder to behold
a carpet of feathers soft to the touch
A mantle of magic and beauty unfolds
The world is still and silent
As the pale sunlight's rays
Fall on the blanket of white
The air is hushed and filled with wonder
The mountains and hills enthroned in
A mantle of grand splendour
So pure, untouched by hand
I stand, in awe at one of nature's pure creations.

W M Martin (Wrexham)

Untitled

It came from nowhere in the hours of dark
Reaping havoc and leaving its mark
Life as we knew it stolen in minutes
Leaving a victim with unknown limits
Shock, trauma, heartache and tears
Numbness, worries and mounting fears
Relief, at life still being there
Anger, why them, it's just not fair
Daily improvements and we are thankful enough
Seeing your loved one struggling - it's tough
Will they ever return to the person we knew?
Strong, independent, carefree and true
As we adapt, and our hearts start to mend
We say thank you that our life didn't end
We will get through this, as others do
Strong in the knowledge of our love for you.

Tina Greenway (Isle of Mull)

Look Oot Burn Broon Troot

Spate torrents sare pounded, sad eyes stark popped
A great marvel hoo yir he'rts no fast stopped
Lang doged otters herons sly guddlers guiles
Sae flegged each time dare cin swim fir miles
Sma wonder yir speckles are nae sickly spots
Whilst shuirly discarded nylon ties yi in knots
Bet yiv seen enough rank bait tae mak maist puik
Impaled on rochest hooks a must aye juik
Puir suite crater sae thin a real shame
A paltry quarry tae the fisher no worth a name
Same gowk wha'll trash hale water up and down
Till face whip stripe parr marks second time roon
Dae beware o' moving shadows keep clean gills
Hope be subjected never tae polluting overspills
Cin trust yill fear when espy wae great ease
Bold gadder angler wae hat o' multi decked flees
Bird encircled fluffed up like some Ascot Jessie
A sicht tae put the wind even up oor Nessie!
Must pity merciless they wha deem unjust just catch yir wink
Or wave o' yir tail before yi I think safe slink.

Tom McConnachie (Dundee)

Origins

Fathomless, without end,
Ever restless feet shall tend
Toward the sea; I close my eyes,
Surrounded by the wheeling cries
Of gulls. Barefoot on the sand,
Before the briny foam I stand,
Gazing out upon the ocean,
Seized by unexplained emotion.
Mesmerised by ebbing tide,
This human form 'neath which I hide,
Grows dim. No more can I suppress
My longing for the soft caress
Of gentle waves; diving deep,
Abandoning my weary feet,
Enchanted by my sisters' song,
I'll swim once more where I belong.

Sarah MacLennan (Inverness)

On Life's Departure

Don't look for me in the cemetery
You'll never find me there
Where the sweet perfume of a thousand blooms
Penetrates the air
Where young and old walk hand in hand
Treading the ground with care
Don't look for me in the cemetery
You'll never find me there
But look for me when you sit alone
Shedding a silent tear
And you feel a breeze upon your face
That's when I draw near
And when you're in the garden
Where we sat for many hours
Although you do not see me
I walk amidst the flowers
So raise your head and give a smile
Believe me this is true
The love we shared for many years
Will always be with you

M S Maldon (Blackwood)

Past Tense

There stood Robert the Bruce and his trusty spider,
With Jean McGregor and her child beside her,
And William Wallace wanting no hassle,
As they make their way to Edinburgh Castle.
The Scots wha hae where Wallace bled,
And chronicles of this are often read,
The timorous beastie by Robert Burns,
Gave nation upon nation a mighty turn.
Those Scots of the past in blazing glory,
And fights with the English were often gory.
But time has settled amidst the dust,
With clans accepting this as a must.
The MacDonalds, the McLeods and McDuff,
The McStays, the McPhersons have had enough,
To live in peace and settle the score,
And to make friends with for evermore.

William D Watt (Irvine)

Badly Broken

Your window has a two-way view,
Outside, is me and inside, you,
A world apart, in terms of thought,
I'm thinking things that you forgot;
Eclipsing gloom hides summer's glow
When your perception fails to show;
A gulf, a gap, some missing part?
Your head is here but not your heart,
And all of life and all it cost,
Is worthless when its memory's lost.
Re-echoed themes are tried and spoken
But the train to the brain is badly broken,
Its wheels and carriages, derailed
When vital points and signals failed;
The words of songs drift and drain,
They haunt and tease a blank refrain.
You hear and touch and look perplexed
By what your window view reflects -
A foggy day, a cloudy spell,
Then a fond embrace and a sad farewell.

Eunice Wyles (Cambuskenneth)

Homeless

I am out on the street,
With nothing to eat.
No roof over my head,
No nice warm bed.
I have holes in my socks,
I sleep in a box.
I shelter from the storm,
Try and keep myself warm.
Sometimes someone looks my way,
Smiles at me says 'have a nice day'.
I think the world is not so bad,
Recall the good times I have had.
I am not as bad as people think,
I am not an alcoholic, I do not drink.
How did I get in this state?
I often wonder what's my fate?

M V Walsh (Cardiff)

Retirement

Many people dread the day of their retirement,
But really it could be a blessing heaven-sent.
Think of all those things you have left undone,
What a time you could have and so much fun.
Take up a new hobby, painting, reading or sport,
You'll soon fill your day if you plan it with thought.
Visit a friend, a neighbour or even a relation,
Do the garden, you will be pleased at your creation.
Take a long-awaited holiday somewhere near or far,
Maybe by plane, bus, train or your own car.
Go to night school and learn a new skill,
It will all help to keep you busy and fill
Your day with so many things to do,
That you will realise the hours are too few.
Take up walking, through the countryside or moor,
It certainly will help your spirits to soar.
Go down to the sea and sail on a boat,
Or simply just swim or lay there afloat.
These are just a few things that may fill your day,
Then you'll realise going to work only got in the way.

Carol Diane Milne (Perth)

Sadness

Born in Paisley it's no life
People dying by the knife
Dirty needles strewn around
Buy a bag for just five pounds
Men out drinking, women battered
The rats have either died or scattered
People shouting, children crying
Junkies robbing, cheating, lying
Broken bottles, cats and dogs
Youths are hanging round in mobs
The sad thing here there's also others
Brothers, sisters, fathers, mothers
The nice, the good, the law abiding
Afraid to emerge they're still in hiding
We all know this has to stop
The good, once more, must get on top.

Joseph Graham (Bridge Of Weir)

Just A Chore

You are just a housewife - that's such an easy job,
you do not have to sweat and slave to earn an honest bob.
No early morning rises, battling traffic in the street,
your job is easy, you've all day to keep your houses neat.
What do you know of heavy work or worry in the city,
you spend your day sipping tea with Jan, Marge or Kitty.
What's that you say? Oh yes I know, you work a little too,
but slinging cakes and buns about is not so hard to do.
Oh yes, I will admit you wash and clean and scrub
and that my clothes from yesterday are ready for the tub.
But really dear, a finger is the only thing it takes,
to make that washing go around, the truth for goodness sake.
Oh yes, I will admit the ironing is a chore
and maybe cleaning out the bath can really be a bore.
And what about the children, oh well now you go too far,
what's that you say? Oh yes I know, you washed and cleaned the car.
Yes I know the decorating and the painting took some time
and the plug I fixed the other day isn't worth a dime.
But darling you must understand that I'm a working man
and you are just a housewife - not a grafter like I am.

Doris Robertson (Kilmarnock)

Sun

You bring your light to Earth each day;
Then silently you steal away.
So constant and without fail;
As revered as the Holy Grail.
No pilgrim more alone than thee;
As travelled over land or sea.
And though your work is never done;
Welcome to thee, oh, friend called Sun.
You travel on as nation's sleep;
Your covenant with God to keep.
No human claims thy fealty;
You shine on man's inadequacies.
To wander over every shore;
Keep thee your secrets evermore.
A greater power guides thee your way;
To serve a miracle of day.

Windsor Hopkins (Bridgend)

No Time In Eternity

In the morning as the sun rises at the beginning of day,
I look to the sky above and see a pattern of decay
Because these things are temporal and not designed to last
With no eternal future only a present and a past
How perfect is this structure detailed, without a flaw
So why do we complain so much as if we had drawn the shortest straw
But what goes up, must come down, that's what Issac Newton said
When the apple fell off the tree and landed on his head.
Think back to the beginning, there was another apple tree
And if anybody touched its fruit they lost life eternally.
Most of us, when we search our soul, have this burden that we share,
Is this existence all there is, or are we going to live somewhere?
Some place above the stars so high, a mansion in the air,
A place of love and joy, a dwelling place to share.
I do believe with all my heart, this Earth is not my home,
And that when I leave this scene of time I will not be left alone
See time is just temporal but time cannot delay
The returning of the Word of Life who never will decay.
So when you look up at the sky, the stars, the moon, the sun
Believe the one who put them there, loves you and everyone.

Joseph Villamuera (Glasgow)

Our Northern Ireland

The beauty of our country takes our breath away
As we view it from our doorstep every passing day.
The colour of the grass, with its many shades of green
Or a crystal flowing river, with its shimmering and sheen.
The buildings of a time that's gone
Are still around, sound and strong.
They blend with modern architecture that scrapes the clear blue sky
And yet their beauty's still beheld by people passing by.
The people of Northern Ireland, with their families and friends
Have that precious love and caring, that never has an end.
With hearts as big as buckets and a will as strong as steel
They'll lift their voice to tell you, exactly how they feel.
We may not be the best behaved
But the majority of us are soundly saved.
We were bought by Him through redemption's plan
And know we'll reach His promised land.

Josephine Quinn (Antrim)

My Garden Now Sparse

The winter fades and spring's due to arrive,
Starting with snowdrops growing outside.
Followed by crocus, some purple, some blue,
Then daffodils blazing a bright yellow hue.
My garden for me is just one sheer delight,
Year after year it keeps my heart bright.
In spring my rockery, with colour abounds,
Edging the borders with colourful surround.
Pansies follow my daffs in coloured array,
They peep from the borders, a lovely display.
Their velvety petals with little faces I see,
How can I help show my rapture and glee?
July's gorgeous roses in all different shades,
With perfume delightful that comes every day.
Some are exotic and can grow quite a height,
Others are shorter like poised in their flight.
My heart's full of sadness, now beauty is gone,
Wild rabbits are feeding where they don't belong.
Yes, I'm not alone; my neighbours moan too,
Flowers are digested with each morning dew.

Joan Prentice (Elgin)

Look After Our Planet

Have you ever stopped to wonder, the power of mankind
The sort of things that he can do and decisions he can mind
He can push the button for the bomb to make the mushroom cloud
He can make our future no matter if we yell and shout out loud
Who gives these people the right to tell us what to do?
Who gives these people the right to damage our planet
The way they do?
They cut down our rainforests and kill our life on land
Why do they push aside the food of the helping hand?
We could all help to make this world a happier place to be
If only mankind would stop killing, the flower and the buzzing bee
These people should really be put away for good
Or taught to live the good life that good people should
These crimes against our planet don't help any one of us
So, look after your planet, the way we should
And stop creating all this fuss!

Lori Wilkinson (Belfast)

Arthur

I've had it a while now about 1950
A very unwelcome thing, a parasite.
I've called it a few choice words along the way
On my fingers and on my neck like a tie.
It won't let me sit comfortable
On chair or couch.
It hates to be on its own,
Cold day, rainy day, dull and cold,
It likes to be active.
It's the same some sunny days too.
Any climate will do
Just likes to see folk being miserable.
I'm not the only one, there are millions
Of us, small children, teens, middle age
but it loves the oldees best.
When we have worked hard all our lives
Looking forward to some peace,
It has to come and spoil it all.
Oh, it has four more letters to its name
Arthur(itis).

N Shields (Llandudno)

Along The Way

I looked for you along the way
Where youth and love went hopeful hand in hand
And were you there
Along the way somewhere
Searching for me
Somewhere along the way?
Did you wait for me
Among the crowd?
Did you look away
Too soon, too late?
Or were you never there at all
Along the way
Waiting for me?
I never found you and I fear
No one ever waited there for me
Along the way.

Margaret Headley (Orkney)

Like Roses

Her perfume
Fills the room
She'll bloom
Then fade away
And she will die one day
Like roses
Her beauty is beyond compare
And people stop and stare
At her burnished hair
Her skin as pale as cream
But beauty is a dream
And life a fleeting thing
In her stem it has a thorn
That can unsettle and sting
From the day that she was born
That will make you scorn
Comforting dew upon the morn
But the dew soon evaporates
And with it her beautiful state
Like roses.

Alan Pow (Hawick)

My Dream

I had a dream, I saw you there
You sat and smiled from your armchair
'Twas long ago I last saw you
What joy you brought, I hope you knew
No words we spoke, a smile was all
But nonetheless, you sure did call
I woke and wondered where I'd been
This dream I had, what did it mean?
Was this a sign you were with me?
Though many years it now must be
Since you my darling fell asleep
I could but only sit and weep
How fragile was your ageing frame
But oh how good it was you came
So as you rest in Heaven above
Remember my eternal love

Margaret Murphy (Linlithgow)

The Ivy Leaf

No one for chapel in the valley remains,
(left to the vandals, the wind and the rain.)
Precious the pennies for building were found,
from mining, the coal took deep underground.
The old generation, the Lord grant them rest,
another has come which think they know best.
Nails boarded the door and the windows lay shattered, forgotten,
it stood and to no one it mattered.
Neglected, deserted, surrounded by briar
and Eyria Jones passing said she heard the choir.
At night it was ghostly, gone creepy to pass
and sudden a woman would shudder and gasp.
The young folk encouraged the boldest and brave,
go pick a leaf, must come off a grave.
Beware the corpse-candle will rise, follow you,
its sickly blue flame, from dead bodies grew.
Brave was the boy, to return like a thief,
presenting his girl with a snatched ivy leaf.
Found pressed in a Bible an emblem to treasure,
a Welsh girl's proud token of love and endeavour.

A E Doney (Cardiff)

Love Letters In The Sand

Shall I write in words
My message upon the sand?
The tide would wash it away
Like a motion of my hand.
There is no need to say
How much you mean to me.
The sun beats down today
Like it's here to remain.
Oh, my darling, don't you see
There's never been any rain?
I could write a letter
For everything I've said,
Your eyes speak words better,
And the warmth of your hand.
We have no need for words
As we tread along the sand.

C A Keohane (Penydarren)

Midnight Madness

I am a fox on the run
From the farmer's gun
I've stolen a chicken to feed my brood
I know why he's mad, but the cubs need food
I have hunted all day for a juicy rabbit
But I've lost my speed and could not catch it
I am not as young as I used to be
I am losing my sight now and can barely see
Tired and hungry, I found the shed
Through the rotting wood, I poked in my head
And there they were, all clucking about
My biggest feast yet, without any doubt
Not much time to do my deed
At last, I've caught one, now the cubs will feed
As I make my way back, I hear the gun fire!
My heart is pounding, as I run under the wire
His gun has missed me this time
I know I've been lucky
But for one more night
My brood gets Kentucky!

Andrea Trick (Swansea)

Flu

The flu is like a death so near,
A feeling of your life force shallow.
The flu is like a crawling smear
That niggles and upsets,
You feel it in your very blood,
An unclean organism.
It makes you writhe and makes you wriggle,
It makes you so unsettled.
Your heart ticks over way too fast,
But still you daren't move,
'Cause when you do
Your life force feels wretched.
The flue gets in command of your strength,
Causing a total lack of vitality,
And still your energy drives away at you
Causing only a drained zest for life.

Thomas Middleton (Ardrossan)

Britain

That was a nation, that was
But not now, finished, now history
Five shilling for a gallon, ended
Property was cheap, four K
Not now, finished, prices through the roof
Where shall it end?
The prices gone sky-high
Bread almost a pound a loaf
Petrol a pound a gallon
How much more, many ask
Cost of clothes, just as bad
Almost everything going high as a kite
Fewer people carry money anymore
Now it's plastic
One time that was your raincoat
To keep you dry
Funny world, we have got
But fewer people are laughing
They fail to see the joke
And who can blame them?

M C Jenkins (Cardiff)

The First Man

The first man Adam
Was never born
He never had a birth
He was never an infant or a child
But created from dust of the Earth
Father Adam
Could not sympathise with me as a babe
He never knew infancy
He knew not childhood
But was full grown at once
Created, not born like me
He was never little
He began in mid-life
Didn't know what it's like to be small
Adam, the first man on Earth
The father of us all.

Christine Williams (Blaenrhondda)

Separation

Confused state again or PMT?
When will I allow myself to be me?
You cannot pull my strings or reel me in
I'm thinking of me and it's not a sin
I feel at ease doing things I've never tried
Finding myself, after too many tears cried
You did not deserve me, for the way you abused
For the way you lied or the way you used
You believe what you want, I believed in you
Thought we had something honest and true
You did not stop to think, didn't think twice
That grass looks greener, mmm this is nice
You cannot hurt me, I've passed that stage
You will not hurt me, new chapter, new page
I still believe in love, my illusion's not shattered
I will look closer, my emotions still battered
I will bump into love, I will be me
I will find my happy medium, just you see
Confused state again or PMT?
It's time I allowed myself to be me!

Hayley Williams (Trethomas)

Songs Of Praise

With my curtains opened at first light
I thank God for this new day
A robin welcomes morning's glorious light
With its grateful notes of praise.
Grey skies seem dark and gloomy
And the storm clouds may come
But when the heavy rain is finally over
We can share the golden sun.
The summer breeze, so crisp and fresh
Scatters all the clouds away
It takes colours to make a rainbow
And light to make a new day.
Oh! Listen to the song thrush's melodious notes
Here's another song of praise
Saying, each hour of life's a golden hour
Sent by the Lord above.

James McIlhatton (Ballymena)

Laughing Boy

The locals call him laughing boy
He's always on the bus
No matter how crowded it may be
He never makes a fuss
Friendly, chatty, nice to know
He certainly makes our day
And when you hear that lovely laugh
It chases the blues away
He spreads a feeling of good cheer
The whole bus feels the glow
It's just the thing to cheer you up
If you are feeling low
His wife must be a lucky soul
If he's like that every day
Though elderly and with a stick
He shops without dismay
To hear his lovely chuckle
All the people say
He's a tonic on our bus route
And makes a difference to our day.

June Davies (Cardiff)

The Office Clerk

The office clerk
Is really nice
He is a handsome guy
He sits at his computer
And never wonders why
He wears a red tie
And grey suit
And sometimes smokes outside
The office door
Beside the steps
Where other folk abide
He has a big red car now
(the last one was bright yellow)
but on the whole
I really love
The arrogance of the fellow.

Sheona Campbell (Edinburgh)

The Great Wheel Turns

The present bleeds into the past,
The cavalcade of moments pass.
As then, the now and soon to be,
The future reaches out to me.
The experiences of the past
Are wrought in iron and will last.
The present dies on very breath,
The future leads it to its death.
Memory, moment and the morrow,
All our pleasures and our sorrow.
The mystery of time proceeds,
Shaped by our thoughts and by our deeds.
Raw phenomena is broken,
Events begin to coalesce,
Nothing in this world is certain
Save our causes and effects.
Our prayers heard by no distant god,
For karma is the key of truth.
Redemption is a concept flawed,
Consequences, our reproof.

Gregor Neil Cook (Paisley)

Tinsel Stars And Jellybeans In Jars

Well, we've set up tables around the hall
There are boxes everywhere, large and small,
We have books, CDs, vinyl records - these are old
Hats, scarves and gloves when the weather turns cold.
Christmas cards, wrapping paper and tinsel stars
Sweets and cakes, and jellybeans in jars,
We've puzzles, games and assorted toys
Everything to interest young girls and boys.
With carved wooden love spoons on the bric-a-brac stall
Jewellery and pictures - so come in one and all,
Enjoy home-made Welsh cakes and a cup of tea
In the Valley town sale there is so much to see.
A banner has been hung on Farmer Jones' fence
Sale 10am today - Entrance - just 50 pence.
Now if everyone is ready - let's open the door
A warm Welsh welcome . . . good to see you once more.

Jean Mackenzie (Cardiff)

Our Future

If there are inhabitants in outer space
Keeping observation on the human race
Watching the Earth from a far off star
Making sure we don't travel too far.
They may remember when the Earth began
Long before the creation of Man,
A beautiful place with lovely green trees
Birds and animals, rolling blue seas.
They can see, as they sit and stare
That planet Earth is the worse for wear
The ozone layer disappearing fast
Without its protection, our world cannot last.
We've taken all that our world has to give
Many plants and animals no longer live
Our turn will come, that we all know
And we'll be looking for somewhere else to go.
And so, the men of the future will roam
The vastness of the universe, looking for a home
But who will say, 'You're welcome here'
Knowing that we have destroyed our own sphere.

Mary Davies (Llangollen)

The Dress

The dress hangs in the cupboard
No one's allowed to see
The wedding that was meant
Alas was not to be
The boy who said he loved her
Sadly broke her heart
Even though he promised
They would never part
It's been a few years on
And broken hearts do mend
I'm not just her mother
I'm also her best friend
I pray she finds another
And be loyal and true
And the painful years of yesteryears
Her life can start anew.

Nan McInnes (Dunoon)

Moray

Moray is the place you really should be
Mountains and moors, rivers and sea
Wonderful climate, stupendous views,
All sorts of animals and fish too
Dolphins leaping right out of the water
Tony will tell you, if mother and daughter
Seals lying right close to the shore
Seabirds a-plenty, who could ask for more?
Watching the osprey over Spey Bay
Gliding and stooping, the salmon their prey
Eagles occasionally float overhead
Deer on the footpath, with so light a tread
Squirrels of red, a very rare breed
Up in the pine trees, after the seed
Blackcock, pheasant and large capercaillie
Strut in the forest, and call loud daily
You must tread softly if you wish to see
All of the creatures, when you visit me
Up here in Moray, not far from the coast
In sight of the mountains, we'll happily host.

Sylvia Chandler (Elgin)

Haphazard

Earth with her natural beauty
Nurtures and provides,
What do we give her in return?
CFCs and pesticides.
Life flows down a poisoned stream
And meets oil spills in the ocean
Upsetting the eco system
In addition, causing a total commotion.
She bares the gifts of paradise
And is abundant all year through
Yet we are on a countdown to suicide
By the likes of you and me.
Therefore, when are we going to take action?
Moreover, start cleaning up our mess
Wiping away the toxins
That is causing so much distress?

Donna Salisbury (Tonypandy)

A Friend Indeed

I want to sit and listen
I want to sit and hear
but not really knowing
the ones who really care.
That is my biggest problem
not knowing who is who
not knowing who my friends are
the ones who are really true.
Nobody really understands
what it means to be a friend,
always on the ready
to be of help, no end.
Sharing so much laughter
so much to be gained,
no reason to even try
cos your mind is always trained.
Feeling that you are wanted
or being in the way
cos no matter what is what
a friend will always stay.

Susan Miller (Pembroke Dock)

Juvenile Delinquent

Biting his fingernails anxiously,
He sits forward in the chair.
The values he has learned at home,
Are the reason why he's there.
His father is long gone,
His mother cannot cope,
A reasonable job or home?
For him, there's not a hope.
So he's turned to petty crime
Just like his father did,
He's on the slippery slope,
And downwards he will skid.
His son will come to court,
So the cycle will roll on.
The odds are weighed against these kids,
From the moment they are born.

Elizabeth M Humphreys (Penarth)

On Top Of A Double Decker Bus

Riding on top of a double decker bus
There's no one up here, only us
People in the street below look so small
It makes me feel quite big and tall
I can see inside people's houses but, they can't see me
I even saw someone eating their eat
We have to get off now, there's shopping to be done
My day out with you is such fun
Hold on to my hand so I don't fall
I really am only quite small
When we finished, we got back on the bus
This time there's more than just the two of us
There are other children with their nans, just like me and you
I wonder if they had fun too
We get back to your house and tell Grandad where we've been
The shopping we bought and the things we've seen
As we sat down to have our tea
I saw someone looking at me
From the top of a double becker bus
How rude. Did we do that? Surely not, not us.

Jo Stimpson (Prestatyn)

Your Rubicon

Stand not in doubt on yonder bank,
Old age will not your youth's decision thank
But will pour ridicule
On those that turn their back,
Courage, insight, hope and enterprise they lack
Cross your Rubicon at once,
For if fearful hesitation holds sway,
The deadly wind of time
Your spirit will decay,
With a kick from the deadly Reaper on course;
He who makes no distinction
And honours not the richest corpse,
Like a Caesar, cast the die, hit the nail,
For it you fail, what loss?
Decisions made with courage seldom fail,
There will always be another river to cross.

C O Burnell (Cardiff)

Flash, My Dog

Flash, what can I say
You were my pal, my friend
You gave me a cuddle every day
You protected me no end
No one understood the love you had
Such a big gentle guy you were
You and I had such a rapport
You loved to play and tease
What can I say Flash
A wonderful friend, my pal
So gentle in every way
But you had to go to Heaven
Where you live without pain
Running free, be free
I love you still, I always will
I still remember you
The things you used to do
Such an intelligent face
But the time will pass
I will meet you again Flash.

Christina Hutchison (Dunfermline)

You Are A Star

Sometimes we feel jaded
Surrounded by our fears
Our young dreams have faded
Lost in a veil of tears

Wily old Omar Khayam
He was more with it than I am
He said people were actors
Life was just a show

So think of these factors
When you are feeling low
When rumour is so rife
That you wonder where you are
In the film that is your life
They are the extras
You are the star!

James S J Mannay (Newport)

I've Seen It All

I've seen the down and outs
The troublemakers, the lager louts,
I've seen the factories fall
Through my life I've seen it all.
I've seen death and destruction
I've seen cheating and corruption
The ups and downs of city life
The breaking up of man and wife
I've seen poor with outstretched hand
The confused who couldn't understand
I've seen the calm before the storm
The sun come up on a summer's morn
I've seen the toll of winter's cold
Generations begin to unfold
I've seen the brave walk away
I've even seen the light of day
I've seen the power of the might
The horrors of the unfair fight
Through my life I've seen it all
I've seen the crumble of life's wall.

Peter Thomson (Paisley)

Chiaroscuro

The sky drew dark
As storm clouds gathered overhead
And, in a moment's chill
A raven, harbinger of doom,
Alighted, wings outspread
And murmurs of despair infused the trees.

But then a shaft
Of sunlight arrowed through a rift
Of gold and shimmerings,
Bright as a bluebird's wings,
Mellowed the breeze.

The past is history.
Tomorrow is a mystery.
The present of today's no gift
To squander ill at ease.

I Goodall (Dundee)

At The Club

(From old Naval Officer - with apologies to Alfred Lord Tennyson)

May there be *much* moaning at this bar
When I put out to sea.
Let voices cry: 'Where's dear old Fred?'
And saddened voice reply, 'He's dead.'
Let all their faces fall,
All conversation pall.
Remember, friends, for more than sixty years
I've had my jokes, my whiskeys and my beers
Beside you; celebrating life
The day I met my wife
The day our eldest son was born
To wet his head - now mourn.
Yes, I think I'm worth a tear or two
So honour me, with your special brew
Of port, year '63, and drink to me
I shall be there, in spirit, silently.
Afterwards let conversation flow
More jokes and laughter - I would want it so.

Kate Wilson (Garth)

Lighthouse Park

St Bride's is situated by the sea,
Five minutes to the Bristol Channel.
To sit on the rocks and muse
And gaze across the water
And enjoy its stunning views.

Western Clevedon, Portishead,
Newport, the Severn Bridge, in the distance,
Along the beach, fishermen hoping for a catch,
Birdlife everywhere, mallards, seagulls
Flying across the sky.

Even on a rainy day
To listen to the waves crashing on the rocks,
The sounds of nature everywhere,
To feel content, this is the place to be,
The wonder of living by the sea.

Terri Brant (Newport)

Homework

Homework is so boring
That it makes me
Fall asleep
And it makes
Me nervous when
My mum tries
To peek

Homework freaks me out
Because there is too
Much to do
And we'll never
Get out
To have
Some fun anew.

Boring as ever
We'll never get it
Done
I'd rather clean than do *homework!*
It's no fun!

Eoin Brady (6) & Sophie Brady (9) (Londonderry)

Life

Life is very precious,
But maybe, that is very obvious.

It comes and goes, but no one knows
What is around the corner, I suppose.

Friends and family will be at a loss,
But that is what your life cost.

You will be laid out to rest
And you will deserve nothing but the best,
Because in God's house, you are the guest.

Years will pass by and by
And there will be no more goodbyes,
The only thing asked will be, why?

So, be careful in all you do,
Because you never know when you are going to go.

Sinéad Mooney (Antrim)

The Widow

Sometimes, in the silence of night,
You come to me in a dream with your arms outstretched;
And I, forgetting The Great Divide which lies between us,
Run to meet you.

Sometimes, we are young again and sitting together
By a water-lillied loch, or walking hand-in-hand over the heather,
Trying not to disturb a nesting moorhen . . .

Or perhaps we are both in uniform under a war-torn sky,
Snatching a few precious days together before returning
To 'Battle Stations'.

Or perhaps you are as on that last day
Coming home to a favourite meal and a chat about our
Children and everyday things - or preparing our
Fishing gear for a trip to sea in our boat.

Nothing of this seems impossible to me until I am
Awakened by the sounds of the morning.
Then I feel the emptiness of a home bereft of its
Beloved - - - - and my heart bleeds!

Chris Morrison (Isle of Skye)

The City Of The Sleepers

Sharp September sunlight on a day clear as meltwater.
Under a slither of fresh autumn leaves lies the city
of the sleepers, still, hushed.
Suddenly, there is a Babel-buzzing, deafening, echoing.
It's grass-cutting day.

Solid, thick stones, reflected in last night's rain,
line the path. Plain, unadorned slabs remember (and suggest)
plain-spoken merchants. Cold angels weep over minor gentry.
Highland Railway officers lie, neighbours for eternity
beside Indian Army subalterns.

Their wives are recorded briefly, mere footnotes in death
as in life. Yet it was they who nurtured new young life
while the men supervised
ballasting or pursued rebel Pathans.

All now lie under the same crisp, wind-troubled leaves.

David McVey (Glasgow)

Seaside Trip

It's Sunday today
Let's get on our way
To the seaside, we all descend

Sandwiches packed
Don't forget the mat
Gramma needs to sit down

'There's sand in the sandwiches,'
Little Tom says,
'Don't be daft,' says Gran
'I made them with jam.'

The sea looks inviting
Let's go for a dip
But watch out
There's a surfer about.

It's time to go home
We had a lovely day
Bags all packed
And we're on our way.

Gladys Evans (Newtown)

Ochil House / The Wallace High

Wallace High means to me
Lots of friends and teaching family
All the staff that helped me do well
Even though I could be cheeky as . . . a monkey

I liked to work, I liked to flirt
I made sure no feelings were ever hurt
As any man was fair game
I made male teachers feel the same

Taught me well you certainly did do
But I like to think I taught you too
That when you give a giggle and a smile
You can take not only an inch but also a mile!

I will miss you all
Each and everyone
As you made school life so much fun.

Terri Hallam (Braehead)

Water Music - The Wells Of Dee - Aberdeenshire

The song of many waters is sweet music to my hearing
The infant river babbles - sings in treble through the clearing.

The limpid liquid chuckles with quiet cadence in the shallows
Past slim, sun-brilliant birches and their flick'ring lacy shadows.

Gnarled pines upon the mountain watch a foaming torrent pouring -
Cascading through the corrie where the rutting stags are roaring.

The river mutters - murmurs - sings the same song as it rambles -
Reflects a thousand changes of the sky, as swift it scrambles

Amid the rocky ledges where the ptarmigan are hiding.
It chatters over gravel where the silver trout are biding

Then glides through misty valley where it bubbles - eddies - billows
To feed the purple orchids and the silver weeping willows,

Then onward to the ocean, changing key, to flats and minors
It empties near the harbour and the ocean-going liners.

Frances Reed (Oban)

Make The Most Of Now

(Dedicated to my Mother-in-Law)

How oft have we said,' I wish' or 'if only'
Put off 'til tomorrow what we should do today.
How many times said 'I'll do it later
I'm busy, exhausted', and then walk away.

Today I would ask you to pause and consider
Is running in circles what you want to do?
Take time to look around and decide what's important,
You might find you'll take a different view.

From this moment on please stop and reflect
On the things in this life that are precious to you
Grab hold of them now and make that decision
The chances to go backwards are few.

Eileen M McCulloch (Lanark)

The Sea!

First time I saw you
I was intimidated by you!
Your majestic, powerful waves . . .
You looked empty, yet you gave me
Plenty of splendour
I was drawn to you immediately!
The force and the power was so intense
Yet I never saw anything more peaceful . . . ever!
You make me shiver, but I am drawn to you
More and more
It feels so peaceful when I am touching your sand
With my bare feet!
You feel like an oasis of peace, in this
Troubled world
Your waters are so calm, yet they know
So many secrets
They give me back my freedom; they show me love . . .

Have you ever felt you belong somewhere?
I belong near you!

Ana-Marie McKeever (Londonderry)

Ships That Fish In The Night

Windswept shore bereft of sun still akin to passage of time.
In the background a silent figure weathered as was his - in prime.

Long ago memories he held so dear - close to his heart,
vision of a pert young lad's fishing line bent in flowing flight.

He had taught him all he knew of fish and ships combined,
watched battles of the raging seas yelling with all its might.

So had he bestowed his learnings to his only beloved son
who fished and sailed in many ships the same as he had done.

He recalled this as he launched the ship in a glass bottle
with the cold, cold ashes dispatched on the last voyage.

A salty tear ran down his cheek as he watched the bottle drift.
A ship on the horizon and a dolphin's rainbow leap.

The knurled hands displayed the grief of countless fishing years,
knowledge that he'd too succumb to ships that fish in the night . . .

M L Damsell (Llandysul)

Too Bad, So Sad

I pity you
You're unrecognisable
She changed you
You're a *liar*
She controlled you
You're a *cheat*
She blinded you with her money
And she sucked you in
Worst of all, she diseased you . . .
Together you all but destroyed me

But

I've bounced back
Better than you knew
I'm strong, free and *clean* . . .

I pity you
You're trapped by her now
Too bad, so sad
Farewell!

Cyra Armstrong (Castlederg)

Grozny Girl

A clown's face
Smeared chalk-white
Streaked with running red,

Hands out held
In dumb appeal
For my pity.

With a small thrill
I thought you to be
A still from a film;

With a dull chill
I saw you to be
Simply a pawn for the kill,

On the chequered screen
Of the dull routine
Horror of real News.

Frances Fairweather (Lennoxtown)

The Ozone Layer

The Earth is the planet, on which we live,
It's full of beauty with plenty to give,
We should take more care of the beautiful place,
Instead our behaviour is such a disgrace.

We need to learn to put back what we take,
Before we make a terrible mistake,
We have to begin to repair,
The all too delicate ozone layer.

The powerful countries don't seem to care,
They dump their rubbish anywhere,
As long as it's not on their front door,
Money talks . . . rich over poor.

Time is running out,
We'll all suffer without a doubt,
The world's population needs to come together,
Scientists must try and discover,
A way to begin to repair,
The all too delicate ozone layer.

Julie Sutherland (Glasgow)

Nature That I Dream Of

The stars twinkle like glitter in the dark night sky
I wonder how they got there, who put them there and why?

The grass it grows so green, from in-between our toes,
The fish swim so freely, in the river as she flows.

The sun shines his rays, gives us warmth and makes us smile,
The children playing happily, making life feel so worthwhile.

Racing through the meadows, hair blowing in the breeze,
Haystacks piled up high; I think I'm going to sneeze!

Little baby badgers, undisturbed, so tranquil in their sett,
Next door the rabbits laze, what would happen if they met?

Horses run so open, uninhibited on the sand,
Besotted lovers embrace, so tenderly hand in hand.

Thoughts of a country pasture, or a cottage by the sea,
With the nature that I dream of, selflessly enveloping me.

Kelly Kinross (Cowie)

Homeward - Bound

To walk along the banks of my favourite stream, for me
Is one place I cannot wait to be
To sit in the shade of the old oak tree
I've been all over the world, seen all there is to see
But there is no place on this Earth, like Ulster for me

The very thought of her beauty, calls a wanderer home
On the boat now, on the final lap, to step onto home shores
I won't look back on the past slice of my life, I'm happy it's o'er
It was a young man's foolish dream, nothing more
At the joy of my return, oh how my heart soars

I so long to see my old Ma and Pa once more
Many times I feared they'd be called through Heaven's doors
Before I could wrap my arms around them once more
I'll make up to them for years gone by
Never again will I cause my dear mother to sigh

Never again will I leave my native shores
No never, ever again will I wish to roam
After too many years, I thank God to be home.

Elizabeth Moore (Limvady)

Nature's Beauty

Down by the river, the sweet river Tay
We stroll in silence at peace with the world
In pleasure we come on this bright summer's day
And watch as life's tapestry is slowly unfurled.
The sun will sparkle and dance through the trees
Nearby a lark sends forth her sweet note
And from the wild flower, the hum of the bees
And a splash as the oarsman brings round his boat.

Soon the sky is aglow with the setting of sun
And the cattle and sheep in the fields softly graze
The labourer wends homewards, his day's work is done,
Now over the river lies a shimmering haze.
The river is flowing, ceasing never
As she journeys onwards, on down to the sea
Nature's circle goes on forever
As God has always meant it to be.

Liz MacSporran (Campbeltown)

Motherly Love

Whilst walking through the forest
I saw a sight so rare,
A vixen with her cubs
Outside her woodland lair.
She watched them so attentively,
She wouldn't let them stray,
She kept them close behind her
While they leapt about in play.
They jumped and they rolled
And through the bracken raced
Till they tripped on one another
In their excitement and their haste.
I'm sure that she heard me
And knew I was close by,
For she stared in my direction
With a keen and wary eye.
I turned very slowly and quietly moved away
And left the loving mother
With her children still at play.

Marjorie J Dorber (Gwynedd)

True Beauty

In many forms does beauty come
And where it's least expected
Like in the smile of that special needs child
Innocent, trusting, although sometimes rejected.
In the face of an aged old person
Each line telling its tale.
In the kind and loving words of a trusted friend
When needed, when all other words
Just seem to fail.
The dying leaves of an autumn tree
Bringing forth their glorious splendour
In a small note, a touch of the hand
And a blessing that comes from its sender.
There is surface beauty and inner beauty
Surface beauty fades and grows dim
But the beauty that stays is the most precious of all
Because it's the beauty that comes from within.

Anna Powell (Craigavon)

New Story

The breeze shimmering through the branches
gently pulling the leafy patches
coloured now with autumn glow
all leaves must hurry down before the winter snow.
Once a proud and fully leafed tree
then a skeleton standing dejectedly
full of sorrow, day has gone
iced up branches start to bend,
perching robin, tree's only friend.
As winter's grip ploughs its furrow
no woodland creature passes now,
all forlorn they stay in their burrows
all creatures hope for winter's end.
Gentle breeze whispering through trees
branches, skipping, whirling, in short dances.
Singing children stop their play
marvelling at the wondrous way
blooming now in all her glory,
start again, tree's brand new story.

G McNicol (Johnston)

Life And Death

One thing in life which fills me with fear
Is one little thought, just why are we here?
God, who is He and what does He do?
Does He lurk out there in the skies of blue?
Is there an address so we can write a letter?
If we pray, can He make things better?
Is there such a thing as life after death?
Does it really matter how you take your last breath?
What will you be next, a dog or a cat
A mouse, a spider or maybe a rat?
What about the dead, are they turned into stars?
Or are they swallowed up by something and banished into Mars?
Is there such a place as Heaven or Hell?
Is Heaven bright and fluffy and does Hell really smell?
So what's out there, we'll never know
You're young, you've got life
So just let it show.

Jodie Lee Stephen Harker (Turriff)

Poverty Row

Standing by a broken window, looking down below
Watching half-clad children play on Poverty Row,
Who cares about their future, if they should survive?
They are doomed like all of us - break away or die.
Remembering the 'good days' not so long ago
Before flowers and trees turned to stone on Poverty Row.
Crippling depression's taken over it seems,
Festering as an abscess, poisoning each dream.
What became of the laughter that brought a glow -
Despite heartaches and hardships on Poverty Row?
A thing of the past, just like yesterday's rain,
Even eyes have stopped crying - it's all in vain.
Prisoners of painted boxes behind closed doors
Pacing floors as on this ice, on Poverty Row.
Victims of circumstance, helpless to rise
Or climb back up the ladder - hunger the price.
Time to get started before daylight goes -
Don't look back, there's nothing to lose
Just Poverty Row.

Meg Brighton (Anglesey)

Childhood Memories

As I sit here in sheer delight
And watch the birds pass my window in flight
My mind goes back to my childhood days
Of happy moments, so full of play!
Never a care in any way -
No unkind words, or worry or pain
If only those days could return again
We danced and ran about in the sun
And hid behind bushes away from Mum
Now I am in the autumn of my days
But memories are sweet
And come what may
I'll return once more to my place of birth
Where my happy past was so full of mirth
With brothers and sisters - all now gone
Love and joy I remember -
Sadness none.

Hazel D C Powell (Cardiff)

Llandovery

Paradise is
a state of mind
it can be anywhere
that you find
A special place
with chemistry
that isn't just a memory
Llandovery with its
charm and history
is a place
that seduces me
Friendly people
with smiling faces
a market town
that embraces
all the best
from Mother Nature
with the kindness
of your neighbour.

John Simons (Llandovery)

Spring And Waves

One of those delightful lengthening days which herald the approach of summer
Soft sunlight caressed distant hills
The air bearing the sweet smell of greenness had a mollifying summer mildness about it
A warm breeze gently flurried the fresh crop of young leaves
That bedecked the trees after their long winter nakedness
A flock of geese flapped in unison overhead
Wheeling gleefully across the blue sky in celebration of glorious sunshine
The warmth of the spring day allowed everyone the luxury of sensual thoughts
Walking in the long grass in some secluded meadow
Wallowing in the sensual touch of sunlight
Now the sun is sinking, casting long animated shadows on the beach
Gazing at the waves as they crashed onto the wall
Listening to the thud and roar, watching the flying spray
The sea fascinates me, to me it's like a great animal, powerful yet gentle
When you know how to make friends with it, sometimes it's angry and cruel
Then at other times it's sweet and loving, playful as a kitten
Swimming in the sea makes you feel refreshed.

Ramire M J Macpherson (Potterton)

Carnock Road, Dunfermline

Carnock Road
Where I used to stay
in Doreen Cottage
Where the sun shone
On each lovely day
I will remember you forever
In my heart
You will always stay
A dream that goes on forever
In the same old way
Five years of happiness
A wonderful place to be
It will last always
I will love you forever
My rabbits I can see
My lovely donkey
I know you loved me
Love lives forever
Inside of me.

Gordon Forbes (Dumfries)

Home

Shone out across the darkest night,
I'm bathing in the brightest light,
From out across the untold lands,
Where fortune and fate forever stand,
With valley deep and mountain high,
I cannot dwell where you will lie,
For all the time my heart sings for you
And weeps the tears, sadness dew,
Freedom has sung,
Yet still I long,
For the one true thing I cannot have,
Find a way,
What if I could,
To push back time and fate,
What if I could,
I knew I would,
To dwell upon where you lay.

Nicholas James Haslam (Wrexham)

The Storm

The pale moon is in the sky
The big dark clouds are riding high
Angry winds like a lion's roars
And trees are cut down
Like a knight with a sword
Grass is waving like a roaring sea
And the rain is beating down on me
Lightning flashes like laser beams
And I stand still as if in a dream
The sound of thunder
Brings me out of that trance
And what a beautiful sight
As I watch the leaves dance
The leaves the colour of orange and gold
That an artist brush could not be as bold
The rain is ceasing, the wind now low
The thunder is fading and now I must go
But for a moment, as I stood still
My thoughts went back to that storm on the hill.

Jean Sutton (Barry)

The Garden Of Eden

The elemental child of time
Flutters and falters in the undergrowth of the ancients
'Neath the serpent of souls
In the forbidden orchard of Eden
She deceived as life weaves
Its spells on treacherous and sanguine pleasure
The leaves are wilting in environmental sin
As mankind burns a hole
In the prospector's pot of gold
For he has raped the planet of its goodness
Only to be replicated
By the barren winter of the mind
And the castigated ones of the new generation
Will curse the sour figs
Their forefather's have eaten
One awaits the banquet of Christ
Not crumbs from the industrialist's table.

Finnan Boyle (Limavady)

Last Of The Seven Samurai

I, who once ruled the magic corridors of the East
Who in all things jade, ruled like an emperor
Am reduced to this.
I, who in the heyday of my youth, bestrode the silver screen
Like a colossus
Am shrunk to this size.
I, who from dawn to dusk, championed at no extra cost
Freedom, justice, eternal optimism
And anything else you care to mention
Am catapulted into obscurity.
I, who was once, almost nearly, made sub-editor of wishful thinking
At the emperor's palace
Am doing this.
Demonstrating the most noble and ancient art of pear-splitting
In all places, Glasgow.
May the ancestors of my genes forgive me.
God, what next? Lecture tours at sunrise?
Banzai!
Banzai!

William Gilfedder (Clydebank)

Little Old Lady

Who is this person I'm looking at now?
The years have gone by and I've missed her somehow
Is she the one who was soft and flowing?
Where is the girl who was so outgoing?
No wrinkles or marks that were ever showing
Can the years have taken it all without knowing?
She was the girl with the pretty face
Could nature not substitute something with grace?

I'm sure that's not me with the silvery hair
It cannot be me who was once so fair
Now with sunken cheek and fading eyes
The mirror they say that it never lies

I'm just seventeen inside my body
Though outside I'm just a little old lady
Teenager for sure I'll not be again
Still I think my charisma will just stay the same.

Grace Campbell (Glasgow)

My Angel

Oh, my angel!
Enfold me in the softness of your wings . . .
And life me high,
Away from this torment . . .
That makes me feel that I want to die,
In the softness of your wings,
I can feel safe and secure,
Of your guardianship and love . . .
I'll always feel sure,
There keep me safe and secure within,
Keep me there . . . until I can begin,
To absorb the strength I can get from you,
Your love and comfort to help me through,
When you feel that I am ready to go,
Unfurl your wings . . . oh! . . .
But don't let me go,
Stay by me for eternity . . .
My beautiful angel . . .
Don't ever leave me!

Erica Gordon (Downpatrick)

Separate Ways

Arm in arm, we walked down the aisle,
Joy and laughter in our faces,
As the sun's rays lit one another's eyes for each other,
You were everything I wanted
And happiness was showed for each other.

Now I write this all alone,
Happiness is replaced by sadness
And the sun is replaced by darkness
We have now drifted so much apart
And both our hearts are sore and broken.

I wish love would return,
But that is long gone
I wait for hope that will never be
The vow we took, 'Till death do us part',
But parted we have
And both our lives have to go their separate ways.

Peter McGaughey (Belfast)

Step Into The Light

One pace forward and bright the ground
Step into the light
And all things are found
Walk from the shadows and glorify the day
You are the spotlight
Central focus I pray.

Pass from the dark of life with its pain
To a brightness of love
With so much goodness to gain
Come out of the gloom and feel warmth in the glow
Light up yourself
As you meet those where you go.

Step into glory for light has its day
God knows you thoroughly
For that is His way
Walk into sunshine and show what you're worth
For life has its bright spots
For you a rebirth.

Stewart Carruthers (Haddington)

A Lone Man Will Grow The Love

A lone man sits on the stage and strums his guitar
The crowd so close yet in their heads so far
He's taking them to places only he has seen before
He's taking them to games where only he decides the score
Everyone's heads swaying in an unconscious tidal wave of thought
Smiling to themselves, thinking of the lives they've got.

A lone man sits on the stage and strums his guitar
Everyone now knows his pain but only he bears the scar
He plays for hours without a break to let his soul mend
This man is alone but with thousands of friends
Every now and then he raises his head and smiles at the unsuspecting front row
These people are leaving with a new lease of life, they came feeling so low

A lone man sits on the stage and strums his guitar
The crowd so close yet in their heads so far
His words are hard to understand yet somehow the heart seems to know
His music is the love and the crowd help it grow.

Chris Flett (Annan)

You Were My Friend

You were my friend
The one I turned to
The one who saw through me
The one I would have told
The friend I needed
You were my friend

You were my friend
In my hour of need
When I needed a friend
You help me see myself
I need you more than ever
You were my friend

You were my friend
Where are you now?
Nowhere to be found
I need you here
I miss you so much
You were my friend.

Lynda Forsyth (Kilwinning)

The Story Of A Princess (War Child)

Ghosts of my friends play in the bombed-out street
Where they were dragged to their graves in front of me
Their souls rise through a haze of broken memories
At war until their souls are free

The sounds of spilling blood can be heard
Through bombs and hired guns
Politicians and congressmen never hold their tongues
Long enough to understand this blood may one day be theirs

Ghosts of my friends play in the bombed-out street
Where they were dragged to their graves in front of me
You watched this story unfold on the BBC
For your entertainment, Reality TV
The sound of spilling blood can still be heard
Through bombs and hired guns
As the propaganda fills your minds with that TV on
But if the truth be told, this blood may one day be yours.

Lewis J Palgrave (Montrose)

The River Of Time

The river of time, it flows like a rhyme,
An endless, eternal, infinite line
From the moment you're born, you fall as a pawn,
In the game of the river of time
We flow in solution, in divine retribution,
Whether good or committed to crime.

While our parents have slept and our ancestors wept,
We are swept from cradle to tomb
On we go; where? We don't know,
Through gorge, cataract and coomb
The river sweeps on, we are there then we're gone
As the river of time eats all life
It gives and it takes without feeling,
Like a kiss with a slash of a knife.

You cannot swim against its flow; you cannot climb its bank
On and on and on you go, no matter what your rank
So river, take me on over rapids and still waters
As we feed your hungry maw with our sons and daughters.

Ian Hughes (Carmarthan)

A Troubled Man

As I sit and watch the day turn to night,
I think of all the pain that I can't escape,
A pain composed of fear and rejection,
A pain that can't make all the wrongs, right.

I'm a walking cliché of a troubled man,
A cigarette in one hand
And nowhere to feel at peace.
The angel of my dreams is in my sight,
But as in a two-sided mirror of fate,
She cannot see me.

I carry a cross for all my mistakes
And one day I will be crucified upon it,
But I worry not, because there I will undo
The bad I have caused,
For in death I will be remembered a good man,
That is all I ever wanted to be.

Dale Alun Duggan (Newport)

Birthing The Spirit

Life breathing free
letting go softly
opening to the unknown.
Life breathing free
sighing, sounding
calling your spirit home.

Breathing out
each breath
a deep surrender.
Breathing out
each breath
a letting go.

Life breathing free
expanding, dissolving
returning to oneness.
Life breathing free
birthing the spirit
melts into lightness.

Lesley Downie (Findhorn by Forres)

A Touching Place

The little waves, breathless, rush to kiss the sand,
Come so far on ocean's breast,
For that brief caress of greeting,
One world touching another, fleetingly,
Meeting for a sunlit blink,
Till, turn of tide, retreating,
Carries the great surge once more,
Far, far away from this homely shore.

You move now in a vaster sea,
In the shining depths of evermore,
But sometimes by the splintered edge,
Of waterworld and land,
There flashes, sudden, a touching place
And once again your hand
Clasps mine, across the fragile borders
Of eternity and time.

Nan Inkster (Argyll)

Reflection

Is there a man who can be said,
Could others guide - the righteous tread?
But he himself was easily led,
And often strayed.
Here linger at this resting place,
Wherein he's laid.

The wretched dweller here below,
With dextrous mind was wise to know,
And sharply felt the welcome glow,
And cushioned flame,
But grave misdeeds, with crushing blow,
Did bring him shame.

So read the lettered stone with care,
And let thyself - thyself beware!
The lesson heed, that's here portrayed -
And give it voice
For circumspection here abounds,
As wisdom's choice.

Padraig - 1996 (Cumnock)

As I Wake

Sleep brings peace,
Yet, as I wake,
Shadows of foreboding
Glide into my consciousness.
Depression's black dye
Seeps again into the fabric of my happiness.
A thrill of fear
Flutters its threat of homelessness.
And, once again, I reach the edge
Of insecurity and tears.

Fragile roots, new-grown
And seeking to secure my life,
Parched of love and tenderness
Are dry and shrinking
So easily torn from their bed,
Leaving me unanchored in an uncertain world.

Jenny Brennan (Cardiff)

Dementia - In The Nursing Home

Total chaos - confusion in collapsing cells,
Cessation of coherent thought.
Conflicting images creep in and out
Of cerebral consciousness.
Needs uninterpreted, drive to distraction -
'I must - I must' - must what?

Feet floundering on foreign floors,
Frail fingers trace the edge of hostile furniture.
Hands, flattened, push on frightening doors,
Which gape ajar into uncharted rooms,
Or stop the frenzied fist, like iron bars.
And language, so familiar once,
Unfathomable now to brain cells battered
In a mind adrift at sea -
Harbourless.

But still, among the flotsam of sensations surging,
Inherent recognition of an outstretched
Human hand.

Joan Conway (Holywell)

For Raymond

Passed away 4/11/07)

Love's legend triumphed
Life's stormy weather
Our passage held sacred
Journeyed together

The flavour of laughter
Measured false fears
Vows cherished - truth constant
Gave us the best golden years

Surreal now is living
Perchance dreamlike each day
For you are gone, dear Beloved
Yet in my heart, always stay

Irene Gunnion (Perth)

Choices

We all make choices every day,
When conflict comes, we ask, 'Which way?'
Sometimes they are small, like, 'What's for tea?'
Sometimes they are big, like, 'Marry me!'
Yes, all make choices every day,
When conflict comes, they ask, 'Which way?'

The choices we make mould our living,
Whether selfish or whether giving,
Whether we tread a lonely path,
Or with others, we weep and laugh:
Yes, the choices we make mould our living,
Whether selfish, or whether giving.

How can we know which choice is right?
Just ask the Lord to shed His light;
Pray for His guidance every day,
Then you're more likely to know, which way,
One way to know which choice is right
Just ask the Lord to shed His light.

Irene Hart (Haverfordwest)

Waterfalls And Bluebells

(Inspired by a walk to Glyn-Neath waterfalls)

Flourished foliage; new as dawn
Silvery streams that sunset's sheen,
An idyllic scene to gaze upon
With eyes that ne'er such beauty seen.

Bluebells blossom; for meadow's grace
Grass green with dew-sweet drops,
An air of calm and freedom felt
Beneath the oak and elm treetops.

White waterfalls; upon aged stone
Eager eyed, the falcon glides,
An elder of an era gone
Behold this glorious countryside.

Craig Hope (Merthyr Tydfil)

Dear Granda

(The most special man that ever walked the Earth (My Hero, My Granda)
John Bain xxxxxxx)

A face, the face of a million shades
The one I long to see
That face of someone long ago
Who passed away from me
Close my eyes once more
There you are again
Standing smiling gently
The pictures wearing pretty thin
Smiling back at you before you fade to grey
The shade with which I shed a tear
And wish you back today
Although we shared a million wishes
And every one came true
The one wish that I wished I'd kept
Was to wish to be with you

Deborah Gorman (Greenock)

Nappies On My Neighbour's Washing Line

Six weeks before the birth
of her third child, my young neighbour
hangs out great flags of nappies.

Peg and dip, peg and dip,
crescents of sky
between the white on white,

in her garden of plastic play shapes,
red, yellow, blue,
their strength unbleached by sun.

At night she leaves the nappies out.
Moonlight lets through curves of dark,
the white squares glow.

Such a row of perfect symmetry,
it stops my breath.

Sue Moules (Lampeter)

Life

Where do we begin? From before our ancestors' birth
Somehow I never could believe in Charles Darwin's
Theory since cross-matching of species does not seem
The right image.

Back through time to the very first person, the Bible says
Was Adam. Yet then again, who fashioned him? Everyone
Would say God formed Man in His own image.

Yet, God is our creator we are told, by church and state
He is pure in spirit and not of flesh like us, so where would
His own life begin, from where? Somewhere out there I imagine.

Nothing comes from nothing, so life must have began somewhere
Out there? What is life? we must believe it was God who found
Life? He passed it on through Adam and Eve, as the story goes.

What is life? in which our being alive, still the question
Remains, what is life? We can only imagine where the actual
Spirit, spark or substance came from, we can only imagine,
What is life?

Janet Middleton (Falkirk)

St Cadoc's Church

Old and majestic, silent and grand,
Standing here with a grand regal look,
Is the church of St Cadoc (an ancient priest)
Mentioned back in the old Doomsday book.

The bells in the tower call all to prayer,
By their sound, we sinners are led.
They call out their message and beckon to us,
To enter and worship, take wine and bread.

On this site it has stood nearly 400 years,
An emblem of courage and might,
The outside seems stern and austere,
But the inside is calm and a beautiful sight.

May St Cadoc's reign on forever,
May its walls never crumble or fall,
When the voice of the bells call our numbers,
May we always answer their call.

Farina May Jenkins (Pontypool)

Song Of The Future

I dream of a world where the barriers are gone,
Where everyone, everywhere, will always belong
No matter the shape or the hue of his face.
Everyone, everywhere, each creed, each race
Walking abroad with no fear in his heart,
Safe in the knowledge that he is a part
Of the new world I see
When I dream, when I plan
For renewal, rebirth, a new age for Man.

I see all the children, the children to come,
All different colours walking as one.
Called from each nation, one banner unfurled,
Children of peace who will rule the world.
One rhythm, one harmony weaving through
The song of the future, clear and true.
On the keyboard of life,
I compose in my mind
A new song for the future, the song of mankind.

A M Atkins (Merthyr Tydfil)

Fields Of Spring And Summer Days

To sit and walk
these fields of spring and summer days to hear all birds of song,
from troubled towns and city runs, to hear the sound of running
streams, far from a noisy city and town, into calmness and clean
air, all around, how sweet the air does taste far from city and
town, amongst all hedgerow, alive that of nature's crown,
where blackbirds and song thrushes, sing with nature's way
of sound in calmness.

In the morning
as I sit and walk these fields of spring and summer days,
through the morning, and its dawn chorus, far from the noise
of town and city and watch the sunrise of gold and reddened
sky, as it rises high, far from city and town, one day we might
miss because of a climate change with floods all around,
no more of spring and summer days, and nature's crown
in these hills and as I walk around these fields, with running
streams and birdsongs around.

A May (Newport)

The Rose

Rose-world: so beautiful, beautiful.
Dark red flowers, or pale purple, ice-white,
Soft yellow, bright pink.
Perfumes that delight.
Bush roses, climbers, miniature flowers;
Roses in country hedges and rich men's gardens.
The most popular flower,
Known as a sign of love.
'Peace', 'Queen Elizabeth', 'Josephine Bruce';
Beautiful, beautiful rose-world.

And now another Rose I tell -
Who died to rescue us from Hell.
Thorn-crowned, He hung upon a tree -
Taking the punishment for you and me.
Our sins He bore upon a cross -
Mightiest victory that seemed all loss.
These truths must be to you unfurled:
The choicest Rose in all the world!

Wendy Prance (Cardiff)

Queen Of The Underground

Good afternoon, Queen of the Underground
And may your stop at some point arrive.
I wish it soon, oh good afternoon,
Your Highness of the Underground.
I hear your cries and commands,
Thrusting that sceptre here and there
Have mercy! Your majesty, please alight
The next stop is almost in sight.

Our rapid stares are at anything but you
So quit your belly aching,
Get off! Get off! You mad old bitch,
Your disturbance is quite too much.
Our gritted teeth and bulging eyes say all
So quieten down.
Here's your stop, take that twitching with you,
Good afternoon, my Queen
And may I think madness took you too soon.

Kate McAtackney (Craigavon)

Happy Days

Happy days
The days we were together
Happy days
Of sun or rainy weather
Ordinary days
When passing time rolled by
The days we shared together
You and I
Happy days

Happy days
With family all around
With cords of love
To one another bound
Changes come
Each go their separate ways
Thanks be to God
For memories
Of happy days.

Dorothy P Aitchison (Bathgate)

Through The Eyes Of A Child

I had my sight, but could not see
The beauteous things surrounding me
Always walking with head turned down
Wearing a continual, mournful frown

Then one day a child I spied
Looking around all starry-eyed
Pointing here and pointing there
Seeing wonders everywhere

My eyes, the pointing finger followed
And I let them linger for a moment
A bird, a tree, flowers the sky
All these things held my eye

Thanks to that child, my life is changing
Now never more to walk unseeing
For all these simple pleasures do abound
If I just lift my head and look around.

R Middleton (Glasgow)

Uncle Ian

Auntie Carol and Uncle Ian
Best aunt and uncle that's ever been,
They've wiped my nose,
and dried my tears,
and cared for me in my three years.
Now Uncle Ian, he's not so thrifty,
now that he's turning fifty.
Auntie Carol's not far behind,
but I don't care and sure don't mind.
'Here's our wean,' is what he'll say,
'what have you been da'en the day?'
He's been out at all the shops
bargains galore!
and Liquorice Allsorts.
So a few short words, we'd like to say
'Happy 50th birthday
Have a great day!'

Yer Lassie

Shirley Easton (Plean)

My Message

Words hanging on the wind
Blowing cold and bitter
Rising in fury
Bursting in fiery exclamation
Simmering as the gentle rain falls

The sea takes voice in my pleadings
Its restless flowing
Spilling patterns of regret
On the trembling sands

The sun warms the message
Into understanding
Floating clouds carry the echo

Moonlight calms
Entreating silently
To link the possibilities
On a silver chain.

Hazel Wilson (Belfast)

The Final Curtain

Death - the final curtain
Is ready to drop
Like the guillotine
And will not stop.
It may come suddenly
It may hover - teasing
Us with fear and dread
With no care of easing
Our misery.

But lo! In our mind's eye
We can find the cord
To lower that curtain
And meet our Lord.
But it will not stay down
As we do not have the power
To seize the crown
Of death
The final curtain.

Caroline Carson (Edinburgh)

Football Crazy

Football, football, in the brain,
Every week it's train, train, train,
Matches here and matches there,
Around the country, everywhere.

Shorts and T-shirts, socks and boots,
On the players how nice it looks,
Running, dribbling all around,
Keep that football on the ground.

Boys and girls, they like to play,
Morning and night and all through the day,
Sunshine or rain, whatever the weather,
The little feet will be kicking together.

Summer holidays are here at last,
Let's get our kits on very fast,
Run around the field all day,
It's time for football, *hooray! hooray!*

Bernadette McGinty (Omagh)

Contentment

Count your blessings every day and trust
That good health is here to stay,
The wonder of nature is all around,
Beautiful colours in abundance abound.

Contentment is a wonderful gift,
Treasure your life whether poor or rich,
Just make the best of what is to hand,
This will surely stand you in good stead,
When unfortunate circumstances arise unplanned.

Life was never meant to be easy,
Fresh challenges herald each new day,
However, if one simply gives of one's best,
They will surely survive the ultimate test.

Time flies on, months turn into years,
Growing old shouldn't raise fears,
Using the knowledge gained throughout life,
Will sustain you through both happy times and strife.

Joan C Igesund (Ellon)

Mid-Spring Morn

The brightness of the morning sun
A great new day has just begun
The purple heather on the hill
Where swallows dive, with speed and skill

This morning as I stand and look
Nature, is my open book
Special scenes, no man can purchase
Like, the trout that breaks the rippling surface

And if I stand and look around
Beautiful colours can be found
Beads of dew on grass so green
Coloured pebbles, in a silver stream

A deer, it rises from its bed
And curlews, skirls overhead
No need to pay for what I love
I look and thank the Lord above

Robert Knox (Ayr)

Legananny Dancers

They offered me pieces of their joy,
Broken bread to ease the hunger in my heart,
The fiddle rang to the sound of little feet
And each child danced and played her lively part.

Then they broke away and left me, one by one,
Sad was I for their going, sad the fiddler's song,
But like a school of dolphins, dancing they return
Whirling in a sea of sound
They danced all day long.

I sit by the fireside, dreaming
A dreaming by the gentle light
I can still see them dancing
Dancing in the ember's bright

All earthly things are passing
All must fade away
But I shall see them dancing
Dancing till the close of day.

Patrick King (Castlewellan)

To A Friend That Touched Our Hearts

The light's gone out in all our lives
You have gone to teach above
You were our friend and confident
Who we all idolised and loved

No matter how many times
We all confided in you
You never told a living soul
No lies, just the truth

There is a place we all know
Where there is peace and understanding
You deserve the very best
We'll miss you Ann, God Bless

You played an important part in our lives
We learnt a lot from you
The way we should be towards one another
We'll keep your work going, we promise.

Rhianan Edwards (Holyhead)

Tora

I shuffle the cards,
Deal pictorial narrative
With my left hand
That forms the Celtic Cross.

I am sealed
By the Star of Solomon
And the elements of Earth
I draw from cups and deniers
Staffs and swords.

I am the High Priestess
Seated between extremes
From which hang
Persephone's pomegranates.

I am the moon:
The observer of tides
That turns
Virgin to mother to widow.

Candice Morgan (Pontypridd)

Summer Memories

As I walk down a country lane
Thinking of you again and again
Beautiful memories come into my mind
Of you and I last summer.

Together we walked hand in hand
Beside the moonlit river
The moonlight lit up your golden hair
As I wished you could stay forever.

I remembered the night we danced
You had stars in your eyes
Later that night we pledged our love
As stars shone above.

Next day you sailed away from me
Across the deep blue sea
You took my heart along with you
I wonder, do you remember me?

Margaret Geddes (Wick)

The Future

In the year one thousand, nine, nine, nine
Nostradamus predicted would be the time
When in our culture many men will cease
As battles commence with those from the East.

In the year one thousand, nine, eight, nine
Berlin's massive wall came down.
Had we decided peace would be best?
Perhaps we had . . . we in the West.

But a dragon slumbers way out in the East
Population explosion has not really ceased.
And China needs space . . . money . . . and life
Through Hong Kong and Taiwan, but that's today's fight.

But, one day in the future
Say . . . nineteen ninety-nine
I think from the past comes a warning from time.
The dragon will come . . . and with a flick of its tail
Make we in the West . . . cower and quail . . .

Sheila Mack (Dundee)

The Sea

Through clear and grey
By night or day,
You'll always find me there,
With wetted feet and tatted hair.

I often go to gaze
Lost, enchanted, in a daze,
Captured by this mischievous array,
Of glittering sapphires in the spray.

Through winter, it's forever churning,
With the seagulls wildly crying.
Its depths coloured murky maroon,
Many ships find a hidden tomb.

In summer, when I like it best
The sea is peacefully at rest,
In aqua-blue, those cunning crystals reappear
I feel calm; there is nothing to fear.

Sophie Fleming (13) (Dromore)

Away With War

A blaze of sword that blinked the eye,
The bloody fight no man must cry.
All doomed to their own private hell,
Where all the souls of demons dwell.
With the coming of another age,
Let everyone forget the rage.
From this generation to the next,
Will it only be written in the text.
That man is born without a sin,
Or a shell for hate to live within.
Lie down and die o' troubled spirit,
And carry not this world within it.
Let all the new and innocent,
Be free from past imprisonment.
Let them know while in the womb,
No more war, no dark, no doom.
Peace at last our children cry,
Theirs is not to do or die.

Mabel McKay (Montrose)

The Gypsies

At a steam rally that we attend,
where we meet our gypsy friend,
he brings his wife and children too,
also his animals, he has a few.
Not far away the horses graze,
a chap with an accordion plays.
Most of the people sitting round
are intoxicated by the sound
of gentle singing good old themes,
nostalgic harmonious childhood dreams.
Great pans of food are cooking
on the fire, with children looking.
Anticipating patiently their next meal,
good atmosphere, traditional child appeal.
Their caravan is an old-time one,
left down from grateful father to son.
It would be strange not to see
the gypsies, with their lives so free.

Ann May Wallace (Isle of Anglesey)

The Rose

Dewdrops glistening on translucent petals
Rounded head on sturdy stem.
Multi shades of red, pink, white, even purple
Leaves of deepest shining curving greens.
Piercing thorns - sharp and pointed.
Perfumes sweet - rich intoxicating.
A robin hops intruding into the space below.
The rose stands tall, erect, towering, magnificent.
It speaks and states, 'I am the king of this domain.'
No one will usurp my place - position.
Comparisons of our wonderful Lord.
Who too stands erect over our land - our lives.
Nothing but nothing will ever contain Him.
He is dominant, majestic, implacable - the Head,
His beauty transcends all around Him.
He shines and like the rose - fills us
With a sweet-smelling savour, aroma
Signalling safety, care. Love, hope and peace.

Richard Ford (Narberth)

Wake The Dragon

Wake him - shake him - rouse the sleeping beast again
So he can fire the souls of those who dwell in his domain.
Too long has he slept, while all around
Corruption and despair abound
Iron masters, coal masters all have taken part
Taking the wealth from our valley's soil
And the spirit from its people's heart
Now the wheel full circle turns
The day we thought had gone returns
The days when Iola Goch once sang of oppression, lust and hate
While at the table Llewellyn sat vowing vengeance for his
people's fate
Those days of old have drifted into the timeless past
The dragon of Cymru who saw that day, will waken up at last
To see his people work again and see them fairly paid
A fair week's wage for a good day's work
Then back to slumbering for many years
Can go our Dragon Coch.

Maggie Pryce Jones (Treharris)

Cheriton Woods (Gower)

A brown path winds its way between the trees,
The woods are warm, sheltered from any breeze.
Leaves high overhead make a whispering sound.
Golden shafts of sunlight slant across the ground.
On one side of the path a thickly wooded rise,
On the other, open glades, shaded from the skies.
Outcrops of grey rocks lay beneath the trees,
Among great swathes of bluebells full of humming bees.
Wood sorrel and anemones blooming in-between,
Pure white stars nestling amongst the green.
Deep gullies of water, trickling down the hill,
Cut across the path on their way to the Pill
That runs along the woodland edge flowing to the sea.
An early butterfly rests, then flutters from a tree.
High in the canopy are tiny birds in flight,
Flitting in and out of shafts of golden light,
Sitting amongst the leaves singing their joyful song.
While, in the dappled shade below, the path goes winding on.

Haidee Williams (Gorseinon)

Those Yesterdays

When I was just a little girl
My mother, she would say
Don't forget to change your clothes
Before you go out to play
I did not wish to miss the fun
So I knew I must obey
I would fold my clothes all neatly
And place them on a chair
My ribbon, I would fold as well
That tied up my long hair
My friends would wait outside for me
To play in the summer's air
Those yesterdays I won't forget
How happy life was then
And people helped their neighbours
Each proved a loyal friend
It's sad those days are passed and gone
But everything must end.

Marina E Cardwell (Dungannon)

Crime-Besotted

When, I walk out, on nature's path,
I hear the world, the din, the wrath.
The noise of children and all their cries,
I wonder where their future lies?
Will the world have time to ponder?
To stand back and look at nature's wonder?
Or will the speed of everyday living,
Cause road rage in motorists, who are driven?
This violent age is crime besotted,
Not just boys, with copybooks blotted.
What makes the young fill up with hate?
No one to show them, it does not rate.
I hear the noise of guns and war,
As they drive about in armoured cars.
The angry young men, of different creeds,
Wreaking havoc on others, by their deeds.
They will have to change, the ways of man,
For man will destroy the world, if there is no plan.

Shirley Thompson (Glasgow)

Africa

Ashla breathed for the last time,
Her arid world, unforgiving.
Three brief torture-filled years,
Longer than most children
Of this rainless land.
Brothers and sisters long departed,
Laughter, smiles, too peppered.
She knew her parents' love,
Her mother's warm comforting bosom,
A father's strong embrace.
How it broke their hearts,
Like lightning cutting through their souls.
No well for their village,
And the warlord,
Sipping from promises of the wealthy
Love has feeling,
Greed has a gun,
Yet still, we feel no shame.

Andrew Russell (Penicuik)

Morning Mayhem

It's morning already and time for me to rise
I moan and I stretch and rub sleep from my eyes.
The clock by my bedside continues to bleep
Should I switch off my timepiece and go back to sleep?
Much as I'm tempted, I know this can't be
So, it's up for a wash and a swift cup of tea.
I still have some time for a fag and a cough
Then on with my coat and I'm ready for off
Into the car and out through the gate
By the look of that traffic, I'm sure to be late.
I swear that each day it gets thicker and thicker
I'm sure that to walk to my work would be quicker
The stress just to get there is taking its toll
Might consider resigning and joining the dole.
Just think, I could lie in my bed most the day
Or nip down the bookies, a bet for me to lay
But then maybe, I'm just as well off as I am
I'll just grit my teeth and sit here in this jam.

L Heatley (Londonderry)

Lost

Been somewhere, but going nowhere
Looking, but never finding
The way, to that somewhere place
The road is never-ending
Turning and bending, up hill and down
I struggle along
Life is the road and I carry a load
That can burden me some, and yet
I can sing along, with happy song and sad
When times get bad, I cry . . .
But in that great somewhere
I find my solace - alone -
Thoughts are mine, memories my own
Emotions are turning round and round
I am lost - in a somewhere place
In a dream, where I want to be found
I awake, and find
I am still . . . lost.

Elen Tai (Fraserburgh)

Untitled

How do I write a love song?
From where do I find the words?
Should I take the song of a sky bird
As the music to sweeten the air?
Then picture you here, standing here with me
See that smile living deep in your eyes
Hear the voice, feel the shiver it brings me
Watch the stars write words in the sky
Add them all to that sweet bird's soft singng
Listen as my heart starts to pound
To hear the song meaning all, you and I
But there never can be any love song
That compares nor can sit down with you
It would fade and its music would die
All the words be bereft of true meaning
Cast in shadow, your grace, your smile
So there will never be any love song
There'll be you with my love for all while

David J A Smith (Aberdeen)

It's Nice To Be Singing

It's nice to be singing when you're happy
It's nice to be singing when you're sad
It's better to be singing when you're happy
Then you know you can be glad
It's nice to be singing in the winter when
The snow is on the ground
But it's better to be singing in the summer
When blooms and sunshine abound
It's nice to be singing in the autumn
When the leaves are falling from the bough
But it's better to be singing in springtime
When the buds and shoots are showing through
So let us be happy, don't be sad
Let us sing in the winter when the weather is bad
Let us sing in the summer through sunshine and rain
Let us sing in the autumn when the fog comes again
Let us sing in the springtime when all things begin
Let us all sing and be happy, let us all sing.

Lionel Brown (Chepstow)

Cry Blackbird

At first I thought he was
Miles away, knowing how sound
Travels on the dusk waves,
But he came each evening
Nearer and nearer, but never
Close enough to hear the words
Filtered out by the
Starlings' atmospherics until
One night I noticed
He'd been there all the time,
A ragged veteran, perched
Uncertain askew in my beech tree.
And suddenly I understood
His crystal notes, though
The sound blurred odd
Through my tears.
He said, 'I made you
These few sad pearls.'

Morris Jones (Chepstow)

My Brave Hugh

(For my loving son)

My darling, how I miss you,
My heart is broken in two,
I never thought the day would come,
When no longer I'd have you,
The special things you'd say and do,
The brightness of your smile,
All these special memories,
Are with me all the while,
The home we shared is empty now,
Everything is dark and dreary,
I wish with all my heart,
That I could have you here,
I know that this can never be,
You are now from pain set free,
You are resting safe in Heaven now,
Beside the timeless sea.

Betty Walker (Newtownards)

Scotland, A Bridesmaid

(Dedicated to my son Paul)

Her veins run fresh with water
With her mountains there all around
Green pastures fit like a bridal gown
No other lady like her can be found
Trees grow around her like a princess' necklace
Grows food like fresh milk from a mother's breast
To feed all her little ones in Scotland
The good God's gifts, they are always the best
God holds the hand of this Lady Scotland
Feeds all His children with the finest of food
Fertilises her body with the water of Heaven
For all His gifts God has given are good
Her sky above is a sky-blue veil
With stars like a tiara for a beautiful queen
With sun warming her body or light of the moon
God made a lady called Scotland for a beautiful dream

Paul Micheal Diamond (Bellsmyre)

Funny Old Life - Isn't It!

I saw it this morning on my washing line
I took a long look - could that be mine?
Flapping in the breeze
Saying, 'Desire me - please'
Funny old life - isn't it!

In my youth I spurned it
When brought one, I burned it
Now wafting in the breeze
It's a tease
Funny old life isn't it!

All right, it's a fair cop
To me now it's essential
I'll no longer pretend
'It's only experimental'
When I bring it in from the breeze
I'll give it a loving squeeze
Funny old life - isn't it!

G M Thomas (Penmaenmawr)

The Quiet Underachiever Rages

I have fifty years of suppression
Oppression
Building like resentful lava
And now it will burst forth

I will strike you all
And walk upon your chests
To stomp upon your faces
Down whose noses you have sneered
For fifty years
Upon me

So take paraplegia
Enjoy your pension-proofed retirement in wheelchairs
Sipping hospital food through straws
And I will have sated
My insults, my sufferings, sadness, despair
Into the physical jail
From the tortured one of my mind.

Patrick Murphy (Belfast)

Soul Mate

Comparison, as if we were in a movie, a film clip, caught in time,
moving silent picture;
as I stood entrenched, whilst you silently go from me gradually
and then the magician, too soon, completely disappear.
One moment you were back in my life at last, you were close
for a split second, gently smiled, looked into my eyes sadly,
before you had to go, for just that time, I had you near.

There were crowds all around, on the peripheral of the scene,
people getting on with their lives, yet from your sensual lips;
there came not a sound.
I walk away, surreal, fuelled with despondency, my soulmate,
twenty-five years previously, I realised then I had found.

Eventually mingling into crowds, I become lost, can't concentrate,
my head is confused, fuelled with regret, inner sadness, want to sob,
my heart is aching,
Must move on disregard, I realised way too late, now aftermath,
you are gone from me, not mine, any longer, for the taking . . .

Karen Gillies (Aberdeen)

Coffee Etc

Coffee, anti-psychotic pills,
The scene is set,
I'll dream tonight,
Ghosts and girls,
All twirled up,
In one big spiral.

The morning comes,
Coffee and anti-psychotic pills,
I'll daydream today.
Cars and planes -
What a display!

Night comes,
Coffee, leave out the pills,
And I'll have a nightmare.
Deaths, dubious monsters,
Drivelling demons,
All coming to haunt me.

Keith Murdoch (Inverness)

Concorde

Gigantic wings of human creation,
Flashing glints of silver cities,
Breaking the silence of vast horizons,
Forming liaisons between distant nations,
True formations amid endless spacious skies,
Lost to the lonely child,
Standing, seeking to find, those silver wings far cry.

Wondrous skies, filled with man's true image,
Planet of age and youth together blend
Born to mould yet another generation,
Past ages, hopes, now those silver wings succeed,

Brought to man this lightning art,
Picturesque, from our heaven above,
Picturesque, from our earth below,
Man's true image now, from long ago,
Wings of travel, precious art of genius hands,
Your thunderous voice echo, through far-off lands.

Margaret J C Coleman (Ayrshire)

Tokens Of Simple Times

We sank along black rivers in the deep snowdrifts of winter
Hair crisp like frosted earth across the white expanse of hills.
Wrapping plastic around small limbs to slide down icy slopes
Like moonbeams in a storybook I once cried about.

Sisters, we could laugh then before the slow decay of childish talk,
My drunken betrayal of blood-trust
That opened distances sometimes we almost crossed
Like diffident kids giggling into danger zones
Or recriminations and word wars
Until the first grey hours of dawn would tear defences down
When already gauche silences have said too much.

And I hear across the water and concrete miles
The roar of the tube train and visualise
You disappearing down some circular blackness
Into the echo of steel impersonal lives
Pinning immortalised smiles of children on damp walls
Tokens of simple times.

Pia Gore (Bangor)

Northern Frontier

Green fields end abruptly at the brow of the cliff
With its fringe of vertical rocks plunging down
To that ocean of impending storm.

The castles of Kinbane and Dunluce -
Two of a kind, but yet so different.
Kinbane, nestling among the lower rocks,
Able to hide from a gathering attack.
While Dunluce flaunts itself like a tiara
On the brow's edge;
A thing of beauty in its ruined state.

As a homing pigeon flies west,
So I too make my journey home of just a few miles,
To relax in the sun, near docile Portstewart Strand.
A garden chair, an infusion in the teapot:
But while I rest and marvel at what I've seen,
I know that in mid-Atlantic
The next storm is brewing.

Mavis Abernethy (Portstewart)

The Star

I looked up at the winter's sky
And saw a shining star
Just like the one the Wise Men saw
And followed from afar

I thought, *this is a special night*
Like that one, so long ago
When the birth of Jesus brought so much love
For all the world to know

I looked up at that winter sky
And knew it gave me hope
I felt the peace surround me
And knew that I could cope

Now I know it was a special star
That shone on me that night
It was Jesus saying He loved me
By showering me with light.

Sally Young (Belfast)

The Navy

The day I joined the Navy
I was overjoyed
From then on I was known
As ordinary Seaman Boyd

I joined the 'Resolution'
A battleship of power
That is when my life turned
I loved it every hour

I had some knotty problems
With ropes and lines galore
I'm glad when I had learned them
No bother anymore

I am now a leading hand
The sailors call me 'Hooky'
It's different when I was called
Just a wee young 'Rookie'.

Rodger Boyd (Paisley)

Wedding Day

The marriage of two people
Is wonderful indeed
They take their vows and tie the knot
And follow every creed

When they say 'I do'
It must be for life
And is so, so special
At last to be man and wife

And then as man and wife
The children will come
And say we have a mum and dad
We'll never be alone

So bless this wedding day, dear God
The happy couple on life's path hath trod
So on this very special day
Good luck, God bless you on your way.

Minette Angus (Irvine)

Reborn

Dawn awakens playful souls
To lives beyond a past
And eyes that used to cloud with grey
With life become ablast

Shadows in the darkest hearts
Fade into the light
And clouds upon the sweetest face
Are swallowed by the light

Songs now break into the silence
And love now breaks the day
And where there once was sorrow
Children laugh and play

A kiss makes life so simple
And shows the better side
And now I keep my head high
When once I used to hide

Stephanie Marshall (Greenock)

What Next?

Sitting here watching TV
Thinking of what I have to do today
Going to hospital
Going to work

Daughter has an appointment
I will go
To help and support
And show my love

After we're done
I go to work
And earn some cash
To buy extra things

It's midsummer time
But the weather's dull
Life goes on
Take each day as it comes

G Arthur (Aberdeen)

Lochgoilhead

I dream of scenes of childhood when I watched the shepherd toil,
As the sun came down in evening o'er the village of Lochgoil.
Such scenes of rarest beauty there is naught for me can spoil,
As in dreams I dream of childhood and my home beside Lochgoil.

Now in memory I stroll once more the Glen More road I knew,
And I walk the banks of Donich where the pines obscure the view.
Or I stand there on Ben Bheula why such scenes on Earth are few,
As the evening sunshine taints with gold the village home I knew.

After school time in the summer as we swam there by the pier,
How such happy scenes of childhood ring the bells of yesteryear.
And if one wish could be granted then that wish to me is clear,
'Tis my one desire to view once more my village home so dear.

Many friends have gone and left her, some are far beyond the sea,
And some lie there in the churchyard resting 'neath an ancient tree.
But before I die as die I will my home once more will be,
In that lovely peaceful haven of my village by the sea.

Hugh Cameron-White (Largs)

Tell Me

I see you walking by me, now and then,
You glance at me and turn away
And distance spreads its wings,
Like a cloak that hides so many things.

Underneath is a shark,
That needs fanned, into a burning fire,
Who will be the first,
To bring, the flame to life.

Could I ignore, the yearning love,
That beats within, this heart
Of yours and mine,
Don't let another day go by.

That glance, that speaks a thousand words,
Will come to life
And tell me why,
We love each other so.

Margaret Reid (Bangor)

Pictures In My Mind

How I long to turn the clock back to when I was a girl
To run wild in the meadow and pick the flowers there
Or listen to the blackbirds that sit high above the ground
Far away from the farmer's crop of corn, or pellets from his gun.

I can still hear the droning of the grey tractor
And horses clopping along the winding country lanes
With straw, or hay, neatly packed
With younger brother perched on top, waving frantically.

How I toiled at stacking mountain turf to dry
Ready for winter fires
I can still smell turf burning as my mother stirred the mutton stew
And listening to the kettle singing its special tune.

Now I have grown older and my youth all gone
No longer can I run through the meadow
And smell the wild flowers that still blow gently on hot summer winds
All I have left, are the pictures in my mind.

Maureen Connolly (Strabane)

Gangs

I don't know why they do it, I really cannot tell
Why young men of today are bent on raising hell
The parents never worry, or wonder where they're at
Take away their money and privileges, it could stop as quick as that

If you let them roam around in gangs, surely you will find
There is not one of them with any sense, they control each other's mind
They congregate and agitate, local people's homes
Shout abuse and obscenities, cause damage with sticks and stones

Don't say these things can't hurt me, they do and always will
Be in the wrong place at the wrong time and one of these will kill
If any of them value their freedom, I'm sure there must be one
And call his mate to come with him then that's a good job done

Maybe the rest would follow, that's if they had the sense
And leave the bullies and ringleaders, sitting on the fence
So parents try to remember your child should not have to die
But outlive their mam and dad and be the ones to say goodbye.

Anthony Mitchell (Barry)

Untitled

Congratulations to your company at Forward Press
You've always done us proud so I say to you God bless
I've been with you for a good number of years
So to each at Forward Press, I say three cheers

20 years of Forward Press, it's time to celebrate
Poetry by the people to which we can all relate
So many different styles making a nice change
There are varied subjects covering a range

Some people may write a poem on a religious theme
Others could describe in detail a country scene
A friendship that has stood the test of time
Or about the blue skies and sunshine

Please keep up the good work, we people need you
To jog our memories into action the way you do
Writing poems and any art is a gift that's Heaven-sent
It will take stress out of life and make you content

Elizabeth Mary Dowler (Bulwark)

Sorrow

Sorrow comes from lengthened years,
Dying loved ones and many tears,
I leave behind the ones who care,
But where you weep, I am not there.

I'm in the clouds up above,
Looking down on you with love,
My body is buried beneath your feet,
My soul hovers until we meet.

Wipe your tears, please don't cry,
Don't torture yourself by asking why,
I feel no fear, I feel no pain,
Take comfort in knowing we'll be together again.

Everyone is equal when they're up here,
Remember me with a smile, don't shed a tear,
Remember me with fondness, a smile and some love,
Because I'm watching you from a cloud of above.

Jackie McGeechan (Lanark)

Adventure Thirst

I yearn to follow the wild goose trail
A'wing to the Arctic snows
Undaunted by the frozen wastes
Or polar storm that blows.

I'd like to search the ocean depths
And treasure ships explore
To seek swashbuckling pirates' loot
From lawless days of yore.

I long to cross the burning sands
Where lurks remorseless death
For careless man or beast who strays
In the desert's fiery breath.

And I must climb the highest peaks
That reach up through the clouds
With untamed scenes, majestic views
Far off from tumultuous crowds.

Robert J Freeburn (Cookstown)

Losing My Way

Many years have passed since I left this place,
Dreams seem a lifetime away, did I leave them behind
Or lose them on the way back, vanished without trace,
To spare the pain of the sadness I might find?

Scared of losing my way, no footprints to follow,
If I return will she be there, still waiting,
Lazing by the burn, living for tomorrow,
To watch the sunrise as dawn is breaking?

And if I were to meet her in a different time,
Would she understand the shadow that remains,
Of the girl I once was, something that was mine,
Living like a prisoner with her heart wrapped up in chains?

Months grow into years and I've still not found the way,
To lead me from the maze that dwells within my mind,
Will she come back, to lead me out on redemption day,
Or has she gone forever, to somewhere I can never hope to find?

Anne Malcolm (Tillicoultry)

Gordon Country

I live in bonny Scotland
In a north east country town
The people they are friendly
Not many scowl or frown.

Surrounded by hills and mountains
And lovely countryside
Woodland trees and rivers
Birds and fish provide.

There is a local 'castle ruin'
With a famous history
Visitors can be shown around
At times throughout the day.

Come and visit my hometown
I am sure you will agree
That when you have a look around
This is a lovely place to see.

I Rugg (Huntly)

Disdain

A jaundiced eye, a vacant stare
Denotes you are no longer there
An eyeball glance without response
Confirms the lack of flair

No interest seems to be about
Instead a feeling is fallout
Impulse tells without revealing
A manifest display of ill-feeling

The haughty flick of a lock of hair
Is an awareness of no longer there
Body language in a solid rock
Infers a total and reticent block

Between a rock and a piece of granite
Compromise is a long-lost summit
To be aware and loathe to retort
A hopeless cause or hopeful resort.

Anthony McGeehan (Carrickfergus)

The Misguided Moth

You came from out of the darkness, like a steady, burning light,
When the days were on the turn again, but daytime still like night.
I suddenly glimpsed your radiance from the place upon which I lay
And I, the misguided moth, just could not keep away.

For two long years, I fluttered just outside your bright glow,
When all my senses warned me not to fly around your halo.
I would not listen to reason and it was hopeless to pray,
For I, the misguided moth, just could not keep away.

So, when I learned about a place where I knew you would shine strong,
I simply had to go there, even though it was so wrong.
And as I stared into your bright source, I did not know what to say,
But I, the misguided moth, just could not fly away.

You never flickered, never wavered, but steadily drew me in
And I, the misguided moth, revelled in my sin.
But, to expiate my pleasure, there was a high price to pay,
For I, misguided moth, suddenly passed away.

Donna Melinda Sloan (Lisburn)

The People's Press

Twenty years of Forward Press,
publishing the nation's verse,
Authors new and authors old,
feeling their thoughts have to be told.

Sometimes hearts hold the greatest sadness,
expressed in words,
when shared with others,
help relieve the broken-hearted.

Those whose hearts hold
Joyous gladness,
spread their joy and
light the darkness.

So good people of Forward Press,
I wish you years of sweet success,
and thank you for putting
my poems to 'Press'!

Anita C Todd (Gourock)

Poetic Rewards

Congratulations, twenty years of publishing!
Well done Forward Press, each and every editor.
One million poets and I'm just one that's blushing,
Because I'm proud to have been a contributor.

For many years now, I have seen my name in print
And yes, it has given me enormous pleasure.
So I hope that many more now will take the hint
And take up writing poetry in their leisure.

Yes, over twelve years and in my seventy-first year,
It comes much easier now than ever before.
So much so, that I have spent time with a group here,
Helping and encouraging, their hearts to explore.

So now today, I will take them your little note,
It may just inspire them the next step to take,
To share with so many others their earnest hope,
That their words may bring a blessing for God's own sake.

Janet Bowen (Milford Haven)

The Waiting Time

Waiting on the edge, standing in the trench
Trying to escape the filth and the stench
Stuck to the trestles, all filled with fear
As the over the top signal draws near

On the duckboards, greasy water laps
Offering salvation for grey furry rats
A quiet voice makes little pleas
Someone please rid me of these fleas

Final prayers are said and done
Make final test on your gun
Look up to the bright sun
Breathe in for that long run

The time is now almost nigh
Last minute thoughts a final sigh
Captain's whistle shrills and sounds
Up and over the furrowed ground

Philip Robbins (Pontypridd)

Seasons Of Friendship

Hot, like grains of golden sand
On a sunny summer beach,
The first ardent flush of friendship
Reaches its peak.

Mellowing, rich in warm tones
Like a russet autumn leaf,
In its second season
Parting can bring grief.

Dormant now, in winter mode
Out of reach and touch,
A time of restoration,
Friendship means so much.

Bursting forth again, like spring
Eager to renew,
A time of celebration my friend,
I'm happy to see you.

Katrina M Anderson (Glenrothes)

The Quiet Mind

Sit down and gently close your eyes
but do not let the light seep in
to spoil the dream you visualise
or thoughts that you may have within.

Your precious daydream in the mind
is yours alone to savour now
no one can steal it, far less find
those thoughts of yours no matter how.

In seconds thoughts, unsure or sure
can change to sad or even glad
yet in a flash another lure
will tempt you from the thoughts you had.

But thoughts can easily slip away
as quickly as the speed of light
yet may return another day
or even in your dreams at night.

Stan M Tweedie (Edinburgh)

War

War is a demon that haunts the mind of Man,
Causing misery and destruction in life's eternal plan.
Our triumphs and our conquests, our laughter and our joy
Can all so quickly vanish in the blinking of an eye.

The planes and the rockets, the tanks and the guns,
Are all Man's creation to bring destruction in our time.
What games are we playing with life, death and trust,
Another futile test of strength, so we can pin medals on our chest.

Perhaps we're still like children who like to play with toys,
Then to fight one another, just to see who'll win first prize.
Our generals and our heads of state just shake their heads and bow,
But it's our men who go off to war and gamble with their lives.

We've fought from the dawn of time, must we fight until its end,
Or look at one another not as enemies but as friends?
Life is too precious to be lost in some damned war,
Better to live our lives in peace and love, than to fight for evermore.

Gwyn Thomas (Merthyr Tydfil)

The Wood

The wood is dark and heavy
You may think it has no meaning
But let me tell you
What the wood says -

Jesus is carrying the wood
He's struggling but won't give in
He's also carrying out guilt, sin, shame
And everything else.

Do you realise what this is costing Him?
The nails are being punched into His hands
And into His feet and His blood is being shed
Then the spear is put into His side

Do you realise what this man has done?
It's not an ordinary piece of wood anymore
It has the greatest love of all
Now carved on it.

Kerry Gibson (Wrexham)

Simply Love

When heartache sharply pierces
the depths none else can know;
when rainbows disappear from view,
and streams of tears o'erflow.

When mem'ry, keener than a blade
cuts through the mind unbidden,
revealing pictures of the past,
of sharing times, long hidden.

Think then of love, received and given;
for love endures forever.
Tho' tender now, this cord that binds
no one, no, none can sever.

This is the pattern of our pain,
the anguish of our grief.
A measure of our life-long love,
let this thought bring relief.

Marjorie Wheeler (Llanon)

Darkest Dark

Dark, dark, dark
People are frightened to go out at night
What lurks in the shadows
Where there is no light?

They say we have peace
What does a knife in the ribs
Or a bullet in the head say
Who is telling fibs?

Where are the lies?
People look at each other
When someone dies
No, not another

Peace, perfect peace
When we all see the light
A peaceful world
Where everything is bright.

Joyce Ambler Evans (Richill)

Longings

Yearning for sun's warm rays, caressing the face,
Expelling the cold, damp air of crueller climes,
Improving life's function, enhancing the mind,
Friend of my childhood through happiest times.

Vast seas of passion, encircling the land,
Framing Earth's landscapes, surrounding its wealth,
Colours of turquoise, the palette of life,
The richness of splendour, the symbol of health.

The blue of the cosmos, enshrining the world,
Ethereal beauty, unreal and untimed,
Mysterious universe, the wondrous of sights,
Elusive, appealing with eternal sublime.

A building, a palace, a corner of land,
Unique in its outlook, a triumph of Man,
Lines of sheer genius, in edifice enthroned,
Epitome of achievement, the Yin and the Yang.

Evelyn Millings Monk Egdoll (Glasgow)

Par For The Course!

I made my way to the garden shed.
Slipped on some ice and broke my head.
I tried to get up, had another slip,
fell down again, and broke my hip!

I tried to get up to raise the alarm,
slipped again, and broke my arm.
A neighbour heard my SOS
and called the ambulance, I guess!

When the paramedics had seen to me
they carried me out - for all to see!
They slipped and I fell off the stretcher.
Now my legs are both in plaster!

I'm still in hospital you know,
all bandaged up, from head to toe!
'Unlucky' is what the nurses say.
But to me, 'twas just a normal day!

Alan G Simpson (Glasgow)

Life

Birthdays come and birthdays go
In-between goes very slow
The years seem to go so fast
When you think of times gone past.

One day, you're a young girl
The next, your life's a whirl
Of dates and dancing all ago
You life's so busy as you grow.

Then you have children of your own
A present off God, just on loan
They in turn grow up and wed,
'Where's the time gone?' is often said.

Then comes the time that we all dread
Through illness, we have taken to our bed
The end of life to be so near
With God so close, I'll know no fear.

Mavis Shaw (Cwmbran)

Before Opening The Gate, At Powis Castle

The scent of flowers fills the air,
Birds sing, the grass is rimed with dew,
The garden's mine, no need to share
The pleasure of this glorious view.

In autumn, spring and summer too,
For five brief minutes I can sit
And watch the garden's changing hue
And fantasise that I own it!

But then the time comes when I must
Open the gate, let others in,
My fantasy must fall to dust;
Not to do this would be a sin.

For others too must see this place,
Enjoy the flowers, the scents, the trees,
The garden's ever-changing face,
The peace to which I hold the keys.

Stephen Parry (Montgomery)

The Fisherman's Bairn

See the yalla meen, mither;
It shines on you an' me.
Is that the meen ma faither sees
Fin he is far at sea?

Hear the nicht win' blaw, mither,
That brings the mornin' rain.
Does that same win' fill faither's sail
Tae bring him hame again?

Ah ken he cares for you mither,
An' that you care for me;
But wha tak's care o' faither
Fin he is far at sea?

Hush, lad. There's anither hand
Looks ower you an' me
An' ilka soul in ilka land
An' faither on the sea.

James D Johnston (Portsoy)

I Will Be By The River!

I will be where it glistens
This place it is the best
The water is tranquil and listens
My problems it lays to rest.

It seems whatever I'm saying
Joins the endless flow
I just sit there wishing
That all my problems will go.

Always it has been my solution
My way to get rid of fears
My problem's the river's pollution
It's flooded with my tears.

I feel my problems and tears trickle away
Never again to be seen
This river has made me feel better . . .
Shame it's only a dream.

Felicity Johns (Pontypool)

Not What It Seems

The noise of the jet planes ring in my ear
As I lie here in the sun
It's off to Europe they go, well nearly everyone
A few weeks of pleasure and fun

That is the picture we see in our minds
But sometimes it's sorrow they leave behind
The orphan hoping to find a new life
The husband running away from his wife

The teenager with only six months to live
Unless someone has a spare kidney to give
Yes, everything is not always what it seems
But that doesn't stop us from having our dreams

We must be realistic in this day and age
We are not living closed up in a cage
Someone has put us here by right
So make the most of life from morning until night.

Marion McKenzie (Irvine)

Storms

Storm clouds hover high up above
As raucous winds fiercely blow
Heavy raindrops dance on ground below
The sky no longer azure-blue anymore.

Warnings of severe weather on the way
Broadcasted continually through the day;
Sea vessels facing perils are homeward-bound
Hatches fastened securely, made safe and sound.

The storms roar on every minute and hour
Thunder and lightning causing damage galore;
Though wind, waves and rain toss all around
An inner peace can still be found.

Amidst all storms, Jesus is found
Addressing all fear, hear His voice sound
He stills the rages in heart and without
'Be still,' assuring words He shouts.

June Pooley (Barry)

Port Lethen

One pace, the rolling pebbles take me there,
Conveyed to an unpredictable sea
A juxtapositional tapestry,
Of foam and surf.

It is March and spring tides heave against this land,
Transitioning what was rock to sand
Sculpturing at nature's command,
This island.

Only the shriek of gull pervades
This watery landscape of wind and waves,
This sea surf polished basalt stage
This foaming ether

Climbing now, I view at last
Cushioned from the North Sea blast
The storm's sea-streaked aftermath,
Consoling me.

William McLellan (Aberdeen)

Why Wait?

Why do we wait till a person's gone
Before we tell of his worth?
Why do we wait? Why not tell him now
He's the finest man on Earth.

Why do we wait till a person's gone
To send him flowers galore?
When a single flower would mean so much
If we'd only take to his door.

Why do we wait till he cannot hear
The good things we might say?
Why put it off? Why not tell him now
And share his joy today.

Of course, we're busy, that's our excuse
But why, oh why, do we wait
To tell a person our love for him
Until it becomes too late?

R G Flack (Craigavon)

For Mark With Love

All encompassing, peace divine
Though humming bees and skylark song,
While rivers of flowers meet my gaze
Sun-drenched orange and blue swathes.

Next to me are cool-toned greens,
Ferns, bamboos, wind-ruffling leaves,
Pendulous grasses and Wollemi pine,
Primula, poppies and seeding columbine.

This garden splendour, the peace of mind
Is nought until it's shared in full
But shared it is through trials of life
He warms my heart and protects from strife.

Life's not been easy, but made more so
By being together all this time,
Life together, in the garden, fills the soul,
Contentment found, the ultimate goal.

Alison Susan Goldie (Menmuir)

The Fear Of Deep Sleep

We all should be loving and giving,
Otherwise, what is the point of living?
You can close your eyes at the end of the day
And the stress and pain might dissolve away.

Whilst floating through time, into the light,
The glory of God is just out of sight.
Life is a struggle, but there is a need to go on
And we honour our duty to be steadfast and strong.

Resting and planning, we then tackle the task,
But, 'Why are we here?' we dutifully ask.
There are good and bad times, but nothing is easy,
The young grow old and the rich are greedy.

Deep in our hearts, we know right from wrong
And following 'God's Rules' we burst into song.
The conclusion of the matter is probably this,
We are afraid of entering the Devil's abyss.

Joan Yvonne Matthews (Swansea)

Tamsyn

On a bright February morn, as fluffy snowflake fluttered from the sky,
Beautiful baby Tamsyn cried loudly when she first saw the light,
Her loving parents thanked God and shed tears of happiness,
For the perfect bundle of joy, their precious, healthy
Little Snow White.

A special star, with sparkling blue eyes
And silky, baby-blonde hair,
Her angelic, sunny smile and cute, affectionate winning ways,
Became the centre of our world and stole our hearts away,
Soon, we proudly watched her first steps
And then it was schooldays.

From the patter of tiny feet, to the clink of computer keys,
From pretty toddler in pink, to fairy-tale princess just sweet sixteen,
A beautiful baby daughter, February's fairest snowdrop,
Has blossomed and become a charming, gorgeous young lady,
A stunning, eighteenth-birthday Queen.

Angela Moore (Londonderry)

A-Z of Authors

Forward Press Information

We hope you have enjoyed reading this book - and that you will continue to enjoy it in the coming years.

If you like reading and writing poetry drop us a line, or give us a call, and we'll send you a free information pack.

Alternatively if you would like to order further copies of this book or any of our other titles, then please give us a call or log onto our website at www.forwardpress.co.uk

Forward Press Ltd. Information
Remus House
Coltsfoot Drive
Woodston
Peterborough
PE2 9JX
(01733) 890099